I

Den + Beverley Lewis

Braehead

THIS BOOK IS
FOR MY FAMILY
WOODY, MONIQUE, DOUGLAS, MICHELLE, NICOLE
WHO BELIEVED

Special recognition is given to Molly Mitchell, who worked tirelessly with the author for two and a half years on the conceptualization and research phases of the book. Her creative ideas and dedication to the project were an inspiration the author gratefully acknowledges.

BRAEHEAD

Three Founding Families in Nineteenth Century Canada

Sherrill MacLaren

McClelland and Stewart

McClelland and Stewart Limited
The Canadian Publishers
25 Hollinger Road
Toronto, Ontario
M4B 3G2

Canadian Cataloguing in Publication Data

MacLaren, Sherrill.
  Braehead

ISBN 0-7710-5409-2

1. Cross family. 2. Drever family. 3. Macleod
family. 4. Prairie Provinces – Biography.
5. Prairie Provinces – Social life and customs.
I. Title.

FC 3238.M24 1986   971.2'009'92   C85-099877-8
F1060.3.M24 1986

The publisher makes grateful acknowledgement to the Canada Council and the Ontario Arts Council for their financial assistance.

Printed and bound in Canada by T. H. Best Printing Company Limited

Contents

PART THREE:

1896-1932
Dear Brewer

Acknowledgments

During the past five years while I was researching and writing *Braehead*, a network of supporters evolved. It was inspiring to me that accompanying their collective expertise was a tireless enthusiasm for the spirit of this story. In particular was the enduring faith of Jack McClelland himself and that of his staff. I also wish to extend heartfelt thanks to the many others who helped:

To IBM Canada Limited, Western Region, specifically Veronica Bell and Gary Brisebois, Principal Group Limited, Pacific Western Airlines, Canada Council Explorations, and the Ontario Arts Council for the financial assistance they each gave.

To Michael Reford, great-grandson of Alexander Cross, who arranged the judge's seven trunks of letters and documents into comprehensible files; and Emma "Criss Cross" Morton, daughter of Harry Cross, Wyoming, who collaborated with her father in writing his memoirs. Both Michael and Emma unhesitatingly turned over their work for my use.

To the Cross, Drever and Macleod families across the nation, in the United States and in Great Britain for their help and hospitality: in particular, Michael and Tewky Reford, and the children of Ernest and Nell Cross: Jim, John, Sandy and Mary; Alexander Cross's great-grandchildren, John Durnford, David Dover, Don and Shan Cross, Julia Cross Gerwien, and Marmo Cross Shakespeare's children, Mary Shakespeare, Sidney Madden and Jane Horner; and to Adam Drever, great-grandson of Helen and William Drever. It is a measure of the families' collective integrity that in no way did they interfere with the contents of this book.

To the archivists of research institutions both in Canada and in Wyoming, too numerous to thank individually: specifically, at the Public Archives of Canada, Patricia Burkett, Joanne Frodsham, Larry McNally, Douglas Whyte and Barbara Wilson; RCMP historian Stanley W. Horrall; at the University of Guelph, the department of history and the Veterinary College, Dr. C. Barker; at the Manitoba Provincial Archives, Vera K. Fast; at the Glenbow Alberta Institute, Calgary, where the bulk of the available source material was found, Hugh Dempsey, William McKee, Douglas Cass, Lindsay Moir and Georgeen Klassen; at the Vancouver Public Library main branch, A.

Kevlahan and his staff; the University of British Columbia main library, departments of microfilm and special collections; and at the Greater Victoria Public Library, Barbara Elford.

To L.G. Thomas, professor emeritus, University of Alberta, who read the manuscript for historical accuracy; M. Greenwood, associate professor of history, University of British Columbia, and the Honourable J.V. Clyne, for their interpretation of nineteenth-century law, Quebec; Professor D. Guth, faculty of law, University of British Columbia, and A.B. Russ, Latin scholars.

To Douglas Gardiner, former vice-chairman of the Royal Bank of Canada, for reading and clarifying the business sections of the manuscript; the Honourable Hartland de Montarville Molson for his reminiscences on the Pine Avenue home, the Montreal General Hospital, and Cacouna; Brigadier-General G.J.H. Wattsford C.D. and Brigadier-General C.L. Kirby C.D. of Kingston for their military expertise on Chapter 5; Dr. Michael Rigg, for advice on communicable diseases.

To Harry Brayne, aged 107, and Joe Ryan, aged eighty-plus, former a7 Ranche hands; Dolbie Turner, sister-in-law to Willie Cross, and Dorothy "Dodie" Watney, long-time Victoria residents who lived also in Pincher Creek, Alberta; A.D. "Peter" Elliott, former chairman of the Alberta Liquor Control Board; several brewers from British Columbia to New Brunswick who shared their personal memories and their wish to remain anonymous.

To Anna Richards French and June Brander-Smith for extraordinary research; Sandra Brander-Smith and Mary Carey for their translations of French documents and near-illegible English letters; Denise Turnbull for researching Alexander Cross's and James Hutchison's nineteenth-century land holdings in Quebec; Diane Way for researching Martin Macleod's letters; Gretchen Creery for developing the index; E. Dipple, former secretary to Ernest Cross, for her reminiscences circa 1930-32; George Mueske and his staff, Information Services, Woodward's main store, Vancouver, for their time-saving assistance on the IBM printer; Gordon and Pat Gray for their enthusiasm and hospitality.

To my editors, whose help was truly priceless: Ruth Fraser, who guided me patiently through the first three years, and Diane Mew, who, with extraordinary skill and good humour, helped ease an agonizing 133 pages from the "final" manuscript. Anything which may be deemed excessive remains at my insistence, and while I have aspired to accuracy, any errors are mine alone.

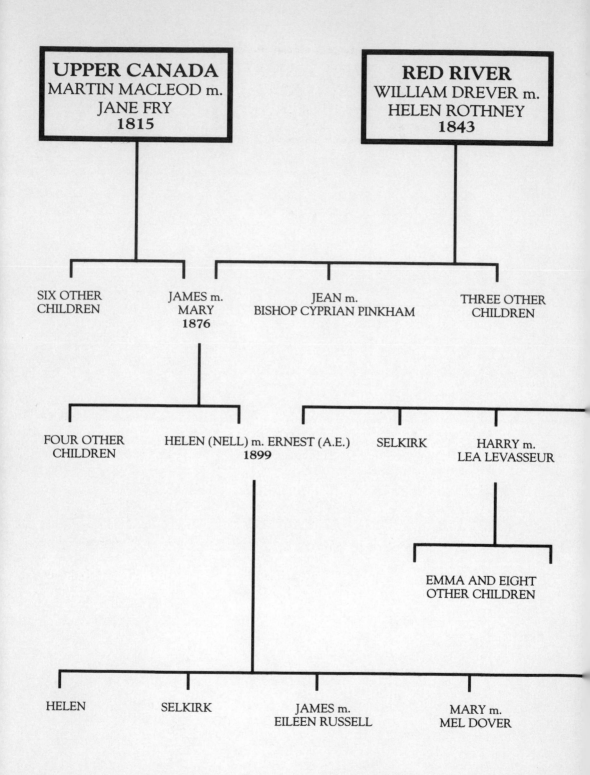

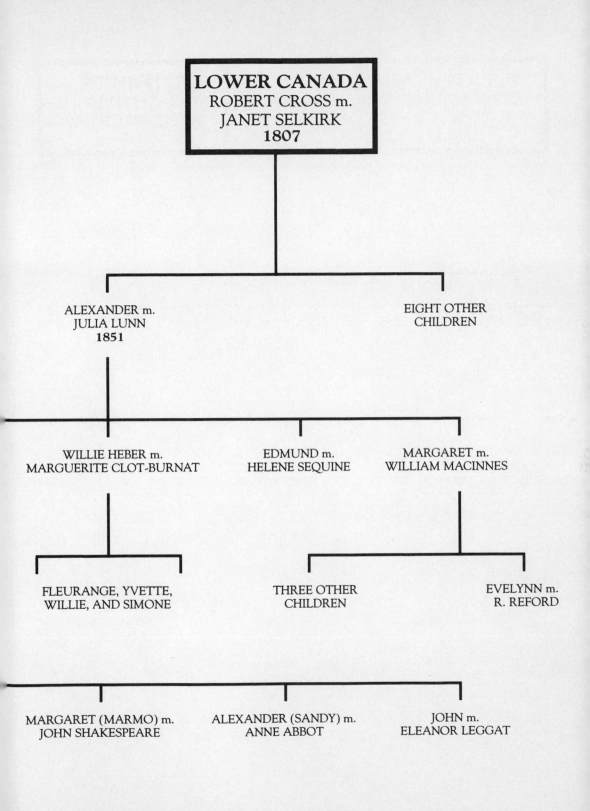

LOWER CANADA
ROBERT CROSS m.
JANET SELKIRK
1807

ALEXANDER m.
JULIA LUNN
1851

EIGHT OTHER
CHILDREN

WILLIE HEBER m.
MARGUERITE CLOT-BURNAT

EDMUND m.
HELENE SEQUINE

MARGARET m.
WILLIAM MACINNES

FLEURANGE, YVETTE,
WILLIE, AND SIMONE

THREE OTHER
CHILDREN

EVELYNN m.
R. REFORD

MARGARET (MARMO) m.
JOHN SHAKESPEARE

ALEXANDER (SANDY) m.
ANNE ABBOT

JOHN m.
ELEANOR LEGGAT

Prologue

"A good many think this is humbug but I believe we should know who our people were."

Ernest Cross, 1916

From 1820 to 1845 three Scottish families unknown to each other uprooted centuries of tradition and emigrated from their homelands. Settling in Upper Canada, Lower Canada and the Red River Settlement, the Macleods, the Crosses and the Drevers brought little with them but talent and heritage to implant in the new land. Some brought poverty with the ideals of duty and responsibility, others combined their ideals with the ability to accumulate wealth and hang on to it, and all brought religion and a sense of position. Their tools were a Presbyterian work ethic and an indomitable belief in the value of education. Driven with the vision of creating greater opportunities for their children, each couple relinquished comfort in favour of hardship, and conviviality in favour of isolation. As such, no generation existed detached from the next, and as individuals died, their influence remained to haunt or inspire their descendants.

By the third generation the Cross, Drever and Macleod families had merged through marriage, and despite roots in Quebec, Ontario and Manitoba, were solidly settled in the North-West Territories and Wyoming. As they helped change both land and society from frontier hardships and political upheavals to an age of industrialization, they encapsulated Canada's formative years into a private portrayal of her history. Their experiences illuminate Canada's strengths, weaknesses and ultimately the hope founded in her people.

During the last century, history flung itself at some generations like flash floods. "Ordinary" men and women were able to shape the flooding river, to place the sandbags, to alter the flow and irrigate the lands. An evolving civilization wrestling with the forces of confusing jurisprudence, disparate cultures and sometimes violent politics created challenging frontiers of remarkable diversity for the characters within this story. In the West, the isolation from central Canada combined with the encroaching American influence from the south eventually infiltrated the Scottish roots of these immigrants. The result was the emergence of a character known as "western Canadian." While James Macleod was frustrated by these influences, it would be Ernest Cross who would come to personify this identity. Today, the Crosses of Alberta are the quintessential westerners.

This story tells what drove a century of one family to seize the challenges and while often intimidated, why most were rarely beaten. On the way, Nature humbled them but they refused to succumb either to death or to mediocrity. They believed that what they did counted.

Their experiences are documented in over ten thousand letters, in balance sheets, unpublished memoirs, and in the reminiscences of family and acquaintances. Collected from Quebec to California, the material was found over a five-year period in libraries, archives, attics, dispatch trunks, garages, cardboard shoeboxes, basements and even behind the bricks of a fireplace.

The narrative perforce ebbs and flows with the available source material, sometimes rich in intercommunication, sometimes frustrating with decades of soliloquy. For example, Justice Alexander Cross's vast collection of Quebec letters between himself, his wife, his children and his colleagues gives an intimate portrait of a nineteenth-century pater familias. On the other hand, the only letters remaining from the home of Captain Martin Macleod in Upper Canada are 1,100 of his own. In their own right, however, and supplemented by the childhood memoirs of his daughter Maggie Baldwin, they were invaluable to Chapter Three, and to Chapter Five on James Macleod. Later, while Mary Drever Macleod saved over five hundred letters of her husband James, he obeyed her instructions to burn all of hers. Inadvertently he extinguished two decades of extraordinary social history.

The papers of Alexander Cross are a frontier in themselves. They reveal nineteenth-century legal and real estate practices as well as hinting at the tangle of pre-Confederation laws and the decades taken to codify and reform them. And while this is largely a Canadian saga, the extensive memoirs of his son Harry provide a unique insight into life in early Montreal and on the American frontier. In marrying a French-Canadian girl and heading for lawless Wyoming Territory,

Harry typifies the socio-political contrasts on either side of the border. He and his pals first outrode warring Sioux then later gunslingers and cattle rustlers long after James Macleod had negotiated a gentleman's peace with the Blackfoot Nation.

The Drevers' life in the Red River Settlement in the mid-nineteenth century was almost devoid of letters. I supplemented the memoirs of Jean Drever Pinkham and her husband, Bishop Cyprian Pinkham, with the history books and family oral history. Later in Alberta, the turn-of-the-century letterbooks of Ernest Cross show the frenetic pace of the western industrialist. Ernest could be so circumspect, however, that I used the letters of his globe-trotting friend Billie Cochrane to provide a kaleidoscope of social history and hilarity from western Canada through Europe during the early years of the twentieth century.

The art of letter writing flourished in the nineteenth century. Children learned it in school, boarders wrote that obligatory Sunday letter home. Writing was the most important form of communication, more enduring, more committed than the future telephone. Some of the letters are lace-thin from wear, thumb-printed and earth-stained as if read and reread during sweaty breaks behind the plough. Some look as if they were carried in breast pockets out onto the range where men battled loneliness and cold with heartwarming messages from their parents or wives. Many of James Macleod's were written from legislative assemblies and superior courts, diversions from lengthy hearings or ordinance draftings.

The handwritings are bold with conviction, wobbly with heartache, nearly illegible from drink, yet most often written with scholarship. Some are encased in handmade linen envelopes; in others, primroses and bluebells still lie pressed between their pages.

Most touching of all, the letters were saved. Except for Mary Macleod's letters, few individuals if any in six generations destroyed the records of their ancestors. Something always seemed to stop them. In 1961 when Ernest Cross's Calgary Brewing & Malting Company sold out to Canadian Breweries, two beer trucks were loaded with uncatalogued Cross papers which were then trundled off to the Glenbow archives. The rest were dumped out in the back to await a garbage pick up. Espying the cartons, Ernest's son James had them trucked out to his Bar Pipe ranch south of Calgary. Cross stored them in his basement and forgot about them. When I first called him about this book, they had found their way to the garage and another expectant dump but again, something had held Jim Cross back.

Treasures of the heart, prisms of the soul, the letters portray the faith that built this nation. This story belongs to those characters who committed to paper their love, joy, disillusionment, tragedy and trivia. Perhaps the letters were not intended for future generations but somehow it seems they were. Some characters in this book might smile shyly over sharing their story, but others almost demand their say. If alive today, I believe that Helen Rothney would insist her story be told. James Macleod would fervently defend his actions both in 1858 and 1874. Alexander Cross actually published arguments justifying his points of view in family altercations. And in breaking from the strictures of nineteenth-century disciplines, James Macleod and Harry Cross could well be two youths in the twentieth century. That they eventually achieved extraordinary goals underscores the contemporary value of their tales.

While much of this book centres on the West and specifically upon Alberta, this is not intended to be a regional work. Ernest Cross's great-grandson, heir to vast western land holdings and the responsibilities intrinsic to a dynasty, chose first to return to Montreal to the university of his great-great-grandfather, Alexander Cross. His quest for his roots provides a pipeline to our national heritage and to contemporary readers seeking their own roots.

Two hundred years ago a Highlander's destiny lay in his ancestral lands. His sense of permanency was absolute. In this story, each of those original immigrants struggled to re-establish that immutable heritage. In today's world of uncertainties it is the sixth generation of those families who preserves that sense of permanency. Ranging from central Canada to the American and Canadian Wests, they can be found in Ontario and Quebec as Reford and Durnford; in British Columbia they are Shakespeare and Semeyn; in Alberta they are legendary as Cross, Drever, Dover and Macleod; in the United States they are the Crosses of Braehead and the Wyoming State Legislature.

"Braehead," which means riverbank, was the name given to the Cross ancestral home established on the Clyde River in Scotland in 1721. Throughout this story it symbolizes the flow of generations, and the riverbank homes provided a refuge from the floods and frozen waters they endured or confronted over more than a century.

I have never intended this book to be an emulation or an exposé of any characters. Its strength lies not in individual renown but within a spirit which binds the family continuum. In sharing their story, the Crosses, the Drevers and the Macleods have provided us with some historical vision of two nations, and perhaps with a glimpse of our own ancestries, whatever they are.

S.M.

Winter 1985

PART ONE

1820–1870

Contract with the Land

Thou shalt inherit the holy earth as a faithful steward,
Conserving its resources and productivity from generation to generation.
Thou shalt safeguard thy fields from soil erosion,
Thy living waters from drying up,
Thy forests from desolation, and
Protect thy hills from overgrazing by thine herds,
That thy descendants may have abundance forever.
If any shall fail in this stewardship of the land,
Thy fruitful fields shall become sterile stony ground and wasting gullies
And thy descendants shall decrease and live in poverty
Or perish from off the face of the earth

Cross Papers

1

The Crosses of Scotland and Lower Canada, 1820-49

For centuries Glasgow had teemed with action. Almost one-third of the country's population had crowded into the city and its surrounding parishes. In good times, craftsmen had built a multitude of products ranging from clay pipes to square-rigged windjammers, and vendors with carts bearing coal, lead, clay and even gold had crowded the streets. By 1826, all that had changed.

About three miles east of the city and just above the River Clyde, stood a mansion called Braehead Manor. From its windows a six-year-old boy named Alexander Selkirk Cross could watch the waters transport emigrants downriver to the sea. To the dark skinned, ebony-haired "black Scot" it was a sight filled with constant change and excitement. Alexander knew that these adventurers sailed from Glasgow for the British colonies of India, the West Indies and Canada, but he was too young to understand that they were desperate to escape the poverty of their homeland and a dismal future.

To the intense, bookish boy, his century-old home might well have seemed a palace. Servants and silver graced Braehead hallways, while purebred cattle and Clydesdale horses grazed beside the manor's grain fields. His family had always been well suited to a region where skilled merchants had ensured Lanarkshire's reputation as the most successful commercial centre in all the British Isles. In the seventeenth century some competitive English businessmen had sued Lanarkshire merchants for fraudulent dealings. During the hearing the bench cited the Scots' only crime as a remarkable ability to turn a pound into a guinea. This could well have described the Crosses, their success in agrarian and mercantile worlds underscoring their disciplines of education, religion and work.

Alexander's great-grandfather had lived in Glasgow during an era of ecological purity and economic prosperity. In the sixteenth and early seventeenth centuries the River Clyde had flowed with the clarity of a mountain stream. The nearby city of Glasgow was Scotland's leading shipbuilding port and by 1690 the Crosses were considered one of the five wealthiest families in the city. Alexander's great-grandfather John was dean of the Glasgow Guild in 1694-95. Major partners in the Easter Suggaries Company as well as landowners, silversmiths, chemical importers, seed farmers, and benefactors of the merchant's hospital, Crosses had already contributed their entrepreneurship and community spirit to two centuries of thriving economy.

Towards the end of the century, tougher rules and stiffer trading penalties had piqued the Crosses. Heavy duty on sugar exports compounded by the danger of pirateering increased the liabilities of the Easter Suggaries Company. The rules had become restrictive to a family which preferred to do things its own way. In 1765 the Crosses and their group of "wealthy aristocrats" sold the Easter Suggaries business, withdrawing temporarily their faith from the vagaries of trade to place it in the longevity of the land.

By the nineteenth century times had grown hard for Alexander's father. Robert Cross had watched the beginning of the industrial age, restrictive trade laws and Napoleonic wars disrupt his business and drastically alter the complexion of his land. By 1821 and the birth of Alexander, eighth child of nine, streams were poisoned by lead and the encroaching smog and pestilence from the smelters had so darkened Lanarkshire that it was called the "black country." By 1825 Robert's oldest brother, Thomas, had emigrated and re-established himself in the wholesale groeery business in Canada.

Alexander's parents decided to emigrate in 1826. The economy was fluctuating wildly as some thirty British banks collapsed and the nation teetered on the brink of bankruptcy. Men were ruined overnight. A good education no longer guaranteed a professional career, and working coal mines or manning printing presses was not what Robert and Janet Cross envisioned for their children. They ranged in age from eighteen-year-old John to the baby, Jean, aged one.

While Robert saw no future at Braehead, leaving marked a monumental sacrifice. Aged sixty-five, he had little time left to re-establish his wife and children in a colony where enterprise could still be rewarded by opportunity and gain. Two areas of America appealed to him. Alexander's maternal great-grandfather, John Witherspoon, had sailed for America to serve as president of the College of New Jersey and found Princeton University. He had also signed the American Declaration of Independence. Crosses were prominently established throughout the United States' east coast. But Thomas had probably taken his Cross inheritance with him to Canada, and Robert elected to join his brother in Montreal.

Lower Canada, and Montreal in particular, was a favourite with Lanarkshire merchants, and many of the scions of the North-West Company were Scots. They had used their broader education and financial skills to gain ascendancy over French Canadians both in the fur trade and in the business world. This society would be just right for the bilingual, enterprising Crosses. Leaving the eldest, John, to complete his law studies at Edinburgh University, the rest of the family sailed for Canada, docking in Montreal on September 21, 1826.

Montreal was a wealthy city of 22,000 people. Its blend of cultural attractions was complemented by limestone cathedrals, the newly founded McGill University, and the fur traders' mansions located outside the city on the slopes of Mount Royal. The Beaver Club welcomed members to elegant soirées. The legitimate stage was thriving. On the outskirts, tanneries, breweries and mills churned out their products. Plans were under way for canal systems, railways, expanded port facilities. Mount Royal's forested slopes welcomed folk from the bustle of the city for weekends of carriage rides, promenades and hunts. As the major port and the commercial hub of Canada, Montreal must have promised an exciting future for the Crosses.

The newly named Cross Brothers Limited on St. Paul Street was close to the docks, enabling Robert and Thomas as produce brokers to swiftly transport their merchandise from the ships. The surrounding countryside also held potential for a new Braehead, and Robert Cross intended to rebuild his ancestral home on another riverbank.

During that first winter, Alexander and six brothers and sisters attended the "British and Canadian School," the first Protestant school in Montreal. It was founded by the Englishman William Lunn, educator, entrepreneur, alderman and magistrate. Alexander loved the world of learning as taught by this demanding taskmaster. It was Lunn who impressed upon him that academic excellence, rather than position or wealth, would some day separate the office boys from the statesmen.

As the winter snows melted into the spring of 1827, then gradually gave way to stifling summer heat, Montreal reeked with the stench of sewage. On rainy days, pedestrians who ventured forth in long skirts and polished leather boots were splashed with mud and offal flung up from horses' hooves and carriage wheels. No one had any clear understanding of how infection was communicated, but it was thought by some that the smelly gutters might hold the secret. Many citizens shut their sick in rooms with windows tightly closed against the foul city air. Overworked nurses in the four-year-old Montreal General Hospital wrestled as well as they could with endless cases of cholera, diphtheria, pneumonia.

Compounding the fear of disease were the destitute immigrants, often sickly before they embarked from the old country. Covered with open sores and wracked with illnesses by the end of the voyage, they crowded into Montreal with nowhere to go. They wandered the congested streets of St. Lawrence and St. Paul begging for food, and stopping at the lush vegetable and fruit stalls of Cross Brothers Limited.

As financiers accustomed to efficiency and control the Crosses knew that if stricken by disease they were as helpless as the indigent. On September 26, 1827, just a year after the family had arrived, Alexander's father contracted typhus and died. His family's dreams came to a shocking halt almost as quickly as they had begun.

Alexander's forty-one-year-old mother was left a widow with eight young children to comfort, house, feed and clothe. Janet had little cash and her capital was invested in the shares of Cross Brothers Limited. She was forced to withdraw her children from Lunn's school. At the time, it must have seemed almost impossible for her to provide her children with the opportunities envisioned by herself and her husband.

Janet Selkirk Cross was no ordinary woman. Slender and black-haired with spirited blue eyes, she possessed a sense of adventure like the famous Lord Selkirk of Rupert's Land whom she claimed as an uncle. This was fortunate, for the Thomas Crosses were sympathetic to her plight at first, then soon drew away from their brother's less fortunate family. Janet would have to make it alone.

Some time during the winter she determined to leave Montreal before the spring thaw. The fear of cholera from ships and sewage-ridden streets terrified her more than the unknown. She believed that fresh country air rather than stifling sick rooms and primitive sanitation would give her family a better chance of survival. In choosing an area in which to live, she was influenced by her native land and people.

Five years earlier a group of Lanarkshire weavers, shepherds and farm labourers, all French-speaking Scots, had settled on the banks of the Chateauguay River southwest of Montreal. Members of a serving class in Scotland who might once have polished Cross silver, Janet recognized that they had re-established their Highland culture and work ethic. She decided to join them.

In the spring of 1828, Janet purchased two properties on either side of the Chateauguay River: lot No. 2 in Ormstown, and a long sliver of land in Point Round. By then, Ormstown was already a thriving community complete with a school, a church and several potato whiskey distilleries. It lacked only a general store.

With the help of her sons, Janet built a neighbourhood store and started again. The older children dredged clay from the Chateauguay River to make bricks for their home, a task which grew exciting when the boys dug up two American rifles, reminders of the 1812 War and their proximity to the border. They ploughed a road which wound through willow trees between the riverbank and the future house and barn. Nineteen-year-old John Cross, graduate lawyer, arrived from Edinburgh to assume responsibility for the large family. Hired as Ormstown's town clerk, he shelved dreams of a law practice until his mother was established, and he became Alexander's surrogate father and mentor.

Their Georgian-style cottage was simple and rather severe with the exception of the attic. There the boys inserted a skylight and left a ladder standing free for access from the second floor. A child full of curiosity and dreams, Alexander could climb up the ladder, push back the trapdoor and scramble into a dusty world of mystery. Light filtered in from the perpendicular skylight almost to the far corners of the roof lines. There the Crosses stored their trunks, boxes, buffalo rugs and extra books. A mud wasp's nest appeared soon after construction, and eventually its petrified clay clung like a cornerstone of the house. Bees and flies brought life to this hideaway, but save for the hum of insects the sun-drenched attic lent silent space to a dreaming child.

The boys constructed a cavernous barn with two-foot-thick stone foundations. Next they built the livestock barn, including spacious standing stalls to accommodate their Clydesdale horses. With profit always in mind, Janet intended the twenty stalls not only for their own horses, but for the neighbours' as well. The barns became a lively centre of the farm, with the children mucking the stalls, breaking ice on the water buckets, mixing warm mash, spreading fresh straw around the massive hooves of the draught horses, all before walking or riding off to school. Each Sunday they attended church in Ormstown after which Janet taught the children Gaelic and Highland dancing.

For the next decade the "Widow Cross," as Janet became known, worked long hours building her merchant reputation. If some thought she worked harder than she needed just to make ends meet, they could not know the depth of her intentions. Each child would be educated. Each would learn industry from the land and in the store. In time they would re-establish the lifestyle the family had known at Braehead in Scotland.

Janet's sons farmed and traded peas and pork in exchange for currency or for dry, hardwood ashes. In the early 1830s they added an ashery to the store, combining potash with animal water to make soap, or selling it at ten cents a bushel to be processed into potassium. The girls learned how to spin the wool and weave breeches and jackets. The one exception to this lifestyle of physical labour was Alexander. His penchant for studies reflected both his dislike for farming and his reaction to his mother's incessant work. He would never forget the change from manor house to simple farmhouse, from servants to manual labour. By the time he was ten, he showed an exceptional mind, and his brother John paid for him to supplement his studies by taking lessons from Mr. Cowan in Ormstown.

By 1835, when Alexander was preparing to read for the profession of law, twenty-seven-year-old John felt free to pursue his own career. He had been offered a partnership in a Philadelphia law practice, a magnificent opportunity and one well deserved. His other brothers were now competent young men managing both the farm and the Ormstown store. But Janet was ill from overwork, and John feared leaving before she was cured.

Occasionally he wrote his Montreal relatives to explain that his family could continue to run their own lives, but would the Thomas Crosses please send some elixirs for his mother? Janet was suffering from anemia, in the 1830s a debilitating disease that shortened the lifespan of many a pioneer woman. John hastened to assure his uncle that, "through our own industry we have managed to see all nine children receive a share of Education." Janet might have been annoyed had she known of her son's letters asking for help. Crosses did things on their own.

In 1835 Janet watched helplessly as her youngest child, eleven-year-old Jeannie, fell ill and died. John remained to comfort his heartbroken mother and to continue handling business matters. Then, early in 1837, he finally packed to leave for his long-dreamed-of profession. But in the mysterious and brutally swift way of those times, he was stricken with pneumonia and died two years to the very day of Jeannie's death. For the rest of his life Alexander could not speak of his oldest brother without a catch in his voice and tears filling his eyes.

In Janet's world there was little time for grieving, and her visions reached far beyond John's funeral on the Chateauguay River that day. Alexander was still growing out of his clothes and lost in a world of novels, but he would have to take John's position as family counsel. Other brothers would care for the farm and protect the Cross interests from the rumbles of rebellion and American invasion. Janet gave Alexander her blessing and immediately sent him to the Montreal College of Law.

In the nineteenth century teen-agers could apprentice in the legal profession and complete their studies in four to five years. A young man in a hurry could be building a law practice before his twenty-first birthday, and Alexander approached his studies like a youth possessed. The dreamy child disappeared within six months of John's funeral. He was so impatient with the slow pace of his law classes that he dropped out and entered the offices of twenty-three-year-old lawyer John J. Day.

The seventeen-year-old Alexander Cross epitomized the young idealists of the era. Six feet tall, slim and intense, he was already styling his black hair and stubbled cheeks into shadows of mutton chops. Many of the youths did, making them look a little older than their years. One of Alexander's ebony-coloured eyes wandered slightly, making it difficult to tell exactly where he was looking. Decades later his colleagues would quip that it seemed to be everywhere.

Political involvement was accepted as a fact of life by Alexander and his contemporaries. They had never known Canada as a peaceful country. Lower Canada in particular was confused by disparate groups arguing for absolute British rule, equality for French Canadians, or annexation to the United States. By 1837, Montreal was boiling with political turmoil. Protestant Loyalists clashed with French Catholic militants. Both sides formed radical organizations and staged riotous demonstrations. Law students listened and argued about the conflicting views of the street-corner politicians and of the leaders of the day.

Especially impressive was the French Canadian, Louis-Hippolyte

Lafontaine, a wealthy young lawyer and former supporter of his more explosive leader, Louis-Joseph Papineau. Lafontaine had become a man of compromise, calling for parliamentary reform, for Canada to become responsible to herself rather than to Great Britain and for moderation by the British in their dealings with the French Canadians. His logic appealed to Alexander, who often joined other law students to hear him speak.

On the other hand, the reform approach of Lafontaine was anathema to Adam Thom, editor of the *Montreal Herald*. Graduated from Aberdeen University with a master in arts, Thom was an exponent of absolute British rule. Under the nom de plume of "Camillus," he published harsh attacks against the French Canadians and, despite his multilingual skills, refused to acknowledge or speak a word of their language. His polemics appealed especially to the Montreal merchants, many of whom wished to extinguish the French identity entirely. In such discordant times some believed that he might actually capitulate Quebec into rebellion.

Like everybody else, Alexander read Thom's pocket-sized book and heard the debates. He visited his mother on the Chateauguay River and watched groups polarizing into Loyalists and Annexationists. His old boyhood chums were divided, teen-agers suddenly and sometimes violently expounding their differing ideologies at a time when they might have been fox-hunting together across autumn fields.

In December 1837, rebellion erupted north of Montreal. It was initially quelled, then on November 3, 1838, six hundred men under the exiled Patriote leader, Robert Nelson, staged an invasion of Canada from the United States, just south of the Chateauguay River. Another Patriote force was also advancing with over five thousand men. The Cross farm was in their path.

When Alexander learned of the invasion, he exchanged his pen for a musket and returned to the Chateauguay River. He found his brother George running messages through the enemy lines. Joining Colonel Maitland's battalion Alexander moved on to Beauharnois, where Nelson's men had imprisoned Janet's two Selkirk brothers and an enclave of wealthy British. In the ensuing battle he was promoted to sergeant in the field.

In the subsequent defeat of the rebels, Sergeant Cross was one of the first to rush into the village. Although still a law student, he was immediately appointed clerk of the first municipal council of Beauharnois, an area covering almost four times that of today. So competent was Alexander in running the new institution that he was complimented by guests of the seigneury house – Lord Selkirk and the writer and politician, Sir Edward Gibbon Wakefield.

Not yet twenty, Alexander was already valuable to a colony struggling toward nationhood. Through the influence of men like Lafontaine, his views matured as a reformist rather than a reactionary and he recognized the necessity of political stability for his financial future. A young man who loved his adopted country, Alexander also realized that bicultural harmony was essential in order to sell produce in Montreal or to create a lucrative market for land speculation. How troubling it must have been to him then, when Lord Durham, the new governor of the two Canadas sent out to examine the causes and possible cures for the 1837-38 rebellions, hired Adam Thom as one of his commissioners.

Lord Durham observed that the struggle in Lower Canada was not political as much as cultural. He expressed hope "to terminate the deadly animosity that now separates the inhabitants of Lower Canada into the hostile divisions of French and English." His recommended solution for Lower Canada, however, is believed by some historians to have been heavily influenced by Adam Thom: "It must henceforth be the ... purpose of the British Government to establish an English population, with English laws and language ... and to trust its government to none but a decidedly English legislature."

Alexander's reaction to the Durham Report was to continue nurturing his French-Canadian business connections and developing a notable fluency in Quebec civil law. In 1844, the same year in which the seat of government was removed from Kingston to Montreal, he was called to the bar as a junior partner of lawyers Duncan Fisher and James Smith, a future attorney general. Duncan Fisher had impressive connections. He was a brother of John Fisher, the wealthy auctioneer, stepfather to H. King, future president of the Bank of Montreal, father-in-law to John Torrance, the merchant magnate, and brother-in-law to the multifaceted William Lunn. For an ambitious young lawyer intent upon building a prosperous future this was a superlative introduction to the influential elite of Montreal.

No period in the history of Canadian jurisprudence was more complex or challenging. Following the enforced union of Upper and Lower Canada in 1841, the colony had inherited a tangle of French and English statutes. Only the brightest bilingual minds fully understood, let alone developed a fluency in, at least nine legal systems inherited from the King of France, the British courts, the French jurists, the two Canadas before the 1841 union and the legislature of the Canadas after 1841. Worse, Lord Durham had written that the judicial system in Lower Canada was chaotic and there was not "the slightest confidence in the administration of criminal justice," or "in the honest administration of the laws." With no codification of the statutes, just trying to identify what the law was at any given point was usually a matter of debate.

Alexander moved easily through this jungle. He swiftly built a lucrative clientele and a reputation for statesmanship as he helped develop the Lower Canada Law Reports, review the usury laws, and assist James Smith in studying the seigneurial system of Lower Canada. Of the old feudal maxim, "Nulle terre sans seigneur," the commission concurred with the sentiments of Lafontaine: it was obsolete. Years later Alexander would write that he viewed his responsibility to the law as not merely to interpret it, but to reform it whenever appropriate. And though not implemented for another decade, abolition of the seigneurial system would free large tracts of land for speculators such as Alexander.

Influential government positions changed frequently with the evolving legislature. In 1847 James Smith was appointed the attorney general. The following year, on forming the government, Lafontaine established the Superior Court and immediately appointed James Smith to its bench. In 1849, when Lafontaine joined with Reform leader Robert Baldwin to form a coalition to govern Canada, Alexander's association with the political and judicial powerhouses of the pre-Confederation era progressively deepened.

When Duncan Fisher died, Alexander invited his nephew, F.W. Torrance, to join the partnership. For Torrance it meant influential connections and a lucrative salary, but in fact it was the Torrance name, one of high profile in Lower Canada, that Alexander may have wished on the firm's letterhead. On the other hand, Torrance could not resist joining Alexander, whom he considered "better connected than any other member of the Montreal Bar." It was a significant statement to make of a man only twenty-seven years old.

In 1848 Montreal plummeted into depression. The financial community suffered from the abolition of preferential duties on goods entering Britain and exorbitant freight rates on the St. Lawrence River. Twenty million dollars had been spent on canals just as railways appeared that would render them obsolete. Yet with the opening of the Erie Canal, New York swiftly became the trading centre of the east coast while bankruptcy announcements filled the Montreal newspapers. Notices of auctions from farmland to entire building blocks made the *Montreal Gazette* look like a modern-day advertisement flier.

Alexander's professional interests in civil litigation did not preclude him from taking on bankruptcy cases. In fact that may have become his specialty, with legal fees being paid in land rather than cash. Torrance admired Alexander's "pecuniary skills" in land acquisitions which called for circumnavigating the seigneury law. This complex law required a purchaser to pay a tax to the seigneur, or owner; yet after making expensive improvements the purchaser might find the land appropriated back by the seigneur's son before a year and a day had transpired. The only transaction in Lower Canada that gave irrevocable title to the purchaser was to declare bankruptcy, offer the land up for a sheriff's sale, then have a friend or relative buy it back.

One victim of the depression was William Lunn, Alexander's former headmaster. In 1848, when Lunn was sued by his own family on a bankruptcy charge, Alexander appeared as his counsel. Lunn had bought a magnificent white mansion graced by huge pillars and a massive conservatory on the corner of Bleury and Sherbrooke streets. His landscaped grounds stretched far up the slopes of the mountain and were noted on the 1839 map of Montreal. The Lunn estate bordered what was referred to as the "Golden Mile," the home of Canada's aspiring aristocracy. Influential in religion, education and politics, William Lunn epitomized over-extended new world success. The son of a Portsmouth harbourmaster, Lunn was schooled in commerce, religion and the classics. Holding a reverence for all three disciplines, he was often unable to combine intellect with business acumen. And Lunn's determination to live by divine guidance was equalled only by his desire to live in luxury.

In 1812 the sixteen-year-old youth had read about a merchant ship which had sailed from London only to be captured by an American privateer and taken to Boston. The cargo included crates of Bibles which were subsequently placed in a customs warehouse and forgotten. Seven years later, when offered the job of running naval stores in Montreal, Lunn prayed for guidance on his future. A vision appeared which he described as similar to that of Moses and the burning bush, and on that same summer day he rediscovered the inventory of the warehouse of Bibles. Lunn saw the calling. He promptly paid up the 2.5 per cent duty hanging over the forgotten merchandise, claimed it and headed for Canada.

Upon reaching Montreal in August 1820, he called on the Protestant clergyman, Mr. Bethune of Christ Church, and proposed his plan for a Canadian Bible Society. Bethune joined the venture, providing him with a pew at the head of the middle aisle and promoting the first Bible society in Canada from the pulpit. Thus, at age twenty-four Lunn established immediate credibility and prominence in the worlds of education, religion and commerce. Officially linking the society with those of American, British and Foreign Bible Societies, he sold his warehouse of Bibles, ordered another shipment, then began investing in Montreal real estate.

Lunn soon married the widow and heiress, Margaret Fisher Hutchison, sister-in-law of John Torrance and sister of lawyer Duncan Fisher. Margaret's first husband, William, had been an enormously wealthy Montreal merchant and landowner. As the couple had signed no marriage contract, by Quebec law she shared everything equally, including his vast Scottish holdings. But when William Hutchison had died in Scotland while on a business trip in 1819, his estate became subject to Scottish law, and the oldest son would inherit all. Believing her children, James, Margaret Jr. and Alexander should share equally in the fortune, Margaret sailed for Scotland in mid-winter to contest the will. She lost, returned to Montreal, and five years later married Lunn. Subsequently, she bore four more children, Alexander, Emma, Mary and in 1826, Julia.

By 1848 the lure of St. Paul Street, on which Cross Brothers Limited, John Fisher Auctioneer and J. Torrance Importer were established, had proven too tempting for Lunn. He borrowed from his relatives' estates to invest in the produce business. At first his fortunes expanded, then floundered with the depression in general and in particular from bumper crops in Britain.

By the fall of 1848, Alexander had negotiated Lunn through a reconciliation. While no documents remain, it appears that he advised Lunn to declare bankruptcy in the *Montreal Gazette*, thus enabling the relatives to purchase his mortgaged McTavish property in downtown Montreal. It was heavily taxed and the family considered it a poor deal. In his memoirs Lunn anguished, "I felt broken in spirit but . . . patiently waited on God's kind providence." In the meantime, thanks to Alexander's efforts, family peace was restored.

Alexander became captivated by Lunn's daughter, the twenty-two-year-old Julia. Barely five feet in height, her rounded features wore a look of severity that belied her sense of humour. She was described as both aristocratic and Victorian in style, and an unusually strong-

willed lady. Educated in England, she was considered the brains of
the family. When Alexander began courting her by letter, she was
not at all sure she wanted to marry one of Montreal's most eligible
bachelors. On one occasion, when he wrote to suggest escorting her
to the Shakespeare Club, Julia hastily wrote to inform him that as
the meeting was a closed group, regrettably he would be unwelcome.

Alexander was accustomed to getting what he wanted. Julia's rebuff
inspired pages of heartfelt poetry written to his "lovely Julia." He
confessed feelings for her "which I have never entertained for any
other person," and he signed his poetry with a flirtatious, "AX."

Julia's response must have been as cynical as Alexander's was
lovesick, for following one full-blown rhyme and her subsequent note
to "Mr. Cross," he replied, "The good sense of your remarks has
made me both smile and blush at my own folly."

In 1849 Montreal exuded an aura of imperial elegance mixed with
political turmoil. Alexander was either escaping conflagrations or
attending magnificent garden parties with Julia. His involvement in
both extremes only deepened his ambition to build a personal empire
in the heart of the city's Anglo-French society. "To do business
successfully in Quebec," he would advise his son Ernest, "you must
remain fluent in French on the colloquial level." As his business
interests and his political influence expanded, he never forgot that
each was interdependent. He progressed with the absolute intent of
a man who knew exactly where he was going and so overshadowed
his legal colleague that just six months after joining the firm Torrance
dissolved the partnership.

Torrance felt he had brought Alexander "neither skill nor clients
despite handsome terms of recompense." He was also completely
frustrated by Alexander handling every facet of the practice himself,
and wrote of his need to struggle toward his own professional
connections. In a candid letter to Alexander, Torrance identified a
sine qua non of excellence, and a pervading characteristic of the
Crosses. He wrote, "You must do it all yourself." Throughout his
life F.W. Torrance would wrestle with moral questions not only
concerning his own professional motives but, to Alexander's annoyance, his friend's as well.

Since the spring of 1849 the two men had also fallen into political
disagreement. This may have been the true reason for the dissolution
of their partnership. Lafontaine had introduced in the Assembly the
contentious Rebellion Losses Bill. It proposed to compensate the
1837 rebels for damages to their property. Alexander recognized it

as a necessary step toward responsible government, but Torrance and his Loyalists friends were outraged. They viewed the bill as treasonous to Britain and held angry demonstrations through the streets of Montreal. Along with other Tories, Torrance would sign the Annexation Manifesto recommending a break with Britain and alliance with the United States.

Alexander had followed Lafontaine's career closely, never forgetting the man who had time not only to discuss the country's future with eager young lawyers but also to place them on reform committees. Thus, on April 25, during Lord Elgin's signing of the Rebellion Losses Bill and then later on that evening, he was inside the House observing the historic moment.

Outside the parliament buildings that night some two thousand furious Tories gathered around the main door. It was a strange crowd. The torches lit the faces of a handful of ladies and essentially younger, upper-middle-class Englishmen. Clad in top hats, softly knotted ties enveloping starched white collars, watch fobs shining from double-breasted suits, they seemed more suited for a soirée than a riot. But the mood was ugly. With the House still in session, rioters broke through the police cordon, tore down the main door and stormed the entrance way, bashing their clubs at the gas lamps as they ran. Once in the Assembly, they pitched stones at the Speaker, then set fire to the velvet curtains.

Flames soon roared through the library, turning Canada's parliament buildings into an inferno. Alexander rushed to assist Lafontaine and Solicitor General William Blake, first in trying to save the library, then in escaping. Lafontaine and Blake followed him and a handful of young reformers through smoke and fire toward the mob. Behind them windows exploded, allowing the chill spring winds to fan the flames.

The jeering crowd pressed toward Lafontaine as he emerged from the building. Alexander roared in French, then in English, "Let us pass!" His authority was recognized, for the rioters hesitated, then stepped back, enabling the group to reach their carriages and escape. When the Tory mob regained its senses, it rushed on to burn Lafontaine's home; his library and stables were completely demolished. Not finding Lafontaine himself, the crowd returned to watch the final explosion and devastation of the parliament buildings.

It was a bizarre four days in Lower Canada. Crowds stoned Lord Elgin's carriage while the Tory chef of Dolly's Chop House served steaks to jailed rioters. When it was all over, Lord Elgin would continue to serve as governor general for six more years but so deep was the antipathy of many English Canadians that they burned him in effigy. Although the seat of Canadian government was removed from Montreal to rotate between Toronto and Quebec, the city continued to erupt with dissensions and conflagrations, fired by those Tories still fighting for the official rule of Great Britain in Canada.

To Alexander Cross and other young men involved in the events of those four days, nothing could more indelibly imprint upon their minds the deep ideological schisms between French and English, and between Tories like F.W. Torrance and Reformers like himself. Close friends with diametrically opposed views were in conflict. Young men with flexible political views were also involved; but parliamentary reform alone would not heal the wounds. Whatever Canada might become through the coming century, one fact was clear to Alexander: each man owed some period of his life to public service, to help shape the nation, however tedious the task. Throughout the remainder of the century he would encourage his sons to serve their country in some political capacity, as long as their public duties did not harm their livelihood or their families.

By the fall of 1849 Montreal had survived the riots. The city's enduring charm seemed energized by her dichotomies, her irrepressible, vibrant cultures fluctuating between angry demonstrations and good-natured cooperation. Alexander Cross had lost a partner but maintained a friend in Torrance; he had distinguished himself by leading the way out of the burning parliament buildings and through the hostile crowd; he had allied himself with the surviving Baldwin-Lafontaine government and he was courting Julia Lunn.

Alexander's success had coincided with that of his mother, who had built a larger store in Ormstown. His brothers, William and Robert Jr., had expanded their interests with their merchant brother-in-law, Robert Cowan of Ormstown. The trio joined Thomas Cross to establish a thriving wholesale grocery business named Cowan and Cross Brothers, St. Paul Street, Montreal.

Torrance's father, John, the first man to sign the Annexation Manifesto, made a peace offering to the city. He hosted a garden party for three thousand British and American guests. Held under the auspices of the Horticultural Society, Torrance, assisted by William Lunn, blended Loyalists, Annexationists and Reformers with American businessmen. Only the French were missing. Liveried footmen delivered guests in coach and four to tunes played by the Nineteenth Regiment. Ladies in tulle gowns curtsied to Lord and Lady Elgin, while their escorts doffed the same top hats they had flung with rotten eggs at His Excellency four months earlier.

The *Montreal Gazette* wrote that the English gardeners competed furiously against each other. They had built moss houses and enlivened *jets d'eaux* with extravagant displays of fruit. Despite his financial disasters, William Lunn had kept on his gardener. He won the prize for the largest melons and the best late cabbages but was beaten out by John Redpath's gardener for the best hollyhocks and most unusual dahlias. Shaded from the unseasonally hot weather by parasols and fans, the ladies were entertained by Mr. John Peacock's rare singing birds.

The party was a personal celebration for Alexander: Julia had finally succumbed to her suitor's persistence. When he wrote, "My dearest Julia, my desire for favour in your eyes is subordinate to the desire for your future happiness. Yours, A.X.," Julia replied, "My dear Mr. Cross, Since I have fully made up my mind I shall at once put an end to your suspense by letting you know that I am willing to trust my happiness with you. Ever yours, Julia. *P.S.* If disengaged, come up this evening."

Early in 1850 Alexander made a pilgrimage back to Braehead, Scotland. While there he purchased an entire set of silver for his future home, including two solid silver, eight-holder candelabra. Years later his granddaughter would remark, "He must have thought he was marrying royalty." Alexander probably harboured no such thoughts but was simply rebuilding a lifestyle he had once known as a small boy.

In the custom of Lower Canada, Alexander and Julia drew up a marriage contract. There would be no community property and while Julia would bring some $2,600 to the marriage, she would proffer no dowry. Her cash, stocks, belongings and any future Montreal property that would come to her from her half-brother James Hutchison would remain hers alone. The couple were married at the Montreal Methodist Church on July 30, 1851.

Through careful supervision of his affairs during the next three years, William Lunn was guided by Alexander to financial success. In 1854 the family would sell part of the valuable McTavish property, realizing enormous returns with compound interest. Everyone involved was able to pay off their mortgages on all properties, and still keep what Lunn described as a "very handsome residue." Convinced that his return to good fortune was an example of God's special favour, rather than that of a newly buoyant economy, Lunn would write, "I pray that I may enjoy intimate communion and friendship with Him and feel myself to be a citizen of the heavenly Jerusalem."

Alexander belonged to an extended family boasting clear title to prodigious real estate holdings as well as investment capital. The partnership included William Lunn, James Hutchison and George Campbell, husband of Margaret Hutchison and dean of medicine at McGill University. The clan was even more fortunate in Julia's marriage. Had they not found themselves a financial adviser in Alexander, they may well have been another family to realize and lose a fortune within a generation.

2

🌿 *The Drevers and
the Red River Settlement, 1820-49*

*"To some of us has been given the privilege . . . of early participation in the joys,
the hardships, the struggles, the achievements attendant upon the dawn of
community life in a new land . . ."*

May Armitage, found in
Jean Drever Pinkham's memoirs

In the town of Kirkland on the Orkney Islands, eighteen-year-old
William Drever was the last of four brothers to leave his home. His
three older brothers had sought adventure in South America, the
United States and in the merchant marine. There was no future for
them on the Orkneys, amongst the most windswept and barren islands
in all of Scotland. In 1821, when the Hudson's Bay Company gained
control of Canada's vast Rupert's Land through amalgamation with
the North-West Company, it was the perfect opportunity for the
tall, dark Scot. On June 9, William was hired by "The Company,"
as it was called, for £15 a year; it also paid a £9 debt that he had
accrued. As the teen-ager said goodbye to his mother, she pressed
a lucky shilling into his hand. Other than a respect for good manners
and hard work, and a basic education, it was all she had to give
him. In July William Drever sailed on the *Prince of Wales*, bound
for Hudson Bay, Canada.

On August 23, 1821, the Company's schooner sailed into the mouth
of the Hayes River to its head office of York Factory. Home of the
chief factor, and main port and supply depot for over one million
square miles of Rupert's Land, the hamlet buzzed with activity from
May to October. Each spring voyageurs would row, sail or paddle

downstream with the furs from their winter trapping. The *Prince of Wales* would be reloaded with hundreds of bales of beaver, wolf, mink, marten and black fox pelts intended for the markets of Europe. The black fox alone brought fifty guineas in the finer shops of Aberdeen.

Commerce was York Factory's sole industry. During its brief summer, turnips, cabbages and potatoes grew only the size of walnuts and competed in the Company's vegetable plot with wild cranberry, swamp currants and gooseberries. Only those who learned to live off the land would survive in the harsh environment.

William Drever proved to be such a youth. He worked as a carpenter for just one month before being ordered north for two weeks to the trading post of Fort Churchill. It was no trip for the faint-hearted; even in late summer Hudson Bay could be lashed by gales and sudden snowstorms. But no adventure ever seemed to frighten William. The teen-ager harboured visions of carving a commercial empire from the wilderness, and the route to his goal lay through the Company. William boarded the little ship and headed north.

A squall struck. Winds blew the ship off course, tossing it among the huge icebergs whose shifting masses growled and cracked like rifle shots. William was shipwrecked in a wasteland of blue-tinted glaciers where the wind chill factor dropped to minus 80 degrees Fahrenheit. The fate of his mates is unknown, but Cree and Swampy Indians befriended the Orkney lad. They taught him their language and their survival lifestyle.

William learned how to hunt polar bear and elk, then use fine rawhide to sew garments from the skins. He learned to protect his eyes against snow blindness, to shoot the white hare which darted across the whitened land. He became skilled on snow shoes and in driving dogsleds in air so clear and dense that sound carried for miles. He told of hearing the crack of a trader's whip during that winter, yet it was over a day later that the frontiersman arrived. The two figured the sound had travelled a distance of nearly sixty miles.

In the following spring William returned to York Factory and was given a raise to £25 per annum. For the next eighteen years he worked as a carpenter building York boats. The forty-foot craft were designed especially to navigate the turbulent rivers of the northwest. Acting as postmaster as well, William ordered in dozens of books for the community, in particular the novels of Sir Walter Scott. He and other Orkney men so impressed the chief factor, J.J. Hargrave, that the latter reported them as "... worthy of confidence.... The lives they lead are as free from vice as could be expected. . . ."

News from the Red River Settlement far to the south arrived each spring as the trappers paddled downstream to York Factory with their heavily laden canoes. The story of this tiny village was one of privation almost beyond description. Death by freezing or starvation was as terrible as sudden attacks by warring Indians. Only brave spirits combined with the Hudson's Bay Company's fur trade and annual food supplies – if they arrived – kept them alive. The demoralized and beaten left for the United States. Those that hung in, Scots, French, Métis and Indian, fought alongside each other for survival. Slowly, the settlement took root.

By 1835 survival alone was insufficient in the Red River Settlement. A council was formed which introduced an import tax, oversaw the formation of a voluntary police force, and appointed four magistrates to deal with civil infractions. Settler Alexander Ross wrote that the farming Scots prospered, while the Métis hunters lived for the moment and stayed poor. When times were harsh the Métis blamed the Company for not sending supplies. When buffalo hunts provided plenty of meat and trapping lines an abundance of furs, they blamed the Company for unfair trading restrictions. When Montreal voyageurs brought word of the 1837 Rebellion, the Métis thrilled to the courage of their Canadian brothers, raised their own "Papineau Standard" and chanted patriotic songs. They demanded land grants similar to those enjoyed by the Scots, and freedom to trade amongst each other or with Americans.

Sensing the tremors of a western rebellion, the powerful Sir George Simpson, governor of the Company, travelled upriver to the settlement. He reminded the Métis that the Company "was the legal owner of their parents' inheritance." He urged them to renounce their savage ways and become Christian farmers so that they could enjoy the same privileges as the whites. The main condition Sir George placed on the Métis was that they sell furs only to the Company. Many Métis attempted to follow his advice by farming across the river in St. Boniface. But by 1838 squabblings, fights and even killings broke out anew. As complaints against the Company grew, so did an alliance with the American trappers and traders operating illegally around the settlement.

A judicial structure may have been needed for the community, but in the Company's perception, no one was in greater need of judicial protection than itself, owner of the vast land and the pelts therein. Thus, in 1839, Lord Durham appointed none other than

Adam Thom, Sir George Simpson's friend, to be the first recorder, or judge, of Rupert's Land. Thom had read law for one year upon his return to Scotland and was instructed officially to establish and interpret British jurisprudence as related to civil and simple criminal infractions. Major crimes were to be referred to Chief Justice J.B. Robinson of Upper Canada or to Great Britain itself. Despite those restrictions, with no trained lawyers to balance the arguments of prosecution and defence, Adam Thom was handed the most powerful appointment west of Upper Canada. His annual salary of £500 plus £200 for living expenses underscored the importance placed on the post. The needs of the Company would become synonymous with the law as Thom ensured its interests.

At the same time, the Company also sent to the Red River Settlement a loyal Scot who had proven genuinely friendly and respectful with Indians. He was the multilingual, easy-going William Drever. Although he understood the ways of the French voyageurs and Indians, William still observed the manners revered in his Orkney home and by the Company. His deportment, his acceptance of and by the natives, and his enterprising ways had not gone unnoticed by Sir George Simpson. In 1834 the governor himself had renewed William's contract and more than doubled his original salary to £35 a year. Given one day's notice for the seven-hundred-mile trip to the Red River Settlement, thirty-seven-year-old William loaded his long voyageur's canoe and on July 6, 1839, paddled into the Nelson River.

In 1839, Adam Thom was in his home city of Aberdeen when he received Lord Durham's offer. He accepted, then advertised in the *Aberdeen Journal* for a servant-nannie to accompany himself and his family to Rupert's Land. Thom was looking for a well-educated girl of proper Scottish deportment. He specifically wanted one who had no "friends" or marriage prospects in the new world, for he expected a four-year term of service. Before long he received a reply from a highly qualified girl by the name of Helen Rothney.

Only one "gentleman's seat," or estate, existed in the parish of Insch, county of Aberdeenshire, an area known for its superior farm land. It belonged to the Rothney family. Their home was described as "a handsome, modern mansion ... finely situated on ... the northern bank of the Shevock [river] ... the approach to which from the village is particularly admired."

The Rothneys entertained high expectations for their clever eighteen-year-old daughter. Helen's statuesque height of six feet was enhanced by cerulean eyes and coal-black hair cut to a soft curl.

She was a catch for a man of substance and the Rothneys expected her to marry and raise a family in the genteel country society of nineteenth-century Aberdeen.

Helen had different ideas. Raised in a strict Presbyterian atmosphere, the deeply religious girl also possessed a passionate temperament. She thirsted for adventure. It was in this latter mood that she happened upon Adam Thom's advertisement. The Rothneys feared she had taken leave of her senses when she stormed off to meet Adam Thom. On a map, the Red River Settlement would appear as a diminutive mushroom struggling to grow in thousands of square miles of prairie wilderness.

Thom may have attempted to intimidate his prospective nannie as he described the privations which lay ahead. He was known to pace the floor and wave his arms to emphasize a point, and his appearance alone was sufficient to command attention if not awe. At a slightly stooped six feet, his heavy features settled into his starched white collar, and his protruding forehead gave the effect of a perpetual frown.

As Helen was a fraction taller than the judge, however, she held the advantage of looking down on him. Few others could penetrate his legendary gaze. Whether amused or impressed by her temerity, Thom awarded her the position. Helen returned home and announced her intentions to sail for the new world. Her parents were shocked, her friends amazed, but they knew that no one ever changed her mind. Pledging to return home at the close of her four-year contract, Helen embarked with the Thoms for Montreal via New York in the late spring of 1839.

The party travelled westward through the United States by stage coach, then river boat. They were laden with multifarious goods, furniture and crates of books. Judge Thom would see that his son became as erudite as if he had been educated in the best of Aberdeen schools. Mrs. Thom proved a fragile, timid woman who was apparently relieved to have Helen along. Her servant was frightened of nothing, even her husband's temper. This was not to suggest that Thom ever lifted a hand to man or beast. Resorting to violence would have demonstrated a flaw in his intellect and the judge acted as if he had no defects.

In July 1839, as William Drever paddled southward along the shore of Lake Winnipeg, the Thoms were completing their northwestern journey from the United States. They had suffered heat waves and hailstones, black-flies and mosquitoes. As they crossed the border into Rupert's Land they gazed at billowing prairie grass and, occasionally, buffalo herds as far as the eye could see. Upon approaching the settlement they saw log homes extending for twenty miles between the Upper Fort Garry and the Lower, or Stone, Fort. Their destination was the latter and it proved as noisy as the Aberdeen market. Trappers constantly came and went, delivering their bundles of furs to be packed out in canoes and York boats with the spring breakup.

The Thom residence proved neither as large nor as roomy as the judge had hoped, but Helen and Mrs. Thom settled the family in, hanging wallpaper and gracing their parlour with the furniture which had survived the journey from Aberdeen.

Helen never went without at the Thom home. Most important, she enjoyed a wealth of learning not only from the bookshelves but also from her master. Thom lectured anyone who would listen on his strange theories of mathematical and astronomical links to the Bible or on his multilingual studies of philosophy and languages. She could argue with the judge over any case he brought home, and although few ever won a point against him, no atmosphere from Aberdeen to Montreal was better suited for learning than in this wilderness home under the tutelage of Adam Thom.

Most of the other Scottish homes in the Lower Fort were simple but all were immaculate. The men dressed in clean white shirts, even when planting seed and tilling the soil. Their children were well clothed, their barns were filled with grain and their cattle were protected in stables.

The Métis were less industrious and lived more for the moment. After Sunday church the Scots often had to jump off the road to avoid their swiftly driven carioles decorated with blankets, furs, polished leather and bells. Helen found them a handsome, fun-loving people who fiddled and danced while talking endlessly over gallons of tea. Already fluent in French and soon in Cree, she described their sense of humour as being as bright as their blue capotes and red-belted corduroy trousers. In turn, the fine-boned, slender Métis women befriended the Scottish lass.

Thom might have taken a lesson from the family nannie, for while he soon spoke fluent Cree for the sake of expediency, he never spoke one word of French, and distinguished between the cultures by referring to the English as "exotics." As everyone in the settlement was indebted to the Hudson's Bay Company, Thom's influence was felt deeply, and settler Alexander Ross wrote that from the start they were oppressed by his presence and his harsh judgments.

On August 13, 1839, an outrider galloped into the fort hollering the news of approaching voyageurs. One of the settlers' greatest delights was to meet them at the end of their seven-hundred-mile journey from York Factory. They were the sole contact with the outside world, and the annual letters which they delivered were greatly anticipated by the community. Helen gathered her long skirts and ran with everyone else to the river's edge. Some of the women brought kegs of rum for the thirsty men. As the York boats and long birchbark canoes drew closer, the shouting back and forth escalated to a joyous cacophony and the men finally disembarked to be greeted by boisterous hugs and ladles of rum.

Helen watched a towering, black-bearded man slip his canoe onto the river bank, then jump out. When he stretched like a giant, he looked straight at her with the bluest eyes she had ever seen. A friend saw the look, nudged her and said, "Aye, there's the man for you to marry." Helen stood tall and scoffed, "I dinna care for a man wi' a great beard li' that!" William Drever may have heard her remark, for the next time she saw him he was clean-shaven and, according to her daughter's memoirs, the handsomest Scot Helen Rothney had ever seen.

Adam Thom continued to count on his children's nannie remaining unattached during her four-year term of commitment. Helen had become invaluable to him. Not only could she run an upper-class household, but she was a buffer between the egregious master and his timid wife. To lose her would be unthinkable. But if he noticed Helen's increasing interest in the Company store where William was clerk, his concerns were well founded. Helen and William fell in love. Thom responded by continuing to withhold his servant's entire salary since she had sailed from Scotland in 1839.

Helen's passionate nature emerged in full, and if she entreated her employer to release her from the contract to marry William, she failed. By September 1842, she was growing visibly pregnant and the situation had become intolerable for both parties. She subsequently claimed that Thom fired her without ever giving her a penny of her wages.

It must have been an agonizing time for the twenty-one-year-old girl, raised in the strict propriety of the Presbyterian church. She might have sought instant respectability through marriage to William but that did not happen. More than her shame, she saw that Thom's action was a travesty of justice. Perhaps she recognized that the quality of the fledgling community lay in the fairness with which the law was enforced, for on February 16, 1843, just three weeks before the birth of her baby, she laid formal charges of breach of contract against Judge Adam Thom. With a rare exception, no one had challenged the autocratic man who would be recorded in history books as "the father of the bench and bar in the west."

The settlement's four magistrates were delighted with Helen's charge. Time and again they had been overruled by what they saw as Thom's self-serving judgments, by his ability to twist and untwist interpretations until the conclusion suited his cause. As resentment had increased toward Thom, it had also increased toward his employer, the Hudson's Bay Company. Helen Rothney was the magistrates' tool with which to strike back at both.

After Helen had laid her case before the magistrates, Thom moved to his own defence. He claimed that he had paid her wages to September 1842, the month that she was not fired but rather left the household for six months' sick leave with pay; it was only this last half-year he had withheld. The magistrates did not believe him. In their final decision, they awarded Helen not only full back wages and her passage to Scotland but they offered to seize the Thoms' entire household inventory as assurance that justice would be executed.

The judgment gave Helen the opportunity to fulfil her promise to her parents and return to Aberdeen. But the thought of facing her Presbyterian parish with a babe in arms must have seemed frightening, if not impossible. Her life was no longer in the old world but in the Red River Settlement with William Drever. She made her decision accordingly. Forgoing the magistrates' ludicrously gener-ous offer, she turned to the bench and requested only what she felt was rightfully hers – four years of back wages for dedicated service. Letitia Hargrave, wife of the factor and sister of Governor McTavish, wrote that "the magistrates were indignant at her compromising." A furious Thom wrote a thirteen-page argument demanding a trial by jury. The magistrates refused and the matter was closed.

Almost a century before women would be afforded any legal rights equal to men, Helen Rothney had courageously pursued her concept of justice. The victory of the servant over her master must have symbolized, particularly to the Indians and Métis, hope for greater impartiality in the court of the Red River Settlement.

Shortly after the birth of their son, Helen Rothney and William Drever were married in St. James Anglican Church, on March 30,

1843. Clad in a magnificent christening gown given to him by the wife of the chief factor, the baby was christened William, and later nicknamed Willie.

The Rothney case hardly slowed the judge. Within the year he exceeded his jurisdiction by building a gallows and hanging a Salteaux Indian found guilty of murder. A number of settlers felt so intimidated by Thom and the Hudson's Bay Company that they left the territories to live in what they saw as the friendlier, more unrestricted United States.

By late spring of 1843 William and Helen were completing their small log cabin at the Lower Fort. It would be a far cry from the luxury of the Thom home, and they would have to do it all themselves. As oxen hauled the logs and William hoisted them into place, Helen chinked them with the sticky Red River gumbo. At first William framed parchment windows, then with the arrival of the summer goods, replaced them with glass. William built their furniture and friends quilted them a bedspread. The one-room cabin was dominated by a great stone fireplace. For warmth underfoot they placed tanned buffalo skins on the hard-packed mud and dung floor which was polished to a high sheen. Helen would bear five babies in this log shanty with the help of a Métis midwife. Four children had been born by 1849: Willie in 1843, Jamie and Maggie in 1846, Jean in 1849. Mary Isabella and Christin would follow in 1852 and 1854.

Almost each day of survival in the Red River Settlement was a triumph. In the year that Helen bore two babies, epidemics ravaged the village. First, influenza and measles swept through the whites, then the "bloody flux" or tuberculosis struck both Indians and whites. By the end of two weeks, 324 settlers were dead. Although the Drevers escaped that plague, William subsequently fell ill from typhoid fever. As she cared for her husband day and night, Helen also nursed her baby, born in the same bed in which William lay near death. She was her own physician and mothers believed that if nothing else, breast milk protected babies against disease.

During William's crisis, word spread quickly through the nearby Salteaux encampment that he was ill. The menfolk gathered and surrounded the Drever cabin, only the soft sucking sounds of their footsteps in the mud announcing their approach. They peered through the windows at their friend who had fallen into a deep sleep. Suddenly they began shouting and singing in the wildest way. Helen was frightened and at first begged them to go away. They refused, explaining, "We are driving the bad spirit from your husband's body."

Whether it was the nights of vigil, Helen's prayers, or the Salteaux' songs, William lived. To Helen, every disaster or blessing held a spiritual connotation; perhaps she believed the Lord had a greater plan for her family to serve Him. But perhaps they survived because they stayed isolated from the community and drank nothing but boiled rain water.

During those years Helen longed for a Presbyterian church or minister, but the Company recognized only the Anglican and Roman Catholic faiths. At the Thoms' she had listened to the judge read the Bible during twice-daily services in the dining room, but not even Adam Thom had budged Sir George Simpson on the issue of Presbyterianism. That the Scots were denied their right to worship in the church of their choice was a source of community grievance. For a while Helen held services for her children in their cabin before choosing a formal alternative. She joined the Anglican church and vowed to support it forever. When a Presbyterian minister was finally allowed into the settlement in 1851, Helen remained true to her commitment; and eventually she helped Anglican Bishop Machray to compile a booklet of family prayer.

Around 1849 William and Helen moved to the Upper Fort and built a log house at the junction of the Red and Assiniboine rivers. Three other families joined them. The Drevers, McDermotts, Bannatynes and Rowands purposely built their shacks at the lowland confluence. The other Scots thought the four families were crazy moving to this lonely flood zone. Their only neighbours were the Salteaux and Plains Indians. But William's 1821 dream of a commercial empire linking the Red River Settlement with the United States had never been far from his thoughts. He was also granted Lot 1212 at Point Douglas on the river bank. To William, the rivers were common highways between the hinterland and the civilized world. He believed that the settlement could someday become a city as fine as Montreal.

Soon weatherbeaten a silver-grey from sun and wind, the four log homes blended into the clay-coloured mud like stones sinking into quicksand. Save for stables and outhouses, there was nothing except Fort Garry, the Indian camp and a small village about three hundred yards to the west. Outside the Drevers' cabin a rowboat lolled on its side like a horse secured to its hitching post. It was their only escape should the rivers suddenly overflow in the spring thaw. Beyond the Indian camp endless miles of sepia-toned grass stretched toward the distant sky. A few thousand acres of land lay cultivated between them and the Lower Fort twenty miles to the northeast, but for eight months of the year, the ground lay frozen and seemingly lifeless.

The Drevers shared their lives and their plenty with the Indians. Years earlier when he had lived in York Factory, William had welcomed a hungry Cree to his table. He thought no more about it. One day in the Red River Settlement, seven hundred miles from York Factory, an Indian had appeared at his door. Holding out a beautifully tanned deer skin, the man had said, "Fifteen years ago you fed a starving Indian. I am that man. This is my thanks." Then he was gone. William never saw him again.

When the Indians came and sat cross-legged on the Drevers' earthen floor, Helen told them Bible stories in Cree. She combined her missionary zeal with a motherly visage, drawing them into her spiritual warmth near the old wood stove. In turn, the Indians brought gifts of berries and a treat for Helen's babies: delicious bladders of marrow-fat made from buffalo bones.

Helen arose at dawn's light to cook on the wood stove even on sweltering summer days, to make candles from animal tallow, to pound dried meat, fat and berries into pemmican, to bake bannock, and to prepare her family's clean shirts, aprons and dresses with starch made from the pulp of ground potatoes. Each day she rushed to complete tasks before nightfall. Spring, summer and fall were merely times of preparation for winter. She slept lightly, needing to be one step ahead of nature and its challenges. The essence of Helen lay not only in service to her family and the Lord, but in wresting civility from the harsh land. She embraced old world dignities and new world realities. Her children received daily instruction in deportment, education and religion. Jean wrote that they stood at attention for their meals and learned their lessons and their psalms from their mother. They learned the ways of the land both from their father and from their French, Scot, Indian or Métis playmates. In the spring breakups, most boys and sometimes their sisters secretly played the dangerous game of crossing the river on the tumbling ice floes. Whatever they did, the Drever children laughed and chatted in polyglot Cree and French flavoured with a Scottish accent. And while the girls learned how to curtsey, to them, their mother's stories of finery and carriage rides through the cobblestoned streets of Aberdeen were but bedtime fairy tales.

The Drevers remembered their Red River years by the forces of nature rather than by political turmoil. Everything depended on the weather. On a good summer day a sea of billowing green grass danced about the plains. Squalls scudded along its surface, rippling its flow and changing its sway as spindrift on the crest of ocean waves. The sky at dusk was ablaze with colour and the promise of a fine harvest. But they never took anything for granted. They knew that a dark line on the horizon could appear like the single slash of an artist's charcoal, then spread like a billowing black sheet and shower them with hailstones, insects or snow.

In 1847, with a threatened American invasion, Sir George Simpson requested and got five hundred soldiers of the Royal Regiment for the Red River Settlement. They flooded the economy with sterling and enlivened the social life of the community with fancy-dress balls as in Helen's Aberdeen of yesteryear. Then in 1848, following the signing of the Oregon Treaty, the Canadian government recalled the regiment and replaced it with 140 pensioners too old and unskilled to keep the peace. The Métis, so often criticized for their indolence, were considered better citizens than the pensioner army.

The settlement's economy plunged and squabblings began anew. The aging Governor Caldwell, so tall that he had to stoop when entering the Drevers' door, impressed young Jean as a delightful gentleman. To the community, however, he was so utterly lacking in leadership or administrative ability that Judge Thom remained the most powerful man in the community.

In the spring of 1849 four Métis were caught trading furs amongst themselves on the shores of Lake Manitoba. While this was expressly forbidden by the Hudson's Bay charter, the Métis and Indians considered the furs theirs by birthright. Judge Adam Thom slated the trial for May 17, Ascension Day, a Roman Catholic religious holiday. The date was an insult to half the population. The trial was symbolic of native grievances against British rule and the Métis' desire to trade independently from the Company. Such an event was of paramount interest to everyone in the settlement. While they sympathized with their Métis friends, the Drevers supported the Company's policy of absolute power over the charter. Fearing an American invasion, William and Helen believed it was the only way for Rupert's Land to remain a part of the British Empire. Moreover, the Drevers were as curious as everyone else in the Red River. Gossip was almost a staff of life and while the telegraph was still thirty years away, news travelled so swiftly that the 11,500 settlers scattered over twenty miles were informed almost as soon as an incident occurred.

That morning Louis Riel Sr. had delivered a fiery oration against the Company from the St. Boniface Church, then incited the Métis to head for the trial. His young son Louis, the same age as Willie Drever, was probably witness to the church meeting at least, if not to the ensuing scene. Hundreds of shouting Métis left the church, crossed the river, then scooping up stones and clubs raced to surround the court house. Within the hour, nearly four hundred Métis, French Canadians and Indians had gathered in the village square. Only the bravest Scots joined the crowd, but the Drevers could easily hear the cries for "Le commerce libre!" punctuated by gun shots. At exactly two minutes to eleven Judge Adam Thom appeared and strode directly through the angry throng into the court house. Alexander Ross wrote that his bellicosity caused even the armed to step back and allow him to pass unmolested. As usual, Thom tried the French-speaking Métis in English.

In the innocence so characteristic of the Métis, accused Pierre-Guillaume Sayer encouraged his son to tell the truth about the fur trade on Lake Manitoba. In so doing, the boy condemned his father by the rules of the Company. Subsequently addressing the court in his broad Aberdonian accent, Adam Thom pronounced the four Métis guilty, then in a jumble of verbosity acquitted them and returned their furs. Future trappings, he reminded them, would still belong to the Company. Misunderstanding the judgment, the Métis rushed out to the street shouting, "Le commerce est libre!" and shooting their guns in acclamation. The words reverberated throughout the village, across the river banks and downstream to the lower settlement before the judge was out of the court house. When the Métis finally realized that Thom had meant nothing of the kind, the bitterness culminating from the frustrations of a decade were unleashed against him. More than ever he symbolized Company oppression. Adam Thom was lucky not to have been killed.

By way of chance or perhaps by some greater design, Helen's association with the erudite if difficult Adam Thom had strengthened her courage and increased her faith in the future of the Red River Settlement. Her passionate character had matured into one which also encompassed discipline, tenacity and foresight. In building her family's foundation, she epitomized the fundamental values which nourished a fledgling nation.

3

The Macleods of Scotland and Upper Canada, 1844-49

"I have an unsurmountable ambition . . . to place my wife and children in a position where they, by their own efforts, may obtain independence, which in this country is impossible to accomplish."

Captain Martin Macleod

The best time of day for eight-year-old James Macleod and his ten-year-old sister Maggie was after school. At two o'clock they would coax their cantankerous Shetland ponies near, slip bridles over their heads and ride toward the hills. The children's choice of adventure was endless on some twenty thousand acres of their Drynoch lands on the Isle of Skye. From the lower pastures the ocean surf deafened them as it thundered against the stone wall surrounding their home. Mindful of the stones underfoot and the tricks of their ponies, James and Maggie trotted through fields of hay, oats, potatoes and turnips that stretched all the way to the foot of the hill called Ben Dhu. They waved as they passed Behac, one of Drynoch's nine dairymaids. Behac (Gaelic for Rebecca) taught the eight Macleod children how to milk the Ayreshires as they stood untethered in the fields.

As the children rode higher, they could wander freely among thousands of black-faced sheep and black cattle which grazed on unfenced pastures. Their Loch Brockadale and mountain streams abounded with trout. In spring primroses and bluebells lined their path. In summer they jumped off their mounts to gather roses and bog myrtle. Heather and bracken on the slopes sheltered untold numbers of birds and it was not extraordinary for their father and his party to bag three to four hundred brace on a good day.

A favourite goal for the children was Croach Martin to the south of Drynoch. It was a misty, eerie place with ruins at the top, and hermits were not uncommon in the Highlands. Each time James and Maggie met the superstitious old hen-wife, she would stab her finger at them and try to frighten them with her moans.

Upon returning to the stable they would rub their ponies down, using the fresh-scented straw just pulled from the stack. If the rain had been falling, as it so often did on Skye, steam would rise from the bodies of ponies and children alike, filling the stalls with a delicious musty stable smell. James and Maggie were mindful that caring for their ponies before themselves was a family rule. "Someday your lives might depend upon your mounts," warned their soldier father, Captain Martin Macleod.

Their tasks done, James and Maggie ran down to the rambling old stone and wood home of Drynoch. Before they could go inside, they had to make up a quick poem in Gaelic or French and shout it into the wind. It was a game. Once approved by their parents, they entered for tea and oatcakes with the fifteen others living at Drynoch. There were mother, Jane Fry of Ireland, father, Martin Macleod, retired from the Moiras Regiment of India, the children: Norman – already a man – Henry, Catherine, Lexi, Beth, Maggie, James, then Donald. Then as well as Grandmother Macleod and Aunt Sibella, there were two governesses, the music and dancing masters, and the Reverend William "Bill" Greig, who was both the Episcopal clergyman and the boys' tutor.

The children began their day an hour before breakfast with their classical music lessons: Norman on the cello, Henry on the violin, Beth and Lexi at the piano, and James on the flute. After breakfast the girls would walk four times around the garden path with bottles on their heads to improve their posture. Then they would return to the house for school. In the evenings after dinner, arithmetic and dancing lessons continued. They had music every night. Just before bed they held evening service in the dining room. Standing with backs to the sideboard, each child recited a psalm. Then together all eight children would say good night and run off to bed.

On Sundays everyone drove the eight miles to Caroy Church in an omnibus drawn by two big horses, a postilion riding on one. Bill Greig's chapel accommodated six families there on the shore of the Bay of Caroy. Maggie wrote that their worship and singing was as simple and as true to the old Scottish faith as she believed any could be. Afterwards the children ran back up the hill into the omnibus, reached under the seat and pulled out a parcel of sweet oatcakes baked by their servant Hannah. At the age of seventy, Maggie wrote, "Dear old Drynoch was full of love, and it was the sweetest place under the sun to us."

The children's world was encompassed by Drynoch and the marvels of Croach Martin. They were oblivious to the fact that their island was swamped by poverty and religious decay. Upon Martin's return to the windswept island in 1832, having served as an army captain in the Caribbean, India, Canada and France, he had learned that his father had bankrupted Drynoch. His brother had expropriated funds from the Bank of Scotland and his brother-in-law was suing for a promised but undelivered £500 dowry. Out of ten thousand sheep less than three thousand were alive and all were suffering from the scab. Heavy rains and gale force winds had destroyed the crops. Yet, despite economic ruin, Martin's clan chieftain and cousin, Norman Macleod, kept land rentals high.

Another tragedy for the Macleods was the demise of Presbyterianism and the emergence of the Scottish Free Church. In 1832 Jane had given birth to a frail baby. They took the infant immediately to be baptized, but two separate ministers demanded first that the Macleods conform to the beliefs of the Free Church. When they refused, neither would conduct the baptism. With babe in arms, Jane and Martin returned home in their open cart. A heavy rain was falling. Their baby grew feverish and died. Martin and Jane buried him beside his ancestors in their loch-side churchyard. Stricken with grief over what he called the fanaticism of the new lay preachers, Martin withdrew the entire family from the Presbytery. Eventually he invited the Episcopal minister, Bill Greig, to live in their home.

Skye had become Martin's prison, his walls the sea, his warden his own cousin Norman Macleod. His sons' only future on Skye lay in the repressive military which he claimed had broken his health and killed seven of his brothers from tropical disease. Suffering from recurring malaria and spinal rheumatism, the embittered man vowed he would never see even one son return from foreign campaigns with diseased livers and enlarged spleens.

The Highlanders' clan system compounded the difficulty of breaking free from an insular and ancient culture. A man of stature both in height and integrity, Martin felt committed to his chieftain, who in turn feared the disintegration of a centuries-old way of life. By binding Martin to Drynoch, Chieftain Norman Macleod knew the entire village of Brockadale was sustained.

In 1832 Martin requested and received a grant of crown land in Canada, a colony where his children might carve out their own lives free from the military. Through correspondence with a friend, he was attracted to the area known as Richmond Hill, Upper Canada. There, numerous retired army officers enjoyed a new world environment with old world civilities. In nearby Toronto, excellent private education was available, although the cost was high.

Martin's hopes of emigrating repeatedly soared only to be dashed by myriad stumbling blocks. The chieftain advertised an inflated rental fee to prospective lessees of Drynoch. Martin's mother never told him that his father had left the entire estate to him and thus he could have sold it. He assumed the crushing expense of caring for the entire household, the villagers, and of clearing his father's and brother's debts.

By 1842 most of the Macleods' children were young adults beyond the age of formal education. But there was still a chance for Henry, James and Donald to study professions and escape the army. Martin wrote of his ambition to settle his children in Canada as educated, country people. They were determined, he concluded, to quit an island they saw as damned.

Two years later the Macleods were still on Skye. That spring Martin climbed through the hills with his sons and the shepherds to count 740 dead sheep. Suppurating boils appeared on James' shoulders and the back of his head. They spread to the girls. There was no doctor on the island, so Martin wrote to Loch Borsdale and arranged for a vessel to bring a doctor to Skye. James was temporarily cured but the infection would always remain in his system. At the time, the simple absence of a doctor underscored the isolation of the island.

In 1844 a windfall came to the Macleods. Jane received an unexpected legacy from a deceased uncle and without a word turned it over to Martin. He repaid immediately his father's and brother's debts, gathered £2,000 from the sale of the remaining sheep and convinced his clan chieftain to take the 20,000-acre Drynoch off his hands for £150. He found his mother and aunt a comfortable rest home, for none of his other brothers or sisters would have them. When the landlord reneged because they were so old, a guilt-ridden Martin demanded that his brother Charles take them in and arranged to pay for their keep.

With a faith born from tradition and honour, Martin entrusted the £2,000 to Chief Macleod, arranging a 4 per cent interest to care for his mother, Aunt Sibella and his sisters. The chieftain and his banker in Portree agreed to send increments of the capital when required in Canada. With the promise of crown land secure, Martin saw little need of immediate funds other than the £700 with which he embarked.

By spring of 1845, some thirteen years after his decision to emigrate, Martin and his family were free to go. Nine-year-old James and eleven-year-old Maggie were wildly excited. Maggie wrote that they dreamed of maple sugar pouring from the trees and played Indian adventures through the copses. When sheep wandered near their playground by the river they herded them as buffalo instead.

For others, the move came hard. The Macleods were leaving behind their ancestral home recorded in the graveyard from Donald Ghu's murder in 1615 to their unchristened child buried in 1832. Beth Macleod had fallen in love with the Reverend Greig, but as he could not accompany them, they broke their engagement. Their servants wept and for the villagers it was a day of tragedy. The old hen-wife told the children that one day the natives of the new country would eat them if they had the chance.

Maggie wrote that on June 24, 1845, Skye was at its sunniest. The family packed great quantities of blankets, bedding, yarn, cloth and wine down to the dock. Anchored off shore was the *Roderick*, the ship which would take them to Glasgow on the first stage of their journey. But first, Grannie Macleod and Aunt Sibella would sail to the mainland where Charles lived. The children knew they would never see them again, and Martin did not want his mother to bear the agony of a final farewell.

Sending James, Maggie and Donald off to nearby Culore with a pet lamb to give to a poor girl, Martin told them not to return until they saw their grandmother's vessel set sail. Running to the top of Ben Dhu they could see the little Green Boat come in for their grannie. Maggie wrote that her father waved the sailors aside and, gripping the oars with his own rheumatic hands, rowed his mother and Aunt Sibella out to the *Roderick*. The children heard the clack-clanking of iron as the sailors hauled up the anchor and set sail. Then they took the lamb to Culore.

When the *Roderick* returned, Bill Greig boarded with the family to give the blessing. The evening psalm was the 104th, which said, ". . . yonder is the sea, great and wide, which teems with . . . living things both small and great. There go the ships. . . ." Maggie remembered, "Mr. Greig found it hard to read."

Bill Greig returned to shore and the captain pointed the ship out of their beautiful bay. Maggie wrote that as they sailed from the lee of the island, the *Roderick* heeled over in the fresh winds. The sailors hauled rhythmically on the sheets to hoist fresh sails, singing old boat songs and adding words of their own, "Sweet Isle of Skye, Oh, Oh! We bid you Goodbye! Oh, Oh!"

Following a fortnight in Glasgow the Macleods embarked on the 471-ton *Albion*. When they eventually arrived in Toronto via Kingston on August 27, 1845, Martin wrote that the Atlantic trip was so pleasant they could have made it in the Green Boat with a lighted candle. He found Toronto a fine, if expensive, town with broad streets and hundreds of brick houses under construction. Renting "a good looking home" for £30 a year, he planned to search for land immediately in the surrounding countryside.

First, Martin enrolled Henry and James at Upper Canada College. He was impressed by the school's character, discipline and the fact that it was not on the "rapid go-ahead system." It was costly, but for him the quality of education taught by the Anglican clergy made his struggle to leave Skye worthwhile.

On the stage coach from Kingston, Martin had met a half-pay officer who told him of a magnificent section of land available in the vicinity of Richmond Hill, eighteen miles north of Toronto. It belonged to the Comte de Chalus of France who was selling out several sections each for £1,500. The officer also informed him that during the five weeks of the Macleod's voyage to Canada, the offer of crown lands to retired soldiers had been rescinded. For thirteen years the assurance of land in Canada had kept Martin struggling to leave Skye. Even while en route through Glasgow he had been assured that lands would be available upon arrival. Appalled at the news, he was certain that paperwork was simply amiss.

The Macleods went out to see the count's forested land and were captivated by it. The 650 acres stretched along both sides of Yonge Street in the townships of Vaughan and King. Gentle slopes swelled to the highest level, which promised shelter from the north winds. Martin predicted, "We will have a delicious panoramick [*sic*] view from Toronto across the end of Lake Ontario to Niagara." As they strolled through the forest of silver maple, oak, birch and willow, they spotted squirrels storing nuts and even a fox sneaking along a fallen log. Thrushes and warblers sang unperturbed by the cries of hawks and jays. From a thirty-acre lake, trout leaped after gnats and other insects.

Not only was the property well situated, but the neighbours were of aristocratic British stock and the unofficial ruling class of Canada. Just to the north lived John Beverley Robinson, one of the most influential Canadians as the chief justice of Upper Canada. The lands of William Baldwin, brother of Reform leader Robert Baldwin, were just to the south.

Martin promptly bought the land without looking at any other. The count's attorney accepted £1,000, £250 down, the balance to be paid within sixty days. Martin wrote to his Scottish banker urging him not to lose a moment in sending the balance. He regretted not bringing all his funds to Canada, for the £2,000 would have earned 6 per cent interest.

His Canadian funds exhausted, Martin wrote the adjutant general of the Horse Guards in England reminding him of his promised land. Not for a minute did the retired soldier believe he would be refused. Then he and Jane called upon the bishop, joined the Anglican church some eight miles away, and arranged to meet the parishioners. As first cousins to Chief Norman Macleod, they were immediately accepted into Toronto society with kindness and respect. Martin wrote that they wanted no part of politics, and in those matters were delighted to find Upper Canada perfectly tranquil.

During the fall, the Macleods cleared the woods to build their new home. They had chosen the highest hill just above the lake, where a well from the glacial waters gushed fresh springs. Martin hired an architect, and found a craftsman who made his bricks at $3 per thousand; he carted them from the city for $5 - $6. Before the snow fell the family had explored the surrounding countryside as far as Lake Huron, satisfied they had made the best choice in all of Upper Canada.

By mid-winter they were all so impatient for country life that they moved from their Toronto home into an old log house on their property. They banked up the seams with clay and papered the three rooms to fend off the draughts. The women kept the wood stove and fireplaces burning constantly but it was still bitterly cold, so Jane sewed layers of red and blue flannel underwear with folds from head to foot. Delighted with the ridiculous outfits, the children turned the underwear into costumes and spent the evenings creating skits and playing charades.

One freezing February evening, the carpenters completed the tin roof and told the young Macleods that part of their new home was habitable. Returning to their log cabin the children mysteriously ordered Jane and Martin to remain by the fire. Rushing outside, they loaded two sleighs with bedding, then hitched them up to the oxen. Adding a picnic feast, they set off towards their partially finished home. There they stumbled about, lighting candles, spreading the blankets around the floor, building a roaring fire in the grate. When everything was as comfortable as could be, they returned with a sleigh festooned with bells and drove their enchanted parents back over the hills to their new Drynoch. Martin wrote in 1846 that the Macleods of Drynoch, Upper Canada, could hardly have been closer to all that they had held dear in Skye.

As for hunting, the Macleods considered themselves expert woodsmen, but upon venturing out for their first shoot promptly got lost. Landmarks once so familiar to them on a rainsoaked Skye were obliterated in a snowbound Canadian winter. They would repeatedly recross their own tracks before consulting their compasses. Then they would find that they had been snowshoeing southward when they ought to have been heading north. It was on one such occasion that they met the Ojibwa Indians. John Snake simply appeared out of the forest. He stared at the Macleod men standing awkwardly on their snowshoes, beaver caps perched on furrowed brows. Then he turned and without a compass pointed out their exact bearings. Martin was astounded and later wrote that John Snake repeated his performance even in poor weather with neither sun nor shadow. He could always lead them immediately to their destination.

Martin described the Snake family as gentle folk and unparalleled as hunters. He enjoyed their company and marvelled that John Snake could "trot through the densest forest with the agility and precision of a fox." The Indian had a way of uttering a call to make the deer stand still, even with the snarling dogs bearing down. Neither Martin nor his sons ever learned to master this, so their only chances to shoot were when the deer bounded away. As the Snakes' guns were often in disrepair they delighted in borrowing the Macleods' rifles, most careful to return them by evening. The Snakes repaid the kindness by acts, rarely gifts. Once when Martin's dog chased a deer deep into woods and became lost, one of the Ojibwas followed it for two days and eventually brought it home.

While his older brothers helped establish Drynoch, it was James who befriended John Snake's young son and delighted in their hunting treks. From this Ojibwa family, known as "the Great Serpent," he learned the language, their keen sense of direction, how to survive a freezing night in the woods and how to move swiftly amongst the trees on snowshoes. He found their wigwams warm and comfortable even in the dead of winter. John Snake lived in one with his cousin, their wives and their entire family. Their floors were layered with small branches of hemlock, pine, flat leaves and mats. A fire blazed in the centre. Their hunting implements were arranged on hooks attached to the poles which supported a covering of birchbark. Outside venison and other meat hung from nearby trees. At least a dozen hard-working, nondescript dogs roamed about, accompanying what Martin described as black-eyed, brown-skinned children who were always smiling.

Jane Macleod found the Indians "very civil fellows." When they were unsuccessful in a winter chase, she would invite them into Drynoch for a meal. Sometimes she gave them clothing, which they valued highly. To the Macleods' delight, the Indians expressed their thanks in music. Martin wrote that the Snakes' wild, sweet airs mesmerized him. Even their speaking tones pleased him, "so mellow were the cadences of their language." In turn the Ojibwa were intrigued by the Macleods' soft-spoken Gaelic, and they appreciated the Macleods' singing accompanied by their instruments. To Martin, the Indians represented more than friends. He wrote, "I was particularly enchanted by them. There was something about their simple life, so free from the cares of class restriction, which appealed to me."

Martin's tranquil moments were short-lived. In 1846 when the total cost of building Drynoch and its outhouses reached £1,000, he wrote cheques against his bank account on Skye. As his mother had died, the capital was his. He was thus both appalled and confused when the contractor, the architect and the bricklayer all complained that his cheques were dishonoured. Writing for clarification, he could but wait and watch the steadily mounting bills. He owed nine scythe-cutters who had worked the fields and helped clear more woods. Carpenters were still working on the barn, granary and poultry house. Never before had Martin owed a man a penny. He had remained in Skye to pay off his father's and his brother's debts, not his own. The laird of Drynoch was as shamed as another man might be who had committed a crime.

Eventually he learned that after they had left Skye, a blight had poisoned the entire potato crop, including the seedlings for the coming year. The Skye folk had plunged into a state of dreadful suffering and starvation. When Britain failed to send sufficient funds and food to meet their needs, without permission Chieftain Macleod had used Martin's money as well as £18,000 more to help feed his people and to meet some of his own staggering debts. Regardless of the need, it was unthinkable to Martin that his chieftain had embezzled his £2,000.

Deeply embittered, Martin used the tragedy to impress upon his children the concept of justice. No circumstances had ever angered him more than "this utterly dishonourable act." Suddenly a land grant or retribution became not only a question of honour but a matter of necessity. He had even invested his remaining cash funds into his oldest son's farming operation beside an expanded Drynoch.

In a bureaucratic run-around Martin was referred in turn to the Canadian Commissioner of Lands, the Commissioner in London, his member of Parliament, the Canadian Commissioner of Crown Lands again, and the Governor General of Canada. Martin wrote them all and anyone else of account and influence. All were gentlemen to whom he had been formally introduced and he felt sure his request would be honoured.

In the meantime, he could no longer meet the Upper Canada College education fees and brought his sons home. His daughters Mary and Kate, one betrothed to a son of the influential politician, John Ross, and the other to the Reverend James de la Touche, had neither dowry nor trousseau. Begging secrecy, a humiliated Martin wrote the gentlemen and cancelled the weddings. His only relief was that his sons would never have to enter the military, and that they had quitted a doomed Skye on the eve of the famine.

When earthly cares grew almost unbearable, Martin would pick up his "Old Rifle" and seek out the Ojibwa. An irrepressible spirit dwelt within him and he described himself as "yet the old man whose heart lifted in the forest." One evening he returned home for dinner with the entire Snake family. They all huddled around the fire, shadows dancing and blending on the walls. The flickering candlelight diffused colour of skin and cut of cloth so that the Macleods of Drynoch and the Ojibwa of the forest became one family, bound to each other and to the land. Martin turned to John Snake and said, "I am one of the Indians of the Old Country, of a tribe of warriors who are now disappearing, like yourselves, before a new people who possess the knowledge of turning the earth upside down. . . . I wish I could speak your beautiful, harmonious language, but it is better for me that I do not. The temptation of going along with you to the far, far West is less this way. You are not afflicted by protested Bills or any of the dreadful anxieties of what is called civilised life!"

Martin's financial disaster forced him to alter a centuries' old lifestyle. He let most of the servants go save for the Gaelic-speaking

Hannah, who had never learned the English language. Lexi, Beth, Maggie and Mary helped with the household tasks and kept their own flower and vegetable gardens; they already knew how to spin, milk and cook. James and Donald cared for the horses – a duty they loved – and fed the pigs – a duty they hated. Henry and Norman worked alongside the remaining field servants with their "splendid" draft horses and a pair of oxen. Martin grimaced at the sight of his sons performing such menial tasks, but when his neighbours expressed no surprise he wrote, "fortunately in this country labour does not detract from respectability."

Before long, Martin rolled up his sleeves and picked up his hoe alongside his sons. He described Jane as his "exemplary wife who joined me in the fields with amusement, she with a scarf fetchingly tied around her lovely face." From dawn's light they walked the long black furrows, sprinkling seed from baskets onto their land. Martin's rheumatism improved and they slept better. When a sickly-looking cousin came to visit, Martin forced him out into the fields too, delighted that within two weeks he looked healthy and well. When measles and scarlet fever broke out among the children the doctor said he seldom if ever saw so large a family get well so quickly. Martin credited their health to the outdoor work.

In the fall of 1846 Bill Greig arrived to a joyous reunion and to wed Beth. He was astonished at the change in the Macleods' lifestyle. After marrying, the couple settled in Kingston where Greig was appointed the minister for St. Mark's Anglican Church.

A year later, the Macleods had turned fears of agricultural failure to exaltations of success. Their horses were so overworked by farming operations that on Sundays they were too exhausted to carry the family the eight miles to church. As a compromise, Martin donated four acres of Drynoch to establish another Anglican parish. Through a community effort funds were raised to build a small church on Yonge Street. It was consecrated St. John's.

After Sunday service they returned home to tune up their instruments and gather their choral music. Martin wrote of "delicious concerts at Drynoch" attended by their singing neighbours, the William Baldwins and the J.B. Robinsons. Romance among the children and grandchildren would blossom through the years along with their favourite musical score, Handel's *Messiah*. Entrenched as the ruling class of Upper Canada in attitude if not in fact, this Family Compact choir blended voices as powerful as their social positions.

The Macleods of Drynoch were soon renowned for their musical talents. In 1847 when the Toronto Philharmonic Society was formed, Norman and Henry were invited to perform on their string instruments. Martin and Jane could never convince their daughters to exhibit what they considered their brilliant piano overtures, but what evenings they had when a concert was on! Loading their sleighs with wolfskins and buffalo robes, the Macleods donned coats, caps and gloves of bear for the seventeen-mile trip to the city. The bells on their horses' harnesses jingled as they trotted through the fluffy snow. Immediately after the concert, they returned to Drynoch by midnight, and it seemed to Martin that the stars were always shining and the moon was always full.

By the fall of 1848 the Macleods had cleared and cultivated three hundred more acres of the heavily wooded half section across Yonge Street. Their harvest included nearly seven hundred bushels of apples, some of which, Martin claimed, measured fourteen inches round and weighed one and a half pounds. They sent a few bushels to a Dutchman down the road who made them into sweet cider.

Before the ground froze, Martin and his sons ploughed a carriage lane stretching from their home down a gentle half-mile slope to Yonge Street. They lined it on both sides with silver maple saplings planted fifty feet apart. The freshly budded leaves shimmered delicately in the chill evening breezes. Martin wrote that he saw himself as he did those newly transplanted trees, their leaves dependent upon the strength of the substance contained in the root ball of their old clay. He felt that same tug and struggle as the saplings, for his success also depended on the new soil, but his lot was cast in the autumn of his life.

Martin may have felt the struggle, but the neighbours claimed that Drynoch already resembled the home of a Skye chieftain. He had even brought out black cattle from Scotland and raised sufficient funds to return James to Upper Canada College for his final year of school. He wrote that he was looking two hundred years ahead, building for his children's grandchildren. As for the saplings, he predicted that in fifty years great maple trunks would link those frail branches, shading one of the finest carriage ways in Upper Canada. The only difference between Drynoch of Skye and Drynoch of Canada was that the Macleods had done it all themselves.

After the seeding in the spring of 1849, Martin renewed his campaign for a remission instead of crown lands. With rheumatic fingers clenched around a scratchy pen that blotched his papers, he wrote to Robert Baldwin, John A. Macdonald and the governor general.

He held little sympathy for the beleaguered Lord Elgin, who had signed what he described as the "Rebel Rewarding Bill." To his mind, those in government should honour their word or such men of title were unfit to rule. Martin remarked that he knew not how to deal with politicians who granted retroactive compensation to insurgents, yet feared granting remission to an old and loyal soldier.

He never stayed angry for long. Often he would begin a letter with an expression of disaster only to interrupt his thought with a glorious description of nature. Inadvertently he would nullify the severity of his straits. Once, in mid-complaint, Martin raised his head to see James dash over the hill, a shadow balancing fishing lines for the evening rise. "Fresh trout the size of whales for breakfast!" he interjected before sealing his missive in wax and pressing home the Macleod insignia, "Hold Fast."

During his long and unsuccessful fight for crown land, Martin impressed upon James never, ever, to abide injustice. Neither father nor son would ever understand the processes or implacability of government. It would remain incomprehensible to them that politicians actually traded favours or made private deals. In 1849, however, James probably held more interest in his hunting and fishing, or that their spacious home was kept warm and dry with cheerful fires of split dry beech and maple. Despite a thermometer which occasionally stood at 10 degrees below zero, pipes leading from a hall stove to the bedrooms made Drynoch a cosy haven. Martin wrote, "Ours was a happy and blessed home. Our only surprise was how rapidly the seasons slipped away."

4

❀ The Third Generation of Crosses

"Ignorance makes a man timid."
Alexander Cross

The year 1867 was a grand time for the Crosses and their nine children to live in Montreal. The advent of railroads in the 1850s and a reciprocity treaty with the United States in 1854 had rejuvenated the economy. For Alexander in particular, 1855 to 1867 was a time of constant personal and political change. Governments were dissolved almost as quickly as they were formed, with leaders fluctuating between the Reform party and the Tories. Both included varying groups of French-Canadian activists. Alexander's appreciation of Lower Canada's cultural idiosyncrasies made him valuable to politicians of all persuasions. At forty-seven, his hair and mutton-chop whiskers fading to silver, he could reflect on financial success, a burgeoning legal practice, membership in the council of the bar since 1852, and appointment as Queen's Counsel in 1864.

One of his most significant associates was Sir George Etienne Cartier, a politician who supported the concept of the English monarchy while maintaining his French-Canadian roots. Cartier worked tirelessly toward a viable confederation of the provinces. In 1858, when he established a committee to codify the myriad laws comprising Canadian jurisprudence, he asked Alexander to assume the position of secretary. While he shared Cartier's conservative reform approach, Alexander deemed that politics should never interfere with a man's privacy or his business and refused the official appointment.

Having established his independence, including the dissolution of another partnership in which he "enjoyed all claims," Alexander then proceeded to assist his colleague J.J. Abbott in the task of establishing tariff legislation and drafting general legislation. Among his work was the first statute passed in Canada for the abolition of the usury laws. His theories on popular representation were said to have been well received and he was publicly commended by the crown for their originality and depth of thought. He also advocated the formation of a Dominion army.

By 1864 it seemed that the constitutional deadlock between the two Canadas might be resolved and a confederation possible. In preparation, Alexander worked with future finance minister Luther Holton to devise a Canadian currency. Favouring a number base of sixteen over one of ten, Alexander wrote a detailed paper supporting his argument, but was simply a century ahead of his time. Today, the hexidecimal system is the interior language of most computers.

Throughout 1864-67 notes were exchanged between Alexander, Cartier, and finance ministers Sir Francis Hincks and Luther Holton. Most were obtuse if not cryptic, but it appears that Alexander's views on politics had softened, for he sought the position of attorney general in the Macdonald/Dorion administration. Holton replied that he was impressed with Alexander's frankness and professional ability, and Cross shared the top of the list with A.A. Dorion, leader of the French-Canadian wing of the future Liberal party. Holton closed with comforting words to Alexander: "I don't forget my obligations to those to whom I owe my public position."

Admitting to an abruptness of manner, Alexander replied, "Each should stand alone. . . . Let there be no motive [other] than choice of free will." Subsequently, the position of attorney general was awarded to Dorion. Alexander would refuse the proffered position of finance minister, apparently preferring the freedom of a backroom negotiator. His decision may have centred simply on his talent as an independent financier, his impatience for political committees and a desire for privacy.

In 1867, when Justice S.W. Monk's seventeen-acre forest and Georgian home came up at a sheriff's sale, Alexander purchased the Côte des Neiges estate for $6,500. The mansion and outhouses were situated high up the mountain with an uninterrupted view of the city, the river and the distant mountains. The estate bordered the 485 acres of Mount Royal Park.

Although Julia could hear the church bells pealing continually from the city below, she wept over moving so far out of Montreal. She was involved with her city, in volunteer work at the Montreal General Hospital and with the orphanage asylum. But Alexander was determined to re-establish the country lifestyle of Braehead Manor, Scotland. No lover of mucking out stables or chopping wood, he instructed Julia to hire a staff of servants including married couples to run the home, grounds and stables. Inspired by the surrounding forest of whispering evergreens, they called the estate "Pine Avenue."

Alexander had not only returned to the country, he had established his family on one of the choicest pieces of real estate around Montreal. He had his own farm with cows, chickens, stable, the upper garden, the lower garden, orchard, forest – the compleat country life, all within commuting distance of his offices on St. James Street or the Palais de Justice. Never again would a Cross in his time suffer from want. Never again would Alexander sniff the foul stench of city sewage as he had forty years earlier.

The only scents assailing the nostrils of Janet and Robert Cross's son were those from his English country garden, tended and manicured by James Middleton, William Lunn's British gardener. Hollyhocks, hawthorne, roses, wisteria, graced the shaded lane near the house. Paths led to the croquet plateau and on down to the lower garden of vegetables, orchards and stables. Beyond, the tangled branches of basswood, oak, maple and birch exploded into a wildness of forest animals and birds.

During the fifties and sixties Julia had borne a large family. Her first son, Selkirk, 1852, would become a man of letters at Oxford and join the legal profession. On the occasion of his christening, Janet Cross sent to Alexander and Julia feather bed pillows and six sheets to express her "regard for their comfort and welfare." She wrote from Ormstown, "My dear Son Alexander. . . . I feel deeply indebted to Mrs. Cross [Julia] for [her] kindness in remembering the old Country Lady in giving the name of Selkirk to the little fellow – may he live to be an honour to us all." Janet continued that she was still "regulating the affairs of such a houseful of young men and servants." She did not attend the christening for she was not sure she could bear the fatigue of a journey.

The second child, George Harry, born in 1854, was slated by Alexander to become the family banker. Charles was born in 1856 followed by William Heber in 1858. In 1860 another baby, Julia, arrived and was described by Alexander as the most perfect child he ever knew. Until then they had been blessed with a healthy family, but in 1861 five-year-old Charles suddenly died. A shattered Julia gave birth only two weeks later to Alfred Ernest. He would be followed by Edmund in 1865, Margaret (Maggie) in 1867, and the darling of Alexander's eye, Robert, born in 1871.

The children's Pine Avenue home reflected a quiet wealth and was impressive without ostentation. Its front door faced northward toward the forest where Cedar Avenue would eventually slice through the upper third of the Cross's property, and the main hallways were always scented by fresh floor wax and flowers. The dining room with its bulbous Victorian table led to the double drawing room with its two marble fireplaces, a grand piano, brocaded draperies and English chintz. There, Julia would await Alexander's return for tea or, in winter, a few fingers of scotch. Double doors led from the drawing room to the verandah overlooking Montreal.

Alexander's study was walled from floor to ceiling with his leather-bound books. Besides his tomes of law, there were the classics which he had enjoyed since childhood: twenty-one volumes of Shakespeare, fourteen of British poets, fifty of Walter Scott and others. His desk drawers were filled with the letters of his ancestors. Alexander and William Lunn were intrigued by history and fascinated by their ancestry. To them, history was the teacher of what to imitate and what to avoid.

On Sunday evenings only, the children dined with their parents, the two flaming silver candelabra illuminating the wood-panelled dining room and wine-red decor. During the rest of the week they took their meals in the pantry where a dolly dropped down to the kitchen in subterranean depths. There, rock foundations jutted between joists and cupboards, lending a medieval atmosphere to the domain of the English cook. A giant wood stove crackled and belched to the accompaniment of the clang of the servants' bells. Warm in winter, cool in summer, the kitchen was never considered dungeon-like, and Cook sent culinary marvels of hot soufflés and brandy sauces up the lift to the black-uniformed maid in the dining room.

Ten bedrooms on the two upper floors provided unparalleled views. In one of the spacious tiled bathrooms a parrot named Lolita squawked in bilingual irreverence. Sometimes children or servants would open the cage and sneak her down to the drawing room for tea. Pine Avenue, or The Homestead as ensuing generations would rename the home, would remain a haven for the peripatetic family over the next eighty years. From the verandah and bedrooms Crosses would watch Montreal mature from Confederation simplicity to a changing skyline of multi-storied buildings and jet aircraft.

Julia's challenges lay in the efficient management of her French-English staff and growing family. A conciliatory woman, she organized a disciplined but cheerful atmosphere for the seventeen to twenty people living on the property. While the gardeners and cooks were invariably British, the maids and sewing girls were French-Canadian.

The Crosses believed that hiring the children of the habitant farmer exposed them to jobs and comfortable living quarters in Montreal usually impossible for those from the large Catholic families. It also provided their own children with unlimited bilingual practice. French was spoken as naturally in the Cross household as was Gaelic in the Macleods.

The children's lives during the 1850s and 1860s were ones of rigid discipline softened by love and every luxury a child could desire. The freedom to explore their own woods and ride their own ponies more than compensated for the rigorous expectations of a proper Victorian upbringing. Clad for outings in warm woollen dresses, white velvet leggings, velvet coats with shiny little buttons and always bonnets on their curly black hair, Maggie and baby Julia were indulged in by their parents and protected by the boys. The girls eschewed their brothers' wilder antics, preferring to play on the manicured grass in front of the house.

The boys, dark Scots all, sported about in rough wool knickers and jackets, soft tweed caps and leather boots. In winter their wooded hill became icy toboggan runs, tree trunks looming treacherously at every curve. A massive iron gate at the foot of Sherbrooke Street beside Grandfather Lunn's protected them as they flew down the mountain, out of the trees and toward the carriage wheels and horses thundering along the main street.

Another favourite sport was hitching their St. Bernard to a cart and chasing the peacocks into the woods at breakneck speed. The screeching birds were a gift from their Uncle George Campbell, dean of medicine at McGill University and a public advocate of hemorrhoid shrinkers and sarsaparilla.

One day, Harry and Willie Heber purchased a goat for 50 cents and dragged it home. At first refusing to keep it amongst his thoroughbred horses, Alexander soon gave in. He took to driving goat and cart around his estate. At times the goat would disagree with its master on the route to take, two stubborn characters clashing in a contest of wills. More than once Alexander found himself dumped into a bed of zinnias or turnips, the goat's head cocked and teeth bared in a kind of infuriating grin.

The Cross boys spent hours with their friends the Allans, Galts, Morrises, Simpsons and the Stephens, playing in St. Pierre Creek. They'd rig pieces of birchbark with stick masts and let them go high on the creek. Then they raced downstream where two giant elms stretched their branches over the water. The boys scrambled onto these undulating bridges just in time to watch their craft sail beneath them and on to uncharted seas.

Selkirk and Harry remembered taking newspapers to the farm on the Chateauguay River. They would rush to their grandmother's bedside, hugging her until her wig was knocked askew, then giggling as she gleefully nudged it back into place. The grandchildren may have remembered Janet with childlike indulgence, but to Alexander his mother was the force behind his success, the woman who had freed him to re-establish the Cross name in financial and commercial worlds.

In 1863 Janet Cross died, forty-three years after she had arrived in Montreal. Alexander and his brothers buried her at Point Round where they had defended their home in the 1838 rebellion. George Cross and his wife remained to run the farm.

Julia's mother, Margaret Fisher Hutchison Lunn, also died in 1863. James, her bachelor son, had cared for the woman who had braved winter storms from Montreal to Scotland in order to secure his fortune. Mrs. Lunn left the high-flying Uncle James, as everyone knew him, immensely rich. Grief-stricken over his mother's death, Uncle James stayed on at the Sherbrooke estate, but dined frequently with the Crosses. When he ran the liquor bills far beyond the grocery costs, Alexander passed the whiskey and port account to him. The children adored Uncle James and he returned their affections like a perennial Santa Claus.

Religion formed a cornerstone in the Cross household. Less vocal than the voluble Lunn, Alexander nevertheless may have believed that his financial successes were aided by his religious disciplines. Certainly Julia did. The children were exposed to daily scripture readings, grace at every meal, and visits from the top-hatted minister who took tea with her. Their place of worship was the venerable St. Gabriel Street Church. Knowledgeable in canon law, and recognizing the importance of self-government within the church, Alexander went to the Supreme Court in 1867 to frame an act of

Parliament which would successfully bring the church's constitution and land titles home from Scotland.

In matters of education, each child was expected to achieve bilingual and scholastic excellence, and to understand that an industrious nature, religious training and expedient politics would decide their fate and the future of the Cross name. Selkirk was the first child to attend boarding school. Alexander took his fourteen-year-old son to Lennoxville in January 1866. The town and its private educational institutions were Canada's counterpart to England's Windsor countryside. Lennoxville's stone schools reflected the quintessence of a British education. There, stern masters with excellent minds dinned into a boy, by caning if necessary, equal measures of learning, manners, religion and a stiff upper lip on the rugby field. Most significant, each uniformed boy, proudly chorusing his school hymn to the majesty of the organ in the ivy-covered school chapel, was indoctrinated into the code of an elite society, one which could be used as a network of influence throughout his life.

At first, Selkirk hated it and told Julia that the other boys were smelly, the brick walls were cold and forbidding, and he expected to die of the privation and cruelty. When that didn't move his mother, he wrote in desperation, "My dear Mamma . . . I feel awfully lonely here. If I could only get home I would live on bread and water for days if you wish. This is a horrible place. I can't learn my lessons. Plenty of the boys at school curse . . . one boy has ringworm. Show this letter to Uncle James. I went to school today and had to come home because I had such a very bad pain in my stomach. . . . If you want me to go home, just write me a letter that I can show to the rector. I can hardly keep from crying when I see the train pass because I want to go home. Your affectionate and loving son, Selkirk Cross. PS. My stomach is better now, but it might come on again."

On July 1, 1867, Confederation declared Canada a nation. Canada West was renamed Ontario, Canada East, Quebec, the Tories became the Conservatives and eventually the Reformers, Grits and Liberals would unite under the latter name. It was a festive day in Montreal, with the older Cross boys joining jubilant citizens to march through the city. Harry wrote of the sight of flags draped from every building and the sound of brass and drums playing on every street corner. At night fireworks showered the city in brilliance.

Alexander could look down on the celebrations with the satisfaction that he was a silent force in the financial and philosophical worlds of the new Dominion. Still, he could see that underlying the pulsebeat of a city self-confident with prosperity drummed the anxieties of two cultures almost irretrievably divided. That French and English citizens had looked beyond themselves in the 1864 coalition government to realize the 1867 Confederation paid tribute to their collective statesmanship, but the current of anger was omnipresent.

In 1868 Alexander Cross was elected batonnier, or president, of the Montreal Law Society. It was a significant position. For the past two decades he had been recognized as a man capable of juggling intellectually disparate points of view, of appreciating the French Canadian's identity in a jungle of cultural survival. He understood how politics, law, culture and business could be successfully blended to attract future stability in Quebec.

Holding no expressed intentions for personal wealth or fame, A'exander's financial moves seemed designed for his descendants. Although his faith in real estate was immutable and his timing superb, he rarely indulged in profits and, unlike many of his friends, he refrained from buying into the often scandalous railway plans. Instead, he built carefully but persistently, expanding his equity and foreclosing on unpaid mortgages. The only visible signs of his increasing wealth were in the monogrammed black coach with footman, and the superior bloodlines of his livestock.

By 1868 many claimed that Montreal was not only the most exciting and wealthiest city in Canada but the one which incorporated all the charm of a European town. The population had swelled to over 90,000. Port facilities were expanded, bridges built, macadamized streets were widened and beautified by fountains and trees in flagstoned squares. Some thought the grandeur of Sherbrooke Street surpassed that of New York's Park Avenue. Alexander and Uncle James built the Standard building on St. James, a street hailed as one equivalent to the most fashionable in London. They expanded their landholdings by purchasing farms in the neighbouring areas of Verdun, Hudson Heights and the Beaudette River. They also bought property with a building on King Street in Toronto.

Housing construction in general mushroomed. Montreal had spread well beyond the original city limits, engulfing many of Alexander's land acquisitions. A consequence of the maze of wooden homes were appalling fires, each of which razed hundreds of buildings before inadequate water supplies brought them under control. The resourceful William Lunn praised the Lord as he made another fortune selling fire insurance throughout the inflammable city.

Each summer the Crosses boarded the Grand Trunk Railway which sped them to their cottage in the resort village of Cacouna. Located 120 miles down river from Quebec City beside Rivière-du-Loup in the lower St. Lawrence, Cacouna sheltered the crème de la crème of British society. The Cross children's summertime friends (and future mates if their spinster aunt, Emma Lunn, had anything to say about it) formed the social register of Canada. Galts, Kings, Molsons, Stephens, Macdonalds, all wiggled toes in the sand, sailed homemade rafts, sneaked their first kiss and got sick on chewing tobacco. The Allans of the shipping line owned a mammoth summer house where children played by day in drooping bathing costumes hitched up to knees, then changed to navy jackets, boater hats and voluminous skirts for evening.

Essentially a Roman Catholic, French-speaking community, Cacouna introduced the Cross children to the eight Levasseur girls, daughters of the village mayor. Cultural differences vanished and time stood still in those lazy, magic summers. Chattering in French, the Cross boys swept up the coquettish Levasseurs in their haycart rides and evening bonfires. When they grew older, they climbed to treetops and swore everlasting love. At the end of each summer the Crosses would wave goodbye to the Levasseurs for another year, returning to their British private schools, their city luxuries and all the strictures and expectations for future achievements.

In September 1868 eight-year-old Julia died as swiftly as had her brother Charles. Grief-stricken, her mother embarked on a winter voyage to visit Selkirk, by then at Exeter College, Oxford. In her absence Alexander felt such heartbreak that living seemed unbearable. He expressed to Julia his powerful "desire to reunite with her whom I have looked upon as the most perfect child I ever knew." But he reminded Julia of their many other children who required their "most earnest and affectionate solicitude. For the sake of them we are bound to labor, to watch, to pray and to abuse none of the good gifts to us that can promote their welfare. . . . May God bless and preserve my dearest wife. . . ."

All in all, Alexander had orchestrated his life into efficiency and harmony – with one exception. Some of his sons displayed vagaries of personality that evaded his control. The boys were not entirely subject to their father's iron direction. What Alexander may never have seen was that the very behaviour patterns which puzzled and at times annoyed him were simply manifestations of the innate drive which had made him so successful. A loving father, he was nevertheless inclined to meet any signs of temerity with greater discipline. Harry was the toughest and the most rebellious. After attending Montreal High School with his brother Willie Heber, he went on to Upper Canada College, excelling in rugby and lacrosse. He always managed to just pass, ever wary of his father's warning, "Ignorance makes a man timid." Harry had no intentions of ever being intimidated by anyone, not even his father.

By the end of the 1860s Alexander expected Harry to study banking or law in Montreal. Admonishing his children to "keep in mind that French is a most essential part of education for a Canadian," he enrolled Harry in the French-speaking school at Nicolet. Harry sneaked off in boats to picnic on Lake St. Peter and once observed with pointed objectivity that "a number of boys were expelled for drunkenness." He considered himself lucky to have survived the school and was glad to eventually leave.

By 1870 Alexander and Uncle James Hutchison had sold part of the Bleury Street property to be excavated for the Hôtel Dieu, named a newly subdivided street "Hutchison," and purchased more land in the St. Anne Ward. They went on to subdivide along Bleury, St. Catherine, Peel, Sherbrooke. Alexander was weighted down by his bereavement, his burgeoning practice, his involvement in the backroom politics of the nation, and a wish to maintain the privacy of his family life. Apart from a secretary who drew up some of the wills, he conducted his own voluminous correspondence and business transactions himself.

More than ever he saw the need for his young sons to prepare for future responsibilities in the family enterprises, to run things when he occasionally went snowshoeing with the St. George's Club, duck shooting at Rivière-du-Loup, or indulged in his passion of fly-casting in New Brunswick's gin-clear Restigouche River. If the fishing was slow, he would turn his interest to the woods. He once mused over a porcupine that had crept from the bushes, nudging it gently with his fishing rod as he inspected its temperament. In one short season he and two friends together caught 299 salmon. Fortunately, Alexander and his colleagues had little time to fish.

5

 The Errant Son

"All one needs to be a successful lawyer is the gift of the gab."
James Macleod

In 1851 fifteen-year-old James Macleod was graduated with honours from Upper Canada College, then passed the entrance examinations for Queen's College, Kingston. Martin and Jane were as relieved as they were overjoyed. They had had to supplement his education at the local school with tutoring at Drynoch and James had only returned to Upper Canada College for his final year. Expressing the pride of the entire family in James's accomplishment, Martin gave him credit for hard work rather than good fortune, and acknowledged that with James's "buoyant, merry heart (it) must have been irksome." He also reminded his son, "The reward by God's step is ever certain."

That fall, Bill and Beth Greig welcomed James into their Kingston home, pleased to act as his guardians and tutors while he attended Queen's College. Martin's master plan was for James to study arts and commerce for three years, article in a law office under the auspices of Osgoode Hall, then write his bar exams in 1858. The plan was well ordered, just the way Martin would prefer to organize his own life. What no one anticipated was the rebellious energy of his son.

Just under six feet and sportingly fit, the golden-haired James was much in demand. His love for girls, wine and revelry was exceeded only by his sudden disdain for studies. By the end of 1852 the scholar had sunk from honours level to a mediocre standing of seventeenth in a class of thirty-one. At first James resolved to study harder and carouse less, even praying with the Reverend Greig for help in mending his ways. His high spirits, however, were rarely consistent with his

76

resolve. The smoky taverns and frolic of Kingston proved too tempting. The university town was filled with bright young minds freed from parental supervision for the first time, with glee, drama and sports clubs, with the pageantry of the military marching out from Fort Henry to the tune of regimental bands. Something was always going on and James was usually part of it.

The Greigs worried over their charge until James suddenly became intrigued by a Professor George and his lectures on logic and moral philosophy. A man who openly struggled with lusty temptations, the professor spoke challengingly on the value of doubt as an aid to reason, and on the veracity of nature in all her manifestations. James wrote to his father, "Professor George's lectures ... are the most interesting I have ever heard."

As much as James admired George's arguments, he admired more the beauty with which the professor articulated and delivered his lectures. As to the daily oral quizzes and weekly essays expected of him, James felt that he had presented many respectable papers. It seemed immaterial that George expounded theories identical to those of Martin. From his father philosophy was a lecture, from George an inspiration.

Delighted by James's change of attitude, Martin was certain that his son was heading for a brilliant career. He believed Professor George's claim that in no country was there fairer prospect for well-educated young men than in Canada, and especially for graduates of Queen's College. Martin's raison d'être for struggling to leave Skye was epitomized in James. But these expectations laid too heavy a mantle of responsibility and achievement upon this spirited son. James had simply responded to an intriguing teacher. In other subjects taught by duller masters, he grew bored and sloppy. One day, when faced with the reality that future courtroom fame must be preceded by studies in Greek and Latin, he decided to quit law in favour of civil engineering. James quipped that dead languages were a waste of time when the gift of the gab was all that was necessary to be a successful lawyer.

Martin shot back, "Extensive knowledge, a sound heart, and business habits are what lead to eloquence and grace of expression." Disapproving of civil engineering, he pointed out that few men rose to eminence as engineers, and he had not come to Canada to promote mediocrity in his children. "It is with my greatest effort that I try to dissuade you from these foolish intentions. . . ." James dutifully continued his law studies but with an increasingly wilder attitude. He kept late nights and begged to study in Toronto. His father refused; he could not afford the city board.

Martin would soon have to find more cash. Norman's crops had failed and Beth Greig had admitted to large debts. To help make ends meet, Bill Greig took on the clerical charge of the Kingston military prison as well as fulfilling his duties at the church, but that brought the Greigs income to only £300 per year. It was insufficient to care for themselves and for James as well. Martin suggested that the Greigs return to live at Drynoch and James find a Kingston shopkeeper who would board him in exchange for labour. So concerned was everyone over James's behaviour, however, that the Greigs remained in Kingston and Martin continued to wrestle with everyone's debts.

He also continued writing to his friend Lord Elgin, the governor general, in hopes of receiving retribution for the land promised to him twenty-three years earlier. Martin's connection to Lord Elgin is noteworthy. At the time, Great Britain was the most powerful nation on earth. Her royalty enjoyed a reverence bordering on adulation, and as the Queen's emissary to Canada, the position of governor general commanded enormous influence. Following an invitation to dine with Lord and Lady Elgin at Government House, and a visit by their excellencies to Drynoch, Martin presented the governor general with some freshly killed birds with excellent skins for his collection. Reminding Lord Elgin of his land grant, he chided, "My claim cannot equitably be denied." His gifts were appreciated, his request denied.

Martin continued orchestrating each step of James's education, explaining, "It is not your buoyant, merry heart that is the object of complaint, but inattention to your studies and duties." He admonished the youth to follow two disciplines in particular. One, to submit weekly lists of his every activity from dawn to dusk. Two, to commit portions of prose and verse to memory. Of the latter, James was to find a sequestered place in the country where he could speak the lines out loud. He was to begin moderately low, developing inflection as well as strength, and to "take great care not to overstrain [your voice] and crack it. . . . Elegance in speaking is of the greatest consequence to you."

With the combined efforts of Professor George, the Greigs and sudden attention to his studies, James graduated in the spring of 1854 with an honours B.A. in classics, moral philosophy and logic.

Subsequently, to everyone's horror including his own, he failed a law school entrance examination on ancient geography. His academic progress had ground to a halt for failing a course on what he saw as obsolete countries. Martin was staggered by his son's failure. Sending a geography text to Kingston he admonished James to aim for the Christmas entrance exam to Osgoode Hall.

James failed the examination again. Writing of his inexpressible disappointment in his son's "absurd letters" and worse attitudes, Martin warned James "to push this winter in sincere study . . . instead of passing evenings in the frivolous and very foolish gaieties of a Town life. . . ." James responded by returning to Toronto with his friends and carousing through an entire weekend. There was some adverse publicity surrounding the antics or even disciplinary action by the university. His father was informed.

Martin wrestled with the intention to bring James home to "feed the pigs for the winter," as he put it, and the desire to let his son remain at Queen's College. Of James's future Martin wrote to Greig, "The sound of an empty barrister may be loud but it will be little heeded if he may discontinue [sic] to disregard the admonitions of you and his dear sister. . . . We have real cause of gratitude and thankfulness to Almighty God that, of all our family, James is the only one that gives us cause for serious anxiety."

Festivities surrounded the Christmas holidays of 1854 at Drynoch. Martin had returned to Skye for the summer, faced Chief Norman Macleod and received some government compensation for his financial losses. (James had written of his "inexpressible joy" at the news of his father's safe and triumphant return.) He had cleared many of his debts, given Kate her dowry for marriage to the Reverend de la Touche, then had plunged back into financial difficulty again by expanding the lands of Drynoch. During that holiday, James's sister Maggie married William A. Baldwin, the widowed brother of former prime minister Robert Baldwin. This union linked the Macleods with one of the most powerful families of pre-confederation Canada.

James loved Drynoch, but chafed for freedom. He may have viewed his parents as old-fashioned, coming as they did from a more disciplined age. The generations grew increasingly fractious. Two years of James's life are unaccounted for. He may indeed have spent much of his time feeding pigs and caring for the horses with Norman. Or perhaps he spent his time between Kingston and Drynoch, detouring through Toronto or escaping whenever he could to hunt with John Snake. Like Martin, James was a woodsman, never happier in winter than when tramping through the forest on snowshoes, or in summer when stepping softly on fallen pine needles along the deer paths.

In the winter of 1855 Bill Greig suddenly died. A heartsick Martin wrote that few people were aware of the depth of his virtues, and that his equanimity had proven the only steadying influence on James. The tragedy so heightened Martin's concern over his son's behaviour that he borrowed money to liquidate Beth's debts, enabling her to stay in Kingston and supervise her wild young brother, who had been accepted back at Queen's College.

No sooner was this arrangement completed than James borrowed money from a stranger to buy into an insurance company. The loan was called, James went into debt and wrote to his father for help. For the first time Martin refused the plea, advising him to pay off his own debt at £20-£30 per annum, increasing it when possible, and always regarding the fund as sacred. Martin also advised his son to lay a certain sum aside every year as a provision for his future family, then add the interest to the capital along with the annual sum. He assured his son that in time it would grow, providing that nothing induced him to meddle with it. Such perspicacity was completely foreign to James. All his life he would prove a man of the moment, caring not so much for the future as for the joy of each glorious day as it came.

On November 17, 1856, James passed his examinations and was admitted as a student in the Upper Canada Law Society. Despite his honours standing in his bachelor of arts degree, he had lost the advantage of his early university entrance. He was unable to grasp the urgency of a professional education, aspired to more by his father than by himself. On the same date as his acceptance as a student of law, he was also accepted into the tutelage of Alexander Campbell, a Kingston lawyer whose first partner had been the Conservative leader, John A. Macdonald. The latter was so deeply involved in politics that he had failed to maintain his share of cases and the lawyers had amicably dissolved the partnership. However, as their friendship and professional association remained a close one, James found himself in proximity to two future Fathers of Confederation.

Life at Drynoch settled down for a few months. Martin and Jane prayed that now their son was settled into a law office he would become accustomed to confinement, his mind more easily moulded to the task at hand. Nothing could have been further from the truth. James longed to leave the parochial Kingston in favour of Toronto.

When Martin again vetoed that idea, James promptly joined the Kingston Voluntary Field Battery as a lieutenant. He loved the showmanship of the militia as much as he enjoyed the camaraderie of the men. Martin was furious. He had brought his children to Canada precisely to remove them from any military influence whatsoever. Father and son clashed again, but in his worst nightmare Martin could not have imagined just how far apart they were.

One Sunday Chief Justice Sir J.B. Robinson and the William Baldwins arrived at Drynoch for an afternoon walk before returning to a roaring fire and tea. William Baldwin chose the convivial moment to announce that Governor Sir William Eyre, commander-in-chief of the forces in Canada, and the Honourable John Ross, brother-in-law to William Baldwin and president of the Legislative Council of Canada, had awarded James a commission in the regular army.

At first, Baldwin probably mistook Martin's and Jane's stunned expressions as pleasurable surprise. Army commissions could only be purchased and that was beyond the Macleods' means. When Martin found his voice he expressed gratitude and pride at "the generous and munificent offer," then stated, "Of course, Jamie must be respectfully allowed to decline." No son of Captain Martin Macleod would ever enter the military. As soon as the visitors left, Martin rushed to his desk to write James. "My dearest fellow, you must know the causes of my horror and great objection to young men to enter the British army in times of peace." He reminded James that promotions came only from purchase and that as they were not a family of means, the son of Martin Macleod would be destined to associate with those of manufacturers and tradesmen. Furthermore, shuddered Martin, "the loathsome tropics are the sure destiny of a British soldier. There men rot and die like sheep of Braxy. Am I not one of eight who returned from serving in his country?" He instructed James to write a letter gratefully declining the honour. He was to send it to Drynoch. After Martin had checked it out, he would take it by hand to the governor general.

James was livid over his father's interference. To receive a commission in the regular army without buying it was a unique honour. The father-son relationship could not survive this clash of wills. James dutifully declined the offer, but for two years, apart from mailing bills to his father, did not write one line home.

Before long, the hot-headed youth crossed swords with his militia commanding officer. Required to meet for only ten consecutive days in the year, James and his men drilled regularly during the whole of winter at least one night every week. They became exceptionally fit, proud and cocky. Two of them in particular, James and a Lieutenant Wilkinson, earned the animosity of their colonel. James relished wearing his uniform to public functions, an honour unsanctioned by Colonel Jackson. Ignoring the order to dress in civilian clothes, he continued attending Government House parties in uniform. Originally the capital of Canada both in politics and defence, Kingston continued its long and colourful tradition of pomp and ceremony. Exposed to this drama as a young man of twenty-two and a member of the Upper Canada elite, James had become a swell.

In the spring of 1858 Colonel Jackson reprimanded James yet once again for wearing his dress uniform about the city as well as to the governor general's ball for the Princess Royal. James exploded. Under the guidance of his mentor, Alexander Campbell, he was learning to split the finest of verbal hairs, to transform a trivial complaint into a valid court grievance. The only drawback to his eloquence was his bull-headed temper. For a lifetime his efforts to resolve his sense of thwarted justice would be conducted without regard for the simplest political expediency necessary to survive. Ignoring the lines of protocol in lodging a formal complaint, James penned an eleven-page letter to Baron de Rottenburgh, adjutant general of the militia. He complained, among other issues, that he was not asked to sit on the platform at a soirée along with Colonel Jackson and another lieutenant, "an honour I would most certainly have declined." Also, he claimed he had just been promised a promotion, then denied it. James felt he was being discriminated against, and although he had attempted a reconciliation, the colonel had refused to meet with him. He ended with, "I cannot believe that Colonel Jackson will be allowed to treat us as his caprice may dictate."

The correct procedure in lodging a complaint was to submit it via one's commanding officer who was, of course, Colonel Jackson. James waited for almost two weeks before discovering that the colonel's aide, a Lieutenant Kirkpatrick, had been too terrified to deliver it. Allegedly James called Kirkpatrick "a damned coward," whereupon the letter promptly reached its destination. Following another period of silence, James received a strange note from Colonel Jackson. It stated that a letter slanderous to himself and signed by James had been sent to the *British Whig* newspaper. A copy had fallen into Jackson's hands and he in turn had sent it on to the baron. The colonel enclosed another copy, saying he would await both James's remarks and the baron's response. To James's horror, the letter made an obtuse attack on Jackson as a coward. It began with the lines,

"All things are infected, that the infected spy,
And all look yellow to the jaundiced eye . . . "
    Please insert the enclosed and ineffably oblige your most sincere friend, J.F. McLeod

James wrote to Colonel Jackson insisting the letter was a fraud and requested the document so that he might take steps to clear his name. Colonel Jackson refused to let him see it, saying he had sent it on to Baron de Rottenburgh. James caught the next stage to Toronto and went straight to the baron himself. Upon learning that the adjutant general had never heard of such a letter, James rushed back to confront Colonel Jackson and his bluff.

James sent the baron a copy of his complaint, then approached the editor of the *Whig* and asked him to identify the handwriting of the slanderous letter. Impossible, claimed the editor, because someone had stolen it from his office. Nevertheless, familiar with James's handwriting, the editor did not believe the misspelt signature to have been his.

Certain that Colonel Jackson had framed him, James feared he would never be allowed to march with the militia again. He believed his military career was finished unless he could extricate himself from the mess with honour. On the other hand, as the colonel's reputation was also at stake, he, too, renewed his attack on James by cutting him out of parade. When the battery marched to the railway station to meet the baron en route to his regiment, Lieutenant Macleod was never informed. Upon hearing of the march past James wrote to the new governor general of Canada, Sir Edmund Head, and demanded a formal hearing to clear his name.

James had underestimated the traditions of the British army while overestimating his legal rights. Junior officers never, ever criticized their commanding officer. Not only had James done that, he had gone over the head of Baron de Rottenburgh, who had decided to ignore the issue and let it die. Following two months of silence, James wrote the baron and asked what action the governor general had taken regarding his complaint. The baron was astonished and annoyed that James was still penning letters and ignoring protocol.

Nevertheless, Colonel Jackson received a letter from Sir Edmund's adjutant general on September 10, 1858, saying, "It is obvious that the Battery cannot retain its organization if the feeling now existing not be checked in some way." He instructed Jackson to take measures to hold a formal inquiry under the office of the governor general of Canada. At the last minute, Colonel Jackson postponed the hearing so that he could attend the Provincial Exhibition. He rescheduled it for September 29, a date when Lieutenant Wilkinson had to be out of Kingston. Perhaps fearing another cancellation, James accepted the altered date without his chief witness.

At the hearing, James brought his charges of discrimination against Colonel Jackson. In turn, he was formally charged with a long list of misdemeanours. With the exception of the *Whig* editor as witness and his own defence, James had no case. The court decreed that James "did not appear to substantiate his charge." He was subsequently reprimanded by the governor general, a more devastating humiliation than the original charge. Sir Edmund Head hinted to James that a letter explaining his situation might modify the unfavourable opinion he currently held of his conduct. Responding in a nine-page letter, James thanked Sir Edmund for considering his complaint, but "felt his severe reprimand bitterly." Believing he had presented a clear case of overt antipathy, he stubbornly requested yet another formal hearing when Wilkinson could testify and clear the accusations made against him.

Instead, Sir Edmund thanked James for his explanation and advised that the sooner the matter was allowed to drop, the better. No further hearing was granted. James was crushed. As a junior officer he had challenged an institution of British society which had proven more powerful than the process of democracy – the military hierarchy. Only time would tell whether or not his career would survive. Furthermore, he still had his father to face. First he had defied Martin by joining the militia, then he had broken the rules of the discipline he had chosen.

The news hit his family, as usual, just before Christmas. On December 21 Martin wrote to his son, "More than any of the others you have caused deep pain and anxiety to your good mother and me. I endeavoured to provide you with the best moral and intellectual training to be got in this country. I wonder whether your mind has become so slippery and alienated that you can no longer lay hold of it and make it act with some degree of thoughtfulness."

More terrible than James receiving a commission into the regular army was Martin's fear that his son might be dishonourably expelled from the militia. He wrote a personal apology to the governor general, a plea as a father and a captain of the Moiras Regiment, that his son not be judged too harshly. He described James as "an angry young lawyer suffering from a vast lack of discretion." Martin continued that he was touched with the paternal manner in which the governor general had dealt with his son rather than pronouncing instant dismissal, a move which would have proven an unbearably painfully blow to himself, his relations and his friends. He closed with the prayer that James be given a second chance, "to strive to the utmost of his power ... to deserve to be left in the possession of his present honourable post, so that he may deserve his Excellency's approbation [and] that he may look forward for promotion in the Active Force of our most gracious Majesty in this noble Colony." Martin had actually said it. If his son wanted a military life that badly, he could join, that is if the army would still have him.

Then Martin implored his son, "Be a man, my dear James, by candour, honesty, and above all, keep your present disposition." He begged him to avoid revenge against Jackson, to "let never a disparaging word be issued from thy lips against the man." Martin then drove from Drynoch to Toronto and delivered his letter to the governor general by hand. As for Jane, she had no part in this quarrel. Her role in life as mother was to love, to nourish and to endure.

While he publicly laid the issue to rest, inside James boiled with anger. For another two years he and Martin sparred, and at times James might have wondered if he was preparing for his own life or for his father's. Once, when he listed some thirteen law books which Alexander Campbell had advised him to purchase and study, and marked the six most important, Martin lost no time in obtaining them all. His son's success had become his consuming passion. Gradually James mellowed, and during the latter part of 1859 and into 1860, refused all parties, studied hard and in the words of his father, "wound up his courage" to successfully write the final examinations at Osgoode Hall. At twenty-four, he was called to the Upper Canada bar in the Easter term of 1860.

At a Sunday reception held for him at Drynoch, the extended Macleod family rejoiced that their wild brother had finally met with success. Chief Justice Sir John Beverley Robinson, by then father-in-law to Martin's granddaughter Margaret, made the congratulatory toast to James. Shortly after, Martin wrote, "Jamie, be assured, your merry and youthful heart is forever a joy to us when balanced with a sense of duty and morality."

A few months later Martin assigned James one of his first duties as a lawyer, the writing of his will. He chose heavy dusk-blue paper, the colour of the lake when the sky had a high film of cloud. His words were those of a man at peace with his world. He probably lit a pipe, filling the Drynoch study with smoke before paying tribute to "my exemplary and good good wife, Jane," and dictating to James, "my funeral to be most private, my body to be carried to the grave in a farm wagon, my coffin to be made of pine – painted black – to be laid in the earth by my four sons should God be graciously pleased they survive me."

In his estate Martin left for Jane's lifetime their Drynoch home and the orchards. In the Scottish custom, he left to his oldest son Norman the farm on the west side of Yonge Street and control of the family purse. To Henry, the next oldest, he left the farm on the east side of Yonge Street. Nothing was to be sold until the death of their mother, and if any cash remained, it was to be divided among his daughters, with one share to go to James. As there would be little cash, in essence what he gave to James was freedom.

It must be curious to write your father's will and be left his love as your only legacy. However, James may have felt a sense of relief. He had already received his inheritance through his education and his debts during his Kingston years. He had no wish to shoulder the heavy responsibilities expected of Norman and Henry. Money was a commodity which was always slipping through his fingers, and the lands were a fetter of which he wanted no part. It seemed unlikely that he would spend his life chained to the uncertainties of Drynoch or buried under piles of legal papers in a law office.

Far from done, Martin borrowed funds to establish James in the town of Bowmanville, east of Toronto. He even prevailed upon Norman to help, though his oldest son's crop was only half in the barn, the other half lying sodden under heavy rainfall. Norman contributed £5 and Martin's friend, Archy Cameron of Toronto, lent £150. Thus, James left the office of Alexander Campbell and was rerouted to another town far from the city. Martin cautioned his son, "A very great deal of valuable time has been hitherto lost."

James headed for Bowmanville and a practice with a lawyer named Cubitt. During the next ten years he apparently practised law and remained active in the Oak Ridges Cavalry, Richmond Hill. Other than the occasional newspaper report of him marching with his militia, no records appear to have survived. For him, the brightest spots in that decade likely were the 1861 Trent affair and the Fenian raids on the Canadian border. He served with distinction in both and by

1867 was promoted to the rank of brevet lieutenant-colonel. It seems he kept in touch with Alexander Campbell and Prime Minister John A. Macdonald, hoping to join any expeditionary force heading for the frontier. There was much talk of one toward the end of the 1860s. Martin wrote no more complaints of his son's military leanings, perhaps feeling that the discipline was good for him.

On December 16, 1863, Martin Macleod died. Following his wishes his four sons painted a pine box a flat black, placed it on the farm sleigh, then drove the greys down his carriage way towards St. John's Church. The saplings planted by Martin in 1848 had become sturdy young trees although spare without their leaves in mid-winter. Following the service, Norman moved into Drynoch with his wife and family. Maggie took her mother to live for a while at the Baldwin home of Masquoteh.

6

 Settling the Red River

"Courage and love made toil and privations bearable."
Jean Drever Pinkham

William Drever retired as an employee of the Hudson's Bay Company on August 13, 1851. In her memoirs, his daughter Jean wrote of the Company, "We trust them to the fullest extent. They are our bankers and lawyers, and they are true and just in all their dealings. May the time never come when their word will not be as good as their bond. A pew is reserved for their officers in St. John's Church and they attend wonderfully well, always paying tribute to the Lord's Day by unfurling their flag every Sunday morning."

To honour William's long and dedicated service, the Company offered to pay his way back to Scotland, or he could remain in Rupert's Land with a land grant as a bonus. Both offers would include his pension withheld by the Company during his tenure and amounting to one-third of his total earnings. It was the land William had waited for all those years, the reason he and Helen had built in the flood zone on the river bank. He chose the river lot on which he had built his log cabin. Registered as No. 249, it was two chains wide, and ran back from the Red River 159 chains, or two miles. To legalize the gift, the Company's standard regulation required William to pay £15.18 for fifty acres of the lot. As the chief factor gave him no date by which to pay everyone forgot about it and William got on with his life.

The Drevers built a two-storey log house further back from the river and named it Clova Cottage, after the country home of Helen's family in Aberdeen. Although a more refined, cosier house than the cabins in which they had spent the last eight years, once again they were the butt of village jokes. Why would anyone build so far from the river?

Ever since the Pierre-Guillaume Sayer case in 1849 the Company had relaxed its ruling against independent traders. Aware of plans to build a railroad linking St. Paul, Minnesota, with the eastern United States, William could realize his dream of trading on the international market. Every six months he led a procession of two hundred Red River carts, each filled with nine hundred pounds of furs and other goods, to St. Paul. To minimize the risk of Indian attacks and of deep rutting in the gumbo, the train travelled like a bunched-up buffalo herd. News of the men's homecoming was telegraphed across the prairie by the squeal of the huge ungreased wheels. Drivers would shoot gophers to stuff into the axles for temporary lubrication, but there were not enough bullets or rodents on the plains to deafen the sound of some eight hundred wheels. Long before fathers and sons appeared over the horizon, children would leap on their ponies and gallop out toward the eerie squeal.

During their two-month round trip, wives and children pitted their wits against the vagaries of frontier life. Women were tough and toddlers grew up fast. While young James and Willie Drever helped their mother care for the animals and chop the wood, other tiny hands would keep the wood stove burning. Maggie, Jean, Mary and Christin held soft wool as Helen spun, wove and sewed all their clothing.

Sometimes Helen had to remain inside cradling a sick baby in her arms. Then she would watch her young sons struggle through her chores. A Salteaux boy from the Indian camp might run to help. In the spring thaw or on rainy days the boys hauled their loads through sticky mud called gumbo. Heavy water buckets sloshed over onto cowhide leggings, grey mud oozed into moccasins. The boys bantered in Cree as they slipped and sloshed about in the gumbo. If Helen wanted to run and help she contained herself, letting her children figure out the ways of the land. Eventually the life took its toll. Jean remembered one long period when her mother had to milk the cow while fevered, nauseated and jaundiced. Helen's physical endurance had been sapped in the struggles of the new world. Her brave spirit could not protect her from physical exhaustion. Lines creased her lovely face, and she looked older than her years. A photograph of her shows a pinched smile, as if she had forgotten how to laugh.

Despite the settlers' growing civilities and comforts, nature remained their real adversary. One night in the spring of 1852, huge chunks of ice jammed the melting river. The water rose seven feet in an hour, then suddenly broke over the banks and rushed through the homes. A pregnant Helen collected her children and jumped for their rowboat already afloat and tugging at its painter. The river rose up the stairs and flooded their bedrooms. Escaping to higher ground with three thousand five hundred others, the Drevers watched the river become a twenty-two-mile muddy sea. Alexander Ross wrote that everything the settlers had worked for was submerged. On June 12, they returned to their gumbo-sodden homes and began again, their only tools their faith, tenacity and friendship. On October 11, Helen bore her third daughter, Mary. She would grow up to be a tall, black-haired, perennially weather-tanned beauty like her mother.

In 1854 Adam Thom left the settlement. Although he still enjoyed his handsome salary, four years earlier he had been demoted from judge to court clerk for misusing his judicial privileges. In an adultery case, he had acted both as attorney for the plaintiff and as the judge. In 1854 the Métis threatened to burn down his home or worse. Thom was enticed back to England by an undisclosed financial gift from Governor Simpson. He sailed on the *Prince of Wales*, the same ship on which William Drever had arrived thirty-three years earlier.

Helen expected all within her home to learn the Protestant ways. Jean wrote of the servants which they were able to hire for ten to fifteen shillings a month, "They are halfbreeds, of course. Mother is always as kind and considerate but their work must be well done. She advises them about the spending of their money and on [the importance of] having good, useful and comparatively cheap clothing. She insists on their attending Church once every Sunday and in the evening assembles us all around the dining room table, servants and all. We have to read a chapter from the Bible, verse about, then my father gives prayers."

Plains hunters regularly visited Clova Cottage for Bible lessons spoken in Cree. One tiny, very old Indian woman called Wifie used to hobble in on two sticks. The white patches on her face and breast were, the children suspected, leprosy. As a precaution against infection it was Jean's duty to spread Wifie's special little blanket on the kitchen floor.

The only doctor that the Drever girls ever remembered in the settlement was Dr. Cowan, the Hudson's Bay Company factor. He had the perspicacity to vaccinate the settlers against smallpox, and as Jean had "a good take," her mother volunteered her daughter to vaccinate the community from her arm. Jean wrote, "So off we went, the doctor driving me in his buggy, and I feeling myself a very important person. It was probably a very risky thing of my mother to allow, but no harm came of it."

Books were still a rarity but they were always in the Drever home. Initially, Margaret and Willie were educated by their parents. While James attended the new St. John's School started by the settlers, Jean, Mary and Christin attended Miss Davis's school. Jean remembered their lunches of sturgeon and sea pie often served without salt, the latter a commodity processed by the Indians.

By the late 1850s twenty-five houses stood around the site of the original four log cabins. In 1856 William had become the postmaster, but as it paid only £5 annually, he soon handed the job over to Alexander Ross. The Drevers' finances had improved so much, however, that William was able to bring new luxuries home from his treks to the United States. One item was their first coal-oil lamp, which Jean had the honour of lighting. She wrote of the excitement it caused, "Some of the neighbours thought our house was on fire and came running first in alarm, then to see the effect. We were all a little frightened of it but thought it was a wonderful light."

In 1859 the Hudson's Bay Company trading licence expired, allowing competitive businesses to flourish. The ox trains swelled. Sixteen-year-old Willie began accompanying his father on the trips to St. Paul. At the time, American Indians beat their drums in anger over the influx of white settlers to the United States but Willie could look after himself and more. He had grown tall and powerful, his dark features framed by long black hair tied back with rawhide. He had the litheness of Helen, the incisiveness of William, and the native wit of his Métis and Indian friends. Willie also had a frontier wildness about him. Amused by his son's bravado and proud of his multilingual fluency, William Sr. gave him the best of ponies and rifles. Willie became a superb hunter, guide and interpreter. His sister Jean wrote of him, "Willie was always a morose individual when cooped up, happiest when on a horse, and he could be very valiant. Once when he was riding in a lonely part of the country and came upon an Indian abusing a young girl, he rode to the scene at a terrific pace, hit the Indian on the head, swept the girl in front of his saddle and rode off with her to camp."

On these southern trips the Drevers watched the railroad creep toward St. Paul and saw that the ensuing influx of settlers would lead to the gradual devastation of the Sioux nation. By 1860 the American Indians were starving and liquor consumption was leading to brawls and deaths. Government promises of reservations never materialized, yet when the Indians complained, they were imprisoned for their temerity. Tensions increased and travel grew dangerous. The Drevers counted on their wagon trains getting through but they knew that if the unrest continued the market to the south could cease entirely. Yet tolerated by the Sioux, the Red River settlers managed to continue travelling south of the border.

One day in 1862 when William and Willie Drever were south on a trek, a party of warring Sioux killed thirty soldiers at the American post, Fort Ridgley. Then they rode on to neighbouring farms, torturing and plundering the whites. Whole families were burned alive in their homes. In Fort Abercrombie on the Red River south of Fort Garry, settlers were scalped indiscriminately. In retaliation, fourteen hundred United States cavalry massacred the Indians and burned the prairie grass as they went. Hundreds of Sioux managed to escape across the Canadian border and headed for the Red River Settlement. The Drever children would never forget their effect on the community, which had neither police force nor soldiers. Some thought the Sioux were coming for ammunition. The Drevers thought they came for protection, hoping that the American soldiers would not pursue them across the border.

When the Sioux arrived at Fort Garry, they were still in war paint. They moved about the village sporting the spoils of war. Some wore fair-haired scalps swinging from their rawhide belts. One young warrior chief wore a pale blue crêpe de Chine shawl with its deep fringe around his loins for a breech cloth. Wide-eyed families stared from their windows. Jean wrote, "It was exciting for us children, but we felt very much at their mercy. There was no going to Church. The merchants gave them tea, tobacco, and other things, fearing that if they did not, they would probably help themselves."

William and Willie had yet to return home. At dusk Helen gathered her children around her by the fire with Dasha, their black retriever, and began reading to them. The candlelight made their shadows flicker eerily on the log walls, but Helen warned them to show no fear. Suddenly the children heard a metallic clicking at their windows. War-painted Sioux peered in at them, tapping on the windows with the knives they had used to slaughter the American settlers. Then they opened the Drevers' door, for none had locks in the settlement. Hardly pausing for breath, Helen continued reading in a steady and audible voice. Jean remembered the Sioux moving silently among them, a terrible stench coming from the scalps dangling from their belts. Eventually they left as silently as they had come. Helen opened her arms and gathered her children to her.

The next night a settler chloroformed Little Six, one of the most wanted warriors. He put the Indian onto a Red River sled and sent him over the border to American soldiers. The remaining Indians were enraged, and determined to find the settler who had drugged their leader. Jean wrote, "They stalked the man with the wonderful stealth habitual to an Indian, coming around our houses, watching, watching. . . . We sat in terror with all the lights out. Every now and then we could hear them tapping, tapping on the windows with their knives."

When the first snows fell, the Red River settlers allowed the near-starving Sioux to settle outside Fort Garry on Salteaux land. Fights broke out between the two nations. Christin Drever told of a fight between Sioux and Salteaux near Clova Cottage that ended in a gruesome scalping. By the end of 1863 nearly six hundred Sioux wandered about Fort Garry. Some of the whites considered themselves in a state of siege but the Drever family continued their lives as usual, refusing to be intimidated by anyone. In reality, the Indians were so destitute that the settlers distributed blankets and cast-off clothing. The Grey Nuns of the Convent of St. Francis Xavier even purchased an Indian boy and three girls for 120 pounds of pemmican.

During this period a Dr. John Schultz arrived in the settlement. He was a member of the Canada First party of Ontario and was dedicated to extending the influence of Anglo-Saxon protestantism to the West. Instead of practising medicine, Schultz built a large store, traded in furs, speculated in land and after buying the Nor'Wester paper, used his pen to create internal dissension within the French-English community. It was the first hint of reactionary politics in the Red River Settlement.

In 1863, with the help of James and Willie, William Sr. constructed what Jean described as "quite a pretentious [oak] home, 50 x 30 x 22. . . . We called it Rothney Cottage, in honour of mother." William then began building his own store to compete with the trading company of neighbour Henry McKenney. Once again the settlers joked over these stores built at the confluence of the Assiniboine and Red rivers. They figured it was a matter of time before these fools were all washed away again.

Ignoring the village snickers, William competed with McKenney in earnest. A heated controversy arose. In dry weather the main trail of the town passed directly between the two stores and equalized their opportunities. But in wet weather when the route became an impassable sea of gumbo, the Métis drove their heavily laden carts around the back of the Drever store onto higher ground. When this occurred, William got all the business and McKenney none.

As McKenney also happened to be the sheriff, he ordered a survey crew to establish a permanent road. The surveyors chose the route between the two stores, appropriated eighteen feet of William's land, then announced that his store stood eighteen feet out into the new road. They ordered him to tear down his store. At sixty years of age and a premier citizen of the Red River, William refused.

McKenney took William to court for deliberately blocking what was now a public right-of-way. At first Judge Black agreed. As the court fidgeted in indecision, the Hudson's Bay Company's chief accountant suddenly whispered to William that he didn't even own the land. The 1851 agreement still read, "William Drever, allowed to occupy during the pleasure of the Company...." Everyone had forgotten all about the £15.18 which he was still owing the Hudson's Bay Company. It was September 19, 1864, fifteen years later. William stood to lose everything.

Squatters and land claims are confusing issues in the evolution of any new community. Saying nothing about the outstanding bill, William rose and delivered an eloquent plea for the home he loved and the land on which he had settled. The boy from the Orkney Islands completed his remarks with a query to Judge Black and the jury, "Can the public take possession of a man's property any time they choose?" While the jury debated the issue of land tenure, William slipped out of court and paid his 1851 bill. He returned with the receipt and the jury returned with a moratorium in favour of William. It added that had certain other evidence been available, they might have reversed the decision. The road crew promptly designed the streets destined to be named Portage, Main and Notre Dame, the latter jogging around Rothney Cottage and the Drever store.

William's fussing over buildings faded into the shade with the advent of the family's first wedding. Seventeen-year-old Margaret married an English-Indian, the Reverend J.A. McKay, destined to become the Archdeacon of Saskatchewan. Maggie wore a gown of silver-grey brocaded moiré which Helen imported from England. Jean thought it looked more like the dress of an elderly duchess than that of a young girl. The couple headed north for York Factory, the Reverend McKay's new parish.

Those were good times for the Drevers. Jean wrote of the parties, of sewing a muslin dress in the morning for a dance the same evening. She admired the Indian women for their skilled bead, silk and quill work, writing, "They dyed horse hair, and the quills of the porcupine working them up in all sorts of patterns on the mocassins. We wore slippers of deer skin, embroidered in silk, beautifully tanned and white, as soft as chamois . . . many a pair I have danced into holes."

Their greatest excitement was to drive out to the McDermotts' at Sturgeon Creek in a cariole or cutter. Three bachelor sons were a strong attraction for the Drever girls, who were growing as tall and as beautiful as their mother. Everyone went. Mothers tucked their babies into moss-filled deerskin bags. The communal supper consisted of buffalo and corned deer tongues, moose nose and beaver tails.

Red River jigs, four- and eight-hand reels, polkas and the Sir Roger de Coverley kept the settlers dancing the night away. It mattered not that Sioux Indians and wilderness dangers hovered just outside their door. Jean's memoirs are lively and remind one that the families not only pioneered the west, they had fun doing it. It may be some kind of record that the Red River settlers conducted their lives surrounded by all cultures in various levels of wealth or poverty without major crimes.

In 1866 typhoid fever, which had broken out in York Factory three years earlier, finally reached the Red River Settlement. With terrifying swiftness it raced through the community, striking down James Drever in his seventeenth year. The bookish child, who had grown so tall and thin, faded quickly. Jean remembered: "It happened so fast. He just became very ill and died. Mother never recovered from his death."

A devastated Helen was briefly cheered when Willie fell in love that spring. A hellion who could outride the Indians and was considered an outstanding scout, her son was petrified of courting. The object of his affections seemed to be Jane-Eliza Still, the governess for the children of Archdeacon and Mrs. Maclean. One day he rode up to their home with a gunny sack slung over his saddle, jumped down and knocked on the door. When Jane-Eliza answered, Willie thrust the sack at her, mumbled something, then leaped on his horse and galloped off. Jane-Eliza reached into the sack and withdrew a crumpled, silk gown. No garden party or parakeet-filled arboretums could have made her happier. They were married almost immediately. As a wedding gift, William and Helen gave to the couple Clova Cottage.

In spite of the happiness engendered by the wedding, a listless Helen became bedridden. Her face was a reflection of the land, the once lovely mouth tightened with determination, and her features sharpened as if chiselled by the winds. Soon after, exhausted and spent at the age of forty-six, she just slipped away. Her children were still in their teens, Christin just twelve. Jean wrote: "Her death was a terrible loss to us all. She was a splendid mother and had gone through so many privations with a strong heart. She had taken the greatest care of us all, bringing us up very strictly for which we have all had great reason to be thankful. She was always ready to help those in need. Dear old Judge Black said, 'Your mother was a wonderful woman, and the country can ill afford to lose her.'"

As if nature wished to underscore the family's grief, a cloud of grasshoppers appeared. For three more years the insects shrouded the land, laying their larvae for each ensuing spring. The summer of 1868 was the worst. Millions of locusts flew in hoards, so dark they blotted out the sun while devouring the crops. Their staccato din assaulted the settlers' hearing night and day like an incessant hailstorm striking a tin roof. The sound drove horses and cattle mad. The insects crawled into the cabins through the cracks in doors and windows unsuccessfully blocked with flour sacks. They ate whole envelopes and letters. They fell down the chimneys and crawled into pots and pans. The Drever girls slipped their feet into locust-filled moccasins and put their arms into sleeves filled with the insects. They worked their way down Willie's gun barrels. Whenever the Drevers were forced to open a door, thousand of them would swarm onto their clothes and faces. When the insects finally began to die the stench grew disgusting. William and Willie helped shovel the rotting bodies into carts, then they hauled them out to the prairie and burned them in great, stinking piles.

During that stifling hot summer, the Anglican parishioners hurried to complete the new Holy Trinity Church at the west side of the village. In July, on the Saturday night before the consecration, three young carpenters remained to work on the chancel throughout the night. Eventually they just fell asleep on a pile of lumber. Around two o'clock Sunday morning, thunder, lightning and heavy rain awakened the town. Then everything ceased and a lull settled for a moment.

Suddenly, sheet lightning brightened the sky. A dark funnel spun across the land and rose thousands of feet into the air. With a terrible

Robert Cross, who died of typhoid fever in Montreal, September 1827, and his wife, Janet Selkirk, "The Widow Cross," who took Alexander and eight other children to the Chateauguay River, 1828.

Alexander Cross, 1877: rebellion fighter, backroom politician, landowner, justice of the Court of Queen's Bench, patriarch of the Cross family of Pine Avenue, Montreal.

Julia Fisher Lunn Cross, 1877: daughter of William Lunn, wife of Alexander Cross.

The Cross children, celebrating Confederation, 1867: front, left to right, Ernest, Julia, middle, Harry, Willie Heber, back, Selkirk.

751 Pine Avenue, the home of the Crosses from 1867 to 1949; today the site of the Montreal General Hospital.

Adam Thom, the writer "Camillus," during the 1837-38 rebellions in Lower Canada, later judge of Rupert's Land and employer of Helen Rothney.

Helen Rothney, about 1840-1845: the youthful nannie to the Thom family and lover of William Drever.

An aging William Drever, after the 1870 Riel Rebellion, his frostbitten feet encased in huge, unlaced boots.

An exhausted Helen Rothney Drever, 1866, age forty-five, worn from the hardships in the Red River Settlement.

The Riel Rebellion, February 1870: the escapees arrive at Fort Abercrombie "more dead than alive" en route to testify in Ottawa. From left: Dr. Lynch, Willie Drever, Charles Mair, John Setter.

Clova Cottage, Red River Settlement, the home of the Drever family from 1851; first home of St. Mary's Academy, 1874.

The corner of Portage Avenue and Main Street, about 1870, site of Rothney Cottage, and the stores owned by McKenney and William Drever.

Willie Drever clad in uncharacteristically formal dress on his wedding day, 1865.

Bishop Cyprian Pinkham, 1900 or later: husband of Jean Drever and founder of many churches and schools throughout the North-West Territories.

Jean Drever Pinkham in London, 1911, dressed for the Coronation of George V.

Captain Martin Macleod, about 1832.

Drynoch, "crown of thorns," the Upper Canada home and farm founded by Martin and Jane Macleod, 1846.

Mary Drever Macleod, 1880s, surprising James with her "delicious photograph."

Commissioner James Macleod of the North-West Mounted Police, circa 1870s.

The Macleod children with their nannie, Auntie, hired by Mary off a Missouri riverboat, circa 1889. Front: Mary, Roma; middle: Auntie, Jean; back: Nell, Norman.

Mr. Justice Macleod, 1895. Plagued by illness, James presses on with his whistle-stopping courts.

The Macleod daughters, taken during James's last summer, 1894. From left: Roma, Mary, Jean, Nell.

Fort Macleod, James and Mary's first home, 1878.

Calgary's muddy main street: Stephen Avenue, 1883.

beauty it sucked earth up into its blackened vortex, curving and weaving in the middle like a wind-whipped blade of grass. Suddenly the twister altered course and came straight for the settlement. It struck Holy Trinity Church, lifting it in a mass from its foundation and smashing it on the ground in a heap of broken timbers. One of the carpenters was crushed to death. Like the Red River flood, the twister raced on unchecked. It smashed a church spire, tore off roofs, shifted entire buildings and ripped up miles of fencing. By some whim it spared Clova and Rothney Cottages, merely whipping shakes off the roofs of the stable and store. Then it was gone. The villagers cared for the injured, buried the dead, then immediately began building another Holy Trinity Church.

Conditions worsened in that year. Buffalo hunts failed and fish were scarce. The rabbit and pheasant disappeared and the crops were ruined from three years of locust devastation. By fall, starvation was rampant amongst the natives. The Scots organized ox trains to head south for food and to wire for help. For the first time in its history, the world beyond stretched out a hand to the Red River Settlement. England, Canada and the United States sent in over £7,000 to purchase seed, wheat, flour, fish hooks and ammunition. The ox train returned laden with the provisions from St. Paul.

By November 4 Holy Trinity Church had been rebuilt and was consecrated for divine service. William Drever was the first rector's warden. Jean provided the church music on the family melodeon carried over from Rothney Cottage. During the service Archdeacon Macleod noticed that Jean took special note of the young curate visiting from St. James Anglican Church, just three miles west on the banks of the Assiniboine. Cyprian Pinkham, age twenty-two, was fresh from St. Augustine's College, Canterbury, England. Soon afterwards, the archdeacon arranged a dinner to introduce Cyprian to the Drever girls, but they arrived to find the curate out cold on the couch. He had consumed enough Hudson's Bay rum to inebriate two men.

The handsome curate floundered at first, surprised and somewhat reluctant to find himself in the western frontier. A native of St. John's, Newfoundland, Cyprian Pinkham was a man of urbanity, used to the cobble-stoned streets and hallowed halls of Canterbury. He had studied Sanskrit and Tamil along with theology, intending to become a missionary in one of the British parishes of India. But by a series of curious turns, Cyprian found himself swatting mosquitoes in Winnipeg instead of flies in Calcutta. He was the youngest curate in the huge diocese, which extended from Ontario to the Rocky Mountains, and from the United States border to the Arctic Ocean – the entire area of Rupert's Land.

On their second meeting, Jean Drever and Cyprian Pinkham became engaged. Unable to find a wedding ring in the settlement, Cyprian took an American $5 gold piece to an old tinsmith, who made Jean the ring she would wear for a lifetime. They were married on December 29, two months after they had first met. It was a bitterly cold day, but following the wedding breakfast Cyprian and Jean drove in an open cariole to St. Andrew's parsonage, sixteen miles north of the village. They returned to Rothney Cottage for the winter, then in the spring moved to St. James parish on the banks of the Assiniboine River. Jean thought her bungalow was the most beautiful place on earth. She wrote: "There was a little rapid opposite the house which we loved. There was quite a bit of land and a very nice grove of trees and we soon made it a very charming home. Our income at that time was 750 dollars a year so we could not do much in the way of furnishing. Nearly everything was home-made and we lived very simply."

Jean ran Sunday school and held a girls' sewing class. Cyprian became involved with the St. John's Collegiate School, and began looking for ways to expand the educational facilities of the community. The Drever girls baked for summer gatherings on their lawn where the parishioners danced and played games. They were joined in the main by other Scottish settlers. While friendly with all races and undiscriminating to a point, the William Drevers and friends established their own British society in the Red River Settlement. It was the spring of 1869.

7

Rebellion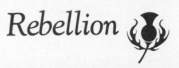

"It was a reign of terror."
  Jean Drever Pinkham

During the hardships of 1868, Charles Mair, a friend of the *Nor'Wester* editor John Schultz, had arrived from Ontario. He subsequently wrote to his brother in Toronto describing the Red River Settlement as the richest country in the world. Mair saw the settlement as ripe for development both as a gateway to the frontier and as a link to the south. His letters found their way (some insist by design) into the Toronto *Globe* late in 1868. A member of the Canada West or Canada First political group from Ottawa, Mair wrote to entice settlers into the area and to convince those already in the Manitoba Territory that Canadian confederation was better than annexation to the States.

Mair described the soil as inexhaustibly fertile, with the absence of wood the only drawback to settling. That problem would be solved, he explained, with the advent of railroads and the harnessing of enormous timber reserves gracing the North Saskatchewan River and the eastern slopes of the Rocky Mountains. "This is a great country and is destined before ten years to contain a larger population than the Canadas," he predicted.

Mair considered the Red River Métis to be "a harmless, obsequious set of men and will, I believe, be very useful here when the country gets filled up." Soon tiring of what he referred to as a motley crowd of halfbreeds playing billiards and drinking in his hotel, Mair moved in with John Schultz.

The editor played on cultural disparities real or imagined by writing in the *Nor'Wester* of the encroaching advance of progress and adding, "The wise and prudent will be prepared to receive and to benefit

... whilst the indolent and the careless like the native tribes of the country will fall back before the march of a superior intelligence.''

No one escaped their pens. Mair delved into the gossip of Winnipeg, writing of jealousies, of intermarriage to halfbreed women with no coat of arms, of wealth earned from filthy lucre, of the facade of British decorum. Having had his fun with the people, he went on to say that farming was a pleasure and there was no toil to it. Never had he felt such fine weather in Canada in November. It was 1868. Five thousand natives were starving.

Mair moved from attracting central Canadians to frightening the Métis by asserting that their lands were in danger of seizure by Fenians. His message to the Métis was, join Canada or be annexed to the United States. As news of political turmoil drifted south of the settlement, armed Fenians did gather south of the border only sixty miles away in the post of Pembina. They were prepared to invade the Hudson's Bay Company's land.

When Mair's letters in the *Globe* made their way back to the settlement by the spring of 1869, they infuriated French and English alike. The blend of races and cultures had lived there for nearly thirty years in relative harmony. Settlers like Helen Drever had shared her knowledge and religion with the Indians. No Drever man ever had a quarrel with a native. Willie understood the Métis' love of hunting and knew that progress would not only spell the end of native freedom but his own as well.

One incident in particular that year underscored the mutual respect between some of the loyalist Scots and the Métis. Across the river in St. Boniface, the St. Francis Xavier Convent burned to the ground. The settler that the French-speaking community turned to was none other than Willie Drever. He and Jane-Eliza, possibly with a little pressure from William Sr., turned over Clova Cottage to the Grey Nuns as a temporary school. It is believed that Bishop Taché celebrated his first mass in the settlement in Clova Cottage.

But Mair's letters and Schultz's articles tore into the settlement's foundations. Settlers began viewing each other with suspicion and isolating themselves into distrustful groups. Some were against American annexation, others considered it. The Métis were frightened that the encroaching farmers and fences would destroy their hunting lands.

Willie Drever found the heavy-handed Mair and Schultz amusing and simply too colourful to ostracize. In particular, he became a lifelong friend of Charlie Mair. Compared to Willie's hulk clad in buckskins and racoon hat, Mair's tailored eastern suits and diminutive size made the two a striking pair.

Trouble escalated in August 1869. The Rupert's Land Act passed by the British parliament freed the Canadian government to purchase the territory from the Hudson's Bay Company for £300,000. Survey crews under Colonel Dennis arrived without warning to lay out the same narrow township design used in Ontario. Their tactics in the Red River Settlement were akin to an invasion. The only two men who were delighted to see the surly crews were Charlie Mair and John Schultz.

Mair hired on as the government paymaster, distributing wages of $15 a month. Instead of paying cash, he handed out purchase orders to be spent only in John Schultz's store at Oak Point. As the Canadian wage for the survey crew had been established at $18 a month, someone was pocketing the difference. The disgruntled crew began fighting among themselves.

A scrappy surveyor named Thomas Scott, and three other workers, struck for higher wages. Scott and his men threatened to drown their foreman unless their demands were met. Later, when twenty-six-year-old Louis Riel Jr. challenged the survey crew not to trespass on private land, the men threatened him, too, as well as the Métis who accompanied him. Christin Drever remembered that Scott had an altercation with Riel at the door of a saloon.

As one of the four original settlers of Winnipeg, William Drever resented this intrusion of the crews as well as the Métis. Ties between the Drevers and the Riels had been strengthened by the Grey Nuns incident and both families wanted the territory to become the province of Manitoba in the Dominion of Canada. Both were united in their anger toward the crews trespassing on Métis land and the insensitive tactics of the government. Yet they were destined to remain on opposite sides. Riel had allied himself with a St. Boniface settler, O'Donoghue, who was encouraging an alliance between Riel and the Fenians south of the border. The Drevers remained loyal to British principles, fearing the other route would result in a loss of Rupert's Land to the United States.

During those unsettled months, messages were shuttled between the settlement to Fort Abercrombie across the border where they were telegraphed to Ottawa. Colonel Dennis specifically requested Sir John A. Macdonald to explain his government's actions to the entire Red River Settlement before further action was taken.

Claiming some of the fastest horses around, Willie raced communiqués to Fort Abercrombie. Just north of Pembina, Riel's men would stop and search him at their blockade. Any information en route to Canada telling of settlement conditions was seized, as were buffalo guns and ammunition being carried northward. Lieutenant-governor elect, William McDougall, had also reached Pembina with a military escort and an entourage of family and servants. He had brought the ladies to witness the historic moment on December 1, 1869. At that time, he would take control of Rupert's Land in the name of Canada. Instead, when the prime minister warned McDougall not to proceed until the issue was resolved, the lieutenant-governor was forced to sit at the muddy border town with nothing to do but play whist. In the meantime, on November 2, Riel and a hundred followers simply walked through the gates of Fort Garry and settled in for the winter.

In Ontario, news of the unrest began filling the newspapers. Rumours of 200,000 armed Fenians collecting at the border reached Ontario. Whether it was the Mair letters, the general interest in the frontier or a stuffy law office, for James Macleod nothing would suffice but that he head west. Acknowledging that his future was as a soldier, not a Bowmanville lawyer, he wrote to Prime Minister Sir John A. Macdonald on November 10, to request a military commission on any force heading west. Patronage was his only hope, for James could not afford to buy his officer's commission, and never again did he intend to be beholden to any superior officer who had bought his.

Macdonald, as minister of justice, had long been formulating a force to control Rupert's Land once the Hudson's Bay Company sold it to the government. It was simply not a published fact, but James was aware of it, probably due to his association with Alexander Campbell. It must have been an anxious wait for him, even though the reply came within two weeks: "My dear Macleod, I have yours of the 10th. Before its receipt all the arrangements had [already] been made by Sir George Cartier at Kingston ... Believe me, Yours faithfully, John A. Macdonald."

James must have been bitterly disappointed. He had either been in the wrong place at the wrong time, drilling with the militia in Bowmanville instead of Kingston, or the scandal of twelve years earlier still hung over his head. As the preliminary force headed west without him, the once rebellious student could only continue performing his legal duties in what must have become an increasingly tedious practice.

On December 1 governor-elect McDougall took the law into his own hands. A thoroughly bored entourage may have spurned him on. By dawn's light he slipped across the border into Manitoba Territory with a group of soldiers. Claiming his governorship, he read the royal proclamation which officially, but illegally, transferred Rupert's Land to the Dominion of Canada. As an aide unfurled the Union Jack, a watching rebel from the Pembina blockade raced to Fort Garry with the news. When the *Nor' Wester* hung up the published proclamation, Louis Riel and his furious rebels tore it down and stormed through the town. All the children were collected and taken down to the Lower Fort. Several armed loyalists prepared to fight the rebels and barricaded themselves inside the Schultz home. Instead of fighting, Riel laid siege to the house. Cut off from wood, water and food for three days, the loyalists became chilled and hungry. Three women, including a pregnant Eliza Mair, wife of Charlie, suffered particularly from the cold and the unsanitary conditions.

William Drever was sixty-three. As a senior citizen of the settlement, now being called Winnipeg, he found himself in the role of negotiator. He sent seventeen-year-old Mary to Riel with a note asking him to meet in Rothney Cottage, possibly to encourage him to join the loyalists in a united appeal to the government. Riel refused. Impatient for action, young Willie then handed a petition of protest around the village. Riel specifically warned Willie not to sign the document. Although he recognized the sincerity of Riel's fears for his lands and his language, Willie would not sanction his tactics. He signed the protest.

When Riel wheeled the fort cannons toward the Schultz house and threatened to blow them up, the loyalists surrendered and were herded off to the jail. Riel showed concern for the women, but stuffed the men into six cells little bigger than closets. Many of the resident prisoners were suffering from scurvy and other diseases. Lice crawled on everyone. One man panicked in the crush and smashed a pane of glass, hanging his head out in the freezing wind to keep from suffocating. There was no heat and the 25 below zero temperatures soon turned the stone cells into tombs. Just before Christmas, Eliza Mair was released and moved in with Willie and Jane-Eliza Drever at Clova Cottage.

On December 11 a group of drunken rebel soldiers burst into Clova Cottage and searched it for weapons. The Drevers had hidden their guns and Riel's men found nothing. Angered, they arrested Willie and marched him off to jail.

The next day Riel raised his Provisional flag with a shamrock beside the fleur-de-lis. In the weeks that followed, the rebels drank their way through the Hudson's Bay Company rum and furnished the fort by raiding the prisoners' homes for cutlery, china and furniture. Many of the settlers were afraid to defy them in case they were jailed for being sympathetic to the loyalists. Not so the Drevers. On Christmas Day, Mary Drever and her friends took roast beef, six plum puddings and tarts to the jail. The prisoners, who by now included A.W. Graham, a young itinerant traveller who inadvertently got caught and kept a journal of the events, began talking of escape. The cold was unbearable and the conditions disgusting.

Although fearful for his son, William Drever made it clear that Rothney Cottage was a home of refuge for any loyalist in need. But he dared not be taken prisoner himself; it was bitterly cold for an elderly man. William sent Mary to demand Willie's release from Riel. The Drevers had learned that an angry woman intimidated the rebel leader more than man or musket. On one occasion when Riel had burst into the Schultz home with an armed guard, Eliza Mair aimed a gun at him and told him to get out. The gun was obviously missing its hammer lock, yet Riel appeared cowed and left. This time Mary won her brother's release along with six others.

Two days later Willie volunteered for New Year's Eve patrol. Partying grew wild in the settlement. As Willie and a friend walked down the snowy tracks of a village path, a group of Sioux Indians appeared. Whooping and yelling, they raced toward the pair with tomahawks raised. Even the redoubtable Willie turned tail and ran. The Sioux howled with laughter. They had come to town to collect their annual New Year's presents.

The following day, despite wind and snow, the settlers held two horse races and a ball. Two nights later, while the remaining prisoners shivered in shirt sleeves and talked of escape, Mary and her friends baked files into cakes and delivered them to the jail. Then the girls drove away to Alexander Logan's house where they danced until four o'clock in the morning.

By January 1870 Riel had become increasingly volatile. Following any act of kindness or after losing face, he would fly into a rage and retaliate. One day he slapped Mair on the shoulder and said, "I am very sorry, Mr. Mair, but we can't save you. You must prepare to die." Mair was escorted back to his cell by a sympathetic guard who gave him a drink from a cask.

The prisoners agreed that Mair's threatened execution would not be the only one. Using Mary's files and knives smuggled from a meal, they began working on the iron bars. That night was intensely cold, the windows thick with frost. Around midnight the chilled guards joined their relief around the stove in the guard room at the south end of the court house. At the north end the prisoners managed to force an opening in the bars so narrow that one man would have to remain to shove the other through by force. One by one the men were pushed through the narrow opening, falling head first to the snow outside. A shivering Charlie Mair was third out. He hit the ground in his shirtsleeves and headed straight for Clova Cottage. The Drevers poured brandy into him, gave him a woollen hat, a coat and mittens. They believed that the time had come to escape to Ottawa and plead for military help. Willie agreed to join Mair south of the border in Fort Abercrombie, but suggested they leave the village separately and rendezvous later. He gave Mair the best Drever pony in their barn, and soon Mair's sled slid through the rebel lines. Before he was clear, the alarm sounded at the jail.

Young Graham was caught crawling out of the window and hauled back. About twenty guards grabbed torches and guns and rushed off in pursuit of the escapees. Hearing them come, Mair drove his pony off the track and straight into a rebel settlement. Ignoring commands of "Arrêt!," he continued on at an unhurried pace as if he belonged. Eventually he reached Portage la Prairie. Most of the other prisoners were caught, exhausted and freezing, about fifteen miles from the fort. Fearing Eliza Mair would immediately be taken as hostage, the Drevers dressed her as a halfbreed, then settler Sam Bannerman put her into a sled and drove right through the Métis patrol and on to a rendezvous with her husband.

Stung as much by lost friendships and loyalties as by any duplicity, Riel demanded that the Drever family surrender. When they refused, he ordered a cannon wheeled out of Fort Garry and aimed at Rothney Cottage. Mary stood fiercely in a window and refused to leave. William Sr. sat in full view of the rebels, calmly eating his breakfast. His long white hair made him look very old. Riel backed down. He would not blow up the house with the Drevers inside. Instead, his men strode into their stables where Willie was with the remaining horses. His sister Christin also was there and remembered one of the rebels demanding of Willie, "The president requires your horses." They took them all save for a deformed mare with one foreleg longer than the other.

Riel then ordered his men to storm Rothney Cottage and arrest William. Jean Drever Pinkham remembered of her father:

They hurried him away from the breakfast table in his ordinary clothes and with only slippers on his feet. They kept him in the guard room ... answering to the charge of sheltering prisoners and helping them to escape. They finally let him off but he suffered so much from the cold in his feet and legs that he never recovered from the effects of it, and was obliged to walk with two sticks for the rest of his life.

At any hour of the day or night Riel would search Rothney Cottage with fixed bayonets. The rebels would go from room to room looking for refugees. They also plundered the store. It was a reign of terror. The French halfbreeds were beside themselves with rage and as they were in a drunken condition most of the time, it was hardly safe for a woman to be alone on the roads.

Donald Smith, the future CPR magnate, had arrived in the settlement and identified himself as a messenger of the prime minister. Eventually allowed to hold public meetings from which evolved a bill of rights and a provisional government, Smith failed to inform the loyalists that he had also been sanctioned to offer perquisites to Riel if he left the country. The loyalists had no way of knowing that a peaceful solution might be in view, and as Riel refused to release the prisoners, they continued to defy his Provisional government.

When one of the prisoners, Dr. Lynch, struck one of the guards, Riel put him in irons. Mary Drever and Mrs. Schultz baked another pudding to hide a knife and a gimlet for boring holes. Perhaps a recalcitrant wood stove was their excuse to the guards for producing the heaviest pudding ever made in the settlement. On Sunday, January 23, 1870, John Schultz used the tools to remove a window and bars. He cut a buffalo robe into strips for a knotted rope and began letting himself down, but when a knot gave way he plummeted to the ground. He sprained an ankle but managed to struggle over the wall and limp through a blizzard to Clova Cottage. Willie Drever found another horse and cutter and soon Schultz cleared the village.

The following morning the French pursued Schultz in vain. An infuriated Riel called the prisoners "rascals and trash." A row ensued in which the prisoners, warmed by rum, threatened to attack. Riel's men loaded their guns and threatened to shoot them all in five minutes. They didn't, but it had been easy to trace Schultz's tracks through the snow to the Drevers. Riel vented his anger on them. It made matters worse that Willie Drever had signed another petition; he was arrested again and this time William Sr. feared for his son's life. He paid what Jean referred to as "the kingly sum of £400 sterling" to the rebels to get Willie released.

Upon returning to Rothney Cottage, Willie determined to escape to Canada. To leave must have been a hard decision. Jane-Eliza, his ailing father and his sisters, all of whom had resisted an increasingly unpredictable Riel, would be left without a man around. Perhaps he felt confident that the hot-tempered Mary was sufficient protection.

In Portage la Prairie the other escapees, including Thomas Scott, rallied behind a Major Boulton. Word of a rebel treaty made the major hesitant to attack, for he counted on the rebels' honour. Then a young rebel, Parisienne, was shot and killed by a loyalist. In a coup, the rebels captured the entire party. Riel immediately sentenced Boulton to execution unless John Schultz was recaptured. In that case, explained Riel, Schultz would be executed instead. Two hours before Boulton's scheduled death Archdeacon Maclean, the Bishop of Rupert's Land, Mary Drever, and some other members of the community convinced Riel to spare the major's life.

Riel vowed he would have John Schultz dead or alive. On February 21, with all roads leading to the United States guarded by Riel's men, Schultz and an English halfbreed named Joseph Monkman escaped by the unthinkable mid-winter route across Lake Winnipeg, through the Lake of the Woods, then over the unknown country of northern Minnesota to the head of Lake Superior. Riel's men pursued on snowshoes for a while, then gave up.

That evening Willie slipped out of the settlement and headed south. Charles Mair had also departed from Portage la Prairie with John Setter, Dr. Lynch, two guides and two dog trains. Expecting Willie to catch up, they headed for St. Paul, Minnesota.

At daylight the alarm was raised for Willie. Riel's men chased him as far as Portage la Prairie, where the weather closed in to a blizzard. In retaliation, they searched for the pregnant Eliza Mair. The minister's wife concealed her from the troops and they returned to Winnipeg empty-handed. Louis Riel turned his wrath on the man who had once thrown him out of a bar and intimidated his people, the abusive Thomas Scott.

Innumerable rumours abound on the death of Thomas Scott. He was certainly tried in French and shot, but whether or not he was buried alive will remain a matter of conjecture. Christin Drever remembered that they tried to see what was happening in the fort from their upstairs window. In the dense, cold air, they heard the shots ring out. Graham believed that Scott had been buried alive and wrote, "The news of Scott's death and the manner of it sent a chill through every heart." Many settlers got passes and left, willing to walk away from their homes and livelihood.

The courage and endurance of the fragmented groups of refugees heading for Canada in mid-winter – Schultz to the northeast, Mair to the south, and Willie somewhere en route – were superhuman. Leaving unprotected families in their besieged community and striking out in wind-chilling temperatures was their only way of fighting for their conviction that Manitoba Territory belonged in the Canadian confederation rather than in the United States, and that it belonged on their terms as well as those of the rebels.

Willie and Mair had escaped in a blizzard which steadily increased to a howling gale. By March 11 Mair's group was lost and suffering from snow blindness, hunger and exposure. The remaining provisions were flour mixed with butter and snow, which they made into a paste over the fire. As they stumbled into the tiny settlement of Grand Forks, Willie Drever arrived, having overtaken their sixty-mile lead. He had plenty of food and provisions and, acquainted with the route since the age of sixteen, knew where he was going. Willie sent the frightened guides back to Portage la Prairie. Mair, Lynch, Setter and Willie resumed their trip together.

The storm built to a howling fury. Mair struggled through the drifts without snowshoes and collapsed with exhaustion. Setter left camp to search for better shelter and was lost for an entire day. The horses they had obtained at Grand Forks in exchange for their dogs and sleds died in their tracks. Even Willie thought he was lost. The blizzard that had enabled them to escape from Riel now threatened to kill them. Eventually they stumbled onto a settler's home where, Mair later wrote, they drank several horns of good whiskey. They also learned that they were on the right route and within forty miles of Fort Abercrombie.

One month after escaping from the Red River Settlement they completed the 450-mile journey. Mair wrote that they reached the fort more dead than alive. Ignoring exposure and exhaustion the foursome rested for only two days before catching the stage to St. Cloud and a train to St. Paul. En route they recounted their stories to the *Pioneer* newspaper, which telegraphed their story east. Only later did they learn of Scott's execution. It must have been frightening news for men who had left their families behind.

While the men were making their way eastward, life in Winnipeg continued in a curiously normal fashion. The mail came and went, balls were held, children returned and played in the streets while their parents played a game of oneupmanship with the rebels. In a conciliatory mood, Riel ordered the Union Jack hoisted. O'Donoghue ordered it taken down. When Riel threatened O'Donoghue with jail, the loyalists cheered the rebel leader. Then some rebels dug out Dr. Cowan's flag post, took it to the fort and raised both the Union Jack and the Provisional flag (on the taller post). After dark someone cut the Union Jack down. It was raised again with the halyard tied too high to be reached. In the midst of this patriotic duel, Mrs. Begg ran out and raised her shawl on the Begg flagpole. A frantic rebel soldier galloped down to see what treasonous ensign was being hoisted in the settlement.

By spring the murder of Thomas Scott had set Toronto afire. Political activists in the Canada First party held indignation rallies, whipping the citizens to a state of frenzy. On the evening of April 6, when the Red River refugees and John Schultz arrived almost simultaneously in Toronto, over five thousand demonstrators welcomed them as heroes. While Willie looked on, Mair, Schultz, Lynch and Setter took turns expressing outrage at Riel's murder of Thomas Scott. With each pause, the crowd roared its indignation.

If the crowd had looked, probably the most interesting refugee was Willie Drever. Dressed in buckskin jacket, leggings, moccasins, with a coonskin hat covering much of his thick black hair, he moved with the litheness of an Indian, yet his stature was typical Scot. While the orators worked their audience to a pitch of patriotic zeal, Willie just looked into the crowd intently, missing nothing.

Following the Toronto rallies, the four men travelled to Montreal, then on to Ottawa. On April 21 Willie testified at a special Ottawa hearing packed by members of Parliament. He described to the hushed room how he and his father had been repeatedly taken prisoner, the deplorable conditions in the jail, and how Riel had threatened other prisoners with shooting. Willie related how his family homes had been searched and pillaged. His knowledge of the inner fort, of Riel's unpredictable temper, and of the settlement itself was excellent.

As the refugees called for the government to take prompt measures to restore law and order, James Macleod knew that arrangements were already under way to send a military force to the Red River Settlement. The plan had been kept secret so that no information would reach the Métis rebel delegates who had also arrived to testify in Ottawa. Sir John A. Macdonald did not want it to appear that the government was preparing for war whilst professing to seek peace.

Finally, James's time had come. He was thirty-four years old. On April 28, he was appointed brigade major for the expedition with orders to raise, arm and equip two battalions of 350 non-commissioned officers and men, half to be taken from Ontario and half from Quebec. Although no one had any real concept of what lay ahead in the 1,500-mile trek, the troops were carefully selected from hundreds of volunteers. The French Canadians proved so reluctant to fight against their countrymen that James made up the remainder with discharged men from the Royal Canadian Rifles.

The leader of the expedition, Colonel Garnet Wolseley, ordered the contingency to prepare for a "howling wilderness." His intended route was considered impossible by many experts. The first two hundred miles west of Lake Superior had never been traversed by any vessels larger or stronger than a bark canoe. Wolseley's expedition consisted of 1,200 men moving 140 boats, each containing 4 tons of freight, 51 tons or 102,000 pounds of rations, cannons and hundreds of horses, oxen and cattle.

James's battalion left Toronto by train on May 14, arriving at Sault Ste. Marie on the sixteenth. A three-week nightmare followed, caused by political hassles, a drunken ferry captain and torrential rainfall. The men hacked their way through miles of forests and built jury-bridges over rushing streams. They repeatedly unloaded their boats, carried them through a sea of red clay, then reloaded them. Struggling through the mud, almost the entire herd of horses and oxen went lame. Exasperated as much by the politicians as the unfinished road, Colonel Wolseley blamed the Canadian government for squandering money and for duplicating jobs in Ottawa "so that patronage may be distributed amongst their friends." For James, Colonel Wolseley was the ideal commanding officer. He possessed that wonderful edge of insanity that inspired men to dare the impossible and he proved fearless when battling with his bureaucratic superiors.

Completely frustrated with the delays, Wolseley attempted the impossible. He ordered the boats hauled through thirty-three miles of rapids and up one falls which was 120 feet high. Experts said it couldn't be done. That kind of challenge suited James perfectly, especially when Iroquois Indians replaced those voyageurs who tossed down their paddles and returned home. For the next eight days the force dragged and lifted the heavy boats with their ten tons of gear to an accumulated height of 800 feet. One chief constable, Sam Steele, wrote of James's contribution to the portages, "Major Macleod, a tall, graceful man, was the first of all of us to shoulder a barrel of pork, a heavy load, each barrel weighing 200 pounds." Under the officers' guidance the men treated the job as a competitive game.

James had christened his boat "La Belle Manitoba." Larger and more ungainly than the others, it was as clumsy to steer in the rapids as it was to haul up a waterfall. His men nicknamed it the "Bummer," yet they laughed and sang their way up the walls of dripping granite as if each one was just another obstacle in a game. The second most cumbersome boat, named "The Flying Dutchman" by Sam Steele, was bringing up the rear. It was not by chance that Wolseley had appointed James in charge of these two giant iron kettles, as Steele called them. A lesser officer might never have got them through.

In June the expedition's scout, Captain William Butler, arrived in Frog Point just below the Manitoba border. His mission was to assess the strength and morale of the six hundred armed rebels guarding Fort Garry, then report to the approaching Colonel Wolseley. Upon boarding the northbound steamer the *International*, Butler met Willie Drever who was also returning to the settlement. As the *International* crossed the border at Pembina en route to the Red River Settlement, Riel's patrol spotted Willie. Wheeling their horses, the riders galloped for Fort Garry to inform Riel of the approaching men. Willie believed that Butler could be in greater danger than himself. He suggested they escape from the *International* and head for family friends at the Lower Fort. They would be hidden while they planned their next move.

That evening as the weatherbeaten *International* plowed from the wider Red River into the narrower Assiniboine, the turmoil of the currents began to push her bow toward the village bank. Willie and Butler would have seconds to leap ashore just 200 yards east of the Fort Garry dock. By eleven o'clock, the moon was hidden by drifting cloud. Willie, clad in buckskins and moccasins, and Butler, cloaked in a great cape, waited near the bow. When the captain suddenly shut off the steam, the current briefly nudged the *International* against the shore. The men jumped and rushed up the steep, clay bank. Beyond them, the plains stretched flat into the blackness of the night. Willie led Butler along the path leading from the river bank to the whitewalled cluster of houses.

Having called for men "not afraid to fight," Riel boarded the *International*. In their search for Willie and Butler, his guards broke down cabin doors and smashed windows. A terrified passenger soon cried that the two fugitives had jumped ship and pointed toward the confluence of the rivers. In a fury, Riel screamed, "After him!

Bring them in dead or alive!" He imprisoned the ship's captain and confiscated Captain Butler's baggage as rebels rode off in pursuit of the escaped men.

Willie rushed home to Jane-Eliza at Clova Cottage only to find Riel had taken the last of his horses. Sending Butler on toward the Lower Fort and assuring him that he would follow shortly with mounts, Willie rushed on to Rothney Cottage. Butler disappeared toward the first bridge leading away from Winnipeg.

At Rothney Cottage Willie again found all the horses gone. His father told him that Mary had taken the lame mare and buckboard down to the Lower Fort to the Gardiner family, the home Butler was seeking. Winnipeg was already alive with rebels swinging lanterns and searching homes. Before Willie had a chance to escape, Riel's men broke into Rothney Cottage with fixed bayonets and marched him off to jail. Riel ordered a gallows built immediately to hang Willie Drever.

Butler was pursued but evaded the rebel force and by dawn had reached the home of the Reverend Gardiner. Startled from sleep, Mary and the Gardiners looked through the window to see an unshaven, dishevelled giant pounding on their door. When the captain managed to convince them he was an English officer in hiding, the loyalist underground and all its facilities opened to him immediately. Convinced by the settlers that he should not risk going to the Lower Fort, Butler continued on to the Ojibwa settlement at Lake Manitoba. Somehow, word of the six hundred armed rebels at the fort had to be sent to the advancing troops and also to Ottawa. It was Mary Drever who offered to take Butler's messages to the captain of the *International* and thereby get word out of the settlement.

Slipping the papers into her blouse, Mary began the twenty-mile drive back to Winnipeg. The lame mare limped along the road as if neither had a care in the world, but no sooner had Mary driven into Rothney stables when a party of watching rebels strode in and searched the buggy.

"Did you see a stranger at the Rapids?" they asked her.

"No," Mary said, the papers still in her blouse.

"Are you sure you passed nobody between here and the Rapids?" They looked her over. Remembering the Sioux in her cabin, Mary fixed them with a steely gaze and insisted emphatically, "No."

They dared not search her clothing. Mary was let go, and the message reached Colonel Wolseley and Ottawa in record time. Mary believed

the Indians had helped relay the messages. Of Butler's successful
escape, settler Alexander Begg recorded in his journal, "the Drevers
and all their crowd were in great glee."

Free to leave for a Lake of the Woods rendezvous with Colonel
Wolseley, Butler learned that Willie Drever was about to be hanged
in Fort Garry. When Riel's messenger arrived with an invitation to
visit the Upper Fort, the word "invitation" suggested that Riel wished
to negotiate. Taking the initiative, Butler agreed to meet with Riel
on the conditions that Willie Drever be set free, that his confiscated
baggage be restored to the *International*, and that the Provisional flag
be removed. The following evening, a messenger arrived in the Indian
encampment to tell Butler that all would be as he wished. As Butler
drove jubilantly through the settlement in a buckboard, a freed and
grateful Willie Drever joining the villagers to cheer him on.

The subsequent meeting between Louis Riel and Captain Butler
gave the officer a new perspective on the siege. He noted the ill-
kempt condition of the fort and the low morale of the force. Riel
appeared as Butler and a guard were playing a game of billiards. Hoping
to lure him into picking up a cue and joining the game, Butler silently
continued playing. Riel seemed to await Butler's pleasure, grew
uncomfortable, then meekly departed. Butler immediately stood tall
and summoned Riel back, thus controlling the interview and realizing
that Riel could easily be intimidated. Mary Drever had known this
when she had refused to leave her cannon-threatened house. Eliza
Mair had known this when she had pointed a broken gun at him.
What no one could assess was how Riel might retaliate.

Later, Butler simply left the fort with some Ojibwa, headed east
up the Red River into Lake Winnipeg, then continued on to the
Lake of the Woods and a rendezvous with Colonel Wolseley. He
reported that the fort could be taken with relative ease. Wolseley
had never thought differently. The expedition pressed on toward Fort
Garry.

Wolseley and Butler entered Winnipeg on August 24 to find it
empty. Riel had withdrawn to become a fugitive rather than risk
a fight. As James Macleod and Sam Steele brought up the rear of
the expedition with"The Flying Dutchman" and "La Belle Manitoba,"
they missed the historical moment. Their crafts were being guided
through the worst of the Winnipeg river rapids by a powerful Iroquois
bowman named Big Mike. After "The Flying Dutchman" successfully
negotiated the boiling rapids, the soldiers climbed out and up to

cheer from the cliffs above. Big Mike walked back, boarded "La Belle Manitoba" and, with its terrified crew, gleefully charged into waves up to ten feet high.

As his company approached the mouth of the Winnipeg River, James demonstrated once again the inspiration and soundness of judgment which made him one of the most popular and valuable officers on the expedition. After crossing innumerable portages in torrents of rain, the six remaining boats had to cross yet one more obstacle – the Yellow Mud portage. "La Belle Bummer," as the men now referred to it, got stuck on the wet clay hill. Steele remembered, "As the entire company got on the lines to haul this Ark, another company with lighter boats pushed ahead, jeering good-naturedly as they passed us."

After ordering the men to rest a moment, James said, "Do your utmost boys, one more heave and we will get her over. Let the others go ahead. We'll cut wood, dry ourselves, have a good feed and rest, and we'll beat them in the morning." Steele wrote, "Although the mud clung to our craft as if it could not bear to part with her, we hauled her out of its clutches and halted for the night. The poor fellows ahead, in a heat to complete the portage, got caught in the dark. Too late to cut wood, they were worn out, soaked and hungry by daylight. We passed them with a cheer and got into Fort Alexander at the mouth of the Red River five hours ahead of them."

Driving Riel away from his breakfast may have been an anticlimax for the troops, but to the people of Winnipeg it was cause for unbridled celebration. When James and Steele arrived two days later, the muddy village roads of Winnipeg were littered with bodies of drunken settlers, Indians, and one pet bear on the loose. Jean Pinkham wrote of the liberation, "the excitement was terrific after the struggle to keep brave hearts. . . . I do not think there were many dry eyes."

Willie and James met almost immediately. Great-grandchildren claim that the Drevers were still ladling out rum in front of Rothney Cottage when James arrived. He was invited into the civility of Rothney Cottage and the company of the spirited Drevers. Compared to the dirt and rigours of the trek, the Drevers' scrubbed home with Victorian furniture, bearskins and the fiery Mary must have been a welcome respite.

Recommended as the best scout in the village, Willie was hired to race the news of the expedition's arrival to the St. Paul telegraph. His accolade came from the *Manitoba News Letter* when it published, "Our worthy townsman, Mr. William Drever (junior), has finally won the spurs as Prince of Travellers. Mr. Drever was entrusted by Colonel Wolseley with important despatches which he succeeded in delivering at St. Paul in six days, and he also made the return trip in the same unequalled time."

James and his men policed the settlement and set the fort in order, returning to the settlers their belongings, and reconditioning what guns and cannon could be cleaned. The overnight saloons soon disappeared and with hundreds of aching heads, the soldiers began the immediate task of returning to eastern Canada.

On September 6, when he was installed in office, Lieutenant-Governor Archibald complimented the soldiers on the "magnificent success" of the expedition. He added that "the men who have so triumphed over such difficulties must not only themselves have worked wonders, but also must have been well led." In a separate farewell to the militia, Colonel Wolseley recommended that James be awarded the Order of St. Michael and St. George for outstanding leadership on the expedition. Referring to all the men as a "force second to no corps in Her Majesty's service," he said, "I can say without flattery that, although I have served with many armies in the field, I have never been associated with a better set of men."

James remained at the Lower Fort as second-in-command of the remaining troops for the winter. He found the men high-spirited and easily given to scrapping. Tougher drilling only amused them. It was child's play compared to hauling a boat or a 200-pound pork barrel up a waterfall. Whereas James had once defied his father, he now became a parent to an entire force, upping parade to three times a day, marching the men with 70-pound packs and ammunition. Afternoon drills to the tunes of the regimental band were soon called "Ladies' Parades." With the other girls in Winnipeg, Mary Drever sat watching from the north side of the parade ground. With ladies at a premium, the soldiers outdid themselves on these manoeuvres, delighted to have an audience other than mosquitoes and black-flies.

Such rough and ready soldiers were almost bound to fall into controversy. During the winter they were allowed into the town on their honour, and became mixed up in the remnants of ill will caused by the rebellion. One day a man called Elzear Goulet, allegedly the one who commanded Thomas Scott's firing squad, was seen running from the hotel with a crowd yelling and throwing stones at him. The terrified Goulet jumped into the river and drowned. Two young militia buglers who had joined the crowd, allegedly out of curiosity, were blamed in the death. On the following day the entire company was called to parade and was fiercely reprimanded. As no official inquiry had been held and no man was able to defend himself, James considered the allegations unfair. In this episode, or during a subsequent incident, he clashed with a future attorney general, J. Clarke, over what he considered the unjust treatment of his men. Clarke would not forget James's interference.

All in all, the militia was well accepted by the English in Winnipeg. Dances were held, amateur theatricals and minstrel concerts were staged with the officers and men often taking part. James escorted the lovely Mary Drever to many. In fact the thirty-four-year-old soldier/lawyer was flattered that the impetuous young woman was around more often than not. When he attended a concert or a dance alone she always chose the seat beside him. James looked dashing in his dress uniform, even if he did dance in moccasins with his shoes tucked under his arm.

Throughout the winter, James passed his spare time with the Drevers at Rothney Cottage. Each member of the family made his or her own special contribution to frontier life and to the building of Winnipeg. Willie served as courier and guide to the militia. The Reverend Pinkham's parish of St. James on the Assiniboine became unrivalled in popularity and the Pinkhams were indefatigable in their ministrations to the families in their vast parish. The *Manitoba Free Press* lauded Cyprian for his humour and for his ability to "embody in a few words the thoughts which other men require sentences to express." William Drever Sr. was appointed a magistrate.

Whenever possible, Mary and James rode through Winnipeg and down to the Lower Fort, enabling James to observe Mary's riding skills. She was both fearless and proud, dignified yet with a toughness of spirit peculiar to frontier women. Mary once told James that her mother was the finest example of strength and fortitude. Nothing ever seemed too difficult for a Drever woman, and Mary's volatile temper matched that of the colonel himself. James wrote to his mother about this excellent young woman and finally mustered his courage to ask for Mary's hand in marriage. She accepted. The Drever family was thrilled, and James wrote that he was overjoyed to think that "a lovely woman of eighteen would marry an old sod like me!" As winter passed into spring, Mary wrote to Scotland for her wedding dress while James requested future orders from his commanding officer before settling the nuptial date. By now he knew his life belonged in the military.

But the well-connected, gentlemanly Colonel Gosford Irvine was put in charge of the Fort Garry militia, and James was ordered to return to Toronto. It was a devastating blow. Not only was he in love with Mary Drever, but Captain Butler was relating disturbing stories about Saskatchewan Territory.

Recently returned from the west, the captain reported a winter slaughter in which 170 encamped Peigan Indians were murdered. Smallpox was racing through the tribes. American traders were openly trading alcohol, arms and ammunition to the Blackfoot on Canadian soil. Payment was made in ponies and young Indian girls. Butler recommended that the government establish a permanent force of about 150 men in the West, a civil magistrate such as the British had established in Ireland and India, and treaties in which the 27,000 Indians would officially give up their vast lands. The West was at a crossroads of dynamic change. It needed men with a love for the military, a knowledge of the law and an appreciation of the Indian. Winnipeg had grown to a population of 215 permanent residents. With Manitoba and British Columbia considering entering Confederation, plans were moving ahead to link Canada by rail. Winnipeg would be the jumping-off centre for railway surveyors and supplies. Red River carts would soon become obsolete as rival companies fought over transport on the waterways.

James asked Mary to return to Toronto with him, but he had not counted on her iron will. She would not leave her ailing father and James would not ask her to wait when he might never return. They broke their engagement by mutual consent. Leaving Fort Garry with a contingent on June 11, he arrived in Toronto on the morning of July 14, 1871. Requesting of Postmaster General Alexander Campbell that he negotiate a western assignment for him, James would soon discover that not even patronage would get him a commission.

In May 1872 the first Legislative Assembly of the new province of Manitoba was saluted by an honour guard of the Ontario Rifles. Initially the Manitoba Act protected the Métis' Roman Catholic schools and the use of two languages in government. But the Métis received no lands, and at the end of the century the federal government would abrogate their right to separate schools. The province of Manitoba was introduced to Confederation with the same cultural disparities as Lower Canada had experienced some thirty years earlier.

8

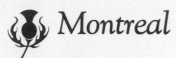 *Montreal*

"On the continent . . . eat . . . sleep . . . and take your satisfaction . . . in French."

Alexander Cross to his sons

In Montreal, fifty-year-old Alexander Cross commuted to the Palais de Justice in his black coach with gold family crest. It gave him plenty of time to mull over his children's progress. He believed the boys' futures depended upon their education and he embodied this philosophy in letters to his oldest son, Selkirk. He once wrote: "Education gives a man confidence and makes him fearless of competition." The concept held merit, for Selkirk had not only survived the smelly boys in Lennoxville but by 1872 was excelling in academics and sports at Oxford.

Alexander also made it clear that, "In the great struggle of intelligence, assiduity is what makes the impression. Talent does not go for so much as it generally gets credit for . . . most persons find they could have accomplished far beyond what was fallen to their fortune had they labored for it." For this reason he encouraged Selkirk's interest in rowing, just as long as it did not interfere with his main purpose of attending Oxford. The exhausting, precision-demanding hours spent with seven other men in a shell could only increase his son's sense of concentration and self-discipline. Selkirk won his rowing colours but got thrashed in football at Wimbledon. Finally, Alexander considered the study of law essential, for it was a foundation which would support a man in any profession and get him far in politics.

So far, Selkirk was the only son completely amenable to such guidance. The second son, eighteen-year-old Harry, exasperated his parents with a temperament Julia described as listless. He was so absent-minded that he got caught as a smoker after slipping his pipe and tobacco into Alexander's coat pocket. To please his father, he enrolled at McGill University, but soon left. He became a junior clerk at the Brockville branch of Molson's Bank and spent his free time with hard-drinking youths who dreamt of little else but the wild American frontier. Their dreams were fuelled by Harry Stephens, an expatriate American friend from Montreal's wealthiest family. Stephens intended to return to Colorado and invest $5,000 in a cattle herd. Barring Indian massacres, rustling or, at worst, death, the irrepressible youths figured they could pool their capital and realize a profit of $80,000 within five years. Harry Cross, the dreamer, signed his letters with a variety of beautifully executed signatures.

Willie Heber, the fourth son, was educated partly in Christ's College, Blackheath, England, but mostly in the salons of Paris. He travelled the continent with Julia's sister Emma, a woman of extraordinary wit who sketched the English character with an hilarious if ascerbic pen. Had it not been for his increasing intrigues with French chambermaids and European cuisine, Willie Heber might also have achieved academic recognition. Two sterling attributes he did possess were a love for his Pine Avenue family and a sense of humour which endeared him especially to his younger brother Ernest.

Young Margaret Cross, the delightful Maggie, was fluent in French and trained by Julia and Mrs. Smith on matters of etiquette and domesticity. In a few years she would head for the continent and Dresden to a finishing school. Uncle William Noble, Mary Lunn's husband, considered his niece an erudite beauty, but worried that excessive reading would ruin her health and her figure. On the other hand, Aunt Emma pressured Julia to increase Maggie's education, to give her the same opportunities as her brothers. That was never considered necessary.

Edmund, the sixth and most handsome son, grew up pampered and overly dependent on his mother. As a baby he may have been comfort for a deeply bereaved Julia, and his father seemed only half-hearted in pushing him. For it was his seventh son, Robert, that Alexander saw as the synthesis of the finest Cross breeding. The child responded with enthusiasm to every intellectual stimulus, and his father responded by guiding him with loving intensity.

It was during this era when Alexander turned his full attention to his fifth son. Ernest was not doing well at Montreal High School, but Alexander believed in his potential. At his son's age he was careening through law studies and heading for a rebellion. What Ernest needed, surmised Alexander, was the influence of a British education. In June 1875 he enrolled him at Haileybury School, England. Haileybury was a traditional route to one of the western world's most influential societies. It was British money that had established Montreal, British cattle barons were financing American grazing lands, and British money would develop the Canadian frontier. Grandpapa Lunn advised Ernest to choose honourable and well-connected friends, as they would be of ultimate importance to his future. An old boys' network stretching from Great Britain through Montreal and on to the frontier was already being established. Ernest was on his way.

Alexander may have judged his son ready for Haileybury, but the British institution was not quite ready for a puckish Ernest Cross. Blackhaired, athletically built, with the same slight squint to one eye as his father, Ernest combined a penchant for fun with a dislike for Greek. Within days of his arrival he charmed a smarter classmate to help him decipher six pages of the ancient language. A loner like his father, Ernest cultivated friends with a detached style. The boys at Haileybury had one common bond – they were economically or socially a cut above the common crowd. Some were titled, others were sons of officers in the Indian army, and all shared a love of fine living. For the next two years Ernest would be as comfortable with the blue bloods of Haileybury as he was with the wealthy British families of Montreal.

Each child was fitting into a niche that pleased their elders; everyone but Harry. Grandpapa Lunn expected him to study calculus and other mathematical exercises for an hour and a half every night. He rebelled, left his Molson's Bank job and headed for the continent. For five months he travelled throughout England, briefly joining Selkirk for a pilgrimage to Braehead, Scotland. Upon his return to Montreal, he succumbed to his father's entreaties and re-entered McGill. Two months later he dropped out again. It seems Alexander had a chat with his Molson's Bank friends, for Harry was then offered a promotion and transfer to Molson's main branch in Montreal.

By the close of his eighteenth year Harry knew that he could not merge his own adventurous dreams with his father's ambitions, and decided to leave for uncharted lands. The Canadian West, a wilderness rife with whiskey traders, Indians and a Red River Rebellion, was either too tame for him or too close to home. Harry looked southward along with three friends, Willie Roy, Fred St. Denis and Harry Stephens. One day he informed his parents that he was leaving

Molson's Bank and heading for the United States. But first he would appreciate a $5,000 loan from his father to invest in cattle south of the border. His request was denied. Alexander saw Harry's trip as an adventure, after which he should return home to banking. Thus restricted, Harry would have no option, or so he thought. Fate intervened in the form of Uncle James Hutchison. Harry and his brothers were in for a windfall.

Suddenly unleashed in his forties following his mother's death, Uncle James had found himself an unencumbered, enormously wealthy bachelor. His carousing and drinking so worried his partners that Alexander and Julia invited him to live at Pine Avenue. The plan was to keep him away from the bottle, but the policing failed in the grand home of a myriad nooks and crannies. Pine Avenue was thrown into a turmoil as Uncle James opened his arms to the servant girls and one day even chased Cook. He showered money on the hired help or any friend or child in need. Signed blank cheques would appear in the hands of delighted maids and dilettantes. "Please cash the following draft in the name of so and so," Uncle James would instruct his banker, "and give him more or anything he wants if he wishes!" he once added gleefully. Huge portions of Mont-real – future city blocks – were in Uncle James's control. No one knew what he might give away next.

Alexander called over his old friend Judge F.W. Torrance, who agreed to assess Uncle James's mental stability. Walking with the judge in the garden that night, an ill-kempt Uncle James suddenly gripped Torrance by the arm and in a besotted whisper allowed that it was himself, not Alexander, who had sired Selkirk. Torrance was convinced of his insanity. He agreed that an interdiction, or judicial hearing, should be held to assign a board of trustees to control the estate until Uncle James regained his senses.

Ultimately, the Campbells, Lunns and Hutchisons looked to Alexander for the final opinion on the drastic move. He gave his blessing. At the interdiction, however, held in the Lunn's Sherbrooke Street home and presided over by Justice Monk, everyone showed up but Alexander. Seeing that his brother-in-law was absent, Uncle James deduced that the Crosses were his sole allies in this hostile deed. He was furious with the others and vowed to have his revenge.

Two years later, about the same time that Harry was heading for the United States, Uncle James regained control of his estate. He promptly wrote a second will. Striking the Campbells out of his legacy, he made the beneficiaries of his entire fortune the children

of Alexander and Julia Cross. Alexander's sons were elated. It was
Harry's assurance of land and of a future Longhorn herd. In the
circumstances, Alexander could only give Harry his love and advise
him to do whatever he did well. Then he could not resist urging
his son to stay in the United States only a few months before returning
home to Montreal and settling into banking. Harry and his three
young friends hopped a train for Colorado Territory. He was nineteen
years of age.

Colorado in 1874 was as raucous as Montreal was civil. Life was
cheap. Settlers formed vigilante groups and hanged men without trial.
Cheyenne City in particular was a dirty, frenetic, gold rush town.
Harry wrote that it was a Hades of fortune-seekers, painted ladies
and gamblers. Of the six hundred saloons, he and his friends
frequented McDaniel's Variety Theatre and Dance Hall. Raised in
the hallowed drawing rooms of Montreal, Harry watched tobacco-
chewers spit black juice all over the floors and was disgusted when
he skidded on the slime.

The Canadians were initiated into the American West with brazen
incidents and phenomenal luck. Harry sported heeled cowboy boots
and American Bulldog pistols slung on his waist. He figured he could
take on the world, and in succession knocked out a gun-slinging
drunk, then was tossed out of the saloon for complaining about a
feather in his turtle soup. He was robbed at gun-point on the east
side of the outlaw town, Los Animas, then held up again by another
pair on the west side. The second time, Harry convinced the outlaws
into giving *him* some money for grub. Shaken, he rode to a saloon
for a drink. He was halfway through his first beer when he was
splattered with blood; a man with a knife had stabbed another man
aiming a gun. The dying man squeezed the trigger, zinging a bullet
right through Harry's hat. Wishing he had gone to McGill University
as his father had advised, Harry slammed his beer down on the counter,
rushed out of the saloon, leaped onto his horse Zeke, and galloped
out of town. Subsequently, Grandpapa Lunn warned his grandson,
"Be very careful in dealing with the Yankees not to be defrauded. . . .
I hope you read the Bible diligently . . . and trust in the Providence
of God. . . ."

Harry spent the winter at the Dowling ranch southwest of Denver.
The Dowlings were cousins through the Fishers from Hamilton,
Ontario. There, he learned not only the arts of wrangling, but also

those of homemaking. Men in the frontier had to know how to cook, sew, clean and build.

Just before Christmas 1874 Harry financed a buffalo hunt. He rode out on Zeke with one of the first breech-loading Henry Repeater rifles shipped west. The hunt lasted six weeks, but after three days of listening to a "chorus of hideous, low bellowing from suffering buffalo," and twice escaping fatal tramplings, Harry returned to the ranch. Of the massive waste of meat left on the plains he wrote to Selkirk, "I thought of the many poor people you and I had seen throughout Europe and how they would relish that abundance of meat; also of the many hungry Indians, and understood their resentment of the white man's wanton waste of their livelihood."

In the spring of 1875 Harry joined the Dowlings on the main roundup. Up to 100,000 Longhorns ran wild over more than a hundred square miles. The riders ranged from ragged criminals to remittance men. Harry noted that, like himself, everyone there had come from somewhere else. He learned to whoop like a Comanche Indian and yell like a Civil War rebel to round up the vast herd. He learned to swing a lariat to let it gain momentum until it "hummed a weird, spinning tune." He learned to chew tobacco instead of smoking, and he slept with his head to the north in case of stampede. If wakened at night his bearings were immediate. At dawn he shook rattlesnakes out of his boots.

Nothing terrified cattle or cowboys more than lightning storms. Cattle horns were conductors of electricity, and on the open plain there was nowhere to hide. One evening thunder crashed across the sky so loudly that Harry became partially deaf for days afterwards. Suddenly a bolt of lightning struck a cow, then jumped crazily from horn to horn throughout the herd. Twenty-one head fell, ten killed outright and eleven stunned. Torrents of rain intensified the sickening odour of burning hair and flesh. Pulling on his new yellow slicker, Harry joined the men rounding up some steers that had stampeded. He wrote that the aroma of dust and burning flesh became impregnated into his slicker, a lifetime reminder of that night.

Harry now knew he wanted his own herd. When he wrote Alexander of his intent, his father replied, "Give it up and come home when you feel you have enough of it. The less entanglement by way of investment the better, but if you still fancy the business, by all means go for it." While he had no intentions of making life easy for Harry, Alexander wrote he would make the following deal: Harry should contribute $2,000, his father would put up $1,000 immediately and another $1,000 for as late as Harry could make it. Alexander closed his letter with, "I expect to return with your Mama from England after the first of September. Soon after that I hope to hear that you have settled and gone into the cattle business, or will relinquish it and come home. Write as soon as possible. With best love, I remain very truly your affectionate father, A. Cross."

Alexander and Julia were going to Britain to visit Selkirk, Ernest and Willie Heber, then return via the Bahamas. Things were going smoothly in the English schools with the exception of Ernest at Haileybury. He and his friend Edward ffolkes, son of a British peer, spent much of the two years reading popular magazine stories about the Canadian West. Ernest failed practically every exam. His thirteen classmates had moved ahead of him. He finally managed to get a good mark in trigonometry, but that one achievement was insufficient to propel him into a senior class. In truth, he was not much further ahead than when he had arrived.

The sixteen-year-old boy may already have become intrigued with a new game from India called polo. Numerous sons of Indian officers attended the school, and the fast-paced riding sport may have been introduced to Haileybury before anywhere else in England. The dangerous game demanded the ultimate in horsemanship. Ernest would grow to love polo as much as he hated the classroom. Harry's letters home from the American frontier must have been further distraction for a youth seeking only excitement.

Deeply disappointed by Ernest's lack of progress, Alexander brought him home to Montreal. But he had no intentions of giving up on his son. The skills of merchandising, finance and entrepreneurship had pumped through Cross veins for two centuries and Alexander intended to unearth them in Ernest. The youth was soon enrolled in the Bryant and Stratton Montreal Business College in Place d'Armes. The school's philosophy of minimum theory and maximum practice in shorthand and French would better prepare Ernest than Greek for a place in the Cross financial empire. In the 1870s secretaries were a luxury, and for the next twenty years Ernest would fill his own letter books with the well-rounded, precisely expressed writing fostered by Bryant and Stratton.

Following two years of business school and the influence of his father, Ernest was dying to head west. From boyhood visits to his grandmother's Chateauguay farm and her Ormstown store, he was able to see merchandising and agriculture harmonized for profit. Each depended upon yet complemented the other. The family farm at River Beaudette provided another opportunity to learn the discipline of hard work, and to study the merits of farming, breeding and of profit through grain.

As Harry had headed for Colorado, Ernest would look to his own frontier – the Canadian West. Its potential suited him as much as it had bored Harry. His father understood Ernest's spirit of adventure but expected him to be educated for every contingency. The railroad had yet to be driven across the prairies, and while his son waited for it to be completed, there was plenty of time for further education, to discover and corral his talents.

In the Cross family business matters, Uncle James and Alexander sold two farms on Mount Royal for $90,000 each, somewhat chagrined that each resold less than a year later for $140,000. Harry had thought it rather imprudent of the purchasers as the property was so far from downtown Montreal. But the city was exploding. The subdivisions by the family on Bleury, Peel and Sherbrooke were under way. Plans for reducing the steepness of Côte des Neiges hill were softened when Alexander advised the city to design a square to beautify the modernization. Politically, Alexander considered running in Montreal West, but his family opposed the idea and he refrained. During this time, he increased his already extensive holdings of Bank of Montreal shares.

Intermarriage and social kinship among the elite families of the time were akin to a private club. John Torrance's daughter had married a son of Sir Alexander T. Galt, and when his son Daniel married Sophie Vanderbilt, the Cross social and business relationships expanded to a father of Confederation and an American robber baron. Emma Lunn divided her time between Europe, where she travelled with George Stephen, the Allans and the Kings, and the New York Park Avenue address of the Daniel Torrances.

Alexander spent his brief leisure time in the St. James Club or with the St. Andrew's Society, and fished or hunted with friends. His snowshoeing activities slowed with the onset of a painful, crippling condition which revealed itself in his handwriting. He would begin a letter with strong, clear handwriting, but by the fourth page it had become shaky and almost illegible. The pain gripped him at his desk, in the garden, or in the pre-dawn hour on the island where he shot geese. Although his pen fingers began to fail him, there was nothing wrong with his casting arm or his legs when it came to standing in a freezing stream. As for the garden cart, it became his favoured mode of transport, the goat his most irascible friend. They resembled a married couple who had fought for years yet continued a disgruntled respect one for the other.

As busy with her charity work as she was with running Pine Avenue, Julia delighted in entertaining Alexander's colleagues at black-tie dinners for fourteen. An excellent horsewoman, she often drove the cutter or carriage through Mount Royal Park with friends. On Sundays she presided over croquet parties in the upper garden. In a letter to Harry, Julia wrote that Sherbrooke Street was so built up it would soon lose its attraction. One day, from Lunn's Georgian mansion and grounds they joined in the celebrations when Governor General and Lady Dufferin came to Montreal, watching the McGill students throng around the royal carriage and run to the university. Later the Crosses and Lunns lunched with the Dufferins. Although the Crosses frowned on extravagance or ostentation, they enjoyed the exclusive camaraderie of the Montreal elite.

In 1876 Uncle James suffered a stroke and was placed under complete nursing care. Alexander requested that Harry return, visit his uncle, and settle down to banking. But Harry did not make it home before Uncle James died, leaving him a fortune.

PART TWO

1872–1895

Heritage without Boundary

"Was it worth it? Were the days of toil and the nights of watching lost? Were the struggles with the bitter elements, the long, long trails across unbroken prairie and rolling foothills without fruition? Was the ministering to hearts wrenched from home ties . . . without reward?

"In those first humble cottages of the new land, courage and love made toil and privations bearable; there, growing things and spreading acres were the stimulus to further achievements; there, the great men of today – many of them – had their early teaching . . .

". . . Worth it? It was a privilege beyond price, a heritage without boundary."

May Armitage, found in Jean Drever Pinkham's memoirs

9

The Invincible NWMP

"The Mounties, as people call us, can travel in any weather."
James Macleod

In 1870 Lieutenant-Colonel James F. Macleod returned from Manitoba to Ontario a celebrity. A hint of vainglory proved no detraction to his charm and the frontier hero was feted at a round of balls and dinners in Toronto, and at Government House in Ottawa. James socialized with friends from Kingston to Bowmanville, reliving the great trek westward and the debâcle upon their arrival. But drink and diversion were insufficient to replace the intoxication of an expedition, the memory of Mary Drever, or the accolades received on returning home. Life turned to tedium and heartache. James yearned for the West, spending weeks at Drynoch, talking with his mother about Mary Drever and life in the Red River Settlement.

Jane Macleod could see that her impulsive son had found in Mary Drever an educated woman who faced warriors and rebels with the same dignity as she executed a curtsey. This was important, for opportunity and position, not money, were what the Macleods of Drynoch had sought for their children. While Jane had encouraged them to play with their Indian friends, she clung to a Victorian sense of propriety, values and connections. Macleods might never be wealthy but they could become influential, and what they accomplished in the new world would be counted. A bankrupt Martin had remonstrated with James over his studies, believing his son could acquire freedom and distinction only through learning. A wisely utilized education would separate servant from gentry, constable from officer. Without it, Martin had believed that immigrant crofters were destined to cling to their ploughshares. With it, a soldier's son and a carpenter's daughter could rule the frontier land. That Mary and James could establish a society worthy of their heritage was unquestioned by Jane Macleod. But with thousands of miles separating the couple and little likelihood of their marrying, such visions might have seemed pointless if not frivolous.

James languished at Drynoch, devoid of prospects for returning west in the manner he desired. Like his father, he was supremely conscious of his social status and the life of a storefront lawyer did not appeal. James would head west only with an official appointment worthy of his self-perceived position. His dreams of a life with Mary Drever were but conjecture, for just as he refused to return a humble man, Mary refused to leave her ailing father and come east to him. Unpredictable and wilful, her laughter could echo the lilt of a chinook wind, but when angry her blue eyes would flash with the intensity of a sudden storm. Daughter of the nannie who had challenged Judge Adam Thom, Mary remained obdurate. The relationship seemed ended.

Having no share in the Drynoch estate, James's Ontario roots loosened. Compared to the appeal of unconfined prairies, his Bowmanville practice palled and by 1872 he appears to have given it up entirely. When his sister Lexi wrote from England asking him to make a new life in the old country with her family, James planned to leave Canada.

Just prior to his departure, an officer at Fort Garry wrote that Colonel Osborne-Smith had left the militia and returned east permanently. The Fort Garry post was open. Was he interested? James seized the opportunity. He wrote to his old friend and mentor, Alexander Campbell, currently serving as postmaster general in the Macdonald administration: "I am extremely anxious to know what will be the result of my application for an appointment in the Militia. . . . I dislike the idea of going [to England] very much . . . but if I am cast adrift by the Militia authorities I have nothing else." He added that Colonel Robertson-Ross, for whom he acted brigade major at Kingston, was willing to write the adjutant general on his behalf. He then delayed his trip, hoping for an immediate answer.

No word came. James waited throughout the summer. When nothing arrived from Ottawa, he suspected that he was again a victim of politics. Finally, with gales beginning to endanger the Atlantic crossing, he wrote Alexander Campbell of his intent to move permanently to England if no job was forthcoming. He concluded, "I have little doubt that my prospects of an appointment in Manitoba have been affected by the hostility of Mr. Clarke, the Attorney General, whose enmity I incurred by giving a very strong opinion, as President of a Court of Inquiry, as to the illegality of his arrest of one of our men.... 'Tis rather too bad that I should suffer for having done my duty. Militia Court Martial and Courts of Inquiry would be worth very little if the members were swayed by the outside consequences of their decisions."

James gave Campbell every opportunity of tracing him, listing his intended moves from Oak Ridges to Toronto, to the Baldwins, until his departure on the *Prussian*. Nothing happened. He sailed for England. Upon learning of his departure, a heartbroken Mary vowed, "If he doesn't return to the West, I'll marry anybody just to be near him."

Family history recalls that James received his Order of St. Michael and St. George from Queen Victoria, then continued on to the Isle of Skye with his sister, Maggie Baldwin. It proved a poignant return. Childhood joys were dampened when they rode through Drynoch. Maggie later wrote of the family graveyard, "It is now a place uncared for, no one responsible for it. The remains of a small Chapel are to be seen. I did what I could to have our graves attended to. I had but a few minutes to stay in the Sacred ground for the night was coming on, the tide coming in to swell the river we had to cross." The horses were restive with the wind and approaching darkness, and Maggie wrote that she felt the dread of ghosts and water kelpies. They turned and rode for old Drynoch at the foot of the Boust. Nothing was left there for this Canadian family.

James was thirty-six. Within months his life had emptied from one of excitement and passion to ennui. He had lost Mary Drever, his Bowmanville practice, and not even one of the prime minister's closest associates had been able to surmount the political stumbling block in Manitoba.

Maggie and her gloomy brother sailed from Skye to the ancestral home of the Mackenzies, cousins of the Macleods, living on the Isle of Mull. James spent his time climbing through scree rock and heather around Castle Calgary. Vast pasturelands undulated toward rugged hills. Streams showered granite cliffs in crystal-chilling elegance. It was a sight James would never forget.

In 1872, the year of James's departure for England, the West changed rapidly. In the aftermath of the rebellion, the new judge, Francis Goodschal Johnson, held court in Rothney Cottage. Calling Christin

Drever to his side, Francis Johnson cautioned, "My child, do you understand the nature of an oath?" When Christin nodded, he administered it, then instructed her to tell the court about the rebels taking the Drever horses. The family received a total of $720 compensation for damages incurred during the rebellion. This included ransom money paid in sterling for the release of Willie, the seizure of their horses, and the goods stolen from Rothney Cottage, Clova Cottage and their store.

William put the rebellion behind him and continued selling and accumulating land, but his timing was off. He had increasingly turned business matters over to Willie, who lacked the innate sense of a true speculator, of holding, juggling and utilizing gains. Nevertheless, it was difficult *not* to make a good deal in those days. Although it was still a few years ahead of the real Winnipeg boom, the town was exploding with activity. Word of the proposed railroad had brought surveyors and opportunists to this jump-off point for the new frontier. Hotels were built, wooden sidewalks criss-crossed the hateful gumbo, and the town was linked to the world through the American telegraph.

As fast as William made money, the lively Willie spent it. He loved well-bred horses and fine carriages. William enjoyed indulging his son; he really did not care about wealth. His legacy was helping to build a city and a province of Canada. He had shown the foresight of settling on what would be the main intersection of a major Canadian city, and had participated in carving a commercial enterprise out of the frontier. At age seventy-two, he was serving as a magistrate and charter member of the Winnipeg Board of Trade. Most of the time he lived with Cyprian and Jean Pinkham at their St. James country home on the Assiniboine River. Mary and Christin helped care for him as he hobbled to his courthouse duties with the aid of two canes.

Mary Drever's days meshed with the Pinkhams' and their young family. Parish life was domestically busy but personally humdrum. Although her friends teased her about her love for James Macleod, who surely would never return, and while eligible men escorted her to rounds of parties and church activities, she swore there would never be another man in her life. While she acted as witness in endless Winnipeg weddings over the next year, Mary had packed her own wedding dress into its cedar box to await James's improbable return. She acknowledged that she had been a bit hasty saying she would marry anyone just to be near him, and occupied her time helping to organize various public functions, particularly the celebration on

November 3, 1873, when Winnipeg was incorporated as a city, with a population of 1,664.

Willie ran a lucrative trade between St. Paul and Winnipeg. He enjoyed the reputation as one of the finest scouts and wagon-train leaders of the southwest trails. In this capacity he was also one of the first to witness the increasing hostilities between the Americans and the Sioux Indians. Only his reputation as a Canadian scout who respected Indians and halfbreeds may have enabled him to hang on to his own scalp as he continued trading below the border. To the south and west of Winnipeg, Indian killings increased as settlers flowed into the frontier. The American Fort Benton on the Missouri was the main focus of violence, with renegades spilling over into Canada at Fort Hamilton, better known as Fort Whoop-Up. Knowing the Indians' craving for liquor and firearms, white traders sold homemade brews laced with ink and tobacco for colour and flavour. They took their payment in buffalo rugs, ponies and young Indian girls. With no law enforcement west of Fort Garry, there was virtually no control over the traders, and no protection for Indians or whites.

John Schultz, now member of Parliament for the Manitoba constituency of Lisgar, had long expressed the fear that settlers would never head westward without military supervision. He had made several impassioned speeches in the House of Commons urging other MPs to support him, and warned that unless the liquor trade was stopped, the fighting was merely a prelude to full-scale murder or war with the Indians.

Short months before the incorporation of Winnipeg, a group of drunken Americans had attacked some Assiniboines on their luxuriant grasslands at Cypress Hills. Claiming that the Indians were horse thieves, the riders had blasted away at entire families. Thirty-six Assiniboines had been killed, many more wounded. Following the carnage, the American traders had recrossed the border to Fort Benton, a sympathetic town that saw no crime in killing redskins.

Colonel Robertson-Ross had also returned from the frontier that year and recommended that a regiment of 550 mounted riflemen be formed to establish law and order in the North-West Territories, to preserve peace, and to protect the hundreds of surveyors, contractors and railway labourers heading west to construct the proposed railway. Sir John A. Macdonald had agreed, and was placing the finishing touches on a proposal for such a force just as word of the Cypress Hills massacre reached Ottawa. His bill for the formation of a western police force passed its readings unanimously.

On May 23, 1873, the North-West Mounted Police became a reality. Its main objectives would be to halt the liquor traffic, gain the Indians' confidence, teach them to respect the law, and collect customs duties from the traders. Unlike the gunslinging sheriff-posse compacts to the south where Indians could be shot on sight, the Canadian force was to achieve a state of peace by diplomacy rather than by rifle. Its judicial powers were sweeping. Stipendiary magistrates would be empowered to hear, judge and sentence any lawbreakers. The Department of Justice, headed by Sir John A. Macdonald himself, would control all activities of the police. As it would be his force, the prime minister would choose his men to lead it.

James Macleod must have come to mind almost immediately. The framework of a civil force under military discipline, combined with the freedom of execution of British law, formed perfect parameters for the justice-loving, authority-hating James. In calling for bilingual men aged eighteen to forty with good character, sound constitutions and riding skills, it was as if Sir John had tailor-made the force for him.

That James had proven a public embarrassment on more than one occasion was precisely the reason which may have drawn the prime minister to consider him for a senior post. James's highly developed perception of justice, combined with his determination to carry it through regardless of personal injury or public shame, was just the kind of quality needed in a huge, lawless country. Whoever rode west with such enormous power must be of unimpeachable character. He must also obey the prime minister, and Sir John knew his man. James might disagree, but ultimately he would do his duty.

It was while striding over the hills on the Isle of Mull that James received a summons from the prime minister. Macdonald offered Lieutenant-Colonel James Farquharson Macleod the position of superintendent third in command, in charge of a division in the newly formed North-West Mounted Police. It was both a reprieve and an offer James could not refuse. He sailed immediately for Canada.

That fall a contingency force travelled west via the American railroad, then rode north for Winnipeg. The troops' arrival was in striking contrast to the mud-splattered, drunken condition of the soldiers at the end of Wolseley's expedition. They were clad in scarlet tunics, blue breeches with white stripes down the sides, white helmets with plumes and black Wellington top boots stretching up the thigh. Encircling each man's waist were symbols of the law and order they intended to enforce: a revolver, Snider carbine and sword. It was James who became the image for the NWMP. Author Longstreth would write: "Macleod was one of the best-looking men of the time. Erect, well proportioned, slightly under six feet with no ounce of superfluous flesh, he presented a figure that his soldiers admired, a bearing that his enemies respected."

The whole town turned out to meet them. James had written Mary Drever that he was coming and asked her to wait for him. His first sight of her was of a beautiful woman of twenty fluttering blue eyes at him from behind a fan. She had feared that he had become more enamoured by the elegance of eastern ladies. James laughed, delighted with her theatrics. They became engaged almost immediately. The wedding dress Mary had sent for in 1871 would be worn the following spring for the only man in her life. One month later Jane Macleod wrote how pleased she was that her "dearest Jim" was to marry the girl he loved so much. As James was stationed at the Stone Fort some twenty miles away, the path between villages was worn bare that winter.

James also spent time with Willie Drever, noting his undiscriminating friendships and special skills. Praising his abilities and wishing him to represent the NWMP in negotiating purchases for provisions required on the trek west, James wrote to Commissioner French: "He [Willie] is ... thoroughly up in this sort of work. ... I am satisfied he would prove most useful, having had so much experience travelling between Fort Garry and St. Paul ... during the Indian troubles in Minnesota." French agreed and Willie was hired.

Early in December James was ordered to arrest and to try whiskey traders operating on the west shore of Lake Winnipeg. After quickly training four men in the art of snowshoeing, the group set out through the woods. Travelling night and day by snowshoe or sled, they surprised the six traders, arrested them and confiscated ten gallons of liquor. Their return to the Stone Fort on Christmas Eve, 1873, was noted in the newspapers as the first patrol ever performed by the North-West Mounted Police.

Winter snows eventually melted into the spring gumbo of 1874. In Winnipeg, far from matters political, Mary and her sisters baked cakes and sewed summer dresses for the pending wedding set for early July. As an enclave of well-to-do British, including the lieutenant-governor, had built summer homes along the river banks in the Pinkhams' parish of St. James, it promised to be a gala event. But on June 1 James was suddenly appointed Assistant Commissioner of Police under Colonel French and ordered to ride south for Fort Dufferin. This changed everything. James faced the possibility of an Indian war, hostile whiskey traders, and a canvas tent for a home. With 300,000 square miles to patrol on horseback, he felt he was in no position to offer Mary even a log cabin. He postponed the wedding and rode immediately for Dufferin. Mary returned her wedding dress to the trousseau trunk.

In Fort Dufferin, James joined the troops arriving by American rail for the trek west to Fort Whoop-Up. A massive stampede of the horses that night showed him that many of the men were still unaccustomed to handling either animals or the elements. The journey began on the following day, the stunning sight of the force stretching from scarlet-coated trumpeters to oxen-drivers plodding several miles to the rear. From behind every hillock and distant wood, armed Indians on both sides of the border watched suspiciously as the military force moved westward. They communicated across the land by smoke signal and drum, providing an eerie tenuity to the peaceful intent of the NWMP mission.

That a fine cavalry troop would soon deteriorate to a ragged collection of men and beasts desperately fighting for survival was testimony to nature's viciousness and to the ignorance of the soldiers. Had they known that hail or blistering sun would beat down within hours of each other, or that food and water would become fanciful visions, they might have confined their dreams to the farms, offices, or gentlemanly lifestyles from whence they came. For Commissioner French and Assistant Commissioner James F. Macleod, morale became the key to their survival. The two would pursue it in disparate ways, French by rigid discipline and Macleod by inspiration.

Mary received her first letter from James camped at the River Morrey. His handwriting appeared rushed, his tone exasperated. Even in uncharted territory he could not escape the hated office. Dispatch orders plagued him more than mosquitoes or sun. Appalled by the "bushels of letters and telegrams" flowing into camp, Commissioner French had requested a secretary, then dumped the task onto James's shoulders. James groused that "I have not had a moment to myself what with boards, investigations and general duty which I am stuck on by the Commissioner. I hardly know where the day ends or commences." He described the difficulty of hauling the inordinately heavy wagons, then allowed his sense of fun to lift his mood. Like his father, James loved to dramatize in his letters and wrote of the previous evening when five ox teams became stuck in the mud at the rear of the train: "[I] took the oxen with my own hands. You ought to have heard me geeing and hawing 'til I was quite hoarse. It was long after dark when I arrived. The half-breeds were awfully tickled when I marched in amongst them. I arranged to get two of the teams into Camp all right and sent a pair of horses to the assistance of the third." In almost every letter he regarded trials as challenges, brushes with death "a lark." He might describe the tragedy of starvation in one paragraph only to marvel at the beauty of nature in the next.

James's attitude was vital to the men as disaster hovered. Starting their fifteen-hour marches at three o'clock in the morning to avoid the terrible heat, men and horses were tortured by clouds of mosquitoes and black-flies. He grew a great, golden beard to protect his face from the sun's relentless rays and claimed that nothing ever bothered him. Not so his men and animals. The scant water supplies they found often remained thick with mud even after straining. Other water holes were contaminated by buffalo. Denied proper feed and water, the horses suffered and began to die. Men fell ill, the halfbreed drivers suffering the most. The latter plodded on some fifteen miles to the rear of the column, their tortured oxen hauling carts filled with gifts for the Indians. Would they were filled with water or beef. James brought up the rear and frowned on the idea of these gifts. He wrote that respect was what the Indian sought, not presents.

In August fierce storms blew down the tents. They ran out of wood and were forced to spend chilling nights in soaked clothing, gnawing the hard biscuits remaining in their dwindling, carefully supervised provisions. Prairie fires burned on all sides to the horizons. Allegedly lit by Indians attempting to impede the force, the flames destroyed pasture land and reminded the men that hostile forces surrounded them. On several occasions when James and Sub-Inspector James Walker rode ahead for food, hay and guides, they were gone for as long as a week.

Many men found the trek a living hell and began to wonder how they would get home. They directed their growing bitterness toward Colonel French. He was seen as the Captain Bligh of the trek while James was the Fletcher Christian who brought provisions, drove the rearguard oxen, supported exhausted horses. They were always relieved when their assistant commissioner finally returned to camp. Recognizing James's ability to inspire the troops, Colonel French commended him to his commanding officer. He wrote, "Macleod is a capital fellow; my right hand. I wish we had a few more like him."

By September 5 force morale had sunk as deep as the coulee in which the troops had camped. They knew they were lost, having followed the advice of an American guide suspected of misleading the force for the whiskey traders. Colonel French had kept his own sightings, however, and commanded the force to head southward. Arising long before dawn the men found the horses too sick to stagger up the muddy walls of the coulee. They threw the wagon traces over their shoulders, some pulling as others pushed the great wheels. They cheered for every inch gained, cursed for each foot slid backwards. Upon reaching the top, they returned for the horses. James and his men placed their shoulders under their steeds' bellies and dodging their flailing hooves, half-lifted, half-pushed them out of the coulee. Those animals that could not be coaxed to remain standing were left to die on the trail.

In early September snow fell. The column was making less than nine miles a day, having travelled 691 miles from Dufferin. Anger welled toward the commissioner and some blamed him for every ill. Joseph Carscaden, an enlisted man, wrote of Colonel French's terrible temper and added: "From what I have seen of our Commissioner, I must say that I consider him wanting in human feeling and without honor. This is hard to say of anyone, but I assert that it is true. . . . It looks very much like starvation, so much so that we must keep moving ahead or sure death awaits us."

On the night of September 9 the temperature fell below freezing. An icy rain shocked them after a blistering heat on the previous day. Around midnight some horses began twitching around the eyes, faces and jaws, increasing to violent jerking. Nothing could be done and most died within twenty minutes. The sight of these dreadful deaths terrified the men. Carscaden wrote that he would never forget the suffering of both horses and men. The two blankets issued to them in Dufferin had the warmth of cheese cloth against the bitter winds, yet Colonel French ordered each man to give up one blanket for his horse. Furthermore, he refused to allow any ox-carts to be burned to heat a meal: they were government property. As Carscaden sat trembling with cold on the freezing ground, fear whipping his anger, he asked, "I wonder, did those MPs who called for a Police Force and sent us out, intend that we should endure such hardships or privations? Not by any means." In Ottawa, with the fall of the Conservative government over the Pacific scandal, nothing could be further from the MPs' minds at that moment than the Far West.

One stormy night while the hungry, miserable sentries shuffled about, someone stole a few biscuits from a barrel. In the morning food count, the loss was noted and reported to Colonel French. The commissioner ordered the night watch roused and brought before him in their overcoats. When a few crumbs were discovered in two of the men's pockets, Colonel French immediately judged them guilty and ordered them put in irons.

James was outraged. Biscuits were often handed out on the march and the crumbs may have been days old. With no thought whatsoever for the code of military procedure, he stepped forward before the force and roared, "No, Colonel French. You cannot by law – and you dare not by justice – put these men in irons!"

If Colonel French backed down he would lose control of his men. If he did not, mutiny was almost certain. Carscaden wrote of the solution, "Our worthy Commissioner is subdued and taught his inferiority in intellect, if not in position, and the irons are not put on. . . . But, will the Commissioner let it drop here? NO, he has one of them brought up and a charge is made out against him for allowing them [the biscuits] to be stolen! The poor innocent fellow is fined $5.00. Now, if this was not the most damnable perversion of Justice, I'm much mistaken!" That James's stand for the accused biscuit-snatchers might have been detrimental to the commissioner's influence on his troops may seem an understatement to military historians. Nevertheless, he was firmly established as the force hero.

On September 11 the force reached the forks of the Bow and South Saskatchewan rivers only to discover that Fort Whoop-Up was not where Colonel Robertson-Ross had said it would be. They had travelled nearly one thousand miles and on September 16 Inspector Denny wrote in his diary, "Can't go much further." But they pushed on in fear of freezing or starving where they stood, cursing each massive wagon wheel as they forcefully rolled it over another hill. Pony hoofprints indenting the near frozen ground were a constant reminder that the Blackfoot were following or even preceding the march, waiting as, mile after mile, wasted man and beast helped each other along. The warriors could ride down on the shabby redcoats at any time, but word sped ahead that the NWMP were coming to protect the Indian from the whiskey traders. So, mounted on swift ponies, the Blackfoot continued to watch this near tableau of man and beast, neither helping nor harming its diminutive progress. Carscaden looked at the horses and oxen who had travelled some one thousand miles and wrote, "Among the men you can hear the question, 'How are we to get home?' "

On September 22 James and Colonel French headed south to Fort Benton in the United States for food and information. The town proved a touchstone to the American West. Guns and light penalties ruled. Both white man and Indian were more aggressive than in Canada, and the latter had no status whatsoever. James wrote to Mary a few days after his arrival: "This is a miserable hole. Nothing but two stores and a collection of whiskey shops." Determined to find the suspects in the Cypress Hills massacre while ostensibly organizing food, supplies and clothing for the men, James found someone who identified them all. To his astonishment, the sheriff had no intention of turning the accused over to the British government for trial. James would have to return armed with extradition orders.

At this time, Colonel French divided the troops; he himself headed for Dufferin, leaving James in charge in the West. In a confidential report to the minister of justice, he buried a growing personal antagonism and commended James's special abilities, but the two would never meet again.

In Benton, James befriended Charles Conrad, the manager of the supply house I.G. Baker and Company, and contracted with them to supply the NWMP. He also hired the Scottish-Indian guide Jerry Potts, whose knowledge of the land and of the Indians was already legendary. Whether in blinding snowstorm or uncharted country, Potts would always bring the men through to their exact destination.

When James returned to the North-West Territories with Conrad and Potts, he found the force surrounded by a herd of buffalo numbering some 80,000. As the riders quietly approached, the docile beasts parted where they grazed, allowing the men to enter deeply among them, as if enveloped by a selenium-coloured sea. In awe of the magnificent animals, James wrote, "I never cared for the sport of killing them." He conceived the idea of imprinting the buffalo head on the insignia of the NWMP.

Accompanied by his men mounted on those horses which could still support riders, James headed for Fort Whoop-Up. They arrived on October 2, 1874. One hundred and fifty men had travelled nearly two thousand miles to rid Canada of the whiskey scourge, centred in this wilderness fort. James ordered the two nine-pounder field-guns and mortars placed in position. The men dusted off what was left of their uniforms, making sure their insignia were visible. Then in a long line, they rode slowly and silently toward the gates. No shots were fired from the rusted cannons on the bastions. Not a person was seen, the world was silent. Halting the line, James and

Potts rode forward. With ever an eye for the dramatic and a sense of the ludicrous, the assistant commissioner startled his men by dismounting and knocking on the door as if stopping by for tea. It was opened by one Dave Akers, who claimed to be a veteran of the American Civil War. Flanked by a couple of Indian women and some dogs, Akers politely invited the NWMP to enter. Warned by the buffalo hunters of the approaching force, the whiskey traders had fled across the border to the United States. No liquor was found.

While other officers may have smarted under the loss of a history-making event, this anticlimax to the great trek eclipsed all the elements of theatrical jest. A lover of charades and Victorian skits, James delighted in the comedy-dramas of his life.

The levity of Whoop-Up soon gave way to anxiety for survival. Exhausted men and horses had to be sheltered and James knew there was little time left before the frozen stubble and snow-sprinkled foothills would be shrouded in freezing whiteness. Three days west of Whoop-Up, Jerry Potts led them to the Old Man's River where a large island rose from the centre. The trail to the Bow River passed nearby, the whiskey traders' route. They would build their fort there.

The island was covered in cottonwoods and provided pasture for the animals. Big game and waterfowl abounded. James noted in his report that the river's rapid current would make it easy to power machinery. He foresaw diverting the river to irrigate the land for raising grain, constructing a grist mill, adding a circular saw for flour and lumber. His own little village took shape in his mind. To the west, beyond the Porcupine Hills, the force would soon view the massive Rocky Mountains, an awesome sight for the central Canadian and British force.

The men threw themselves into building Fort Macleod, racing to beat the rapidly approaching freeze-up. Determined that the horses and sick men would be housed first, James announced that not a single log of officers' quarters would be laid beforehand. The men cut and hauled logs, then chinked them with gumbo. At 10 below zero when the mud solidified between their bare fingers like freezing cement, they switched to other work. Another foot of mud had to be shovelled onto the roofs. With each storm they drove the herd into the woods for shelter and blanketed each animal. But the weather was as capricious there as anywhere on the prairies. Shivering and incoherent with cold, builders might be driven down off the roofs only to be warmed within an hour by what James called a "Coquettish Chinook wind."

As the horses were too ill for a chase, James bought meat from the hunters and billed the NWMP, unaware that in Fort Pelly to the east Colonel French insisted his men buy their own flour and provisions. When buffalo drew near the Old Man's River, success depended on the skill of Jerry Potts and the men on foot. James had them skin the buffalo, then instructed the tailors to outfit all the sentries in buffalo coats, caps and mitts. Lined with red flannel that James found in Indian supplies and transferred to police stores, the coats were a boon to the men on sentry duty.

At the same time as they were building shelter, the troops continued to strike at liquor trafficking. It must have impressed both Indian and white trader to see policemen stumbling through the cold, many still ragged and wrapped in blankets, to confiscate ten gallons of whiskey. No law-breaker was beyond reach of the police. In dispensing justice, James swifty established a reputation for harsh but fair sentences, particularly in the cases of white men trading in contraband or liquor. Ten years later he would also deal severely with Indian rustlers, but in these early days he showed a paternalism toward the Indian law-breakers, who were often unaware they had even committed crimes. Under his hand, the Indian learned of a new justice based on subpoenas and witnesses.

Unlike the shoot-outs in the United States, James's method proved effective if frustrating. In one of his first cases he had the NWMP inspectors sit with him so that they might learn correct judicial procedures. Five traders with a host of contraband had been captured fifty miles from the fort. An Indian named Three Bulls had helped find their cache. As the hearing got under way, James asked Three Bulls to produce more witnesses. Instead, the Indian presented him with a horse. James refused, explaining that it was improper for a judge to take presents from someone who had a case before him. Again, James explained the meaning of evidence. Finally, Three Bulls produced the witnesses, then just as James was reconvening court they all rode off on a buffalo hunt.

Captain Martin Macleod would not have recognized his once impetuous son, for although James had every right to bring the Indians back to the trial, he prepared subpoenas for them instead, wishing to avoid any compulsory action until they understood the process of law. At any rate, the horseless force was incapable of chasing down the Indians. Eventually the trial was completed and in his subsequent report James stressed the need to purchase up to forty more horses to strike blows at the illicit traders regardless of the weather. No reply was received.

Confiscating liquor must have been painful for a man like James who enjoyed his whiskey. A family story tells of James and Jerry Potts spying a keg in the bushes along the Whoop-Up trail. Dismounting, James asked Jerry what he thought it might be. Scratching his head, the scout suggested James sample the contents. Taking a swig, James coughed, saying that he really wasn't sure, but it was vile stuff. Jerry Potts followed suit, guessing that it might be some kind of medicine. The two sat on a couple of boulders, sipping, choking and analysing until the entire keg was empty. Then they pulled themselves back into their saddles and allowed their horses to return them to the post, still wondering aloud what it was they had discovered.

By November of 1874 the men were in a deadly race for shelter, building the hospital, kitchen, wash house, latrine and the constables' mess. The temperatures ran as low as 30 below. Howling winds and heavy, drifting snow battered them from the Belly River to Fort Benton.

During the pre-Christmas period the Blackfoot Indians visited James. The Bloods and Peigans had already arrived but not the Blackfoot. They had hung back, watching the men survive mid-winter chases of whiskey traders and contraband. Then one day an Indian whom James described as "a very nice looking young man" brought a message from the chiefs seeking assurance of friendship. A few days later he recorded the arrival of some "splendid Blackfeet, tall, graceful and straightforward." They were led by Chief Crowfoot, a man of extraordinary courage and wisdom and the veteran of nineteen battles. James wrote that after smoking a communal pipe, he told the Blackfoot that, "we have not come to take their land from them and that they will know the intentions of Government before anything is done." He also gave a general idea of the laws which would be enforced, but told the Indians they need not fear being punished for doing what they did not know was wrong.

Chief Crowfoot expressed his delight with the policemen, and another chief said, "Before you came the Indian crept along, now he is not afraid to walk erect." The Blackfoot quickly came to respect the man they called Stamix Otokan, or Bull's Head.

James wrote that the Indians he had met were intelligent, hospitable, with apparently no objection to white men settling in their country.

His was a trust founded in childhood friendships with the Upper Canada Ojibwa. To the Blackfoot, James embodied the government, the law of the Great White Mother, and the judge. In a letter to Ottawa James wrote:

> It is quite unnecessary to lavish presents upon the Indians. The great thing is to treat them kindly; ask them into the room where we ourselves sit, give them a cup of tea or coffee and a piece of bread and as much tobacco as they can smoke; speak to them about their Camps, the buffalo and their horses, and they go away perfectly contented. If any man of consequence comes to me ... he makes a speech – an art at which they are great adepts – I reply in a few words and give him some tobacco for himself and his braves and he goes off as satisfied as if he were loaded down with presents.

By the end of 1874 James wrote that there seemed to have been a complete stoppage of the whiskey trade throughout the whole section of the country. In a land where desperate Indians were known to slide down chimneys searching for liquor, people no longer felt the need to even lock their doors at night. He was accomplishing through friendship and tact a peace which the use of force was failing to achieve in the nation to the south. Backed by a legal structure, and by a cohesiveness of courtesy and courage inherent in his character, James was establishing a peaceful development of the Canadian West on his word alone. Rarely in the history of British colonization had such a feat been accomplished.

By the new year James and his men still had no news of their families, and apart from one six-week-old telegram appointing James preventive officer in H.M. Customs, the government remained inaccessible. Two policemen had frozen to death on the trail attempting to deliver the mail.

At Fort Macleod the men were fairly well off in food, shelter and morale, but in the outlying posts the mood was mutinous. Diarist Carscaden, stationed at Fort Pelly under Colonel French, renewed his attacks on the commissioner. It was not so much French's inequitable discipline that angered Carscaden, as the commissioner's disdain for the ordinary man. He claimed Colonel French forced the men to pay for basic boots and clothing, and for flour at $15 per bag, as he did not consider such items the government's responsibility. No one had been paid a penny of their wages, and they were forced to borrow from the traders at interest rates of 23 per cent.

On the other hand, with no word whatsoever from the government, James noted in Fort Macleod, "We go on our own here." He purchased when he saw the necessity, for if he had waited for permission before securing horses, oats or red flannel, the force would have been annihilated. Consequently, he ran the government's bills higher than in any other fort, a situation aggravated by an inefficient quartermaster. At the time Ottawa was in a state of flux and some confusion, although the Liberal party under Alexander Mackenzie now formed the government. New ministers and members of Parliament now controlled the finances of a force clad in rags and sole-ravaged boots thousands of miles away.

Throughout that first winter NWMP morale diminished. Carscaden wrote, "Our laws and lawgiver are all included in the one word FRENCH – ." In closing his memoirs Carscaden wrote of him: "The only act he could do which would cause the men of this Troop to feel rejoiced to see him, would be to grant one and all that which they ardently desire and pray for; viz: their discharge from the North-West Mounted Police."

To further discredit the police, traders passed the word that they would be gone in the spring. When troubled Indians came to James to ask the length of his stay, he wrote in his report, "Their delight is unbounded when I tell them that I expect to remain with them always." As well as speaking for the force, he was doubtlessly speaking for himself. Far from the seat of power and domination of superior officers or politicians, he believed he was free to shape his own destiny, to lead his men and to interpret a compassionate law as the basic structure of a future society.

In January 1875 noises of mutiny and desertion started to rumble around James as well. The men had not been paid a cent of their wages. By mid-January James still had no orders or even acknowledgments from Ottawa. It was as if the government had dropped off the face of the earth. Once the Queen's own proud force, the men's uniforms were more patches than dress, and even their vermin-filled underclothing was in rags. They wore Indian moccasins and buffalo hides, for most of their clothing and blankets had had to be burned. Yet they still scoured the countryside in search of illicit liquor. James vowed that duty would be carried out to the letter whilst they still had a horse and a man standing. Despite his messages to Ottawa, "blunt almost to the point of rudeness," and warning that he alone was faced with a possible eighteen desertions, Ottawa ignored them. For the officers and men it was not the hours and hardships which demoralized them – it was the lack of recognition.

In the bitter cold, the poverty, the hunger and the lack of any communication with the outside world, the loneliness of the gregarious assistant commissioner was agonizing. James's penchant for writing romantic letters to Mary was scant compensation. Day after day he worked from five in the morning to eleven at night. Everyone from Indians and settlers to the latrine-cleaning constables came to him with their problems. Anything that kept his mind busy sufficed, duty a panacea for pain.

He attempted to establish a sense of family and place in Fort Macleod much as Martin Macleod had once done under bitter conditions on the Isle of Skye. He settled the men down to a routine which included church services in the mess hall. The NWMP surgeon, R.B. Nevitt, wrote that anyone overhearing the men practise for these services would be treated to hymns liberally interspersed with songs of profanity.

One day James hired a mail courier, then learned that the man was trafficking in liquor. Unable to take one horse out into the freezing temperatures, he sent his men on a fifteen-day snowshoe and dog-sled chase through winter gales. He recognized the desperate need for the men to believe in themselves and in the force. When the police proudly returned with the courier, James exulted, "the Mounties, as people call us, can travel in any weather."

On March 7, 1875, nine months after the force had left Fort Dufferin, some mail reached Fort Macleod. But neither word nor provisions came from Ottawa. The men's morale had diminished to the emblem on their patched uniforms. They were totally isolated from the rest of the world, if one still existed. Was there anything beyond the frozen wilderness of Old Man's Island, save screaming winds and the odd whiskey trader? Faced with the literal disintegration of the Canadian NWMP, James made a desperate decision. He would head for Helena, Montana, and bring back the payroll himself. A round trip of three hundred miles, Helena was the closest telegraph and banking centre to Fort Macleod.

James must have relished the adventure. He was a man of action, not an administrator, and he recognized the vital importance of morale. Heading into an empty land of blizzards that could freeze a man in his tracks was better than standing still and watching the demise of his force. So in mid-March James, Inspector Denny, Jerry Potts and four others loaded themselves with blankets, buffalo robes, boiled bacon, biscuits, tea, oats, and with sturdy Indian ponies (acquired without permission from Ottawa), and headed out of the gates of Fort Macleod. Almost immediately a snowstorm enveloped them. Following their first night at Fort Whoop-Up, the group pressed southward, the horses plunging to their bellies in snowdrifts. Again, James proved both his extraordinary riding skills and his love for danger. He wrote to Mary:

> I was remounted on a horse I had just bought before leaving – a white – a very good animal. I thought I would try if he knew anything about running Buffalo, so off I set after a Buffalo. . . . I got up to him . . . close to his tail, when like a flash he stopped and turned to charge. My horse would, I believe, have jumped over himself if I had let him. You would have laughed till you were tired if you had seen the remainder of the "chase." The rascal was chasing me, and I was going as fast as my horse could go. He followed me about 50 yards, and then turned and gave me up. I had no intention of shooting the old villain. The episode furnished subject for a good laugh at my expense for a long time afterwards.

One slip and James would have been dead. Inspector Denny wrote in his memoirs that the buffalo had ripped a stirrup from James's saddle. That night they continued on until 11 p.m. before bivouacking. They used sagebrush to boil a kettle of snow. Their next night, at Milk River, the temperature fell to a windchill of nearly 60 below. James wrote:

> We broke up an old wagon box and were able to boil water but could not keep the shivers off. I was pretty well off when I turned in but the rest suffered very much . . . we had to guard our horses as the country thereabouts was filled with Indian horse thieves. In the morning it had got up a perfect storm and our guide (Jerry Potts) was afraid to start, so we went to work and dug out a hole in a snow bank, efficiently large to hold us all. I never spent such a night as I spent in that hole. Every now and then I woke up in a cold perspiration chilled to the very marrow. In the morning the wind was blowing a perfect hurricane. It came in from the South. Our snow house was no longer any protection and there was nothing for it but to start right in the very face of the wind and driving snow, thirty miles over the bleakest portion of this whole country.
>
> About six o'clock the clouds rose and we found ourselves just where we wanted to be, our guide had taken us as straight as an

arrow. That evening things looked better, but before we were in bed an hour, the wind cleared to the north, and when I got up in the morning there was a covering of inches of snow all over us. We started without any breakfast, too cold to eat. When we were about half way through the morning the sun came out and we were soon as much scorched with the heat as we had been nearly frozen with the cold.

James's horse broke down about ten miles from the last station at the American border, where they astonished state troopers with their trek. The blizzard howled on. Denny's toes froze. One of the men began slipping into that bone-chilling, dreamy state from which there is no return. He slipped off his horse to warm himself but could not get on again and James wrote that he "appeared not to care whether he did or not." Author J.P. Turner wrote that it was James's magic influence which kept the man alive.

For the only time in twenty years of letters James wrote that his fingertips froze. His face became blackened from sunburn and frostbite and he sustained a red scar across his nose. Eventually they stumbled into Helena, faces, hands and feet painfully swollen from frostbite. Welcomed as a hero out of the wilds, James found that the people at Fort Shaw and Helena were so attentive to him he could not get a moment to himself. He was recognized on the streets and in the hotels. The advantage of Montana was, of course, the telegraph, and James wrote to Mary:

I communicated with Ottawa direct. What do you think of their saying in one of their telegrams that my action was approved!!!! Everything here has been left to me to settle; indeed, they have given me a 'carte blanche.' Just fancy, they gave me authority to draw the money to pay the men up to the last of February. I drew $30,000 and brought $15,000 out here with me. There is no doubt I ran a very great risk, but I was bound to get the men paid and I have succeeded. I don't think I shall run such a risk again.

Upon returning to Fort Macleod, or what James described as "these miserable quarters," he closed with one of the few references he ever made to personal exhaustion:

I have been awfully bush since my return. I will write you very soon again. Thank Mrs. P. (Pinkham) for her kind note. Give Christin my love and remember me to your father, Mr. P. and your brother. With endless love, Ever yours, Jim.

P.S. I recv. your letter with the teletype the other day. Sorry to say it is all blotched and *not* flattering!

James had brought the men's pay back, just as he had always returned with provisions on the original trek. By challenging the prairie winter, flirting with death, and still achieving his goal, he established the reputation on both sides of the border that men of the NWMP were invincible. His men had made a larger-than-life gesture, and James's loyalty and dependability were forever beyond reproach. He became the stuff of legends, underscored later by a comment in a Montana newspaper that the NWMP always got their man. Of this remarkable mid-winter journey, policeman S.J. Clarke later wrote, "Col. Macleod will always keep in memory the Boys of the NWMP as being the best Commanding Officer the Police ever had."

In July 1875 James returned to Helena for the extradition trial of those accused in the 1873 Cypress Hills massacre. He experienced firsthand the difference between Canadian and American law, as well as the bitterness harboured toward Indians in the United States. Ranchers, settlers and outlaws had swelled the mining town's population of three thousand in anticipation of a spectator sport. No red-blooded American was going to allow the extradition of white men for shooting Indians. The scarlet-coated heroes were now so unpopular that they took their meals in their quarters rather than incite riots in the hotel dining room.

Court was convened on July 7. Commissioner W.E. Cullen charged the Cypress Hills defendants with "assault and with intent to commit murder upon Assiniboine Indians at Fort Farwell near the Cypress Mountains [sic], North-West Territories in the Dominion of Canada, on or about the first day of May, 1873." The spectators booed, hissed or cheered depending upon who was in the witness box, intimidating some into changing their stories mid-sentence. Wisecracks ricocheted about the room and on out the door to a huge crowd. When the American district attorney, hired to conduct Canada's prosecution, showed sympathy for the accused, James fired him.

Through the wisecracks and hostilities the real adversary in the case soon emerged. On the second day the defence lawyer suddenly jumped up and shouted that before any of his men were given up to stand trial in Canada, he and his friends would "wade knee deep in British Blood!" Unable to contain himself any longer, James leaped up and roared above the din for "Justice to be done!" The War of 1812 was about to be renewed.

The streets rang with patriotism. No Montanan was going to see one American boy handed over to the British. As James and his men left the courthouse and worked their way through the throng, lurid accusations and ridicule were hurled at them. At night, reporters from the *Helena Herald* scribbled gleefully as a witness, Abe Farwell, embellished his tale. Each barroom blast became front-page news.

In his final judgment, Cullen regretted the publicity and the lack of an impartial trial, but concluded that there had been no premeditated design to kill the Assiniboines. The accused were acquitted. That night a crowd waving bottles of Montana rotgut (rum) held a torchlight procession. They built bonfires on the edge of town and rejoiced in the American victory against the Canadians.

The following morning, as James prepared to return home via Cypress Hills, Helena's sheriff arrested him on a charge of false imprisonment. The vindicated Jeff Devereaux had laid the charge. Helena citizens were delighted by this turn of events. Back they all went to court, this time James in his scarlet uniform and scarlet face in the docket. Justice Wade ruled that James was simply acting on his orders, and prevailed upon the citizens of Helena to extend the goodwill already shown between the United States and Canadian governments on the extradition treaty. So the citizens cheered the departing James, who promptly hired the wily Abe Farwell as mail courier for the NWMP.

Returning to Fort Macleod in August, James was again out of telegraphic contact with Mary. It had been too long. This was not the way he wished to spend the rest of his life. Although he had no wish to leave the West, he determined to leave the force. The trouble was, he still did not envision himself as a storefront lawyer. Furthermore, each time he thought of taking leave and heading for Winnipeg, another crisis arose. In November 1875, seventeen months since James had said goodbye to Mary, he learned that Inspector Brisebois had built a new NWMP post on the Bow River one mile from where he had originally been instructed. Under ordinary circumstances, it is unlikely that James would ever have assigned the task to Brisebois. Both he and Colonel French had criticized the inspector for poor judgment, insubordination and sloppy supervision of his men. But the force had fallen under criticism in the House of Commons for excessive expenditure and poor morale, and Major-General Selby-Smyth, James's old commanding officer, was en route to assess NWMP operations. Knowing the general was heading toward Brisebois's camp, James raced north to catch up with the northward-bound "F" troop at the river. There they lashed wagons together with greased tarpaulins to serve as ferries, and crossed to camp at Tail Creek. James sent Inspector Brisebois north to begin construction of the new Bow River fort, remaining behind himself to prepare a welcoming troop for the general. After two days of drilling the motley bunch relentlessly, James met the general with a small police escort and two hundred Blackfoot headed by Chief Crowfoot. The hastily polished troops presented an impressive show in the wilderness. The general subsequently wrote in his report, "Too much value cannot be attached to the NWMP; too much attention cannot be paid to their efficiency." He also remarked: "The privations of camp life can hardly be overestimated. . . . Lieutenant Colonel McLeod is held in very high estimation; he has gained the respect, esteem, and confidence of all classes . . . as an officer eminently adapted for the post he occupies."

Some weeks later the Reverend McDougall arrived in Fort Macleod to report that Brisebois had not only named the new fort after himself but had also moved a Métis girl into his quarters and commandeered the only iron stove and cooking facility for himself. As a consequence the men had mutinied. Every move Brisebois had made was the antithesis of James's interpretation of what the NWMP stood for. The force had ceased to be the brain child of the government; it had become his own creation, a symbol of his name. He exploded, riding hard for the north with Assistant Commissioner Irvine. It was snowing, but they made the distance from Fort Macleod to "Fort Brisebois" in record time.

To James, the site of the new fort was reminiscent of the magnificent bay pastures and clear running waters on the Isle of Mull where he had received his summons from the prime minister. He requested that it be renamed Fort Calgary. Brisebois was subsequently eased out of the force. Author Hugh Dempsey wrote that from Irvine's report, it appeared that the officers and men "could not bear the embarrassment of having a fort named after an officer who, in their opinion, had failed in his duty."

10

🌣 A Soldier's Son and
a Carpenter's Daughter

"I entirely trust Stamix Otokan . . . I will sign with Crowfoot."
Chief Red Crow, Treaty 7

Christmas 1875 marked eighteen months since James and Mary had seen one another. The assistant commissioner waited no longer and resigned from the force. James had already accepted the offered appointment of North-West Territories stipendiary magistrate. On New Year's Day, 1876, he penned his farewell to the officers and men, expressing a deep respect for them all. Now, after a courtship of five years, he was free to return to Winnipeg, join Mary and be married.

Almost simultaneously, the Privy Council reported that upon Major-General Selby-Smyth's investigation of the force, it concluded Colonel French's services would be no longer required, and that Lieutenant-Colonel Macleod be appointed the new commissioner. James longed to be free from duty and·to join Mary, but he could hardly refuse such an appointment – it was not his style – particularly as it came from the incumbent Liberal government. The dual positions of commissioner and stipendiary magistrate were accolades for a man who had been shamed by a governor general. More important, this was also James's opportunity to establish the law and to shape its moral tone in 300,000 square miles of Canada. Warning that he intended to move the force's headquarters from the site at Swan River to Fort Macleod, he accepted the positions to begin July 20, 1876.

It was early June, and James still had time to ride for Winnipeg and wed Mary Drever. His brothers Norman and Henry were already there, having delivered a tiny ring purchased by their mother. Jane Macleod had written to Mary, "I hope though I am very old, to learn the happiness of seeing you someday. . . . Blessings for you both wherever you are." The news created a flurry of excitement and activity in Winnipeg as Mary Drever shook out her wedding gown for the third time and planned her marriage to the famous NWMP colonel. It would be the gala event of the West. Enjoying one of the greatest events in her life by proxy, Jane wrote again from Drynoch, "Norman wrote that you were preparing The Day. I hope you will succeed in trying to be a great Swell. I would indeed like to see you . . . and Jim dressed for the occasion."

As if Jane Macleod's letter was an omen, Sitting Bull with eight thousand Sioux killed General George Custer and 266 officers and men of the United States Cavalry at the Little Big Horn River, Montana, on June 24. Frightened settlers watched Sitting Bull and his three thousand braves spill over the border into the North-West Territories. Instead of heading for his wedding, James rode immediately for the border site of Wood Mountain and Sitting Bull. In an act of bravery and audacity that astonished the American troops, four red-coated NWMP officers headed by Inspector James Walsh had ridden to Sitting Bull and politely asked the Sioux to lay down their arms. In trust of the Great White Mother and of the NWMP, the warriors had complied.

James recommended to Ottawa that the Indians be induced to recross the border. The collective Blackfoot and Sioux nations could not live off Canada's diminishing buffalo. Sioux roamed through the outskirts of Blackfoot country, shooting their game and antagonizing the Blackfoot. If war broke out, the proposed railroad would go unbuilt and settlers would never come west. Without the railroad, British Columbia would refuse to join Confederation. James headed for Ottawa to give an eyewitness account of western events to the politicians. In the House of Commons he was publicly thanked for his success "in winning the co-operation and friendship of the Blackfoot Confederacy." James tried to impress upon the government the difficulty of communicating with the force, and attempted to convey the very real threat of war in the West.

Having completed his official duties, he travelled westward via Drynoch, where he kept his wedding intentions a secret. He had no wish to disappoint his mother again. Catching the train in Toronto and heading west through the United States, James arrived in Winnipeg on July 28, 1876. Six long years after their first engagement, his bride was taking no chances. He rode up to Rothney Cottage to find Mary literally fastening the stays on her Scottish wedding gown.

Governor General Lord Dufferin and Lady Dufferin would soon be arriving to stay at Silver Heights Lodge in the Pinkhams' parish, and Lieutenant-Governor J.E. Cauchon was in residence. But the long anticipated pomp and circumstance that would have made the Macleod/Drever wedding the closest event to royalty ever known in Manitoba never happened. The wedding took place so swiftly that no one outside the Drever family knew of it. With Christin acting as witness, James and Mary were married at five o'clock that same afternoon in the parish of St. James. Bishop Machray performed the ceremony with Cyprian Pinkham assisting. Old William Drever was delighted to see his fiery Mary married to a man who had helped liberate the loyalists from Riel. No sooner was the ring on Mary's finger than James was off before dark. Mary was left with instructions to head east for a Drynoch Christmas and to live with Jane Macleod until he returned. As Jean Pinkham would care for their father, Mary had no further excuses not to obey. On August 3 the *Manitoba Daily Free Press* noted with surprise the wedding of "one of Manitoba's . . . favorite daughters" and wished the couple well.

True to his astonishing speed, which made him pivotal to almost every crisis in the frontier, James travelled over thirty miles a day to reach Fort Carlton in time to sign Treaty 6 with the Indians, then continued on to arrive within ten days, at midnight, in Swan River. Rousing the force and placing Sergeant-Major Sam Steele in charge of moving NWMP headquarters to Fort Macleod, James rode west toward Sitting Bull before dawn.

Upon learning of the wedding, a surprised Jane Macleod wrote to Mary, "It was too bad not to let me know of his intentions when leaving me only a short time ago. . . . With sincere thankfulness I bid you most welcome, to a fond Mother's love, most fervently do I wish that you may ever be happy with my beloved James."

Living with Jane Macleod during the five months they would be parted, Mary was graciously accepted as an integral member of central Canadian society. She developed an especially close friendship with James's sister, Maggie Baldwin. Although her love for James and her dedication to the West were absolute, the comforts and perks of stately homes and stimulating company with the Baldwins and Robinsons, plus the attraction of superior educational institutions for her children, would so enrich Mary's life that as the years passed they would become increasingly difficult for her to ignore.

At Wood Mountain the international press had arrived to interview Sitting Bull. James was angered by newspaper articles, which he claimed often blew matters out of proportion. He wanted no publicity, but someone in the force was leaking even his discussions to the New York newspapers. He bided his time and watched for the culprit.

James and Inspector Walsh attempted to convince Sitting Bull and his warriors to return to the United States, but some of the refugees tried to induce all the Indians to form a confederation against the whites. When the Blackfoot refused to join, the NWMP spent the fall and winter months tracking scattered bands across the prairies simply to express Her Majesty's appreciation. In return, the Indians gave James their unbounded loyalty. Had he been a politician, James could have named his post and won the country, and had he been less courteous to the Indian, Sitting Bull may have recrossed the border. However, in an American frontier where the whites feared murder and the Sioux feared genocide, it was little wonder that the Indians chose to remain in the British colony with Commissioner Macleod, an officer and a gentleman.

The task completed, James was anxious to make an 1877 mid-winter rendezvous with Mary in Chicago. He rode through blizzards from Fort Macleod to Fort Benton, travelled south by stagecoach to Helena and the Union Pacific Railway at Corinne, then east to St. Paul and finally Chicago. They almost missed each other. Mary had arrived at the station first, searching as other loved ones met and departed. She stood in the cold near the tracks, occasionally showered in soot from a blasting engine, its screeching and shunting reverberating through the hollow building. She probably stamped her buttoned boots on the blackened snow as much in impatience as in chill. Finally the dejected Red River bride hired a cab to take her to the hotel. Her driver had pulled his horse out of the station and was heading down the street when someone roared, "Mary! Mary!" She looked out to see another driver urging his horse to a gallop. James was leaning dangerously out a window and waving at her. "Jim!" she cried. The cabs slid to a halt on the icy street. James leaped out and raced to Mary for a passionate embrace. Decades later Mary would tell her delighted grandchildren that she and her husband were oblivious to staring onlookers.

When James announced that their final destination was Swan River, not Chicago, Mary's eyes flashed in protest. Duty had called again. The first council meeting of the North-West Territories heralding a more permanent form of government with a lieutenant-governor and a council of five coincided with their honeymoon. When he smiled and asked, "Would you rather wait here?" Mary knew she could either join him, remain in a Chicago hotel, or return to Drynoch. She had met her match. With a laugh, the earth child of the Red River Settlement headed north with her husband.

They travelled by train to Fargo, North Dakota, then boarded the stage for Winnipeg. Following a short reunion with the Drevers, the Macleods skimmed along the snow in a cutter to Portage la Prairie. There James hired a Métis guide and dog team to take them to Swan River. Wrapped in buffalo skins from head to toe, or mushing along on snowshoes with the barking dogs, the honeymooners were like the children who had played in the Drynoch woods or along the banks of the Red River. The sun shone on the snow and their laughter rang out across the prairie. When tired, they hopped the runners or bundled back onto the sled, but the driver was a surly man and they preferred to make their own way. They chewed pemmican by the side of the trail, warming themselves with bonfires and sleeping in a small tent, oblivious to the wind howling outside or to their cantankerous driver.

Over three hundred miles later, at the historic council meeting, James lamented the lack of ceremony – not even a cannon – and laughed at the friction among the commissioners. Saying that he proposed a triangular duel to settle the matter, he got everyone on with the job. His sense of humour was at its best when officials lost their temper. Similarly, Mary headed off the dreadful storms which occasionally blew from James. Although she held considerable influence over him, she would never be able to completely save her outspoken husband from himself.

After the meeting, the Macleods returned to Ottawa via Winnipeg and the United States. In the capital they were entertained by Governor General and Lady Dufferin, both great fans of the Reverend Cyprian Pinkham. Links were forming across the vast country. In a few short years, Mary's life had encompassed Sioux stealing through her home, racing messages through the lines of a rebellion, honeymooning by dogsled, and curtseying in elegance before the prime minister and the governor general of Canada. In watching her float through a minuet, few of Ontario's elite realized that twenty-four-year-old Mary Drever Macleod had already experienced more adventures than befell most men in a lifetime.

Leaving Ottawa and heading west with some new recruits for the force meant yet another journey to Fargo and a trip by paddle steamer up the muddied waters of the Missouri River. In a kaleidoscope of colour, a profusion of races and nationalities milled about the American docks. Men were heavily armed and watchful against anticipated Indian attacks. It was impossible for Mary to ignore the fact that her western progression would be almost entirely in the company of men. Indeed, she would be the first white woman in Fort Macleod and the first married woman of a NWMP officer.

On the steamer she was attracted to one of the stewardesses, a big handsome Negress, with a smile and a laugh as broad as her waistline. She wore spotless gingham dresses with a matching head scarf and a starched white apron. She was presumed to be a freed slave. "Just call me Auntie," was her answer to Mary's query of her name. Mary was so impressed by her warm-hearted manner and keen sense of humour that she persuaded Auntie to quit her job and work for the Macleods. Auntie remained with them for years, often boasting, "Me and Miz Macleod were the first white ladies in this part of the country."

Disembarking at Fort Benton, Mary's goods, including her mother's silver soup tureen, some Wedgwood and Crown Derby china from Rothney Cottage, a black walnut table and James's favourite iron-framed chair, were unloaded from the steamer onto a wagon far bigger than the Red River carts. The wheels were six feet in diameter and covered in rawhide. All the freight came by ox-train – up to six wagons hitched in a line – the first one always more heavily laden than the last. Each train was pulled by ten yoke of oxen or mules, urged on by bullwhackers who flicked twenty-foot-long whips over the oxen's backs. For the next six years these bull trains would bring in all Mary's supplies.

The head wagon was reserved for the police, but rather than remain at the front of the column, James often rode the entire line to check the men at the rear and to see how the ponderous oxen were managing. One family member claims that Mary rode sidesaddle beside him, permitted to wear the red coat of the mounties. The first was certainly true; a prairie woman of excellent horsemanship, Mary Macleod gave a particular esteem and dignity to the role of a frontier woman, if not to the entire trek. Little had Helen and William Drever imagined as they once encouraged their young daughter to gallop with the Indians that she would ride with the NWMP from the United States across the border to the Canadian foothills into history. More than one twentieth-century children's book may have been inspired by her image with the famous force.

As the wagon train rumbled toward the west, Mary's first view beyond Fort Macleod was of the foothills. They rolled gently, scented with the freshness of a recent rain and resplendent with myriad bushes of gooseberries, strawberries and prairie flowers. Some forty miles west loomed the magnificent Porcupine Hills. Wagon wheels squealed and oxen splashed out of step to the prancing horses as the entourage crossed the Old Man's River to the island.

Fort Macleod now had two stores: I.G. Baker's and T.C. Power's. The buildings and log homes all flanked by Indian lodges were reminiscent of the old Red River Settlement, but if the proposed railroad passed through the fort, the place would also grow as had Winnipeg. For now, the flow of mail was still haphazard, reaching the outside world by steamboat, stage or railroad via Calgary to Edmonton and the rivers, or via Helena and Fort Benton in the United States. After this trip, Mary marvelled that James had made it to Chicago. She finally understood why letters took so long and probably wondered that they arrived at all. Without personally making the trek, few could imagine the vast distances and the isolation that divided East from West.

Ignoring pouring rain and heavy mud, the entourage rode through the gates of the fort to a salute of cannon fire and an honour guard in full dress uniform. The men must have wondered how Mary would look, how friendly she would be, how conditions around the fort might change with her presence. It was a time when the service considered wives millstones around the men's necks, keeping them from travelling on spur-of-the-moment assignments to remote destinations.

A hastily tidied officers' mess had been turned over to the couple. The mud roof oozed droplets into the room, making dripping sounds like a forest after a rainfall. As Mary watched, a trickle of water formed in one corner of the hardpan floor, hesitated, then urged on by a deluge from above, danced along a trough toward her. James quickly marvelled, "It's an old buffalo track. Ours may be the only home in Canada that has one!"

Laughing at the stream running across her floor, Mary set to work making the officers' mess the first home she and James had known. She fuelled her stove with coal from the Sheran mine thirty miles east, where another village was forming. She covered crates with cretonne or chintz, and placed stones under the wooden legs to balance the chairs and tables on the uneven floors. Once the rains stopped and the warm winds arrived, Mary would scoop the mud blobs up off the furniture in preparation for the swirling dust. Along with the soot from the wood stove, it would settle on the tables, the linen, the beds. Housekeeping was an endless task.

The men saw that Mary placed duty above personal concerns. In all their years of marriage, James would be away more than he was home, yet she extended the colonel's hospitality to everyone who knocked on her door. She rode daily, and when James was home, joined the morning parade. The men quickly became used to her and some of the officers talked of bringing their sisters for a visit. They had their eyes on each other's kin for future wives. Before long the government realized that women could be an advantage and, after a mandatory waiting period, encouraged the men to marry.

It was an exciting time to live in the West. Although not nearly as wild as the United States, crime was sprouting as fast as the villages. Mounted police patrols criss-crossed the land continually. Wagon trains beat paths into roads. Gambling was always around. Liquor was still prohibited for the Indians and restricted for the whites, although few of the latter went without; written permission from the lieutenant-governor was easy to come by. Others drank Montana rotgut. A request to sell beer was cancelled by James. He was against any legitimate sales of spirits. As crime was quickly brought under control, American cattlemen in particular began seeking out sites to establish ranches.

The year 1877 was a good one for the Macleods. Some modern houses and buildings were constructed at the force's sawmill. A handful more women came to live at the fort. They formed dance and drama clubs and held concerts. It was also the first year in several that grasshoppers had not destroyed the crops. Although the summer brought incessant rain and gloom, the irrepressible James wrote of "the splendid countryside of incandescent green, a backdrop for profusions of garden vegetables." As a married man, he was very happy, although he would understate his feelings to his friends, saying, "I am rather comfortable now."

Wherever he was, James and Mary managed to send messages to each other. The commissioner's letters were newsy if at times prosaic, but rarely spoke of business matters. He used his letters to escape the rigours of the job, calling upon his love of drama and eye for detail in depicting scenes of fort life. In doing so, his stories also serve to dramatize the contradictions of his character. James recognized and respected both the Indian and the white man, as long as each kept his place. Throughout his life he would adhere to his parents' Victorian class system:

> Before I left Cypress (Hills) I went in to see Stuttaford and his wife. He is a subconstable and tailor. They have a nice neat little house near the post. Mrs. S. showed me into their bed room – don't be alarmed – she said she wished very much to go to Fort Macleod. I at once thought, "Here is a capital servant for my pet – she is a nice, clean, well-spoken woman." So I said, "would you like to come and stay with Mrs. Macleod; she would be so glad to have you?"
>
> She said she would be delighted. "Well," I said, "I am sure Mrs. Macleod would be glad to get you as housemaid and I suppose you can cook also?" Lord bless us – if you had seen her nose go in the air and such a curve half way across the room. "Ah no," says she. "My people are quite above that. They would never hear of my going as a servant." I very nearly told her that my wife could hardly think of meeting a tailor's wife on terms of equality and that she would not find such society very congenial to her tastes as she had never been accustomed to it. But I simply said, "I never had the least thought, Mrs. S., of receiving you into my house except as a servant." I could hardly contain my laughing till I got out, when I turned round and saw her little husband crossed legged on the table plying his needle and thread on a pair of breeches with all his might and main, but then she is contented with her little *strut* – and he is no doubt enchanted with a wife above people etc. etc.
>
> As I passed out he said he had a request to make, that he might be allowed a half ration for his wife. I replied that the half ration was only given to women who did the washing for the men – did his wife do any of their washing? "Oh no," with a kind of apologetic smile intended to give a proper idea of his wife's exalted position in society. Her people would blow up, bust out, annihilate him, her, the whole family of Stuttaford including the 1/9th part of a man before me if this lady ever soiled her hands with soap suds! The whole thing was so rich that when I returned to the Fort I had all the fellows in fits over it.

James not only had a home and a wife, but as stipendiary magistrate he was free to interpret the law as he saw fit. The West was currently so unsettled that lawyers had yet to arrive and complicate an issue by pleading for the defence. James would hear the evidence from accused and witnesses, make his judgment, then move to the next case. In one letter to Helena prosecutor W.F. Sanders, he boasted of dealing with some ninety-seven cases in less than three days.

One of James's main concerns that year was for the status of the Sioux. Their huge encampment was in Inspector Walsh's territory, just south of the fort of that name. He disliked the inspector's harsh methods of dealing with the Indians. Often in negotiations the Sioux voiced a preference to await the arrival of the White Mother's great chief, Colonel Macleod. Worse than concern for their treatment, however, was the foreboding he held for starvation and war. James warned Lieutenant-Governor David Laird at Swan River that the Indians must be told the intentions of the Canadian government. Writing of their present demoralized condition, he warned, "Hungry men are dangerous whether they be Indians or Whites."

The Sioux grew jumpy and suspicious. They wanted ammunition for hunting, a thorny issue in case they returned across the border to fight the American cavalry. In mid-August when the U.S. General Terry and his commission gathered with the NWMP to arrange some kind of treaty, Sitting Bull had a chance to show the Americans in whom his trust lay. A great showman, he glanced disdainfully at the American troops, swept past them and warmly shook hands with James Macleod. After hearing General Terry advise the Sioux to surrender and return, Sitting Bull showed no reaction. Later he met privately with James, who explained their position in relation to both the American and Canadian governments.

All around Fort Macleod huge Indian encampments of Cree, Blood, Salteaux, Assiniboine, Peigan and Blackfoot would appear overnight, only to disappear on a buffalo hunt the next day. As they came and went, James greeted them as Martin had welcomed guests at Drynoch, and he explained the law as patiently and firmly as the father had once done to the errant son.

In late September 1877, Treaty 7 would be signed at the Blackfoot Crossing, eighty miles north of Fort Macleod and sixty miles south of Calgary. Some Blackfoot were displeased with the treaty, and although James felt that the traders and settlers moving into the lands should wait until the Indians officially relinquished them, it would proceed. Skirmishes and threats were diverted by the tact of the police. As the date drew closer, the trail between Fort Macleod and Calgary

bustled with activity. Indians herded hundreds of horses and trans-
ported lodges, families, food, guns, skins. Traders drove creaking oxen
carts filled with trinkets for the Indians; settlers rode horses and
hauled camping equipment. Miles of dust hovered above the route
for days, an opaque marker for travellers.

James preceded Mary, now pregnant with their first child, in order
to ready the campsite. (Mary probably would have preferred to ride
the eighty miles in the invigorating autumn weather, but she followed
in a wagon with Lieutenant-Governor Laird's contingent and the
strong-box of treaty money.) James and his men marked out the
vast camping ground for the various tribes, and lined up the NWMP
tents in meticulous rows. Just beyond them scores of traders erected
unkempt log and canvas booths, their wagons and oxen sprawling
across the land in disarray. Over five thousand Indians rode in wearing
feather headdresses, beaded buckskin clothing and bear-tooth neck-
laces. Some fifteen thousand ponies grazed along the Bow River. The
huge and colourful encampment would be the last magnificent display
of the Blackfoot nation. As well as an historical event, this was a
social affair of great excitement for everyone. Only six white women
were present. They were usually scattered throughout the territory,
so it must have been an extraordinary pleasure for them to meet
each other.

Up on a gentle rise, doeskin-clad Indian children ran round the
white women as the latter balanced on camp stools and chatted as
if at an Ottawa reception. Mary said that the only time she was
frightened was when a thunderstorm sent Indians and whites running
to the council tent for shelter. Fifty years later she recalled, "It came
to me suddenly how much we would be in their power if the Indians
should take advantage of their strength."

James's words to the Blackfoot were spoken in the name of the
government, yet carried a tone of personal commitment. He assured
them that they would be cared for, fed and educated. The payments
would consist of $25 (annually), plus a coat and a Queen's silver
medal for a head chief, $15 plus coats for councillors, and $12 for
each man, woman and child ($5 a year thereafter), and a square
mile of land for each family of five persons, to renounce claim to
the rest of the land forever. In return government agents would present
each family with ammunition, blankets and miscellaneous items, every
three years providing a suit of clothing, and they would assist the
Indians to establish schools and learn farming.

Chief Crowfoot stood and claimed, "If the police had not come to this country, where would we all be now? Bad men and whiskey were killing us so fast that very few of us would be alive today. The Mounted Police have protected us as the feathers of the bird protect it from the frosts of winter. I wish all my people good, and trust that all our hearts will increase in goodness from this time forward. I will sign the treaty."

Red Crow, chief of the Bloods, added that James had never broken a promise in three years. He closed with, ". . . I entirely trust Stamix Otokan . . . I will sign with Crowfoot."

With those words the Indians gave away their lands to the Queen, represented by Lieutenant-Governor Laird and Commissioner James Macleod. Whites and Indians wrote their names or scratched their X's on the document. It was a proud moment in Mary Drever Macleod's life when James invited each of the white women to affix their signatures. In giving them historical recognition, it was also a statement to the Indians, who regarded their women as little more than chattels.

In closing the ceremonies James said to the Blackfoot, "As surely as my past promises have been kept, so surely shall those made with you today be carried out in the future. If they are broken, I will be ashamed to meet you or look you in the face. Every promise will be solemnly fulfilled, just as sure as the sun shines upon us all from the heavens. I shall never forget the kind manner in which you have spoken of me today."

Years later Major-General Sir Sam Steele wrote of James's relationship with the Indians, "I doubt if any one ever had such influence with them. He kept his place, never accepted a present, never gave one, and was respected by them all the more for it, his word being law from the time he appeared among them."

Now that the Blackfoot lands were opened, the railroad could be pushed through, British Columbia would probably stay in Confederation and settlers would fill the West. If James ever suspected that he might have been a pawn of the government, that a great railway venture rather than the welfare of a defeated race might be the primary interest of the politicians, he never recorded it. In truth, his work had irreversibly changed the West. Acting as a buffer between the government and the Indians, he had paved the way for countless settlers and for the influx of ranchers who would arrive in the 1880s.

Shortly after the treaty was signed, James became alarmed over the treatment of the Blackfoot. Settlers, prospectors and traders swarmed into the country. He wrote to the minister of the interior complaining that one American settler actually asked him if Canadians had the same law as they had, that allowed a man to shoot any Indian who approached his camp after being warned not to advance. James commented, "It is a matter of common notoriety that the Indians are systematically cheated and robbed by the agents and contractors; the former on a salary of $1,500 a year, have many been known to retire with fortunes after two or three years incumbency. The Indians know of these scandals and as a consequence have lost all faith in the Government under which such frauds are perpetrated." The government remained unresponsive to his allegations.

As the wife of Colonel Macleod the treaty-maker, Mary was either welcomed as a heroine or cursed for being the wife of the man who took the Indians' lands away. Separated from James during most of their first year at Fort Macleod and at that time seven months' pregnant, she walked alone daily. One Indian named Bad Boy was unhappy with the treaty and took to venting his anger at Mary. Whenever she walked outside the fort he seemed to be waiting. As she strolled across the chill autumn earth, Bad Boy would wheel his pony and charge her, skidding to a stop and rearing over her head. Mary never wavered a step. Eyes steady, head held high, she would continue walking. A few minutes later she would turn on her own terms and walk steadily back to the fort.

One day when she was sitting by the wood stove sewing for the baby, Bad Boy entered the house. Auntie was out at the store; Mary was alone. Aiming his rifle barrel straight at her head Bad Boy thrust his hand toward her. Mary had never seen him point a rifle before but she had learned her lesson well from her mother: an Indian respected courage and despised fear. Continuing to sew and praying for steady hands, Mary offered her elbow to shake instead. Bad Boy was puzzled and only partially satisfied. He refused to leave. Mary continued sewing. Unbeknown to them James had returned to the fort and was heading for home. When the colonel walked through the door he was stunned to see Mary sewing, Bad Boy sitting cross-legged on the floor at her feet pointing his gun at her head.

"Get out!" roared the colonel advancing toward Bad Boy. Mary had never seen James so angry. As the Indian skulked away he gathered her into his arms and said with all conviction, "It's alright now, my darling, you'll never see him again."

Mary's immediate concerns were for the winter. She put up preserves of jelly, apples, vegetables. While she baked mince tarts for the Christmas season, she learned of the arrival of the first railway locomotive in Winnipeg. Six flat-cars had arrived on barges gaily decorated with flags and green boughs. The engine had been brought down the Red River by the steamer *Selkirk* from Minnesota and was christened by the Countess of Dufferin. And each courier that arrived brought news of the telegraph line pushing its way westward. Mary continued baking, the old wood stove producing wonders under her skilled hands. In a way, she must have looked forward to the winter. At least the buffalo trail would stop trickling across her floor and the mud on the roof would freeze. Only a carelessly chinked log would allow in a winter breeze or a swirl of snow.

With the increasing cold, some of the Sioux lit vast prairie fires designed to drive the buffalo southward. Seeing the flames, American newsmen wrote that a huge tribe was amassing on both sides of the border to murder whites. James denied this, reporting that the tribes were congregating to hunt, not to fight. Angered that someone in the force was still leaking stories, he wrote about these "extravagant rumours" and "embellished stories." He was caught in a tangle between the visible urgency of the Indians' needs and the actions of those who saw dissension as a quick method to increase general anxiety over Indian affairs and thus get the Sioux deported. James considered these "anonymous correspondents . . . [as the] . . . pests of the North-West."

After months of watching, James suspected Inspector Walsh of leaking the news. He disliked the publicity-seeking inspector. On one occasion Walsh had called Sitting Bull's bluff during an argument and had thrown the chief out of his office, kicking him in the rear for good measure. James deplored this kind of treatment and the heroism with which Walsh was subsequently lauded in the New York papers. Confirming that Walsh was indeed providing American newspapers with confidential information, he wrote to Mary, "Walsh has returned with the recruits. I am afraid he is a *snake in the grass*. You remember my telling you about some letters which appeared in the *New York Herald*, and his denial of any knowledge of how the correspondent got hold of them. I made him admit here that he *gave them* and he begged me to give him another chance, promising that he would never do it again. . . . How do I like to have anything to do with a man who is not straight forward. . . ."

James never forgave Walsh. It must have filled him with rancour to see the inspector immortalized in the press as the Indians' great and respected friend. In that same letter James confided to Mary,

Just fancy, Walsh tried to make White believe that it was the right thing to do when you stayed at Indian camps to take squaws to your bed when they were offered to you. That it gives the Indians a good notion of our *manliness* and that they think little of a man who refused the embraces thus offered. Nothing could be further from the true state of the case. Indeed I think that Indians have a very much greater respect for the man who lives as a white man, and does not follow any of their practices. . . .

Somehow I can't get over his conduct. I have treated him well, almost with partiality and ignored the fact that he was not a gentleman, and there is no doubt he has tried to undermine me in a sneaking way, but entirely without success.

Newspapers aside, James became increasingly outspoken in his official reports, warning of the Indians, ". . . they never cease expressing their gratitude for the paternal care the Government is taking of them; but they are already brought face to face with starvation." He pressed that his proposal of emergency supply depots, presented years earlier, be adopted. He recommended that a herd of cattle be bought by the government and kept in the Bow River country. James saw no reason that the Canadian government should not "utilize the magnificent domain lying idle in the West, and have at any moment such a supply of food as would meet any necessity that might arise." His foresight might have saved the Indians or even made the government money, but the latter did not respond to the ideas. It would be left to the penny-conscious ranchers and businessmen of the future to realize the opportunities ignored by Ottawa in 1877.

On February 9, with James in Montana, Mary faced her first childbirth with the same loneliness and determination as any pioneer housewife. Save for the attendance of the NWMP doctor, the officers' mess with its dancing kerosene shadows might have been Clova Cottage in 1855. First labours are often long and arduous, but in time Mary Macleod bore the first white child in the district of southern Alberta. An itinerant American missionary baptized the baby Helen Rothney Macleod. Her nickname, Nell, stuck throughout her life, although she claimed to dislike it as she grew older.

In 1878 the Dominion Telegraph was slung as far as Battleford on the North Saskatchewan River, but communications remained sporadic. Grazing buffalo rubbed against the poles and when the telegraph crashed to the ground they often entwined their horns in the wire. If James was sending a message to Mary, prairie fires or a grazing beast might snap the punch line. Still, news flowed in with the settlers, ranchers and railway surveyors arriving in the High River area. Like other towns springing up, Fort Macleod grew as swiftly as the buffalo diminished.

On October 16, 1878, when Sir John A. Macdonald defeated the Mackenzie government and returned as prime minister, he immediately moved the NWMP portfolio from secretary of state back into his own of minister of the interior. James lost no time in requesting and getting new uniforms of the highest quality. Everything from grey felt hats to new, streamlined saddles were sent west for Sir John's favourite force.

During the heavy snows and storms of 1879, Indian starvation loomed. Purposely lit prairie fires deprived the Indians' ponies of pastureland. Man and horse became too weak to hunt. As James had predicted, the large band of buffalo driven south in 1878 never returned. Once the beasts had crossed the line east of the Cypress Hills, they were hemmed in by Indians in Montana. When the Blackfoot crossed the border to hunt their own herd, they were ordered back by American authorities. James informed Ottawa that "the Blackfoot's condition is deplorable in the extreme."

He now suspected that his government would not fulfil its commitment to the treaties. Even if each and all of their provisions were completely met he believed the dangers could not be averted. He suggested that rather than pay the Indians treaty money, which immediately fell into the hands of traders and horse dealers, with their consent, it should be spent on provisions for them. No response came from Ottawa. James faced the personal dilemma of having to remain loyal to a government that had dishonoured its promises, which, in all good faith, he had made on its behalf. To compound the Blackfoot tragedy, newly arrived ranchers complained of cattle rustling and pointed their fingers at the Indians. James leaped to their defence, writing that not only had the Indians behaved well under the circumstances, but that many of the cattle had simply perished in the winter storms. The stockmen could hardly blame the Indians, wrote James, when they checked their herds only once or twice a year.

In this year of encroaching starvation, Louis Riel returned. Exiled from Canada in 1871 after having been elected a member of Parliament, the Métis leader had taught school and wandered amongst halfbreed settlements and Indian camps in St. Joseph, Dakota. Now Métis were encouraging Crowfoot to talk with Riel first as a mediator for Sitting Bull with the Americans, then to encourage the Indians to gather in a great confederacy to eliminate the whites. Inspector Walsh learned at Wood Mountain that Louis Riel had visited the Métis just before the huge prairie fires which had destroyed the grazing for the buffalo. The Métis were suspected of causing the blaze. For the time being, nothing more happened, but an uneasy atmosphere pervaded.

Watching the rapid changes of the West and feeling bound by the absentee administration of the government, James headed for Ottawa to speak on behalf of the Indians. Mary was pregnant again. She and Nell travelled as far as Toronto, then on to Drynoch, where the attraction of domestic comforts and lush countryside far outweighed the many social functions in the muddy, ugly capital.

James wrote from Ottawa of one reception, "Everyone here looks at me as if I am a most noted personage. Some come up and ask me, 'are you Col. Macleod? We have all heard so much of you,' and then ask endless questions about Indian rumours, one fellow telling me today that there had been a brush between two tribes and 12 scalps taken. They looked astonished when I laughed right out and told them I did not believe a word of it." James attended teas with Lady Macdonald, dinners with the governor general, and the theatre for such obscure performances as "Engapil."

One day he indulged Mary's professed loneliness by sending a horse cab to take her to Toronto. She visited the shops with Maggie Baldwin and attended the symphony. It was enjoyable, but Mary felt lost without her husband, complaining that she could not sleep. Neither could James. One night he fell asleep in a hotel chair. Awakening at three in the morning, he seized a pen and wrote, "It is too bad, dear girl, that you find the bed so hard. How is it that I make it softer? I have an awfully comfortable bed – just spring enough!!"

James left Ottawa briefly for official functions in Montreal. He described the city as in a turmoil preparing for the royal visit of Queen Victoria's daughter, the Princess Louise, and her husband, the Marquis of Lorne, now governor general of Canada. He said that the "great metropolis" was full of colonels, police officers and ten of the governor general's foot guards. Given a seat of honour near Her Royal Highness at the governor general's ball and later at the St. Andrew's ball, James teased Mary, "Aren't I blessed to be kicking my legs under the same mahogany as Royalty!"

The Macleods delighted in mailing each other daily notes and Mary astonished James by wiring him a box of flowers for his forty-sixth birthday. In return he surprised Mary by sending his official photo in dress uniform. On one occasion, James laughed to hear that Mrs. Allan had caught Mary trying to push a letter into a fire alarm, mistaking it for a new-fangled mail box. When they could stand their separations no longer, James would rush to spend a weekend at Drynoch.

For a while Sir John increasingly relied upon the commissioner to negotiate the thornier issues over the Indians. James spent many hours at Rideau Hall with the prime minister and the governor general trying to find solutions to the problems plaguing the frontier. Anxious to have James return west, Sir John told him that Assistant-Commissioner Irvine was a good soldier, but "not the man to tackle a serious difficulty. I have the utmost confidence in your judgment and think we would all feel more comfortable if you were there."

Feeling completely secure in his position with the prime minister, James dined one evening with Sir Richard Cartwright, finance critic for the opposition. He had a delightful time, oblivious to any criticism Sir Richard was preparing against him concerning the sky-rocketing expenses of the force. The next day he wrote to Mary, "I am stronger than ever in Ottawa."

In May 1879 James and the Indian commissioner, Edgar Dewdney (a personal friend of the prime minister), gathered at the Toronto station with new recruits and horses for the West. James searched for Mary in the throng, waiting for the last minute before he leaped onto the train. As it shunted away he leaned far from his window, straining for a glimpse of her. She never came and he headed for the seclusion of the baggage van, his eyes filling with tears at having missed her. As the train shunted along a farmer sat down beside him and said, "I suppose, Colonel, you are feeling pretty lonely just now...." James turned away to hide his grief, and soon wrote, "Oh my darling how I miss you.... May God grant that it may not be very long before we are brought together again."

Mary had arrived at the station to find that the agent had made a mistake in the departure time. Instead of the usual excitement of loading horses and milling policemen, there was silence – and a departed train. She wrote of the station agent that she was so angry she "could have clubbed him." With the famous Drever temper, she gave him a scathing piece of her mind.

Expecting a late December child, Mary left Drynoch in June 1879 and headed west. From St. Paul she and Nell rode a crowded train into Winnipeg to stay with the Drevers. The settlement Mary knew as a young girl was no more. Well-dressed crowds jostled and hurried about. Where hundreds of Salteaux had once roamed around Clova Cottage, only an occasional Indian mother and papoose were seen.

The land William Drever had purchased for £15 and the roads over which he had battled McKenney were almost unrecognizable. The Drevers' homes, once surrounded by prairie and Indian lodges, were now dwarfed by the Red Saloon, real estate offices, and hotels. Rothney Cottage had become the first Dominion Lands Office.

Cyprian Pinkham's St. James Church was a mark of the times. Sunday service was the major event of the week. When bells chimed from city through countryside, pews filled quickly and parishioners crowded to the doorways. Most were men, getting their lands established before settling down. With baritones and tenors of diverse nationalities and accents, church choirs boomed in resonant splendour. "Fight the Good Fight!" gave ringing justification to the cliché, lifting the roof. One Sunday, Cyprian announced to a crowded congregation that $1,500 was needed to winterize the church. The money was quickly raised with rounds of picnics, luncheons and other gatherings, often on the lawns of the Pinkhams' home or at the home of the lieutenant-governor, nearby Silver Heights.

Mary remained with the Pinkhams for the summer, watching Nell crawl over the lawn by the banks of the Assiniboine and worrying over the dearth of letters from James. She could not know that starvation around Fort Macleod was escalating.

James wrote in August to say that he and Dewdney had arrived at the Blackfoot Crossing with flour, tea, sugar and tobacco to find about 1,300 emaciated Indians. A trader was exchanging small amounts of flour for the last firearms and horses. James caused "a flurry of excitement" (and hope) when he entered the camp. Noting that the Indians had suffered dreadfully during the last winter, he credited Chief Crowfoot for keeping them all in check. As he walked into their village, men, women and children flocked round to greet him and shake hands. "The women," he wrote, "brought their children on their backs and [they] held out the tiny little skeleton hands for me to shake." James was heartsick over the deterioration of the Blackfoot's condition. Chiefs Old Sun, Crowfoot and Heavy Shield walked him and Dewdney through the camp, forcing the white men to stare at their own want of promise. At Treaty 7 they had offered friendship and peace on the word of Stamix Otokan. James had promised them food, education, protection of their lands. Now too weak to hunt, they were impelled to eat their dogs and ponies.

Young and old lay in the dust around their lodges, eyes sunken and lacklustre as they awaited their end. Chief Crowfoot turned to James and said in a thinly veiled threat, "If I had not made the treaty we would not have gone begging food from the government." They might have attacked the settlers, or more likely the intruding Sitting Bull and his Sioux. The Indian chief believed they could still survive but only if the police would drive the Sioux away. Headed by an increasingly demanding Sitting Bull, however, the Sioux remained along the border and continued to prevent the buffalo from travelling northward.

There seemed little the NWMP could do. Assistant Commissioner Irvine requested permission to hire an army of Blackfoot, one hundred strong, for 25 cents a day including ponies, rifles and sufficient ammunition to hunt for food. Ottawa refused the request. Shortly after, Dewdney bought a ranch and cattle with government funds to start the Indian hunters on agricultural pursuits but failed to provide instruction or incentives. In his next letter to Mary, James avoided mentioning the Indians, but obliquely referred to the growing differences between himself and Ottawa.

Having doled out the last of the token provisions, Dewdney returned to Fort Macleod with James. Then they took Mary's "dear old Skylark and Blackfoot," and rode for a long time through the mountains, a respite from the ongoing tragedy. Loving the drama of discomfiture, James described "D" [Dewdney] as being "annoyed almost beyond endurance" by the mosquitoes: "He used to tie a handkerchief round his neck then put a netting round his head and keep another handkerchief continually agoing, knocking them off. He used to wonder how I could travel along without any protection only now and then, wiping them off my neck. He got so irritated – but you know my placid temper is proof even against the attacks of mosquitoes innumerable."

In subtle ways, it appeared that Macdonald was tiring of James's conscience over the Indians, and Cartwright was openly accusing the NWMP of financial carelessness. Sir Richard could have brought this to James's attention when they had had dinner together in Ottawa but it was too marvellous a weapon for the opposition. If James was a hero in the Indian lodges, he became the scapegoat in the House.

Mismanagement of stores had long been a bête noir. In 1876 Colonel French had attacked James's accounting in a letter to Assistant Commissioner Irvine. At the time French had believed that James was retiring from the force and barely restrained his hostility toward him. In criticizing what he saw as inefficiency in cost accounting, Colonel French had listed the purchases of horses as one of the excessive expenditures. The colonel did acknowledge that someone in Ottawa should be paid a decent salary to supervise the outlet, but for James, it was the old hateful paperwork, and the need was usually urgent. In stinging tones aimed at James, French had referred to the carelessness of "that Gentleman," then closed with, "I . . . think it advisable to tell you that I am determined to put a stop to such a discreditable State of affairs."

Thus, in the spring of 1879 when the opposition attack in the House of Commons was mounted against the NWMP for exorbitant costs of $344,823.77 (including salaries), James was almost the author of his own misfortune. He could not have known that Sir John was heading for England hoping to close a deal with a British-Canadian syndicate to build the Canadian Pacific Railway. The prime minister was about to commit his government to costs of $25 million and twenty-five million acres of Canadian land. His future and possibly the future of Canada were contingent upon him pulling off the most improbable railway venture in history: to lay tracks across the geographic nightmare of Canada. Painfully sensitive to opposition attacks at the time, the prime minister arrived at his desk one morning in June to see a $5 bill for a Toronto cab. It had been submitted by James Macleod. Sir John exploded. He dictated a letter to James threatening him with everything from firing to disbanding his beloved police force.

Expressing horror over the "prima facie evidence of want of economy," Sir John accused James of thinking more of the efficiency of his service and that of his three hundred men than he did of the public treasury. He listed James's responsibilities, which included the discipline and efficiency of the corps and his double position of a military man and a peace officer. Fumed Sir John, "In all matters of expenditure and cost other parties are ultimately responsible, and you must consider yourself as distinctly a subordinate." He also referred to the "culpable neglect" of NWMP customs officers and suggested that they were also victims to "the wiles of the Yankee traders. . . . From all I have said you can easily understand, my dear Sir, that I am dissatisfied with the state of things. They must be amended or the whole corps must be broken up."

He closed with, "I brought you into the Force and am much interested in your success, and therefore act the part of a real friend in giving you this most serious warning. . . . Believe me, my dear Sir, Yours very Faithfully, John A. Macdonald."

James was totally unprepared for such a letter. His reply was as blunt as the prime minister's attack. During the past six months he and Dewdney had travelled over 2,300 miles by wagon and horseback, witnessing the destruction of the Indian nations so long predicted by himself but ignored by the politicians now criticizing him. A man in the saddle had little time for tallying columns of figures or writing letters. James was outraged that members of Parliament should bandy the quality of his administrative efficiency back and forth across the chamber of the House. Some of those politicians had never ridden to hounds let alone ridden west. How could they imagine the difficulties of patrolling 300,000 square miles of prairie? Sir John himself penned letters from the comfort of his leather-topped desk, missives which a hard-riding courier often passed to James on the trail. Was James expected to reply from the saddle, or in a hailstorm with his tent flattened in the mud? Not even the ubiquitous commissioner could police every fort, store and border crossing at once, particularly when the government issued conflicting orders as to where he should be.

By way of example, James described receiving orders to head for a Battleford Indian Conference. Upon arriving, he received a telegram from the government ordering him to obtain the Treaty 7 payments from Baker & Company at Fort Benton. To accomplish this, he had to ride 450 miles south to Benton. When he arrived, no arrangements had been made for the money. That meant another 150-mile trip to Helena to try and raise it there. Only partially successful, James brought home what he managed to get, returning at a later date to pay the Stony Indians. When he finally returned to Fort Macleod and his desk, a backlog of two months of court awaited him. Had he known ahead that he would have to raise the treaty money, James snapped, he could have planned ahead on everything, and "I would not have been kept away from the work which I had laid out for myself to do."

He also took a swipe at the newest folly of the prime minister – the idea of reverting to the custom of officers purchasing their commissions. James considered it a giant step backward into the eighteenth century, particularly when there were "excellent men worthy of promotion within the force." He also defended his customs officers, declaring they were in no way "hoodwinked by shrewd American traders," and he stressed the necessity of a capable man in Ottawa to purchase supplies of the most durable quality. In all, James claimed, it was the Conservatives themselves who were creating the inefficiencies of which he was accused. For example, he noted that it was they who had built far costlier barracks in Swan River and Battleford than had he at Fort Macleod.

Noting that Sir John's letter bore the same date as his Toronto cab bill, "in which extravagance is imputed to me, and you judge from this that the same want of economy exists at Head Quarters," James explained that when his troops had been stationed two miles from the city, they had required the services of smithies and a surgeon. He stressed, "I was careful to pay out of my own pocket all cab hire which could not be fairly chargeable to the Public."

The letter underscored the geographical and psychological distances between Ottawa and the frontier. In six years the government had failed to appreciate the vastness of a country still unlinked by telegraph. Ottawa was simply incapable of understanding or uncaring of the difficulties faced by the commissioner and his force. James's reply to the prime minister on October 23, 1879, was typically lengthy, but at no time in his life does such a document of his seem more justified. The condition he was describing had no name at the time but the seeds of what would be called "regionalism" a century later had already been sown in the West. The following year the NWMP reduced its overall costs to $322,855.12.

James had spent the majority of 1879 in Ottawa or in the field separated from his wife and daughter, who had remained in Winnipeg with the Pinkhams. It was months before he would see them again. Near desperation crept into many of his letters as he imagined a family reunion. Whenever he reached a spot where Mary and he had previously camped, or when he returned to Fort Macleod, his sentiment burned through his writing: "Do you remember the place where we camped the night before we reached Macleod, where we had such fun? I stood over the place where our tent stood and thought of that pleasant night when everybody else was suffering like the very mischief from the flies. Our happiness was not marred by the above pests...."

Of his "precious little Nell" who spoke more Cree than English, he wrote, "She has entwined herself in the most extraordinary manner in my affections.... My own one, how I sit and think of what you and our little Nell are doing from morning to night ... about your getting up in the morning ... then your breakfasting together ... Miss Nell on my office chair with her own chair on top of it. You would spend the morning about the house whirring away at the sewing machine making all sorts of things, then lunch in the afternoon, a good walk or a drive...."

By December, Mary had returned to Fort Macleod. With Christmas almost at hand she turned her home into a flurry of preparations for the new baby and her husband's imminent return. S.J. Clarke, an enlisted man, decorated the barracks with boughs, red berries and some of the precious and seemingly endless red flannel from police stores. James returned to a tumultuous welcome. At five o'clock on Christmas Eve, the piper filled his bellows as the Macleods led a procession of officers and ladies into the decorated mess hall. James and Mary drank the health of the police and the police drank their own health, all predicting that Mary would have a Christmas baby. Mary had other plans; she intended to be at her own New Year's Eve ball. James gave her a beautiful piece of jewellery which he had picked up in Helena in the summer. After dinner they all marched around the fort in the chill December winds, Mary walking heavily beside her husband.

The New Year's ball, held on December 29, was attended by all the citizens of Fort Macleod and for fifty miles around. About four hundred people arrived and, despite prohibitive measures on alcohol, "Jamaica Ginger" rum was consumed in massive quantities. Many guests stayed up all night singing and dancing around huge bonfires. Around midnight, Mary suddenly went into labour. At one in the morning on December 30, 1879, she gave birth to a boy. When James rushed outside with the news, bagpipes groaned to life with renewed vigour and more Jamaica Ginger was found for the crowd. For James and Mary, who had been separated so many months, young Norman Torquil Macleod heralded a time of hope for peace, togetherness and joy in the new year.

The Macleods' home was already the focal point of the West. Over the coming decade lieutenant-governors and dignitaries would step from their buckboards into a world they'd left thousands of miles behind. Mary's china and silver blended with unpretentious charm when softened by buffalo rugs and the chinked logs of their house wallpapered with the latest *Winnipeg Free Press*. Delicious frontier beef and the best of whiskey was always forthcoming, and out of her trunk Mary unfailingly produced a magnificent if patched gown in which to entertain her guests.

11

 The American Frontier

"Be careful of the Redmen . . . and don't let those Yankees get all your money."
Alexander Cross to Harry

Alexander and Julia's life was filled with the challenges of growing children and the frustrations of absentee parenthood. Their hearts raced with anxiety upon receipt of each letter from the American frontier. Harry wrote that he and his friends had built a shack in Colorado Territory named "Little Canada," then nearly burned it down when a skunk got under the floorboards. His spine-tingling letters described their latest escape from outlaws or hostile Indians. Well versed in Montreal's formal funeral services, Harry now paid scant respects to dead men. "Goodbye George," was all he had said to a Sioux victim before hastily rolling the corpse into its grave and racing off. Grace at meals was "Oh Lord, make us thankful for free land, free grass, no taxes, plenty of meat, and let us keep our scalps."

Harry's letters were not the only excitement in Alexander's life. Storm clouds over Uncle James Hutchison's second will had broken into an angry gale. Offering to reimburse Harry $200 travelling expenses, Alexander implored his son to come home from Colorado and exercise his vote in the Hutchison estate. Uncle James had specifically bequeathed to Selkirk and Harry his Mount Victoria Farm. More significant, Alexander was alone, for Ernest, Willie Heber and Selkirk were all away in England and neither Julia nor Maggie would become embroiled in money matters. It was Julia's family, but she would let the men fight it out. Harry herded a handful of newly purchased Longhorns to the Pine Bluffs station, sold them, then continued by train to Montreal.

Julia's brother-in-law, Dr. George Campbell, claimed Uncle James was insane when he wrote the second will leaving his fortune to the Cross children only. In his opinion it was invalid. Of particular issue were properties bordering Peel, Dorchester, Sherbrooke, St. Catherines, St. James and William streets, farms on the mountain and in Verdun, and farmland throughout the townships. The argument was not only over who owned them, but also whether or not they should be sold off to divide the profits.

Campbell contended that it was Alexander who had arranged the interdiction of Uncle James, then failed to show up at the hearing. In his absence, the Campbells had appeared the aggressors, thus alienating Uncle James and his fortune. Alexander retorted that the interdiction had been Campbell's idea in the first place, that the second will was valid, and his children were the rightful heirs to the Hutchison fortune. As angry letters were exchanged between the two families, Julia's and Margaret Campbell's sister, the childless Mary Lunn Noble, felt so sorry for the Campbell children that she altered her will and named them sole beneficiaries of her estate.

When Alexander suggested an arbitrator be appointed, Campbell expressed an intent to take the matter to the Supreme Court. In return, Alexander published a booklet of the letters and arguments in anticipation of the battle. He deplored the great sacrifice to be suffered by his children if they "relinquished their just legacy."

In the heat of the battle, Alexander's lifelong friend and unsolicited conscience, Justice F.W. Torrance, wrote to remind him of the interdiction, "All were morally and in honour bound *solidairement*, to stand by each other and protect each other from the consequences." Torrance added that he was aware his comments could materially affect the interests of the Cross children, but, "you and I are ... sure of this: that nothing we do or suffer to be done, can have a certain or prosperous issue unless it have its foundation laid in truth and justice."

The rebuke inspired Alexander to fire back a missive filled with legal justifications. Fifteen years later he would still be angry over Uncle James's estate. Nevertheless, he relinquished sixth-tenths of the fortune to the six Campbell children. In the restoration of an uneasy peace, the Cross offspring received four-tenths of the estate. But Mary Lunn Noble had by now become senile and forgot to change her will back to include the Cross children. When she died, the Campbell children received both legacy windfalls, making Alexander angrier than ever. His temper did not improve when his counsel, J.J. Abbott, personal friend and future prime minister, wrote to admonish him for giving up too much.

Harry stayed in Montreal for a few months enjoying the diversion from the wild frontier. He found Pine Avenue unchanged. The assortment of his father's papers and the smell of tobacco still filled the library with a comforting familiarity. There was also a new collection of five thousand leather-bound law books bought for $1,296.86. He told his parents that with luck the reading material out west was Montgomery Ward's mail order catalogue or a three-month-old *Montreal Gazette* which sold for 25 cents in Colorado. As for family routines, young children still sneaked Lolita, the bilingual parrot, down to the drawing room at teatime. There, his mother still presided at the urn before the roaring fire, and the plates of delicate watercress and cream cheese sandwiches on the mahogany stand were a far cry from chuckwagon breaks on the range.

Harry tried to convince Alexander to back a ranching venture in the United States. He had already purchased six hundred head of Longhorn cattle, assuring his father that instead of the usual hand-shake, he had scratched a bill of sale on the inside of one of his envelopes. He admitted that the herd was so motley it looked "as if a freak artist had emptied buckets of many hued paints over them." But knowing the Crosses' love for blood lines, he hastened to assure his family that he could trace their history back to the conquistadors, and time and again he wished that his father could see them. Harry regaled his parents with frontier stories. He told them of brushes with death at the hands of outlaws and Indians, and once by his own hand when he drove an axe into his instep. On that occasion his pals packed the wound with cobwebs, flour and sugar, and moss, then dumped him into a wagon and headed for Fort Collins. A druggist told Harry's friends to hold him down, then poured horse liniment into the mashed instep. It was a month before he could walk.

Alexander may have been convinced that Harry could survive these escapades, but buying land was something else. The Montreal depression continued and he wasn't relinquishing any of his growing empire for a harebrained venture on the American frontier. But if he hoped that he could convince Harry to sell his herd and stay in Montreal, he was wrong. Harry remained for a few months and then returned to the United States.

In 1877 Harry wrote to his father to say that Colorado was overstocked. He had joined Charlie Campbell, who had survived a winter at La Bonte Creek, Wyoming Territory. The first thing Charlie asked him for was some salt – he had been sprinkling gunpowder onto his meat. At the time Wyoming was dangerous country. The war between the Indians, whites and the American cavalry had escalated. Charlie's cabin was built like a fortress. Windows were high, and the six-horse stable was in the centre with doors leading in from the kitchen and bunkroom. Harry was warned to carry his guns ready even to the nearby creek, and they made their own bullets by ladling melted lead into moulds.

In the comfort of his Pine Avenue library Alexander read that in Wyoming at night the Sioux repeatedly tore down telegraph posts, rolled up long sections of wire and tossed them into the Platte River. After dark, Harry and the other youths would muffle their horses' hooves, retrieve the wire, pad their hammers and repair the damage. Their fear was intensified by howling wolves travelling in huge packs across the prairies. Sometimes tens of thousands of stampeding buffalo or elk terrified Harry into thinking that the entire Sioux nation was thundering down.

It probably did not surprise anyone at Pine Avenue when Harry wrote that the confinement had gotten to him. He was forgetting the night terrors and riding into La Bonte saloon with his pals. They played games of pool and drank a rotgut said to be made of alcohol, rattlesnake heads, coffee, red pepper, tobacco juice and water. Late at night they loped off toward home, ignoring the dangers of low-slung telegraph wires that could slice a man's head off, abandoned well holes that could swallow a horse and rider, and the Sioux who were on the warpath.

On one occasion when chased by a large party of Indians, the Canadians lost their herd of horses but made it alive to Charlie's fortress. Soon afterwards, while searching for strays, the Canadians spotted eleven ponies grazing not far from a group of Indians in a ravine. Either in revenge for their stolen horses or in sheer devilment, the Canadians charged. They stampeded the animals out of the ravine and away. The startled Indians gave chase on foot. Lead zinged past the boys' ears and thudded into the ground around their horses. A bullet struck one of the Canadians, "Long Bill" Dailey, and he thunked heavily to the ground. Harry wheeled, leaped off Zeke and stood over his friend. The Indians pounded closer. Suddenly to Harry's amazement, the dead man sat up and shook his head. The Indians bore down. Without a word Harry and Long Bill leaped back onto their horses. They laughed hysterically as they splashed through the

River Platte and away. The bullet had whizzed across Long Bill's belly and lodged in the leather of his cartridge belt. He was left with a six-inch powder burn and the boys with a thirst that dried out the nearest saloon.

Harry admitted to his parents that when surrounded by Sioux he always wished he was at home studying law at McGill or working in the Molson Bank, and on several occasions he believed he owed his life solely to his mother's prayers. But he and Charlie Campbell were enthralled with Wyoming Territory, of the oceans of sagebrush and tall rippling grass, of game abounding in fertile valleys, of grazing hills rolling on forever. With fierce determination they fought wolves and mountain lions while increasing their stock and strengthening the blood lines with good Durham bulls. For the umpteenth time Alexander wrote to him, "Be careful of the Redmen. Take no chances and don't let those Yankees get all your money."

Julia sent Harry long winter underwear and $100 every six months with the warning, "Say nothing [to your father]!" By then the frazzled parents must have realized that in a year and a half Harry had undergone a metamorphosis from greenhorn into seasoned cowhand, bronco rider, rancher, survivor. Instead of panelled drawing rooms and uniformed servants, Harry was happy with stable fortresses or dirt-floored shanties. He had nearly got himself killed a few times and lived to laugh about it.

The spirit of adventure had always dwelt in Alexander and he swore on more than one occasion that if he could, he, too, would have headed west. He promised Harry that when his son was certain what he wanted to do with his life, he would loan the money for land. But it must be repaid.

In 1877 Alexander ran for the Huntingdon provincial seat next to the riding of Chateauguay. He was assured the cabinet position of attorney general by the premier of Quebec, Charles de Boucherville. At the time, the Roman Catholic priests had drawn the church heavily into politics and strife in Quebec had grown more fractious than ever. Alexander's knowledge of French civil law would have been invaluable to the Conservative government; but he lacked a taste for campaigning, fared badly in winning votes, and withdrew before the polls were closed.

Later in that year, Alexander was appointed a judge on the Court of Queen's Bench. Letters of commendation poured into him.

Although he was appointed during the Liberal reign of Alexander Mackenzie, a colleague of Sir John A. Macdonald wrote to compliment him: "The country has an inestimable gain . . . you have great advantage in not having been mixed up in the dirty streams of political warfare. . . ." He also reminded Alexander of the "urgent need for the crime laws to be codified and consolidated." William Coffin, lawyer, writer, and senior civil servant, wrote of Alexander, "No man has ever earned this distinction more faithfully or received it more worthily. It is a credit to the government that merit has been recognized as superior to all other considerations whether national or political."

There was just one catch to Alexander's judgeship: it carried the proviso that he move to Quebec City. Justice Cross accepted the position but privately determined to commute. For the first few years he managed his travels without official comment; but as the province grew, crime flourished and his presence in Quebec City became imperative. At times he had to spend an entire month there for the criminal court alone. Letters from the chief justice imploring him to get on with his permanent move were politely and obscurely answered by Alexander, then the matter expelled yet again from his mind. For him it was unthinkable to leave the cosmopolitan Montreal and his Pine Avenue manor for "that hateful city" of Quebec.

Alexander's duties on the bench meant even less time to attend to his business propositions, and to date, no son had shown himself to have inherited his entrepreneurial talents. Harry was gone, Selkirk was practising law from his fashionable offices on St. James Street. Willie Heber was bright, but struggling through McGill University toward a degree as notary public. (His partying prevented prodigious academic achievements, and as for ambition Selkirk once wrote, "If Willie would pick up some young woman with a reasonable amount of cash it would be just as well.") With Edmund under-achieving at school and Robert too young to be considered as a future partner, Alexander placed increasing pressure on Ernest.

Julia often said that Ernest was the son who most reflected Alexander's personality. Just under six feet, lean and intense, his somewhat aloof yet friendly bearing marked him as a loner. Outwardly affable but increasingly private, his processes of accomplishment would become something of an enigma. By the fall of 1879, the youth had completed two years of business school at Bryant and Stratton and wanted to head west. Nevertheless, he determined to go only with his father's blessing. Under Alexander's direction he enrolled in the Ontario School of Agriculture and Experimental Farming at Guelph.

Ernest soon discovered that his father had not sent him merely to learn how to build a manure pile or even to describe the nervous system of a trout. The headmaster, John Mills, intended to instill in his mind the virtue of wealth and the principles of application. Mills also lent a dignity to a calling that Martin Macleod had once scorned as "manual." He would thunder to his students, "Success in agriculture ensures success in every other occupation; failure in agriculture means failure everywhere else. No argument is necessary to prove that it is the foundation on which the prosperity of this country has been built. If it gives way, the whole fabric is sure to fall."

As much as Ernest hated the classroom, he enjoyed hard physical work. After early morning prayers he moved on to formal studies interspersed with farm labour. He fed cattle, worked sheep, mended fences, cleared bush, chopped wood and endlessly mucked out stalls. Frolicking in nearby Guelph was disallowed. Doors were locked and lanterns snuffed out at ten o'clock. Most of the young men were already asleep.

The subsequent examinations posed questions on political economy and wealth. Ernest had come to learn about cattle, not the philosophy of finance. He failed. When faced with a neurology test shortly after, he failed again. At the end of the year thirty-one students passed. Ernest and five others failed the principal's special exams. Proving he was no quitter and believing his future lay somewhere in agriculture and animal science, Ernest returned for a second year and headed for the barns. At the time, a poorly drained manure pile must have seemed a long way from fame and fortune.

In his second year the sun shone on Ernest. Thanks to a promotional program in England and improved facilities in the college, the enrolment swelled with young gentleman immigrants. One of the newcomers was none other than Edward G. ffolkes, Ernest's Haileybury friend. ffolkes boasted the finest of brandy and imported tobacco. His trunks held changes of black and white tie, velvet smoking jackets, and even a waistcoat knitted by his Aunt Fannie. He hadn't counted on the parochialism of a Canadian agricultural school or on the work load, but cheerfully replaced his tails with canvas overalls and played the game, baling hay in scorching heat or shovelling snow at 10 below zero.

As the class comedian, ffolkes was typical of the ebullient kind of friend with which the more serious Ernest would surround himself throughout his life. He threw his classmates into fits over his debates on the virtues of vanity and ambition. Then one day his marks plummeted and the inertia that had paralysed him at Haileybury returned. He failed three out of five Easter exams, announced that his heart was in the West and left for a Manitoba farm.

How Ernest must have yearned to join ffolkes, free of the classroom, free to spin off his life like his friend or like Harry in Wyoming. But he respected Alexander's decree and plodded on to complete his term. While he continued to place in the last third of his academic classes, he won honours in confirmation judging and in the handling of cattle, horses and sheep. He was a natural with animals.

In placing heavy burdens on Ernest, Alexander was also entrusting to him his empire. He knew that countless fathers had established fortunes only to watch their wealth vanish in the hands of ignorant or careless children. His recipe for success depended less upon exam marks than upon diligence, conservative investment policies, some political bench to help shape the western frontier and sheer street moxie. It was this son in whom he began to see those qualities. Ernest possessed the same self-generating energies and the same insatiable pursuit of excellence as himself.

It was precisely the youth's mediocre standing in the classroom, combined with his tenacity of character, which would impel him far further than his gold-medalist brother, Selkirk. Ernest would never rest. He would always find one more manure pile to build or one more exam to pass. His manure piles would become breweries and oil wells, his exams his public duty of establishing churches, hospitals, a territorial government, a stampede. He would never lose his powerful sense of community nor cease his pursuit of education.

In 1881, at the end of his years at Guelph (renamed the Ontario Agricultural College), Ernest's visions were catapulting him toward the development of the North-West Territories. James Macleod and the NWMP had brought peace and order to the frontier and the railroad was being hammered across the prairies. As soon as the tracks were laid, he intended to take the train west. His father agreed, but, with the future of the Canadian Pacific Railway somewhat tenuous, he noted that his twenty-year-old son had plenty of time for more study; Alexander believed that no one should head into any frontier without the broadest possible education. Ernest enrolled in the new Montreal Veterinary College associated with McGill University.

Established by Alexander's friend, backroom politician and western entrepreneur, Dr. Duncan McEachran, and by his brother-in-law, Dr. George Campbell, the school demanded a longer period of academic pursuit than any other veterinary college from Ontario to Edinburgh. The Edinburgh-trained McEachran had no degree himself but was awarded the title "doctor" by McGill. His students would study with the medical faculty under Dr. William Osler, a man dedicated to revolutionary principles in pathology. Osler's interest may have been inspired by his former mentor, Dean George Campbell, who moved through each surgical procedure wearing an undraped tweed jacket and starched shirt cuffs.

Fascination with Osler's colourful teaching would evolve for Ernest into a lifelong fear of infection, yet occasionally inspiring him to undertake his own research. One night after hearing that a horse had been shot due to a throat malignancy, he and a cohort hitched up a horse and cart and drove up Mount Royal. Locating the grave around midnight, they dug for nearly an hour before Ernest's shovel rammed the horse. The would-be pathologists severed the head, loaded it onto the cart and returned to Pine Avenue. The following day they drove to McGill and unveiled the specimen-equidae for their professor. Osler was delighted with his students, but found no evidence of malignancy. Worse than Ernest's grisly nocturnal efforts, it appeared that the horse had been shot in vain.

Perhaps more significant than the school's association with the McGill medical faculty were McEachran's personal connections with Ottawa and the West. With a $500,000 investment by Montreal businessmen, McEachran had guided the Quebec senator, M.H. Cochrane, in the incorporation of the 109,400-acre Cochrane Ranche Company in Alberta Territory. (In the new district of Alberta, leases of up to 100,000 acres were available under the Dominion act.) McEachran was made absentee general manager while Major James Walker retired from the NWMP to become the local manager. It was the first great ranching company in southern Alberta. For the next three years Ernest would not only be privy to McEachran's medical lectures but also to his commentaries on the foothills and, inadvertently, on the setbacks of absentee ownership in western ranching.

Alexander was pleased with Ernest's new pursuit, but was increasingly concerned over Harry's life in Wyoming. Letters from the American frontier continued to pour in with news that a boom was on and Harry was desperate for money to invest in land and cattle. Settlers were pouring in, school houses were springing up, mazes of irrigation ditches were being dug by hand. Absentee Britons were investing millions of pounds into vast ranches. The Wyoming Stock-growers' Association had grabbed a stranglehold on controlling the size of ranches, who could own cattle and who got punished for rustling. The bigger the rancher, the greater his influence on the association. Harry had to grow or be squeezed out.

Alexander was still suspicious about Wyoming. Montreal had been steeped in depression ever since the real estate and building boom had ended in the 1870s. He replied to his son that, as for the possibility of raising money for cattle, Harry might as well offer a mortgage on the North Pole. At any rate, might his son be too optimistic? Perhaps cattle values might soon peak. Alexander used his own folly as an example: a few years before he had gambled $60,000 in the cotton market and $40,000 in a flour mill. Anticipating lucrative returns, he bought more property before he had his capital gains in hand. Then surplus crops caused the price per pound to plummet. He was caught short in falling commodities and heavily mortgaged land. Just how he manipulated his holdings to stay afloat was carefully documented in his letter, then subsequently chewed out in Harry's cabin by a rat.

Harry would have to wait until the Wyoming market had stabilized. Alexander advised him to avoid expansion until the economic climate in Canada improved. He added, "Be quite assured that you would be helped if there were means of doing so, but I would like you to be moderate in your expectations and be content with what you have for a time." It was tough news for Harry, who stood helplessly by while twenty thousand settlers poured in along with hundreds of thousands of head of cattle and sheep. British businessmen invested nearly $30 million into ranching.

An astonishing cultural stratum evolved in Wyoming. In Powder River country just north of Harry's roaming herd, the Frewen brothers incorporated the huge Powder River Cattle Company. They built Frewen Castle and met their aristocratic guests in a Concord coach driven by liveried coachmen. Moreton Frewen married Clara Jerome, sister-in-law of Lord Randolph Churchill.

The cattlemen soon built the inevitable enclave, named the Cheyenne Club. It was richly appointed and boasted a glass observation tower, the best chef in any American club, and uniformed servants imported from Canada where servility was better understood. Unlike Harry's first cabin, called "Little Canada," the Powder River area of Johnson County was soon dubbed by the cowboys, "England." With thousands of settlers buying plots and fencing in the water holes, Harry could not impart to his father, so sunk in the gloom of the Canadian depression, that available land was diminishing.

Finally, in the spring of 1882, Alexander sent Harry a loan of $1,600, pointing out that it cost him $1,602. He advised him to make careful use of it as it had been hard for him to come up with the money. As he understated to Harry, "The struggle is to prevent sacrificing property, of which there is enough."

Compounding Alexander's worries over his sons was another legal battle between himself and F.W. Torrance. At sixty-two, Alexander was getting a little testy and hated it when his old friend challenged his personal sense of justice. This time, Alexander's brother-in-law and partner, Alec Lunn, had allegedly used the money of his client, a widow, to invest in Windsor Hotel shares. When the widow's son, whose counsel was Justice F.W. Torrance, requested funds from his mother, it was discovered they were temporarily in use. In the ensuing scrap both Alexander and Torrance accused each other of personal involvement in the widow's affairs. The two judges threatened to sue each other in the Superior Court. Claiming that he had, in fact, saved the estate from bankruptcy although he had requested land in lieu of payment, Alexander accused Torrance of creating a wrong impression. Nevertheless, he agreed to put in his share of the loss if Torrance would put in his, and closed with, "I have now made my last appeal to your sense of justice and honour."

The case is an illuminating commentary on nineteenth-century professional ethics. Both a justice of the Queen's Bench and a justice of the Superior Court felt morally correct in collaborating, then scrapping, over an estate which they had overseen as both trustees and investors. They were also quite prepared to go public and settle the issue in court. In the more freewheeling practices over a century ago, the term "conflict of interest" was non-existent.

In the spring of 1882 Willie Heber joined Ernest, who had been given the River Beaudette farm as a practice ground for his agricultural and veterinary studies. When Alexander and Julia visited the farm in June, they were delighted to find a stunning improvement. The crops were in, the cattle, horses, sheep and Berkshire pigs were in outstanding condition. In October Ernest would return for his final year at McGill.

Alexander was also pleased that although Selkirk's reputation as a *bon vivant* was rivalling that of Willie Heber's, he was building a strong professional reputation with the law firm of Ogilvy and

Renault. His oldest son's dealings with the family business took him before the Queen's Bench on several occasions, particularly when concerning their considerable shares in the Windsor Hotel. What may have been unique, even for the nineteenth century, was a son arguing his case before his own father on the Court of Queen's Bench. Justice Cross and two other judges heard Selkirk's case, then Alexander disqualified himself from passing judgment, thus risking a split bench.

In the spring of 1883 Harry returned to Canada for a visit and fell in love. Eighteen-year-old Léa Levasseur of Cacouna now lived at Pine Avenue as the French governess to Robert and Edmund. Harry had not seen the petite, dark-skinned girl since she was seven years old. Time stood still as Léa and Harry chatted and laughed in a melody of French verbs and summer memories. For a man who had spent the last nine years in the company of dancehall girls, Harry found Léa enchanting. But in Montreal an upper-middle-class British Protestant was never, ever supposed to marry a French Roman Catholic servant girl. For the entire holiday Harry said nothing to Léa or his parents, pillars of the Presbyterian church. It wasn't until he was saying his farewells and about to step into the carriage for the train that he drew Léa aside and asked her to wait for him. Only then did he dare speak to his parents.

Had Harry attempted to establish a life with Léa in Quebec, the couple would have stood with a foot in two cultures, two religions, never fully accepted one by the other. If they could get dispensation from the churches, their wedding would be Roman Catholic. Their children's births might be registered "Non-Catholic" on the English side of the civic archives but they would be raised in the Roman Catholic faith. Harry would choose for them the broad education of a British school, while the priests would demand they attend a Roman Catholic school with its heavy emphasis on religion. When the couple died, Léa's death would be registered in the Catholic civic records, Harry's on the English side. Harry's body would be buried in the English cemetery on Mount Royal, Léa's in the Roman Catholic graveyard at Cacouna. The schisms would slice through their mixed marriage as Harry's Wyoming mountains would one day divide his ranch. So Léa agreed to leave her family and head for the American West. There, French trappers had long settled in peace, and as long as you were not black, race, religion and language mattered to no one but the cattle barons. There would be a year's wait, however, for Harry returned to Wyoming Territory to purchase his own land and build a home.

Harry had long known of a place in the foothills some two hundred miles west of Cheyenne called Red Canyon Valley. It reminded him of the Braehead of Scotland that he and Selkirk had visited a decade earlier. Stirrup-high grassland rippled up to near perpendicular walls of rust-coloured rock. Craggy peaks reached up 10,000 feet into heavy rain clouds hanging over Spring Canyon and Tomahawk Bluffs. Buffalo cakes littered the grass like leaves after a fall wind, a sign of good grazing and sheltered winters. Red Canyon Creek sparkled along the valley floor. An elevated meadow well above the creek's spring floods commanded a magnificent view. It would be perfect for a house.

Dreaming of owning the entire valley, Harry rode for Cheyenne and filed for 160 acres at $1.25 per acre, payable in thirty-three months. He got the title late in 1883 and named his homestead "Braehead." At the time, he owned twelve horses and 250 head of cattle. He branded 196 calves and shipped ten head to the Chicago sales. After paying freight, hay and yardage expenses, he netted a balance of $387.50. In his eagerness to return to Quebec for Léa, he paid a neighbour $500 to build a two-room cabin. Before leaving he made one more commitment. He applied for citizenship in the United States. Then, just after Christmas, he headed for Montreal and his bride.

Following the bishop's dispensation, Harry and Léa were married in the Roman Catholic Church, Cacouna, on January 30, 1884. It was a family service and the first time the Crosses had entered the church. Léa's father wept as his raven-haired daughter, resplendent in a white lace gown with satin ribbons, stood with the twenty-nine-year-old Harry, tall, lean, and very much in love. Almost a century before it was acceptable, two dissident cultures and two disparate economic lifestyles were blended in the young lovers. Uncle Robert Cross was not only absent, he would refrain from acknowledging the marriage of his favourite nephew for five years. During the reception the old laughter and conviviality of Cacouna summers were restored when Léa's nephew tugged on Harry's sleeve, and thinking that Wyoming was somewhere near California, pleaded in a shrill voice, "Monsieur Cross, pouvez-vous nous envoyer des oranges?"

Alexander counselled his son, "Harry, you have a good wife. Take the very best care of her and never let the sun set on any misunderstanding." A tough taskmaster, Alexander's love for his children burned through his pen. He had become a formidable patrician but once his sons made their decisions, he stood by them. Both Harry

and Léa reassured their large families that they would make their
fortune and return to Canada. Harry and Ernest also promised each
other to meet in Montreal. Return they would, but separately. For
when these two brothers waved farewell to each other following the
Cacouna wedding, it would be forty-three years before they would
meet again.

Harry and Léa's trip to Cheyenne and then on to their cabin
two hundred miles in the Wyoming wilderness was a saga of survival.
After a bolt snapped on their coach, they continued on by open
buckboard in a mid-February blizzard. They became so lost and frozen
that they gave the horses their heads in a last attempt to find help.
The animals found a cabin. As it was full of cowboys, the newly-
weds got to sleep behind a calico curtain while the men bunked on
floors and a billiard table. The stomping and munching of horses
sharing a stable wall with the cabin kept the teen-age bride wide-
eyed for the entire night.

Each day, Léa wiped the tears from her face and grappled with
flowing skirts and stays in the blizzard privies. Although they paid
for their lodgings at each stop, she assisted the women in cooking
and cleaning. In turn, they taught her how to make bread with
sourdough starter, advising her to keep it close to her body; if it
froze on the trail the dough would be lost. Léa found her language
and culture an asset in this country where so many French trappers
had long ago settled. The rebellious and impetuous Harry was
frequently reminded that he had chosen wisely, both his home in
Wyoming Territory and the woman with whom he would spend his
life. Everything he was doing was a departure from the aristocratic
life he had known in Montreal.

Upon completing the mid-winter trip to their cabin, they found
only a few logs struggling up through the drifts. Snow blew through
holes for windows and their provisions were buried under the snow.
Harry's would-be honeymoon had turned into a nightmare of survival.
They were forced to make the grim journey all the way back to
the Interocean Hotel, Cheyenne. For a month Harry paced the hotel
room and the bar like a caged panther while his bride fought a cold
and hooked a rug. That spring they returned west to their cabin,
finally completed by the neighbour who had set aside the job in
favour of winter trapping.

In her new home, Léa rose before dawn in summer and winter
to milk the cow, make tallow candles, plant fruit trees and dig a
vegetable garden. While she worked alone, Harry ploughed his land

with a piece of old railroad iron behind two steers. He harrowed his fields with a heavy branch tied behind his oxen. Their only visitors were down-and-out grub-liners. Léa never served food to them without saying grace, a custom which often astonished these drifters. They whispered throughout the foothills, "You know those Crosses at Braehead talk to their plates before they eat?"

Someone once told Harry that cow-country was deadly to women and horses; only men and mules survived. Before long it took its toll on Léa. In that first year she survived a horrifying rat migration which swarmed through Braehead like a hoard of locusts. But nothing was as terrible as the loneliness when Harry was away rounding up strays or fetching supplies. One such evening late in September when Léa was pregnant, a covered wagon filled with gypsies pulled up to Braehead. Without warning they entered, opened the cupboards and swept the Cross's winter provisions of sugar, flour and spices into their sacks. Léa hid under the chimney behind the stove with her one bottle of Burnett's vanilla extract. She was spotted by a gypsy woman who screamed a curse at Léa's unborn child, then grabbed the vanilla extract and waddled out the door with her haul.

Léa's sense of isolation and fear deepened with this violation of her home. Soon after an Indian arrived with two horses to trade. She shook with terror, grabbing the rifle and flattening against the inside wall. Her mind spun almost beyond reason and she feared she might have shot him had he not soon left.

The silence got so bad that Léa claimed she could hear the grass grow between the cracks in the logs, and she wandered about the cabin snip-snipping at it with a pair of scissors. It was broken only by the ticking of the clock, the bawl of a calf, or the cry of a crow. Léa loved the birds, for they brought her courage until the eerie sound of howling wolves reminded her of her solitude. She sewed and gardened and wrote letters. When there was nothing left to do, she prayed for courage to accept her isolation. When Harry finally returned they would stand together looking at the stars, so close in Wyoming's dry air that Harry wrote, "one feels he can almost reach up and grab a handful, as cherries from a high tree."

So concerned was Harry about Léa's loneliness, that he sold sixty-two head of cattle just before winter and bought Léa a Beatty organ. Thereafter she obliterated the sound of silence by filling the cabin with beautiful music.

The bond between the handful of frontier women was immutable. When Léa went into labour, her neighbour, Rosa Arrowsmith, came to help. Except for the gypsy and an old lady called Granny, it had been seven months since Léa had seen another woman. Following a rough labour during which Harry feared his wife would die, a girl was born. They called her Margaret, or Maggie, after Harry's sister. For all his toughness, Harry wept in relief and gratitude over their first-born and Léa's survival. The crib they had ordered had not arrived, so for weeks Maggie would sleep on a pillow in the bureau drawer.

Léa quickly learned that she had little milk for her baby, and they had no milking cow. Harry rode for help to their neighbours. A Mrs. Rice immediately picked up her own baby and came to live at Braehead. Despite Léa's initial horror, Mrs. Rice wet-nursed Maggie until her screams of hunger ceased. At Pine Avenue the Crosses had never given a second thought to the fresh milk that the stable man placed twice daily on the pantry door-stoop. That luxury had become a desperate necessity in Wyoming. But Harry's spare money had gone to fencing and the organ; he could not afford a cow. One day, while browsing through Léa's wardrobe, Mrs. Rice came across her magnificent wedding dress. Turning to Léa she said, "I'll trade you one milk cow for this dress." Tears brimmed in Léa's eyes as she gazed at the elegant vestige of her past. A few days later, Mr. Rice arrived leading an old cow, her udders swollen with milk. Mrs. Rice left with the wedding dress.

In Montreal, Ernest's final marks at the school of veterinary medicine showed a superhuman effort. He had squeaked through the written exams in 1884 and fared little better on the orals conducted by Osler, McEachran and other members of the McGill medical board. As the school was not officially recognized by the universities, Ernest and his eleven classmates received diplomas rather than degrees. They were assured by McEachran that thanks to their association with the medical professors, they were more than competent to practice as full veterinary surgeons.

Whether Ernest passed or not mattered only to himself and his father, for at the age of twenty-two he had already been hired to replace Major Walker as treasurer-manager-veterinarian of the troubled Cochrane Ranche in Alberta. There, out of a total of seven thousand head, one thousand had died during the first winter. The Montreal board had held Walker responsible for the disasters. Criticisms from the absentee management had escalated into heated debates. Infighting among the shareholders exacerbated with arguments and accusations flying between Cochrane and McEachran.

Eventually the unanimous choice of Ernest Cross as the new east-west mediator brought temporary peace. The move mollified everyone and raised new hopes for the Cochrane Ranche, judiciously renamed the British American Ranche Company. Ernest took up his post in April 1884, the month following his graduation. Without waiting to hear the outcome of his exams, he headed west the next day. Clad in a three-piece Gibb & Co. suit designed by his Toronto tailors, he rattled and steamed across the land, through Winnipeg and on toward Calgary.

In many ways the town into which Ernest stepped exuded a comfortably eastern flavour. Tents, log buildings and wooden shacks blended with suits from London. Calgary already sprawled across the river and boasted a civic debt of $17.40. Ferries and a treacherous log footbridge linked the two areas. About thirty single-storey buildings in the business section were brightly painted and topped with large signs like a musical stage setting. There was nothing somnolent about Calgary. It was a town ripe for investment and industrial development. In two years the number of cattle surrounding the town had swelled from 3,000 to 75,000 head. Most exciting, the West had discovered gold. Thousands of fortune-seekers readied their grub packs in Calgary streets, looking northward and gossiping about the newest find. Of Calgary's future the *Calgary Herald* crowed in its maiden issue that August, "We do not pretend to the role of prophet, yet it requires little foresight to predict that the city of Calgary will be the largest in the Northwest."

In some ways the 1884 atmosphere of Alberta was reminiscent of Harry's 1878 Wyoming: the British hunts, the cattle barons' white-tie balls, and the multinational, social roundups. Following champagne breakfasts, guests in various conditions and dress were known to gallop smartly out onto the prairie to round up the cattle. A seasoned cowboy would collect strays, gently driving them through streams and over the rolling hills, only to have the whole bunch scattered noisily back into the bushes by a couple of tiddly aristocrats.

For Wyoming, the British crust had been a veneer. North of the border, Alberta *was* British. The difference between Harry's and Ernest's territories was the Queen and her scarlet-clad police force. So legendary were the Mounties that on several occasions a few Canadian "red coats" had proven more influential than an entire Wyoming cavalry. English accents were common in Alberta and Ernest's suit attracted less attention than other men's Stetsons – even when he cut cattle in it, which he would do for a lifetime.

Ernest Cross, MLA, rancher, brewer, posing for his wedding photo in Calgary, 1899.

Helen "Nell" Rothney Macleod Cross on her wedding day, Calgary, 1899.

Helen Macleod Cross, Ernest and Nell's first child, age four, 1904.

Ernest and Nell by their home at 1240 8th Avenue S.E., standing on the edge of their orchard and polo field.

Margaret Fisher Cross when she married
William R. MacInnes.

Willie Heber Cross, entrepreneur, original owner
of the a7 Ranche, circa 1890.

Selkirk, oldest son of Alexander and Julia Cross,
Montreal lawyer, executor of family estates.

W. E. Cochrane
— or —
"Billy" of the
X Ranche
Calgary 1893

Wild Billie Cochrane in the Wolves' Den, the
precursor to the Ranchmen's Club.

Léa Levasseur, childhood playmate of the Cross children, then French teacher at 751 Pine Avenue, married to Harry Cross in 1884.

Harry and Léa Cross, in Montreal en route to Wyoming Territory, February 1894.

Braehead, the Montreal-style home of Harry and Léa Cross on their Wyoming ranch, circa 1900.

Polo in southern Alberta, 1896. From left, H. Critchley, O. Critchley, A. Wolley-Dod, Ernest Cross.

Nell Cross lays the cornerstone for the expansion of the Calgary Brewing & Malting in 1907. Mary, age two, and Jim, age four, look on with Ernest.

Nell at Rhappanock, 1595 Rockland Avenue, Victoria, with Sandy (sitting), John, and Marmo, circa 1921.

The first Calgary Stampede, with "The Big Four" founders, marks Ernest's year of frenzied creativity in Alberta.

The Cross children walking with their nannie at Rhappanock, Victoria, 1921.

Queen Mary Cross demonstrating mountain skills in the pack horse race, Banff Winter Festival, 1927.

The a7 Ranche cattle being driven across the Old Man's River, October 1927, topped the Chicago market, realizing Ernest's 1886 dream of raising "the best steers in North America."

A.E. Cross, 1927, rancher, brewer, oilman, film-maker, hospital builder, Stampeder – a visionary whose do-it-yourself nature helped to build Alberta and to inspire the self-reliant tone still prevalent today.

Helen "Nell" Rothney Macleod Cross, at a time in her life when she urged women to become involved, to "take their place." Drawing by N. de Grandmaison about 1930.

Braehead. Built on the a7 Ranche by Ernest and Nell in 1913, the huge home is dwarfed by its own vast lands.

Courtesy Sidney Shakespeare Madden.

The children of Ernest and Nell Cross, clockwise from top right: Colonel Mary Dover of the Canadian Women's Army Corps, 1944. John Munklands Cross riding herd about 1955. Margaret "Marmo" Shakespeare competing at the Vancouver International Horse Show on "Grand Slam," 1960s. James Braehead Cross, businessman, rancher, sportsman, 1950s. Alexander "Sandy" Cross, centre, brewmaster, rancher, late 1950s.

In Wyoming, range wars were common. In the Canadian territories, fights between ranchers and settlers were deterred by government control of homesteading and land leasing. Monied gentry from Britain and central Canada felt perfectly safe in the Canadian West. A local Albertan journalist put it succinctly when he wrote, "Calgary is a western town but not in the ancient use of the word. It is peopled by native Canadians and Englishmen, citizens who own religion and respect law. The rough and festive cowboy of Texas ... has no counterpart here."

Ernest's Alberta suited him perfectly. If not the synthesis of his collective ancestry, the Haileybury man symbolized the British way. He was more inscrutable than Harry and thanks to the NWMP was able to be more conservative in action. It would hardly have been Ernest's style to slug a gun-wielding drunkard in a Calgary saloon.

He soon met other educated young men on-the-go such as James Lougheed, one of the new breed of lawyers who had invaded the judicial domain of Judge Macleod. Lougheed was just in the process of hanging out his shingle in a small building with a shack attached to it. These men shared an instant camaraderie and a knowledge that their intellectual advantage could propel them into positions of influence.

On June 1, 1884, Ernest swung onto a train for the trip to the British-American Horse Ranche twenty-four miles due west. Almost all trains stopped there before shunting on toward the Rocky Mountains and the Pacific Ocean. There he found the seasoned cowboys standing silently outside the bunkhouse staring at the "eastern interloper." Steeled for some kind of initiation, Ernest breezed through the bunkhouse door to find a toughened bronco rider with a young Blackfoot "maiden," as he later described her. A hearty subscriber to the concepts of racial purity, he was shocked and turned to leave. As he was closing the door, Chief Crowfoot rode up in a flurry of dust to retrieve the Indian girl and return her to the reserve. The chief of the Blackfoot had his own standards of dignity and propriety. Never had Ernest learned a language as fast as he did Blackfoot.

The Cochrane ranch with its absentee management proved a hotbed of friction and confusion. The current manager was not even aware that Ernest had arrived to assume the duties of bookkeeper as well as veterinarian. So for the first month Ernest played the role of diplomat, waiting for Senator Cochrane himself, who would arrive in July to advise and dismiss at will.

Almost immediately, Ernest was called to tend to an outlaw horse about to be broken. He was stunned to watch the rider, Frank Ricks, lay into the horse with his spurs and break flesh from ear to tail. By the time Ricks dismounted the horse was no longer chestnut, but splashed pink with blood and foamy sweat. All eyes turned toward the greenhorn as the men silently wondered how Ernest would get near the crazed animal to treat him.

Ernest lured the horse into the squeeze-gate by jumping into it himself and hooting. Crazed with pain, fear and anger, the horse stampeded toward him, stopping just short of the narrow, confining stall. Ernest stood still in the far back of the stall. In a sudden lunge the horse charged, lips curled back, ears flat. Ernest smoothly leaped out as the cowboys slammed the gate closed. With the bronco locked tightly in place, he cleaned and salved its wounds. While working, he calmed the animal with a gentle, confident voice.

Next, a wild mustang was brought out for Ernest to break. Still wearing his three-piece suit, he halter-broke the gelding, then blindfolded it. The horse stood quivering. Ernest eased the western saddle on, mounted, then slipped the blindfold off. Immediately the horse dropped its head between his front legs, its back bowed up in the air and jumped violently round the corral. Ernest lost both stirrups but managed to "grab leather," or the saddle horn. Within moments the mustang broke out of the corral and galloped eastward. Several miles from the ranch it suddenly jammed to a stop, sending Ernest hurtling to the ground. The mustang raced on toward Calgary. Ernest limped back to the ranch.

Dr. McEachran had talked incessantly about the glorious foothills. He considered the winters to be quite severe, but assured Ernest that the frequent chinook winds which warmed the air allowed livestock to graze without supplemental feeding. If Ernest believed him, he was in for a shock. In January of 1885 when the temperature fell to 40 below, he began driving 2,500 sheep through the canyon and into the hills. He had barely started out with a couple of sheep dogs as his only help, when coyotes attacked. If Ernest raced to one end of the flock, the coyotes attacked at the other. It took him a week to get the creatures to fenced rangeland.

Another night a cowboy burst into the bunkhouse yelling, "The sheep are all dead!" Ernest roused three men, harnessed a team to the wagon and headed for the huge corral up in the hills. No sheep were to be seen. They had used the drifts as ramps, stumbling out of the corral and wandering about in the storm. The men found them freezing to death a half mile away in the lake. Accustomed to roping cattle from the backs of horses, the cowboys were forced to wade into the icy waters and wrestle the waterlogged creatures toward land. Coyotes stalked the shoreline, gnawing at the sheep as fast as the shivering men pushed them onto the bank. All the next day, huge fires unfroze the cowboys' limbs and leather chaps between their struggles in the water. In the end they lost three hundred head but it could have been the entire herd. Ernest wrote to his father, "There is no doubt that sheep will do well here."

In the spring of 1885 Ernest wrote Alexander a thoroughly researched letter about land northeast of the Cochrane ranch near Red Deer. Entrusting his father not to breathe a word of his plans outside the family, especially to the Montreal directors of the British American Ranche Company, he explained, "I expect they will not like me leaving or taking a ranche up this creek, but as the saying is and very truly applied to this country, every man for himself and don't care a fig for your neighbour." If Willie Heber and Edmund claimed homesteads beside his, Ernest continued, they could control all the water and thus the land for miles around. He foresaw all the land being bought up within three years.

Hoping to win his father's commitment, Ernest cheerily ended his letter with the threat, "If you do not care about this project I have another. It is ... to go to South America. From all I hear of Peru, Chili and Brazil there are splendid prospects for ranching, coffee growing, mining etc. for any enterprising man."

Replying that money was so scarce he could not send Ernest a cent, Alexander headed for Europe with Julia and Maggie. It was a "finishing trip" for Maggie, designed to polish any rough edges on an already beautifully rounded Victorian lady. As their itinerary included Berlin, Prague, Switzerland, northern Italy and Burma, it was virtually impossible for Ernest to negotiate with his father. A decade earlier, Alexander's tight-fisted policy had not stopped Harry, but this time it did inspire Ernest to rethink his plans.

During that spring Louis Riel sent couriers across the plains, urging Métis and Indians to form one last great confederacy and force Ottawa to recognize their collective land claims. If unsuccessful, he intended to fight for their rights with an Indian-Métis army. Many were sympathetic to their cause. Even Riel's old enemy, Charlie Mair, had travelled several times from Prince Albert to Ottawa on behalf of the Métis. On March 26, at Duck Lake, forty-three Prince Albert volunteers joined with a NWMP patrol and were ambushed by Riel. Twenty-three men were killed, more wounded. On April 2, Cree Indians at Frog Lake, northern Saskatchewan, swept through the community murdering the settlers. Some whites escaped downriver with the NWMP and made it to Prince Albert. From his headquarters in the town of Batoche, Riel prepared to attack Prince Albert. Settlers throughout the West anticipated war.

On the Cochrane ranch, rifles and ammunition were issued for defence, but the uprising meant only one thing to the men: they sold their worst saddle horses off to the incoming armies. Ernest described the soldiers as "French Canadian sixty-fifth Tommies fresh from the city of Montreal." He wrote that when the Tommies tried to mount the "old outlaws ... they soon flew in the air. Horses and saddles were scattered all over the prairie."

On July 1, 1885, Ernest resigned from the Cochrane ranch. He bought a roan pinto and rode one hundred miles south to visit an old college mate working on the Walrond Ranche, Pincher Creek. Checking into the Fort Macleod Hotel, Ernest and his pal held an all-night Montana Red Eye reunion. The next day, thoroughly hung over, Ernest headed northward without grub or even matches. He soon forgot his agony and became enthralled with what he saw, for he had ridden into the Alberta foothills. They rolled like ocean waves as far as the eye could see. To the west the Rocky Mountains radiated hues in receding shades from Prussian blue to iridescent silver. Ernest wrote of that day, of being "so close to nature, with all the freedom of the unbounded prairie without a living soul.... If you ever experienced it you can never get free from a longing desire to experience it again."

At dusk he dismounted and, using his saddle as a pillow, flopped onto a hill of billowing grass. Red Eye demons still spun in his head. He tied a line from his horse to his wrist, then, chilled, with neither food nor fire, fell asleep. Around midnight, a pack of timber wolves gathered and circled at the bottom of the hill. The terrified horse snorted, then bolted, dragging the startled cowboy behind. Ernest recalled, "I hung on for grim death. There was not a living soul for miles." He got the cayuse under control, then spent a miserable night fearfully pacing about while the wolves prowled nearby. At dawn's first light he continued on, unaware that he was riding through foothills which would one day form part of his own vast ranchlands.

Two miles west of the Fort Macleod–Calgary trail and about thirty miles south of Calgary, Ernest found a stream gurgling over the pancake-flat prairie. It was a natural area for hay and grazing. He filed the $10 registration fee for a homestead, rode on to the Mosquito Creek Stage House for a huge meal, then headed for Montreal.

12

The Canadian Frontier

"Blast the C.P.R.!"
James Macleod, 1883

Following the christening of his second child, Norman, in January 1880, news that Louis Riel was back prompted James to head for Benton and the telegraph. He was reluctant to leave his growing family, and his system was rebelling against the arduous treks and the brandy consumed to fire his chilled limbs. En route to Benton he wrote of his failing health: "That confounded rheumatism knocked me all up my right side and hand then that miserable stomach went out of order and would not perform the duties for which nature designed it. It could hardly have been the whiskey I drank for I only had a few horns just after I arrived, and I have not tasted a drop since. I don't think I ever will as I have taken a great dislike to the very smell of it."

On the court circuit, James took long walks in the evening, but never joined the nightly poker games played for drinks and cigars. He preferred reading by the fire and thinking about Mary. When asleep, his dreams were no less vivid than his memories:

I dreamt such a queer dream about you. You made your appearance in my room with the baby in your arms and said that you had come to see me as you heard I was ill. You had your bonnet on and I was going to jump out of bed to dress myself and go with you to some detached house like the Winders where I thought we lived. You said, "No, the house is all cold. I will just stay with you where you are." With that you flung the baby to the other side of me, pulled up the clothes and jumped in, commenced taking

off your stockings and boots which were all wet with snow. I had
the greatest difficulty in keeping baby from falling out of bed with
my right hand ... but I awoke and found myself alone.

James's visions of the future were recorded only in terms of family
reunions. Rather than adhere to some form of secrecy for fear of
security leaks, it seems that he simply never considered recording
his professional opinions. His family and his career were utterly
separate entities, although it was hardly a case of one not to intrude
upon the other. Dreams of Mary haunted him everywhere. Whereas
some men have trouble leaving their business problems at the office,
James fought a losing battle in leaving his connubial fantasies at home.

With the spring thaw at Fort Macleod, Mary cared for her two
small children and eyed the Old Man's River, which threatened to
sweep through her home. It had broken through a neck of land and
already washed some houses away. One night the muddied waters
raced over the banks to within five feet from the floorboards of
the fort. Shortly thereafter, the Macleods determined to build a home
on their Pincher Creek land some thirty miles west.

In May James was called to Ottawa. He longed to be relieved of
some of his duties and Sir John A. Macdonald had hinted that he
was in line for a judgeship. But he was kept in suspense for months,
a subtle reminder of who was boss. James wrote to Mary of the
coveted bench position, "I know you will like to be told that there
is a chance of my being appointed Stipendiary. This absence from
home is so *intolerable* that I would rather do anything than continue
it."

Sir John fully recognized James's abilities, but he may have felt
that the commissioner's partiality to the Indians was detrimental to
the government. The prime minister's conundrum was to figure the
best way to use James's talents of negotiation and frontier jurisprudence while removing him from the Indians, from the politically
embarrassing police stores and from other administrative positions.
If James were assigned solely to the future bench of the North-West
Territories, the West would benefit and the government could save
face.

While Sir John mulled over his options, James prepared to return
to the West with a new member of the NWMP – his oldest brother
Norman. Norman had developed a lifestyle beyond his means. He
had run through his inheritance and mortgaged hundreds of Drynoch
acres to pay his bills. Martin's dream of holding the Richmond Hill

estate in the family for two hundred years was diminishing within a generation, although some three hundred and twenty acres remained intact. A few years earlier, Norman had left Drynoch to assume various railroad jobs with his younger brother Henry, the latter a successful survey engineer. That worked for only a while. Suffering from inflammatory rheumatism and wishing to avoid a life of labour, Norman appealed to his youngest brother for help. There was no decision for James to make on the matter; some twenty years earlier he had personally recorded his father's admonition that each child accept full responsibility in caring one for the other. James invited Norman to come west, convincing Indian commissioner Edgar Dewdney to hire him into the NWMP. Norman first became postmaster and overseer of police stores, then Indian agent at Fort Macleod.

The choice of Norman to handle James's nemesis of police stores was madness for he, too, hated paper work. Worse, he didn't like Indians. During the years that young James had run in the woods with his Ojibwa friends, Norman had sweated over a plough and other tasks as the future owner of Drynoch. Unlike his parents, who had adapted to tilling their fields, he had found the farming demeaning and aspired more to associating with the right class of people. In the same way, he headed west with a sense of position far above the pending tasks. That he and his eighteen-year-old son Norrie might be unsuited for frontier life became apparent as early as their trek from Ottawa to Fort Macleod. While it would be unfair to fault the Macleod relatives for a disaster of nature, their arrival proved a heartbreaking introduction to the western frontier.

It was during the spring floods that the entourage consisting of James, Norman and Norrie left Ontario with a NWMP escort. Upon reaching Sitting Bull's encampment, James held a council meeting and urged the destitute Indians to return to the United States. At Fort Walsh the family played a few games of lawn tennis and bathed in the creek before riding on toward their destination.

By evening, the group reached the Belly River to find that heavy rains had turned it into a raging sea. James was anxious to reach home for he had caught a chill at Fort Walsh. Accustomed to crossing rivers in any condition, he placed his gold watch in his waistcoat pocket and dropped the treasure aboard the wagon. Then he and Jerry Potts half rode, half swam, to the far bank. James shouted back to the others not to make the attempt with the wagon until morning. Flooding often abated as quickly as it had started. The pair rode on to Fort Macleod.

At dawn, the Belly River still thundered away. Norman and Norrie stoked up a smoke fire to discourage the ever-hovering mosquitoes and black-flies, but just as they were beginning to heat coffee and fry bacon, Constable Hooley hitched up the four horses and announced that they could cook breakfast at Fort Macleod.

Keen to brave the elements but only in a manner of speaking to get his feet wet, young Norrie seated himself high and dry beside Hooley. Norman and the other policemen jumped aboard as the team plunged down the bank and into the churning water. In mid-river the lead horses lost their footing and swerved downstream. Norrie gripped the frame as the wagon tipped dangerously.

With hands entangled in the leather traces, Constable Hooley fought to regain control and hollered, "I can't swim!" He yelled at Norrie to grab a knife and cut the horses loose. But at that precise moment Norrie also realized he was going to get his boots wet. Instead of seizing a knife, he bent over and began to unlace his boots. The wagon lurched and upended, flinging Norrie and the men through the air into the turbulent river.

A tangle of traces, Hooley, horses and wagon disappeared downstream. Upon reaching the far bank, Captain Denny and Norman sent a shaken Norrie on to Fort Macleod for his Uncle James, then headed downriver after Hooley. They found the wagon on a sandbar, overturned with the four drowned horses. The only item remaining on the wagon was James's waistcoat with his gold watch. There was no sign of Constable Hooley. One month later his body was found twelve miles downstream. He was brought back to Fort Macleod and buried with military honours.

That a NWMP constable should be killed in the line of duty was as rare as it was tragic, but the worst disaster of the West that summer was still the massive starvation of the Indians. Norman and assistant agent Pocklington drove wagons of flour and tea around to the various camps to feed about three hundred Indians per day. It was a diminutive gesture when over seven thousand were encamped around Fort Macleod. Occasionally some broke angrily toward Norman and his wagon. When the NWMP supply was reduced to six bags of flour, Chief Crowfoot visited James to report constant deaths and to plead for assistance. Facing the personal dishonour of representing the government's empty promises, James wrote of the Indians to Mary on May 29 and June 3, 1880.

Four thousand Indians [are destitute] ... and the authorities in

Ottawa appeared to overlook the necessity which has been pointed out to them over and over again, that they would be required to be fed or they would starve. Between us, your old skalliwag could have managed things better if it had been left to him.... The poor creatures have been living on fish for some time back as the supplies here are about exhausted, but that source is now failing them, as the fish are pouring back from the creeks where the Indians cannot catch them with their nets....

I am not at all satisfied with the arrangements the Government has made about the supplies for the Indians. Indeed, they do not appear to appreciate in the least the call that will be made upon them this summer. They appear still to think that the poor creatures can gain their livelihood by hunting as if everyone didn't know that there is nothing for them to hunt. The fact is that [the government] are not half doing the thing, and the result will be that the Indians will be dissatisfied and what the government spends will be thrown away.

Norman Macleod felt quite differently about the natives. In a letter to his daughter, Jeanie, he wrote, "My office is never without Indians complaining or trying to overreach me in the matter of grub. I cannot conceive how any person who had ever seen them would write of one single good quality being found in every ten thousand of them. They are everything that is low, mean and vicious, and the more you see of them the more firmly you become convinced of the correctness of this opinion."

Furthermore, Norman could also see not one single advantage to living in Fort Macleod where the only society other than the NWMP was "one of the roughest in manners and morals." Of police stores he wrote, "I am in charge and I hate the sight of pens and ink, and am always glad of an excuse to leave the Office and go on a trip."

James had been criticized for incompetency in running the stores, yet he had placed them in far more unqualified hands than his own. Worse, he so loved the West and everything he had built, that he was blind to his brother's biases. It was inconceivable to him that anyone could dislike this magnificent country or its natives. The policemen, however, were only too conscious of Norman's shortcomings. Complaints flowed past James to Ottawa.

Despite the rumblings or perhaps because of them, James's new appointment came through in October 1880. He retired without fanfare from the NWMP, gave his uniform away and resumed his position as stipendiary magistrate of the North-West Territories. His annual salary would be $3,000 plus travelling expenses. The title changed little, for James remained integral to the development of the West, and in particular to the well-being of the Indians.

As for Norman, NWMP Commissioner Irvine eventually held a formal inquiry into police stores and his performance in general. Irvine subsequently reported to Edgar Dewdney: "The result ... convinced me that Depts. were being swindled before his very eyes. Mr. Macleod was unable to cope with the class of men who did business at Fort Macleod." Norman's clerk got wind of the investigation and headed for the border. He was caught and returned, confirming a consensus that there was a conspiracy to rob the government. It was also the opinion of Irvine that as Norman was suffering from rheumatism, he was, "physically incapable of carrying out the onerous duties of even half of Treaty No. 7." By the winter of 1881 the commisssioner felt compelled to take control of all the Indians in the south.

Asked to submit an assessment of Norman to the prime minister, Dewdney argued that his choice of Colonel Macleod's brother as Indian agent had been designed to please the Blackfoot, who saw in James a sterling character. He believed Norman to be the same. Dewdney added, "I would wish it to be understood that whatever irregularities have taken place since Mr. Macleod was in charge of the Agency, I am confident that he personally has acted with the strictest integrity and carried out his duties to the best of his ability." Ottawa suggested reappointing Norman to the Carlton agency but Dewdney advised against it, believing that he "would be detrimental to public service." Norman had become a monumental problem.

James remained oblivious to the gathering storm even though he was in Ottawa at the time. Commissioner Irvine, Edgar Dewdney and the prime minister did not speak to him about his brother. At that time he was blissfully happy that Mary had safely given birth to twins Mary and Roma in Winnipeg. He subsequently wrote from Toronto that he had shopped for "a beautiful carriage for the precious twins ... the most beautiful thing you ever saw." He dined with Lieutenant-Governor Robinson and lunched with investors interested in establishing ranches near the Rockies. Then he went out to Drynoch. So preoccupied was James with the fun of life that he was shocked and enraged when he received a letter from the prime minister and a copy of Dewdney's letter. He would not rest until Sir John restored honour to the Macleod name.

Seizing pen and paper, probably at the same desk Martin had written to John A. Macdonald in the 1850s, James wrote one of his epistles. In detail he recounted Norman's history: education, farming experience in Scotland, association with the Indians north of Lake Simcoe, a bid to become chief of police in Toronto, positions as an explorer and commissariat officer on CPR surveys. With blinding loyalty, James wrote that Norman had "secured and held the confidence and affection of the Indians. While he acted as Agent I never heard of a single complaint from anyone that my brother was incapacitated by or from doing his work...."

James requested that the prime minister give the adverse charges "a most unqualified dismissal." Then he directed the brunt of his anger towards his old friend, NWMP Superintendent Crozier at Fort Macleod, who had appeared friendly to him while complaining of Norman behind his back. James retorted, "No official in the North-West is safe if he is to be judged by the expert statements of a false friend." In closing he suggested that Sir John give Norman a land agency registrarship, or a timber agency combined with the position of fishery inspector, the latter to be a newly created job for his brother. James then wrote a scathing letter to Dewdney for his disloyal conduct toward an old friend. Not once, even in his letters to Mary, does he entertain the idea that perhaps Norman might have been at fault.

Shortly after, James went to Ottawa to argue on behalf of his brother. It also seemed to him like a good time to request a raise in pay. He lacked the survival instincts to separate the two issues. As a result, his determination both to clear his brother's name and increase his salary was as blatant as the collective ministers' absence. For the first time in his professional career, no one would see him. A friendly MP told James he would not receive a raise. When James asked why he should be treated differently from the others, the MP "read a very lame excuse." The "others," such as Justice Alexander Cross, Court of Queen's Bench, Quebec, received annual salaries of $6,500 plus $1,200 travelling expenses, yet James's jurisdiction and travelling were vaster by far than those of judges in central Canada.

Finally, Sir Alexander Campbell agreed with James that he was being unfairly treated concerning his salary. Encouraged, James went to the prime minister's office to clear up the matter of his wages and, of course, of Norman. He was not permitted an audience. Returning to the friendly MP who again referred him back to the prime minister, James complained to Mary about the run around, "You can imagine how disgusted I am."

James had no political leverage because he had no knowledge of the game. He never spoke of the graft, the vote-purchasing or the payoffs so common in nineteenth-century Canadian politics. Like his father, his code and his perspective were those of an eighteenth-century gentleman. A year later he would return to Ottawa to plead for Norman and a salary raise; again he would be shuffled from office to office with no one agreeing to discuss either matter. Oblivious to the suicidal tone of his mission, James would fume to Mary, "I am ... afraid I am going to wax wroth about their treatment of Norman." Eventually he would receive annual travelling expenses of $1,000, but his pay never equalled that of his central Canadian colleagues.

Norman was never exonerated. He retreated to Winnipeg where Cyprian Pinkham was now the canon of St. John's and the Archdeacon of Manitoba. He and Jean had moved to the St. John's parish and built a new Rothney Cottage. The visit coincided with the Winnipeg land boom of 1881-82, a result of the decision of the CPR to locate its main western depot in the city. Land speculation was mind-boggling. Even Holy Trinity Church held a meeting to discuss selling their prime Winnipeg property and moving further out of town. Thousands of dollars changed hands daily as real estate manipulators worked up the prices. Tent cities surrounded the town. Garbage and teenage drunks littered the streets. It was not the peaceful village Norman had visited in 1876. He returned to Drynoch, a broken, embittered man until his death.

In July 1881 the issue of Sitting Bull drew to a close. Christin Drever, who had once visited the great warrior with James, had remembered him as "a nice quiet man with blue spectacles." Now the beaten Sitting Bull and his people were drifting ever closer to the border, collecting as much flour from the NWMP as they could. Filled with mistrust, the chief finally handed his rifle to a Mountie on July 19, gave a brief speech, then crossed the line and surrendered to the U.S. army. On December 15, 1890, Sitting Bull was killed by the United States cavalry in front of his hut at Grand River, Dakota.

In 1882 the Marquis of Lorne became the first governor general of Canada to visit the prairies. En route to Fort Macleod, he had attended services in Archdeacon Pinkham's parish of St. John's rather than in the cathedral. At age thirty-three, Cyprian was famous for his sermons, which were unfailingly compassionate, humorous and brief. After leaving Winnipeg, the governor general travelled west with the NWMP in regal style, the force a striking contrast to the Indians and halfbreeds left about the land. They arrived to a massive Fort Macleod reception at which the marquis and Princess Louise were welcomed by an Indian interpreter called Dirty Dan. Greeting the governor general in the name of the Blackfoot nation, Dirty Dan acknowledged the marquis's royal connections with, "I'm told the Queen's your ma-in-law on accounta you're married to a daughter of her'n."

During the initial ceremonies, the Macleods were noticeably missing. Lord Lorne sent his aide to Pincher Creek specifically to invite them to a vice-regal reception. But Mary had become so accustomed to formal attire and James's former NWMP uniform for such occasions, she felt they would be inappropriately dressed. The once-moccasined child was now a western doyenne and argued that as James did not own a top hat, he would look ridiculous in an evening suit and stetson. Her own dresses were, she felt, beyond repair. She turned to the aide and said, "We cannot go."

He replied, "I'm sorry, Mrs. Macleod, but this is a command." So James cheerfully strode off bareheaded, and the earth child of the Red River Settlement regained her senses. Mary put on an old black dress with holes in the elbows, swept up her hair and joined her husband. Throughout the entire reception, no one noticed that she had eliminated the holes by blackening her elbows with shoe polish.

So popular were the Macleods and so confident were they of their own position in the West that Mary impulsively invited the governor general and his wife to visit their Pincher Creek log home. Nestled on the bank halfway down to the river, surrounded by evergreens, birch, cottonwoods and poplars, it was a site fit for royalty. Beyond, hills undulated westward towards a stunning view of the Rocky Mountains.

Although he was delighted with the idea of visiting the Macleods, the governor general's hectic schedule precluded the possibility. Then, as if in conspiracy, nature created such a terrible storm that all routes out of the area became a sea of mud. As the royal camp was close to Pincher Creek, Lord Lorne and his princess simply disappeared for two days with the Macleods.

Receiving almost no notice of their pending arrival, Mary raced to dust and decorate her already spotless home. She quickly snipped long strips of red flannel from the children's panties, then tacked them along the edge of their bookcases for decoration. Firing up the wood stove, she roasted a well-aged venison for the dinner. Lord Lorne later complimented her, "This is the best elk I ever tasted." The delighted hostess explained, "I scraped three quarters of an inch of green rind off it before cooking."

The following morning after James's prayer service, everyone stood up but the marquis. He remained on his knees, spellbound by the British newspapers with which Mary had papered the living room. The rain had ceased, the day had dawned sunny. After breakfast the Macleods rode westward into the hills with the royal couple. Upon reaching a high ridge, they looked down onto a herd of cattle grazing in the verdant hills. It was a similar view of splendour which had inspired Lord Lorne to paraphrase Psalm 121 into the famous hymn, "Unto the hills around do I lift up my longing eyes." He exclaimed, "This really is God's country. If I were not governor general, I'd be a rancher in Pincher Creek!" On his return to Ottawa he officially named the western portion of the North-West Territories after his wife's last name, Alberta. Months later James and Mary received a silver cigar box from the marquis with a misspelt "Mcleod" engraved on the top. James ignored Mary's delight, eyeing the error and recalling the ancient foes of the clan Macleod. He remarked, "He may be a wonderful man but he's a Campbell."

The advent of the railway brought dynamic changes to the West. James's judicial responsibilities increased a hundredfold. By the time the rails were slammed across the prairie into Calgary, it was 1883 and some eight hundred settlements had swelled into villages or burst into towns. Court cases in arrears overwhelmed James. He could no longer keep pace with the exploding crime rate and exclaimed to his old friend, Conrad, "I say with you, blast the C.P.R.! It has brought us a sort of bastard civilization.... The women are all frills – bosh and humbug – and the men, well ... such a conglomeration no one ever saw."

To ease the load, the North-West Territories was divided into four judicial districts, one of which became James's territory of Alberta. This reduced his responsibilities to 75,000 square miles. Concurrent with his court circuit came the task of moving the North-West Council to the newly created town of Regina. It had already been moved from Swan River to Battleford, and now Regina, a more focal point in the proliferating settlements. With the Dominion government in control, the lieutenant-governor and resident council of five still presided and, with James, helped to frame legislation designed to guide the North-West Territories toward responsible government.

If James and Mary had hoped a judgeship would enable them to be together more often, they were disillusioned. Their lives became a litany of travel only partially eased by the weekly stagecoach service to Fort Macleod. James's court circuits can still be traced by the postmarks on his letters. He wrote to Mary from Feorly, Lethbridge, Medicine Hat, Regina, as Alberta's population soared to 21,000. But ironically, the railway which brought him home faster than ever also provided the increased opportunity for Mary to head east. Rather than unite them, the railway as often divided them as she visited her children at school in Winnipeg, or connected with established society in Manitoba and Ontario. It is impossible to understand all of her trips, for she convinced James to burn her letters.

Never did James complain that she had gone, only that he missed her. His letters were filled with hope that she would either "come down" or "come up," depending upon which direction of the river she had taken. Reading his responses to the letters he burned, Mary must have been equally as desiring, their love expressed with passionate intensity throughout a lifetime of separations.

James would often sign his letters, "In haste," but they remain littered with vignettes of a frontier society grasping at civility. He refused a wild party at Commissioner Irvine's which ended in an early morning party of blindman's-buff; he described a July ball at Regina's Government House; he sketched a tea and scone scene with Mrs. Forget, the French wife of the future lieutenant-governor; he wrote of completing tariffs and ordinances by candlelight; he marvelled at those dear old Rockies; he complained of those leaky broad-nibbed pens.

One frequent subject of complaint concerned the lack of funds with which to run their expanding household. The Macleods loved to entertain and to drive their "noble greys" or "fine blacks." Perhaps no magistrate's pay east or west could have maintained the luxury of such steeds. In Montreal, Justice Alexander Cross had his practice, his mortgage income and his dividends to support the Pine Avenue stables, but James had never saved. While he attempted to augment his salary by breeding horses for the NWMP and raising cattle, his absences were too frequent and the ventures proved unsuccessful.

In 1883 Mary oversaw the building of their new home, Kyleakin, in Pincher Creek, then took the children east. James subsequently described the progress of their "dear little home," with six-stall stable, a loose box and a carriage house with harness room. When Mary's china and other furnishings arrived, he opened the boxes and congratulated her on her perfect choices.

For the itinerant Macleods, the Pinkhams formed a powerful fulcrum between east and west. Mary often remained in Winnipeg or took along some of Jean's children with her to Drynoch, Ontario. Sometimes the Pinkham children would summer with the Macleods in Pincher Creek. In this way the younger generation met cousins and grandparents across the country from Calgary to Toronto. No one knew who would drop in or where. One beautiful evening, James arrived unexpectedly in Winnipeg, where Nell was attending St. John's School. He gazed in a window of Rothney Cottage to see his niece, Mary Pinkham, playing the piano. Old William Drever sat in his huge black boots, his white hair flowing and his eyes gazing with weariness. At eighty-one, his leathery face and his large gnarled hands looked like the land itself. William was witness to his prediction that the Red River Settlement would someday become the Chicago of the north.

As for the brothers-in-law, they shared common bonds of courage, magnetism and purpose. Just as James travelled throughout his 75,000-square-mile jurisdiction to interpret, maintain and develop the law, Archdeacon Pinkham and Archdeacon John McKay (Maggie Drever's husband) snowshoed throughout the north to care for their parishes. Both were becoming legendary figures – ubiquitous spiritual fathers travelling through frozen wastelands to reach their children.

Jean Pinkham wrote that Cyprian often travelled by dogsled to bring the Anglican service to the Indians. When she accompanied him, neither thought anything of nursing a sick Indian child through the night, an opened umbrella keeping bugs from falling from the ceiling onto their heads. On one occasion Cyprian was travelling by stagecoach when a hurricane wind struck from the northwest. Blinded by snow, the driver and horses lost their way and the passengers suffered frostbite. Cyprian transformed the freezing coach into a chapel on wheels, and throughout the night its parishioners sang all the hymns and psalms they knew. The morning sunrise showed they were some eighteen miles off course, but all were alive. Unfailingly and at times magically, whatever privations Cyprian had experienced en route, he held services in the starched, spotlessly white robes of his calling.

Christin Drever considered the West too unrefined. During a four-month trip to Fort Macleod, she had found Mary's home filled with dust and the countryside howling with winds all the time. She had been raised in the era of relative comfort at Rothney Cottage and was relieved to return to Winnipeg. In 1883, she married John ("Jermy") Pascoe Jephson, a Cambridge lawyer who had arrived in Winnipeg. The couple moved to Calgary where Jermy became one of the new breed of western lawyers.

These youthful, argumentative lawyers came with the settlers. They invaded James's territory and slowed his court proceedings with a multitude of witnesses, cross-examinations and legal bafflegab. Once, in exasperation, he roared, "What we need out west is less law and more justice!" He would always prefer the expeditious one-man trials, himself as judge. On the other hand, as the lawyers enlivened the courtroom scene, James could not resist poking fun at them to Mary: "I held Court last night from 7 o'clock till after nine and disposed of over 30 cases. I had not much difficulty, not withstanding the array of lawyers. One, an English Barrister, I took down somewhat. He wears an eyeglass and carries a huge Barrister's bag (which he lays on the table in the most conspicuous manner) with his initials marked in silk...."

Of Calgary in 1883, James wrote, "There is a general air of prosperity about the place. One of the streets is called after me. I told them I would rather have it called after my wife. They insisted upon having both names. So another is called St. Mary. Was ever so appropriate an addition made to the name of a perfect woman?"

By the fall, James was in Fort Macleod while Mary remained east with the children. Following so many months of separation from his family, he determined to spend Christmas with them at Drynoch. But the demands of the Territorial Council in Regina were heavy and he was kept busy into December. One North-West Territories judge, H. Richardson, said that James was the only man who could push the bills through. Consequently, by holding them up until James returned to council, they created a huge backlog.

In November James wrote to Mary from Kyleakin that he expected to catch the train east during the second week in December. He described his exhausting whistle-stopping trips, hearing one case here, another there. On one occasion when the temperature fell to 22 below he was unable to write because the ink was frozen in its well. Nevertheless, the man who hated paperwork pressed on, developing ordinances for the future Legislative Assembly on a creaky table with three candles, until his hands were too cold to write. No one would disagree that James had done his duty. It was time for a well-deserved reunion.

Early in December Sir Alexander Campbell telegraphed James to head immediately for Edmonton. Six months of cases were backlogged because the judge in that jurisdiction had left the job undone. Under pressure to provide sufficient judiciary, the government could not afford to have James take a holiday. In ten years, James's superiors either had never adjusted to the vast distances and the time involved to reach destinations, or they did not care. One fact, they knew their man.

On December 7, en route to Edmonton, James discovered that an engineers' strike threatened to close down the trains over Christmas. But he remained on the Calgary platform and waved off the last train heading east with a group of laughing friends. No mail was even tossed off for him – it had been taken off by mistake somewhere in Saskatchewan. Fighting back the lump in his throat he watched the departing train until it was out of sight, then started northward. He travelled by wagon as far as Red Deer, then switched to an open sleigh. The first two nights he slept in houses, the next two under the stars with the cutter thrown up as shelter and a roaring fire at his feet.

James raced through the cases in Edmonton, "Holding his own with the lawyers" and planning to catch a Calgary train by December 18. That would get him to Toronto by December 25. He dreamed of his Christmas Eve rendezvous with Mary in Toronto, then out to Drynoch in time for Christmas Day service with the children and his mother. But the rail strike continued and James was left in Alberta. As a compromise, he determined to return to his Pincher Creek home for Christmas. There at least he would have memories of Mary and the children. So on Christmas Eve, James turned southward. He was invited to spend that night in a lodge with his other western family, the Blackfoot Indians. They all slept before a fire in the centre, shadows of white man and Indian flickering and blending like those of the boy, James, and the Ojibwa in his Drynoch home. Fired by the need to reach Kyleakin, he returned to the trail long before daylight. All along the way he "thought of the happy faces ... with all the things Santa Claus had brought them." Throughout Christmas Day he continued sleighing south through Calgary, then on towards Fort Macleod. As he drove along James hummed his favourite hymn, "Lead Kindly Light" but when he came to the words, "... and I am far from home," tears flooded his eyes and froze on his face. He wrote Mary, "It was you of whom I thought, and for a short time I felt quite maddened at the distance that divided us."

On Christmas night, James built a huge fire and camped under the stars. While Mary, the children and Jane Macleod dressed in velvet and celebrated at Drynoch with turkey, fine wines and Christmas crackers, James wrapped himself in buffalo hides, munched bacon and hardtack and toasted them with a cup of tea. He could have stopped at a nearby ranch but preferred this silent communion with his family.

Upon reaching Pincher Creek and entering his empty home, James found Kyleakin so quiet, and a fire would not light. By candlelight he wrote to Mary, "How would you like to be sitting beside me ... just where I am now, close to the window in our old bedroom, with a bright fire burning.... To me ... it would be the supremest happiness.... A Chinook is blowing outside and the only noise I hear is its well known sigh overhead and the light tapping of the loose paper on the walls." Suddenly he discovered two letters from her awaiting him on a table. Fired by her words as if the lanterns were suddenly lit and Kyleakin was filled with gaiety, he exalted, "Darling woman, how a few words from you just electrified me. I think of them day and night – it just fires my blood to read them. Please God, before very many months are over, you will be able to convey your feelings to your heart's content."

Within a day, James returned to Calgary and carried on with court. He bunked at the barracks in Colonel Sam Steele's room. At a New Year's reception for James by his former NWMP officers, a visiting member of Parliament said that no one was spoken of from one end of the country to the other in such glowing terms as James. Following toasts and speeches in James's honour, the twenty men jumped upon their chairs and each with a foot on the table cheered themselves almost hoarse. One guest called out, "Our future Governor!" Others chorused, "He ought to be now!" A delighted James wrote to Mary, "I replied in a short speech and felt that I made rather a nice one! I fancy I hear you saying, 'Egotistical Jim.'"

In the spring of 1885, Mary returned from Drynoch via Winnipeg to find thousands of settlers squatting around the Fort Macleod – Pincher Creek area. She also found the ranchers angered. Like their Wyoming counterparts, they saw open rangeland diminishing. Mary and the children were surrounded by rustling, bootlegging, smuggling, fighting and the inevitable horse stealing. It was not an atmosphere of gentility in which to raise a family, and like a parent overseeing his angry children in their backyard scraps, James dealt particularly harshly with the horse rustlers. He still believed a man's life might depend upon his mount.

When Louis Riel called for a great confederacy of the Indian nation during that spring, James felt sure that the Blackfoot nation would never join such a battle. As the press fuelled threats of a war, he complained of "the usual overblown rumours making sensational headlines in the press." In a letter to Mary, he poked fun at the government meetings and classified information of which he was part: "The outcome of the whole thing, which, remember, is a profound secret – is that we are all going to be swallowed up by the Halfbreeds and Indians – next spring. Early." But despite James's light-hearted comment, the Cree Indians and then Riel's men battled the whites with devastating results. Sir John A. Macdonald mobilized armies: one under the command of General Middleton in Ontario, a militia from Alberta and Saskatchewan Territories under General Strange and Colonel Sam Steele, and the NWMP under Commissioner Irvine. General Strange was a retired rancher who affected flowing white hair and a monstrous hat. From Calgary, James wrote of him to Mary: "Gen. Strange is unremonstrably a little bit crazy. He and I have had a long talk tonight. He tells me that Police were not wanted at Macleod and he was ready to march to Edmonton or Battleford with his whole command etc. etc. I answered by ordering 20 of his men and one gun here."

Reluctant to volunteer for service, as he wished to remain near his family, James went about his work, writing that he still considered talk of a great war "a lot of puffery." Sir John A. Macdonald appointed Dewdney, now lieutenant-governor of the North-West Territories, to negotiate for peace with the Blackfoot, while James was assigned to hear the grievances of the Halfbreed Commission. He wrote to Mary: "I lunched with the Dewdneys today. He spoke to me about a lot of public matters – *privately*. Sir John has told him to do so.... Everything is as quiet as ditch water and there is not the slightest danger of any Indian trouble in this part of the world. Irvine says the Bloods are all anxious to be allowed to go for the Crees."

From Fort Macleod to Calgary some five thousand Indians – Blood, Peigan, Sarcee, Blackfoot, Stony and Cree – paced restlessly. Mary learned what was happening in Riel's headquarters at faraway Batoche by smoke signals which spiralled into the sky in rapid succession across the prairie. They were immediately interpreted by an ancient

Indian woman camped near Kyleakin. Despite the tension, both Mary and Nell, aged nine, understood that white women must never, ever, show fear. They continued planting their spring garden, and each time the winds blew precious topsoil away over the harsh prairie, they stubbornly brought in more.

When Chief Crowfoot eventually sent a message to the prime minister saying, "I have the young men in hand. None will join the Crees," Macdonald telegraphed back, "The good words of Crowfoot are appreciated by the big chiefs in Ottawa ... [and] shall be sent to the Queen." This message was published in the newspapers. It prompted Norman Macleod, back at Drynoch, to comment to his daughter Bessie on the prime minister's "weakness in issuing it [the message] before licking the Métis into submission. By doing so he has made a laughing stock of himself and the country.... The people at home and the newspapers all over the world ... see that the French question and nationality is the millstone which hangs about the neck of Canada and which will eventually drag her down."

Following a battle with General Middleton's army, much of which was missed by Commissioner Irvine and the NWMP, Riel surrendered and the rebellion ended. Of Louis Riel's final, controversial days in Regina, James's remarks remain frustratingly circumspect. During the trial, James wrote to Mary only, "I am still consulted by the Gov. and Irvine about difficult matters and everything has turned out right." It was his only reference to the emotion-charged trial in which Riel was judged sane and therefore guilty of treason.

Did James believe that Riel was actually sane and as such deserved to hang for treason? After worrying about Riel's body either being vandalized or being exhibited as a martyr, he concluded to Mary, "Well ... [at least] he is out of the way." He added that the weight of the entire trial had been oppressive and "I dislike being here more than I can tell you." For Mary, there was no question what Riel's fate should be. Forced to watch her father hobble on canes from his confinement in the freezing Fort Garry jail, the child of the Red River Rebellion had feared that Sir John would get "weak-kneed" and not go through with it.

Immediately following Riel's death, Dewdney reported to the prime minister that James had brought him the translation of Riel's will. Dewdney underscored the following, "It is not the will of an insane man by any means...." The lieutenant-governor added, "I am glad Macleod was here ... with Irvine ... the former has some backbone, the latter _____ ." Willie Drever ended the family discussion of his old boyhood chum and his foe in the 1870 Red River Rebellion with a conundrum. From his home in Prince Albert, he concluded to his children that Louis Riel was insane.

In 1887 Jane Macleod lived just long enough to learn that her "dearest Jamie" had been appointed Supreme Court judge in the North-West Territories. The woman who had worked so hard beside her husband to break from the Isle of Skye in 1845, then to cultivate their Upper Canada lands, died that fall. She had seen her children take their places alongside some of the nation-builders of the country or as leaders themselves. She had seen her grandchildren educated and raised with her old values of religion, work and honour. For a long period afterwards, James wrote his letters on the black-bordered paper of bereavement.

For the Drever family it was also a year of mourning. Anointed Bishop of Saskatchewan and Calgary, Cyprian Pinkham planned to move his family west. Eighty-nine-year-old William Drever would have to accompany them. In Calgary he would be with the Macleods, the Jephsons and his many grandchildren. Everyone else had left Winnipeg. But William wanted no more surprises in his life, no more changes. One day Mary and Jean Pinkham had taken him on a train ride from Winnipeg to Pembina, swooshing down the same trail over which he used to plod with the oxen and Red River carts. Once was enough. Almost in expectation of the Pinkhams selling Rothney Cottage, the Orkney lad who had signed on with the Hudson's Bay Company in 1821 fell ill and died in his home. William's passing signalled the end of a pioneer era. He left a legacy of $12,000 to be divided equally amongst his children. Today, the Drever name at the junction of Portage and Main is unknown. But a block north of the avenues named Bannatyne and McDermot is "William Street." That was all that was needed in those days. Everyone had known who he was.

October 31, 1888, marked the opening of the North-West Territories' first elected assembly of twenty-one members. It was a system in which the federal government still held broad controls over the territories. Frederick W. Haultain, the member for Fort Macleod, was appointed head of the Advisory Council and referred to as the first acting premier. Mary had helped campaign for him. Haultain announced the appointment of James to the Supreme Court of the judicial district of Southern Alberta; his salary would be $4,000 a year plus travelling expenses. Later, James wrote of the history-making event to Mary, "Haultain made a neat speech all about the satisfaction of everybody at my elevation to the Bench." Then he sliced through the pomp and ceremony to poke fun at Edgar Dewdney, the lieutenant-governor: "He looked most uncomfortable in the uniform – his sword would insist upon getting mixed up in the chair when he tried to sit down, and getting between his legs where he sat."

James had become a symbol of justice known to every man, woman and child in the West. He could be seen almost anywhere criss-crossing the prairies with his beautiful four-in-hand black horses and shiny black carriage racing to the next hearing. Like Cyprian Pinkham in his flowing whites, the black-robed James never succumbed to mediocrity. Although the courts on his circuit were the antithesis of the trappings found in Montreal's Palais du Justice, he intended even a frontier tent to reflect the same dignity as would the Court of Queen's Bench in Quebec.

At each stop he worked far into the night, forming judgments or developing ordinances for schools and councils in the growing towns. He cursed the dripping candles and the shaky tables on which he scratched with blotchy pens, but delighted in entertaining Mary with his midnight sketches. His favourite tales were of dinner parties such as one at Judge Richardson's where one lady persisted in farting, and another in which a maid fought with her mistress, then retaliated by washing her hands and dumping the basin of dirty water into the salad bowl. He filled his letters with anecdotes of mini-clashes between imperial dignity and frontier faux pas, and upon learning that Calgary had received its first electric service, immediately called Mary "my electric girl."

Stories of Commissioner Irvine littered James's letters. He lived in Regina at "Poverty Flat," where James often stayed. One time at four in the morning Irvine burst into James's room with a bottle of whiskey, "dancing about like the Lord Chancellor in 'Iolanthe.'" Irvine was still angered that General Middleton was acknowledged as the only national hero after the Riel Rebellion. Sir John A. Macdonald had awarded the general with a knighthood and $20,000 for his brief role while ignoring the militia and the ten-year peace-keeping efforts made by the NWMP. For once, James took a more philosophical view of political hero-hood and the follies of patronage, and cheerfully complained that his old friend was getting to be a perfect nuisance.

James often slept on the floors of his makeshift courtrooms, riding out at three in the morning to rendezvous with a passing train.

Sometimes he just camped beside the tracks until an engine came shuffling by and picked him up for the next court hearing. He often augmented his peripatetic itinerary by using the narrow-gauged private railway built by the Galt family from Lethbridge to Medicine Hat. He was in constant demand in the territorial council and he claimed he could hardly walk from one end of the room to the other without a half-dozen members tackling him with various problems. Expected to attend an increasing number of state dinners and balls, James remarked to Mary on the latest, "I have not the slightest interest in it except it should be numbered amongst the things of the past."

One time when Mary was east, James wrote from their new, larger home they had rented in Macleod. "The barrel and box of china just arrived. My darling ... it is just like everything you do, just the thing.... I hear old Annie [Auntie] has got religion. She is, I believe, one day filled with one kind of spirit and the next with another kind! ... As you asked me to do so, I burnt your letters today after a long meditation."

At times on the circuit, James became so lonely that he paid for his entire family to join him in Regina. His influence on his children was far more benign than his own father's had been on him. One can hardly imagine Captain Martin Macleod ever writing a letter to his son such as the following one James wrote to his eight-year-old Norman. Expressing pleasure over the fact that Norman had got a saddle despite some altercation, James added, "It shows that it was a good plan to give Buff Henry a black eye. You just do the same thing to anyone who does not keep his promises, but take care you don't get one yourself. Write me another letter, you dear little chap. Your fond father, Jimbo."

Over the previous decade the West had developed from a one-man show into complex departments. Various agents now dealt with the multifarious issues, intending to streamline the mushrooming bureaucracy of large-scale settlement. From James's point of view the agents messed everything up, hampering the expeditious and personal manner with which he had run affairs. And although he no longer had official dealings with the Indians, they still considered him as the Queen's emissary, their friend who had given his word at Treaty 7, and who had presided over the treaty's 1883 and 1885 amendments.

Thus in 1888, starving, diseased and barely living through farming, the Indians demanded a grievance meeting with Justice Macleod. James declined. It was no longer his "department." Demands on his time were extraordinary and although few knew it, he was ill. At forty-eight he was suffering from Bright's disease, a chronic condition of kidneys and heart, as well as from a painful stomach destroyed by warming his chilled limbs with too many brandies. The only cure was absolute rest.

The grievance hearing was arranged instead with Indian agents Neale and Pocklington. James met with the government emissaries beforehand to brief them on Indian policy, and was dismayed by their lack of understanding of the issues, and by their lack of interest in general. He complained to Mary that instead of talking about Indians, Pocklington had launched into a story of his latest hunt with the Prince of Wales: "... didn't I have an hour or so of the most *pronounced English*.... I managed to get them back to the Blood Indians and Indian policy generally."

In the ensuing conference, 250 Bloods and North Peigans expressed complaints ranging from infringement of timber rights to James Macleod's desertion. White Calf said he thought it strange that Judge Macleod could always attend to the whites and would not come to hear the Indians. Chiefs Red Crow and Morning Plume also expressed their annoyance at James's refusal to come, and reminded the agents of the promises made at the Blackfoot Crossing:

> Judge Macleod runs this part of the country. The Bloods are talking for their country as Judge Macleod used to talk for his. Why does he not come here and hear us talk?... We think the Queen is not treating us right. Our letters never reach her. They only get half way and are destroyed. Take pity on your children. Don't give us a handful of tea again. Don't give us any more of that tobacco. It smells bad. Write to the Great Mother ... and ask for more rations. We had something to say to Judge Macleod but he is not here.

This was the last known official contact between James and the great Blackfoot nation. It was the end of an era for them both, the proud Indians decimated and James pressing on with the complexities of civilization and a fledgling North-West Territories government. Save for a continuing personal interest in the Indians, he had done all he could.

In 1889 the Pinkham family learned that a rental home was finally available in Calgary. They moved west permanently. Almost immediately upon arrival, Cyprian left for a four-month trip by dogsled to the north. As Bishop of Saskatchewan and Calgary, his diocese was the largest both in Canada and in the Anglican world.

Jean settled their seven children into a small frame house situated in a gravel pit at Third and Sixty Street West. A May snowstorm was raging and some of the windows were missing. She found the frontier town a far cry from the grassy slopes of her Winnipeg parishes. In the ensuing summer drought, she pined for the St. James parish on the bank of the Assiniboine River and the sophistication of Winnipeg. By comparison, Calgary was a "barren wilderness.... I do not believe we had a drop of rain that first year, one dust storm after another, everything gritty, one's eyes, ears and mouth were full of dust." Eventually, when a waterworks scheme was developed, Jean Pinkham found that trees, shrubs and flowers could be grown there as well as in any part of Canada. Their little house, known as "Bishop's Court," became a focus for Calgary just as Mary's home was in Fort Macleod.

As chairman of the new Alberta-Saskatchewan Board of Education, Cyprian continued raising money (often in England) to build schools based on the philosophy of the British greats, Eton and Cambridge. Nevertheless, children in Pincher Creek were not the beneficiaries of this education. Mary and James Macleod wanted Nell and Norman, now eleven and nine, to experience broader academic challenges than were available even in Winnipeg's St. John's College. Perhaps they also wanted them to be exposed to the central Canada they loved. Mary may have used some of her father's legacy to send Nell east to Bishop Strachan's School, Toronto, and Norman to Trinity College, Port Hope, Ontario.

Nell Macleod was growing into a willowy, dark-haired beauty who rode like the wind and seemed as fearless as her mother. She was a combination of frontier toughness and the romantic, recording her love for the simplicity and fury of nature in a grey-toned sketch book. To her, the prairie winds and broad expanse of sky reflected her wonder of the Lord. Her faith ran as deep as that of her grandmother and namesake, Helen Rothney Drever.

Nell's introduction to Alberta society came at a time when central Canadian and British financiers were buying huge tracts of land for ranches. Many of the Montana and Wyoming cattle barons had driven their herds north to Alberta. The influx of beef and money was enormous. Ranches were often run by the titled if black sheep of the family. English and American customs blended, and as in

Wyoming, formal dress for riding by day or dining by night became de rigeur. In Fort Macleod, the Macleods' home often swelled with up to twenty for dinner followed by amateur theatricals and charades.

The Indians loved these events and gathered to watch gentlemen ride in with their evening clothes in gunnysacks thrown over their saddles. They peeked in the windows of the Macleods' home to see ladies dressed in outdated gowns, wildflowers gracing their hair. They watched one doyenne from Ontario stunned to find herself beside an Indian princess with neatly braided hair, a clean cotton wrapper, moccasins, and long white gloves. The guests would usually spend the night, the men curling up in sleeping bags in the halls. On Sundays in particular, James would stand outside his front door inviting any who rode by to come in for dinner. A gentleman scouting for land or playing a polo match was always a welcome guest. Cowboys down on their luck came in the back door where they were fed and allowed to spread their blankets near the kitchen stove.

James was continually broke. He often gave his clothes away to those less privileged and lent money though he had little of his own. He had never heeded his father's admonition to build his own insurance fund. He lived life to the hilt and loved buying furs for Mary. Wealthy beyond measure in ideals and laughter, he could never balance his bank books.

An unknown writer once described James as "A happy combination of the gentleman of the old school and a man of the world and affairs. He had a manner which put a stranger at his ease but at the same time prevented undue familiarity." At home this reserved judge loved to throw on his judicial robes and, flapping his "wings," race through the house playing tag with his squealing children. He often romped on the floor and occasionally turned the garden hose on the children when starched into their Sunday best. In playful taunts outside, they teased their father, "Stomach Sodium! Stomach Sodium!" their translation of the Blackfoot's "Stamix Otokan." The only time Norman ever recalled his father's anger was when he playfully pointed a pop gun at James, yelling, "Stick 'em up!" Seizing the gun, James roared, "Never point a gun at anyone, even as a joke!" Aware that their father was a most important personage, the children were also exposed to his humility as they watched him hold court in his study. Ranchers, Mounties and Indians came and went, while a chronic offender called Turkey Legs sat on the bottom step suckling her baby.

Whether Mary held domestic court in Fort Macleod, with Jean Pinkham or with Christin Jephson in Calgary, the West belonged to this family. Even Adam Thom paid tribute to the memory of Helen Rothney Drever when he ran into the Pinkhams on a London street. Perhaps old Thom was alluding to the enforced salary for his former nannie when he presented Jean with a copy of his book, *The Pentaglot*, inscribed, "From Doctor Thom to Mrs. Pinkham, whose mother and himself, in the spring of 1839, sailed together from London to the Red River Settlement: She to become the founder of her husband's fortunes...."

Whenever James could, he attended Cyprian's church services. He also served on Bishop Pinkham's synod, which in turn encompassed Archdeacon John McKay's diocese of Qu'Appelle. Brother-in-law J.P. Jephson, Q.C., Christin Drever's husband and lawyer for a budding industrial community, cared for any legal needs in the family and often argued cases before James. Known as a lawyer with a brilliant if scathing wit, Jephson had recently become the legal adviser to Ernest Cross. Together with the Drever sisters, these men created a network of influence throughout the West.

13

The Winter of 1886-87

"It Depends on the Weather."
    The ranchers' creed.

Ernest returned to Montreal after filing for his Alberta homestead
and proposed a Cross family venture. He explained that if two or
more of his brothers bought land adjacent to his own, and they took
advantage of the government policy to lease up to 100,000 acres
at annual rents of 1 cent per acre, the Crosses would control the
huge Mosquito Creek water resources south of Calgary. All they
needed, he assured his father, was a little capital combined with energy
and perseverance. If Alexander would supply the former, he and his
brothers had plenty of the latter. He also argued that by starting
with a purebred herd instead of mongrels as had Harry, profits would
be more quickly realized. He painted such an exciting picture of the
life out west that both Edmund and Willie Heber agreed to return
with him.

Alexander was also captivated by Ernest. Within this son lay the
Cross financial spirit and the driving character of his Scottish ancestry.
Ernest's arguments made sense to Alexander, for the British-oriented
West promised greater stability for investment than had the wild
American frontier. He could keep track of his funds more easily
and see that they were utilized productively. He agreed to loan the
boys money to establish a purebred livestock herd. The Crosses
subsequently took out a 60,000-acre grazing lease; but despite their
powerful connections, they never intended to raise funds in Montreal
or England to establish a spread as large as the British American
Ranche. It meant starting smaller, but Crosses did things themselves
and maintained personal control over their ventures.

On the outskirts of Montreal in April 1886, Ernest and Edmund loaded a thoroughbred stud, two young Clydesdale mares, a Clyde stallion and twenty-seven purebred Shorthorns onto their Calgary-bound train. Their finest cow was named Maggie 13th. Waving goodbye to Willie Heber, who was first going to Paris before following in the spring, the brothers set out for Alberta Territory. One week later they stepped off the train at Calgary into a howling blizzard. One of their heifers had lost its balance and had been trampled to death in its boxcar. Undaunted, the Crosses established quarters at the Alberta Hotel, then increased their herd to 334 head by purchasing one hundred British Columbia cows, one hundred calves, twenty steers, eight bulls and eighty heifers. Planning to breed stock for the NWMP, they bought 145 horses and twenty-two colts. Finally, they purchased provisions for their homestead but bought none for the cattle. The custom of the day was to put up some hay and let the herds forage for themselves.

In May Ernest paid the Calgary Dominion Lands Office for his homestead, listed as the west half of Section 12, Township 16, Range 29, west of the fourth meridian. Aiming to one day breed the best beef in Alberta, he was disappointed when his proffered "A1" brand was rejected. Officials figured it an easy mark for rustlers. The alternative suggestion, "a7," was granted on May 26 under the registered name of Cross Brothers Limited. Some claim the "7" stood for the seven Cross brothers.

Believing they had met every contingency, the pair straightened their business suits, then swung into their saddles and drove their herd southwards. En route the seasoned Ernest advised Edmund on everything from protecting a herd against storms in winter and flies in summer to finding a lost horse. He was relaxed and, like Harry, thrilled with his new herd. Suddenly his horse shied, threw him, and raced toward the foothills. As the expert picked himself up, a delighted Edmund gave chase. Following a day and a night of search, a cowboy found the bronco and charged Ernest $20 for his trouble. To Ernest's embarrassment, Edmund told Alexander, who promptly related his son's folly to Harry in Wyoming.

In June the brothers received word that Grandpapa Lunn had died. Lunn had intended to celebrate his ninetieth birthday the following month in grand style. He had survived the original co-incorporators of the Montreal General Hospital, his magistrate colleagues, his fellow aldermen and the members of various Montreal school boards. His religious and educational exhortations, combined with his earthy lifestyle, had been an inspiration to them all. Following a service at the Sherbrooke Street home, the funeral cortège proceeded up Côte des Neiges to Mount Royal Cemetery. There the Portsmouth boy with the entrepreneurial spirit and the warehouse of Bibles was laid to rest.

From Alberta to Wyoming, that summer of 1886 proved a sweltering, rainless nightmare. Hot winds seared the prairie grasses and fissured the dried creekbeds. South of Calgary, Ernest threw himself into preparing his homestead. Upon completing the sod shack and barn, the brothers began harvesting the hay. For Ernest, the back-breaking work was rewarding but for Edmund it was horrible. While Ernest's actions were almost frenetic, the eighteen-year-old pitched hay languidly into the loft. A shady tree with a cool drink was more Edmund's style.

Before long, black clouds began forming on the horizon. While a welcome sight for the parched land, if the hay got soaked in the field, it could go mouldy. Eyeing the clouds, Ernest stepped up his pace and yelled at his brother to do likewise. Instead, Edmund hung up his pitchfork and, complaining that everyone always pushed him around, slouched out of the barn. Ernest pitched hay furiously throughout the day and into the evening by lantern light. He had learned the bitter way how each man's concept of work could differ. Upon returning to the shack at ten o'clock, he fell exhausted onto his straw mattress without eating or even removing his boots. The rain never came. Edmund remained sullen.

In Wyoming, Harry worried that the cattle had lost weight and would face a winter with no body fat. Léa remarked on the abnormal number of spiders crawling about their cabin. The coats of deer and jack rabbits had bleached a lighter colour. All were omens of an early and hard winter. Accustomed to chilling Quebec winters, Léa laughingly quoted childhood jingles that warned of bitter times ahead. American cattle barons grew alarmed at the huge numbers of thirst-crazed cattle on overgrazed land. They drove thousands of cattle and sheep north into Alberta, hoping for better grass, water and weather. The land was there all right, but the weather was the same. While Harry, Ernest and Edmund had no way of communicating with each other, they would soon be inextricably bound in mutual suffering for an entire two-thirds of the year.

Tragedy struck suddenly. One evening in mid-October, the sun set into a grey cloud bank over Braehead, Wyoming. In Alberta, Ernest and Edmund also watched the sky darken. Cattle bunched under trees along the dried creekbeds. Soon the winds roared, sand swirled through the cracks in Braehead, Wyoming, and sparks flew from the stove in the sod shack in Alberta. Rain began to pelt the cabins, then hail thundered down before turning to snow. The next morning the countryside from Wyoming to Alberta was silent, save for the cracking of tinder-dry boughs breaking under a foot of snow. Before anyone could recover, storm after freezing storm swept over the land to immobilize men and livestock. Hungry cows bawled for food that wasn't there. By December the brothers' homesteads were entombed by snow. When Harry dug out and walked along the creek smashing holes in the ice looking for water, he found fish frozen solid. On the banks, the starving cattle had gnawed at and delimbed the trees. Nothing was left save the tall skeletal trunks with a few upper limbs poking upright through the drifts.

As one month blended with another, the moans of starving cattle haunted the Crosses. It was a time of trial that exposed each brother's character as never before. In Alberta, Ernest proved curiously immune to the cold and would toss just one jacket on and head out to do the chores. Edmund was appalled and dressed for the outdoors like a man about to assault Mount Everest. Ernest wrote to his mother describing her pampered son's timid attitude toward the outdoors; Edmund layered his body with woollens, flannels and leathers, then pulled on a fur cap and wound two woollen scarves about his face. Only after jamming two pairs of woollen gloves and a pair of leather mitts on his hands would he waddle outside. By then Ernest had all but completed the chores and was preparing to return. It was just as well, for thus bundled up and sweating, Edmund quickly chilled.

When the two returned inside they were forced to wait for the warmth of the stove to thaw their jackets and pants before they could haul them off. They hung Edmund's pounds of woollens from lines stretched from wall to wall under the sod roof. As the heat from the wood stove penetrated the garments, steam rose and enveloped the brothers in a pungent smell that Ernest would never forget. In the near darkness, oil lamps shining on the line of long johns threw ghoulish shadows onto the walls. The clothes almost obliterated their light while they ate corned beef and drank "tin cow" or canned milk. For luxury they drank Johnny Walker, and Ernest smoked Simon Roosevelt cigars. Their few copies of *Punch* and the *Illustrated London News* became quickly thumbworn. At night they turned in on straw ticks piled six-high with blankets and buffalo robes, then blew out the lamp standing on a trunk filled with Hodgkins shirts from London.

In Wyoming the saying went around that when a man died he went straight to heaven as he'd already been to hell in the winter of 1886-87. During the coming months Harry often wondered if he should have studied law at McGill as his father had wished. Instead he read American law by candlelight. He felt guilty about Léa giving up her planned teaching career, but she was content to have him read stories to her while she knitted by the fire. Temperatures of over 63 below zero broke their outdoor thermometer. Before Harry dressed to go outside, Léa wrapped his body with newspapers: "The power of the press," she teased. But women knew that when their husbands headed for the barns, they might never return. Men lost their way in the blizzards and froze to death just feet from their cabins. Some tied lines between their buildings like umbilical cords to the homestead.

One day Harry found a Longhorn cow in the chicken house. A line of chickens warmed her back. A rooster with frozen legs hobbled around underneath trying to stabilize himself with his wings. On his way back Harry found Bell, the milking cow, frozen upright against the side of the house. Her eyeballs were as hard as marbles. When Léa feared her husband would never return, he burst through the door clenching his teeth to keep them from chattering. With a smile that was more of a grimace, he recited Rudyard Kipling's limerick:

There was a small boy from Quebec,
Who was buried in snow to his neck.
When they asked, "Are you friz?"
He replied, "Yes, I is,
But we don't call this cold in Quebec!"

No cow from Wyoming to Alberta would escape the ravages of starvation that winter. When one absentee cattleman inquired about the welfare of his herd, his foreman was incapable of replying. Instead he found artist Charlie Russell in a bar and asked him to help. Russell's sketch showed a humourless caricature, a collapsing skeleton pushing through folds of sagging hide. Underneath he wrote, "This is the real thing . . ."

One evening Harry returned chilled and miserable, having lost count of his dying herd. Léa stunned him. "Happy Christmas Eve!" she smiled. With what he described as bits of nothing, she had decorated the cabin and prepared a feast. She gave him hand-knitted stockings and wristlets, and Maggie a rag doll with a bright calico dress and embroidered face. Harry just stood there looking at his family. Then he sat down and quickly whittled an empty spool and stick into a spinning top for his delighted Maggie.

In Alberta, Edmund spent his twentieth birthday at Christmas huddled in the sod shack and longing for the Elysian comforts of Pine Avenue. Each day he built his despair into a determination to flee for home with the first signs of spring. On the other hand, Ernest saw the cold as a temporary setback. There were no unbearable tomorrows for him, merely new routes to discover in reaching his goals. There was never any doubt in his mind that he would succeed. Among his papers he kept his father's credo: "Optimism is that quality in human nature which persists in looking on the bright side of every condition in life, and discovering some ray of sunshine in every cloud. Hope, long-suffering, frailty and joy are stronger than their negative forces."

As January dragged into February, Ernest and Edmund watched their purebred cattle die. Their land was flatter than an English saddle with not even a coulee to protect the herd. The hay in the barn was long gone. Seeking nourishment, starving cows sucked hair from the hides of the dead. Gradually they suffocated, their throats, mouths and stomachs clogged with hair. Out of his herd of 345, Ernest counted ten dead, then twenty-five, then sixty. When 150 were dead he went out and tied Maggie 13th to the leeward side of the shanty. It was her only hope for survival.

In January 1887 a long-awaited chinook wind brought relief in both territories. It melted snow and exposed the grass, that amazing root of survival. Prairies turned to slush, cattle began to drink and to poke around for feed. Cows calved. Families stepped outside to bask in the first rays of sun and warmth in five months. Then as suddenly as she had warmed the land, nature snatched back her gift and shrouded the prairies in a watery freeze. A mirror of ice stretched from Alberta to Wyoming. Cattle broke through the glassy surface, slashing their legs with every step. They left trails of blood, wandered aimlessly, then slipped and fell. Soon their udders and scrota froze to the ice. Rooted thus to the earth, bulls bellowed in agony until they died. Early-born calves vainly tried to nurse from their mothers thus crippled. Blinding snow or freezing rain continued to sweep through the land with no further respite.

While their sons wrestled with survival on the western plains, Alexander and Julia suffered their own agony in Montreal. Sixteen-year-old Robert was attending the boarding school, Lincoln College, in Lennoxville. He thrived on the French community, the challenging studies and his music. Whenever he was asked what he would like for a gift Robert invariably and gratefully chose a book such as Homer's *Iliad*, or a newly published dictionary. Often he included his poetic caricatures of the masters or the boys. Alexander and Julia considered their youngest son a gift from heaven. He was the most loving, the brightest and the most motivated of all the children.

In early February, Robert and a number of other Lincoln students developed sore throats. Other boys were being sent home to escape a flu epidemic in the school and Julia requested her son's return to Pine Avenue. The headmaster not only did not send Robert home, he put another sick boy in his room. A day later Robert's roommate showed the dreaded symptoms of diphtheria.

Two days later Robert's fever shot up and he complained of excessive thirst. Although there was a doctor in the nearby town of Sorel reputed to be an expert in the disease, the headmaster never sent for him. Early one morning, five days after Robert first fell ill, a greenish-black membrane in his throat began choking him. Robert might have survived had the headmaster cut open his windpipe. The operation was successfully undertaken by many a desperate parent with many a kitchen knife. But the headmaster was unable to perform the ghastly procedure, and he later explained to Alexander that the doctor was unavailable – unfortunately he was not an early riser. Robert strangled to death.

Following an immediate investigation, Alexander launched a scathing attack against the school. He documented the progression of Robert's illness, his anguish building with his discoveries. In a written report to the headmaster he concluded, "It appears to me that willful stubbornness and gross neglect is involved in the above conduct.... I cannot therefore think otherwise than that his [Robert's] life was sacrificed and it is most attributable to you. The terrible calamity oppresses us to the verge of insanity and is likely to continue to the end of our lives." Vowing that the headmaster's, "unforgivable sins will not go unpunished," Alexander forced Lincoln College to close. All the furniture was sold. The school never reopened.

A few days after Robert's death, Selkirk, Maggie, Willie Heber, Alexander and Julia, braving the sub-zero winds, drove to Mount Royal Cemetery. Robert was temporarily laid to rest in the ice-lined mausoleum; he would be officially buried when spring temperatures thawed the ground. In May 1887 the family returned to their splendid ten-foot-high marble tombstone for Robert's graveside ceremony.

Resolute in his faith that he would meet with his children again, Alexander wrote that they were "A brightness that now moves in another heaven." Carved onto the tombstone in Latin, the epitaph read,

> Charles Edwin the cherished, Julia Mary the precious,
> Robert Arthur the perfect.
> "Album Mutor in Alitem Superne."

In May, eight devastating months after it began, the prairie winter abated. Watching suspiciously for the skies to blacken again, settlers journeyed out to check their neighbours and their livestock. It was only when the Cross brothers rode through the snowdrifts into Calgary and Fetterman for supplies and mail that they found the dreaded black-bordered envelopes. Alexander had written to Harry, "Only my misery and deep-felt suffering keeps my anger from consuming me. . . . Robert was taken from us a cherished youth so deserving of manhood but who was unfairly denied that promotion. He was blessed with a wisdom and compassion from which we . . . all feel persecuted by its unexplained and abrupt absence, causing your mother and I to take once again, that awesome walk that so nears death itself."

Each child was allocated one-sixth of Robert's four-tenths of his Hutchison estate. In desperate need of cash to replace his decimated herd, Harry sold his share to Selkirk. He would thus relinquish any accumulative value of the Hutchison estate. It did not matter to Harry. He had saved Braehead and that was all that counted. Ernest decided not to sell Robert's share, for he hoped to get by on the sales of his horses. The latter had survived the winter by pawing through ice and snow for grass, a skill unknown to cattle. Neither of the brothers requested help from their father.

In Alberta the terrible winter had claimed over 20,000 head of cattle in the country from Pincher Creek north to Calgary alone. Like other cattlemen, it was impossible for Ernest to calculate his losses on unfenced land. His herd was running with thousands of others. He first wrote his father that he estimated a loss of 12½ per cent, then 20 per cent, but it would rise to 60 per cent before his tally was complete. He faced the bitter truth that he had chosen the wrong homestead. The flat, almost treeless land had provided no refuge for cattle. Even the buffalo summered only on the flats and wintered in the more protected foothills. Still, Maggie 13th had made it tied to the side of the shack. If she could survive, so could a wiser Ernest. Bruised but undefeated, he determined to search out new land.

Despite Alexander's insistent queries, Harry just replied vaguely that things were not too bad. He never did record his total losses, perhaps feeling his parents' bereavement was too monumental to absorb another tragedy. But Ernest wrote somewhat cryptically to his father that he had learned much from Harry's disaster. In fact, the overall losses in Wyoming were horrifying and signified the end of the huge cattle herds. An estimated 425,000 of 500,000 head had perished. One cowboy from Bighorn told Harry, "In places a man could walk a half mile on dead cattle and not step on the ground." Roundups that spring were nightmares. Riders might find live cows now and then but they were too weak to be driven. From Harry's Braehead to Ernest's a7 homestead, wolves, coyotes and turkey buzzards grew very, very fat. The air was putrid with the stench of rotting cattle. Some were lodged in the treetops; others polluted the streams and rivers, floating by in bloated reminder that nature, not man, ruled the West.

Alberta's High River roundup that June proved almost as dismal as Wyoming's. Still, the surviving calves and colts gave hope to the winter-worn cowboys, and years later Ernest would see the humour in it all. Edmund had packed for Montreal, then unpacked when he heard Willie Heber was en route to help on the a7. It was the first of many times that the rotund Willie would blow in like a mistral wind to help a troubled brother.

The riders of the 1887 roundup comprised the future cast of supporting characters to Ernest Cross's lifetime. The managers and owners of the outfits were either old school friends of his also come west, or gentlemen who would become lifelong associates with the Crosses. Plenty of Lord, Lady, Sir, Viscount, and black-sheep titles were sprinkled liberally about. One was the Oxford-educated Springett, son-in-law of Sir Alexander Galt. Another friend was Walter Skrine, the Oxford-educated son of an English squire. Skrine would marry the poetess Agnes Higginson and raise a family of six. Ernest would one day write that the Skrines were one of the few remaining families of pure British stock.

The Bar U outfit, financed by the Allans of Montreal, was managed by Fred Stimson and foreman George Lane. No one ever disputed the word of Lane, unofficial boss of the cowboys. Also present was the brilliant rider John Ware, one of two negroes in the North-West

Territories. The Indians called him Bad Black White man; the white men called him Nigger John. His expertise stemmed from his slave-bound childhood when his master had made him ride broncos bareback. If thrown off, he was licked with a black snake-whip. One day Ernest was unable to control a renegade horse. John Ware switched horses and within moments had transformed the outlaw into a docile ride. Awed, Ernest wrote, "He made him stop, trot, walk, anything John took a fancy to doing."

Ernest's favourite outfit was the Little Bow Cattle Company, owned by five wild aristocratic Englishmen and Scotsmen. He described nineteen-year-old Billie Cochrane of that group as having a kiss from the devil on his cheek. Billie would often shrug, "We're a short time living and a long time dead." Known as "Bad Billie Cochrane," to distinguish him from the senator or "Good Billie Cochrane," he loved raising hell in the bordellos of Calgary. Other friends of Ernest on that 1887 roundup were H.B. Alexander, a jockey who had won the Irish Sweepstakes, and T.S.C. Lee, whose entrepreneurial zest for financing Calgary land deals gave Ernest and his father no end of headaches.

The roundup included wild horses as well and was big, each of the outfits providing their own cook and chuckwagon. Early one morning, all the outfits met on a high plateau with Lane sitting in his saddle like a general. Choosing ten of the most seasoned riders to head each contingent, he sent everyone galloping off in different directions like the spokes of a wheel. Most cowpunchers were searching for cattle, while the Cross brothers and their ten riders raced about lassoing wild horses. On the first day they roped a powerful four-year-old stallion. Ernest and several men grabbed the rawhide lariat but the horse ripped it out of their hands and took off over the hills, as Ernest put it, "like a violent Chinook wind." (Two months later they recaptured it and sold it to the NWMP.) Eventually Ernest's riders rounded up about 120 outlaws and drove them whinneying and rearing into a rope corral strung up between the two wagons. Two of the best ropers immediately worked their way into the billowing dust and began breaking the frightened broncos.

One evening Ernest's men camped some seventy-five miles from the nearest cabin. The cattle were quiet; the cowboys were settling down on their bedrolls. Only one horse was saddled and tied up near the men. Horses hate to be separated from the herd, and soon it snapped its head back, tore its reins from the brush, and raced off to join the others. As if the rope corral was straw, the 120 outlaws broke through, stampeded the cattle and thundered into the foothills. Ernest and a dozen men grabbed their boots and raced after them. Accustomed to riding, the footsore cowboys soon dropped behind until there was just Ernest. He wrote, "Somehow I managed – and it sounds conceited to say this – to single-handedly herd off the bunch." He had just quieted them when a greenhorn rushed up with a rope and threw it at one of the lead horses. The herd stampeded again. A Métis cowboy sent the exhausted wranglers back to camp. Hours later, he walked the herd back into the camp's rope corral. That night every man caught and picketed a horse. The following days they rode for hours and often got hopelessly lost. By the end of the roundup, some two thousand cattle were also driven over the fenceless prairie to their respective ranches.

During the summer of 1887, Willie Heber and Edmund helped Ernest improve the homestead. He imported more Shorthorns and a few Hereford and Galloway from Ontario and Great Britain. He bought a herd of wild British Columbia cow ponies and some half-broken saddle horses. Alexander shipped him a Cleveland bay sire to breed body, size and spirit into his horses. With his devastating losses in cattle, Ernest's intent was to sell well-bred, powerful horses to the NWMP. He did so, raising them to three-year-olds, rough-breaking them, then driving them to Calgary police barracks at a pace which tired them out. Subsequently purchased by the NWMP, the horses' behaviour remained impeccable until stabled for a night's rest and buckets of oats. The following day the high-strung mounts threw their rookie riders from one side of the parade ground to the other in a forerunner to the first NWMP musical ride.

The horses proved a good investment that year. Sales to the NWMP paid back to Cross Brothers Limited the total capital invested besides a fifty-head profit. By the end of 1887 Ernest was able to rebuild his Shorthorn herd to 357 head. Compared to other companies with 6,000 head, his beginnings were humble. Nevertheless, Alexander had taken a more lenient approach to helping him and it had made the difference.

Following the fall roundup Willie Heber and Edmund worked their way back to Montreal as cowboys shipping cattle to market. When Ernest had said goodbye to Edmund he never expected to see him back. But Willie Heber had had a great time. Alberta had proven such a contrast to the elegance of the Champs Elysées that he intended to return, as long as he was never trapped on the homestead for too long. The exhausting work had trimmed him down while providing him with that sense of purpose, that elusive purity which he periodically sought throughout his life. Willie Heber had wrestled joyfully with what frontier life had tossed his way; Edmund felt victimized by it.

The Wyoming summer following that dreadful winter encompassed all the hardships of frontier ranches juxtaposed by the boom of progress. Harry negotiated with history's first striking cowboys on one of thirty-one roundups. He wrote to Alexander that miles of barbed-wire fencing were causing hot tempers and fights. Like other ranchers, he fenced in his water to stop the settler, only to be informed of a new government rule making that illegal. He countered by digging an irrigation ditch called Cacouna. A close friend jumped his claim to lands surrounding Braehead. Shocked and angered, Harry figured Braehead's future was finished. Then he cooled down and figured a man had to get political to survive. Taking the friend on as a partner, Harry deepened his contacts with all factions – cattle barons, ranchers and farmers. Then he worked for change. In a neighbour's kitchen, he was overwhelmingly voted in as commissioner for the newly formed Converse County. His duties encompassed those of postmaster, and treasurer to the new school established for the four children ready to attend.

That fall Léa gave birth to her second child, Julia. To celebrate they wallpapered their home. First they pasted cheese cloth to the logs, then glued the wallpaper to the cloth. Trimmed in gold, the heavy beige paper glowed with small white flowers that brightened their cabin and helped keep out the wind. No more grass ever grew through the chinks.

Gradually, the collective trials of the Cross families began to lift. One month everything seemed to underscore what was the worst year in Cross history, the next the sun smiled on them. The Montreal economy improved. Calgary's population boom was so great that housing starts were two years behind; Ernest helped organize the first agricultural fair. Irrigation and greening crops from River Beaudette through Mosquito Creek to Braehead in Wyoming nourished sorrowful hearts and set visions toward future joys. The winter of 1886-87 was past.

14

Beef, Beer and the Ranching Frontier

"We never called 'em farmers. We called 'em sodbusters. . . . If cattle could drink, they'd find plenty to eat. But the Godamn sodbuster fenced in the waterholes."
J. Ryan, a7 Ranche wrangler

Alexander aged terribly in the year following Robert's death, and he wrote that Julia remained in a state of melancholy. In that year of sorrow letters connected the peripatetic family almost daily. The sons tried to buoy up their parents with their adventures, and in turn Alexander and Julia wrote of Pine Avenue and redistributed everyone's mail. It kept Montreal, Wyoming and Alberta close, and Ernest in particular learned from Harry's experiences south of the border. In Montreal, Julia recorded with alarming frequency that "Willie [Heber] is getting very stout."

Maggie, a kindly, devout young lady, travelled in a whirlwind set. She lamented not taking enough dresses to the Adirondacks with CPR lawyer John Abbott and his family. She delighted in some ball or other, and rode off to yet another hunt. "She is," mused Alexander, "what you would call a social success." Other than marrying and raising a family someday, that was all that was expected of Maggie. But she did volunteer work in the church, at the Montreal General Hospital and with the Protestant Orphanage.

In his letters to Harry in Wyoming, Ernest discussed the urgency for water rights and heeded his brother's comments on the pitfalls of stockmen's associations. Ernest was never shy about telling a joke on himself, about giving praise where it was due, or about providing everyone with news of investment potential. When he told his father that he had been asked to stand for the new Parliament of the North-West Territory but had declined, Alexander informed Harry, "I suppose he [Ernest] was frightened by the expense and the neglect that it would entail to his ranch, as both his brothers left him. Both Selkirk and I are a little sorry he declined."

Once when Harry queried his father on the sagacity of money-lending, Alexander warned, "Don't speculate." He explained that a man had to be hard and sharp to take up the pursuit, and only those who did knew its dangers: "One good venture usually puts a man off his guard so that he risks still more. In the end there are few who don't come out serious losers." Harry followed his father's advice, building slowly and steadily, never taking excessive risk, and never realizing the phenomenal financial gains of Ernest or Willie Heber. His contributions would be in establishing Braehead, and in helping to frame the laws of his adopted land.

Alexander was delighted with Harry's first political victory as commissioner of Converse County. Nevertheless, he reminded his son of his priorities: "You will, of course, have good sense enough not to allow your public service to interfere with your more profitable occupation of attending to your ranch. A conscientious fulfillment of your public duty will be a satisfaction to yourself and ought to meet with approval. . . . Above all, avoid drink."

Harry complained that trains to nearby Douglas had brought what one writer called "the rabble of the earth" nearer to Braehead. Rustlers rode amok throughout the countryside but the Wyoming Stockgrowers' Association made few arrests and convictions. Privately owned cattle disappeared off the range as quickly as did mavericks. Harry lost twenty-four in one year alone. Ranchers threatened to form vigilante groups and hang the offenders. Sod-busters, or "dirty nesters," as the Americans called them, flooded the country and fenced off more waterholes. Harry had his hands full but believed that the infractions necessitated a rational word rather than a fighting speech.

The Pine Avenue family loved Harry's story of one of his first territorial duties, which was building a jail. Not long after its completion, the sheriff mentioned that he had locked up a Canadian who was charged with poisoning the drinking water on the stage from Buffalo. Those were days when Wyoming lynch mobs would string a man up on a telephone pole without a trial or murder a lady of pleasure, such as Cattle Kate, without paying any consequences. The Canadian was lucky to have made it to jail.

"What's his name?" asked Harry.

"Osler. He's well-dressed and says he's a doctor," Sheriff Overman replied. Hardly believing it could be their family friend, Harry rode over to the jail to find Dr. William Osler sitting on a cell bunk. The convict jumped up and clasped Harry's hands through the bars. Bubbling with amusement, Osler explained that the stage driver had drawn water from a stagnant creek filled with polywogs. Had the passengers drunk it, they might have contracted typhoid fever. Osler's crime was dropping a chlorine pill into that drinking water. No one would believe that the pill was harmless to man but killed bacteria in contaminated water.

Harry yelled to the sheriff to bring the keys and let Osler out. He was delighted to "spring" the man who would be knighted for his work on the mysterious process of infectious disease, for instigating bedside teaching, for writing textbooks so advanced they are still used today, and for modernizing the Johns Hopkins Hospital in Baltimore. His story might have ended on a tree in Wyoming in 1888.

A deepening respect felt by the entire family emerged towards Harry. Five years after Harry and Léa's wedding, Uncle Robert finally accepted that the black sheep had established a commendable foundation. Writing to wish them well, Uncle Robert apologized, "I have always regretted omitting to congratulate you at the time of your marriage."

Alexander's right hand had grown increasingly wobbly. The first page of his letters would be scrawled but legible, the next almost hopeless, as if he was writing while travelling by train over a rough rail bed. Each time he and Julia visited New York to stay with the Daniel Torrances or with Emma Lunn on Park Avenue, Alexander consulted specialists about his painful shaking. Nothing could be done. He pushed on with his Queen's Bench duties as senior puisne judge, frequently commuting to Quebec City but still fighting the decree to move. Despite his declining health, he was determined to remain on the bench in Montreal until 1892, thus becoming eligible for a $3,000 annual pension paid after fifteen years of service.

In 1888 Alexander wrote several justifications in favour of keeping his Montreal domicile. In a letter to the under secretary of state, he cited other cases in which judges of the Queen's Bench had contravened their orders and remained in that city. He argued that as the bulk of court business was in Montreal where better facilities existed, such as a law library and his own contacts, he was more effective staying where he was. Driving home his coup de grâce with the delight of a trial lawyer, he announced that in fact, due to the tardiness of the Canadian postal system (circa 1877), he had already been sworn into office three days before the decree arrived. As the Statutes of Canada had nothing to say on judges' residences, he concluded that the order was invalid.

The result was a heartwarming letter from his old colleague, Chief Justice A.A. Dorion, noting that the statute requiring that two judges reside near Quebec City had been long disregarded for convenience sake and no one had suffered because of it. Subsequently, the secretary of state wrote to say the governor general had decreed that Mr. Justice Cross could reside at or near Montreal.

During the winter of 1889 Harry, Léa, Maggie and the baby Julia returned to Montreal for their first family visit. The Crosses, Lunns and Levasseurs had never seen their grandchildren. Upon reaching Montreal excitement mounted as their sleigh clipped smartly up the Côte des Neiges hill and through the wooded lane to the front door of Pine Avenue. Maggie and Julia toddled ahead of Harry and Léa to be greeted by their ecstatic grandparents. Edmund and Willie Heber joined in the celebration, but not Selkirk. They were strangely reticent to speak of their oldest brother.

Harry sent Léa and the children down to Cacouna to visit the Levasseurs, then visited "Selk" in his St. James Street home. Selkirk was deep into his brandy. He was in love with a humble teacher of whom Aunt Emma Lunn had not approved; she was, opined Emma, "not one of our kind." Staunch in her pride of race and position, Selkirk's influential aunt had admonished him to terminate the relationship. The entire family from parents to brothers had argued over what Selkirk should do. Finally, in the interest of family solidarity, Selkirk had ended the romance. He promised never to see the girl again but remained devastated. Unlike Harry, he could neither break from his society nor from the family traditions. Sick with the decision but feeling he was of no help, Harry headed for Cacouna.

It was a bitterly cold time to be visiting the sluggish waters at the mouth of the St. Lawrence but Harry and Léa took their youngsters sleighing across the land where they had played as children. The bells jingled on the horses' back as the foursome laughed and trotted over the packed snow. But later on that first day, Maggie started to cough, complained of a sore throat and developed a raging fever. Léa steamed her with Allen's balsam, made her gargle with vinegar and water, then placed a mustard plaster wrapped in soft linen on her chest.

Alarmed, Harry telegraphed the Crosses, prompting Julia and Alexander to write heartfelt letters of prayers for their granddaughter. On the third evening Maggie whispered to Harry, "Papa, would you carry me downstairs?" Harry rocked her gently in his arms. Maggie sighed, "Oh, Mama, I'm so sick." Léa brought her a cup of water. Maggie slurped it down and begged for more. She asked to see her sister. She downed another cup of water, then flopped against Harry's chest, her eyes growing vacant as she died.

Harry telegraphed his parents again. Alexander wrote a heart-wrenching letter asking them to come to Pine Avenue with little Julia. Maggie's death had renewed his own anguish over Robert and he added, "Your mother and I now know no hopeful future to look to. Léa and you are still young and have many blessings to come." Julia wrote a separate letter encouraging Harry that one's duty in life is to live on and be prepared to join their loved ones when called away.

Maggie was placed in a little white coffin with her eight Levasseur cousins serving as pallbearers. Harry and Léa walked beside the white hearse drawn by two white horses to the Cacouna Roman Catholic Church. Following the service, she was placed in the mausoleum in the graveyard beside the rectory.

The next day while Léa gathered Maggie's few treasures into a parcel and prepared to leave for Montreal, Julia flopped listlessly into a chair. By morning she was whimpering with the pain of a sore throat and insatiable thirst. On March 28 she died as suddenly as had Maggie. Harry and Léa suffered the same words of consolation by the same priest, and another diminutive white coffin was placed next to Maggie. Just before the coffin was closed, Harry and Léa had someone take a picture. Although her eyes remained slightly opened, Harry remembered, "It was very natural, as if she was sleeping." Léa begged Harry to take her babies home to be buried at Braehead, Wyoming, but fearing contamination from croup or scarlet fever, he decreed that they remain in the Cacouna graveyard. The undertaker gave them several locks of the girls' hair which they took home and framed.

Returning to Montreal, Harry and Léa stayed one night at the Windsor Hotel rather than expose anyone at Pine Avenue to infection. The next morning Selkirk accompanied them in a sleigh to the station. In a wordless communion of tears, the shattered brothers made their farewells. Gone was the lustre of childhood, of carefree youth and the excitement of men's adventures. Léa was wooden in posture and dry-eyed with shock. Minutes later they were shunting off toward Wyoming, their little family decimated as swiftly as lightning had once struck Harry's herd.

Through spring, summer and fall, Harry and Léa worked with an intensity never before imagined. Léa remained dry-eyed for months. Harry found the empty house unbearable and both felt a pall hanging over the whole of Braehead valley. Once suffusing them with joy, the glorious sunrises and spectacular storms served only to sharpen their pain. Harry rode a little harder and visited the saloons more often. At times his heart was so heavy he felt he couldn't go on. But he would always return to Braehead to build more buildings and dig more ditches. He didn't know how to help Léa, yet he would later credit her with keeping him from wasting his life away in drink. Léa became pregnant but initially it brought her no joy. No longer caring for music, she sold her organ to help Harry's terrible financial losses still hanging on from the winter of 1886-87. Finally, one day when Léa espied Maggie's touque, she burst into tears of grief and relief. In August, she nearly died giving birth to a baby girl. They named her Margaret Julia Mary, joy and sorrow eternally intertwined.

Just before Christmas, Harry wrote his father in a final cry of bitterness. Alexander replied sternly to his son, "I see that you are reluctant to submit to hard destiny and feel that you have been particularly not fortunate. We all have griefs at one time or another. You have now occasion to look around you to find instances of cruel fate much more distressing than yours. With youth, time comes to soothe the wounded heart. New consolations obliterate the wounds of the past. New hopes are engendered, and the things of the past are gradually forgotten. I have no doubt you will be greatly cheered and comforted by your little girl." Alexander included a $100 cheque to start the baby's bank account but urged Harry to use it if he needed it for his "big ditch" or anything else.

From letters arriving at Pine Avenue, Alexander saw that the experiences of his frontier sons were similar, but the laws governing their territories were strikingly different. Harry's Wyoming history had begun about the same time as Canada's Cypress Hills massacre and the advent of the NWMP. Yet eighteen years later while the Canadian West enjoyed relative peace and civility, lawlessness still galloped through the state of Wyoming. The corrupt Wyoming Stockgrowers' Association had become all-powerful in controlling the settlers, ranchers and cattle barons. In Johnson County, just north of Harry's

Braehead, every other man was considered a rustler. There, they had even developed a "hit" list of one hundred honest cattlemen who had refused to turn a blind eye to their crimes.

Not even the advent of statehood in 1890 brought an end to the outrageous rustling. A Live Stock Commission which included inspectors, range detectives and roundup supervisors proved useless. Harry and other desperate ranchers banded together and rode patrol to control rustling. In their escalating fury many ranchers blamed the "dirty nesters," or immigrants who flooded the land the way cattle had done ten years earlier. Men who had run their herds over God's country before ever owning their own land watched the magnificent range whittled away to 160-acre plots. One cowboy looked at the jammed land claims office and grumbled, "Not enough open range to piss on."

In truth, Harry wrote that it was often the ranchers themselves who stole cattle, with sheriffs and the association turning a blind eye. By 1892 the situation was out of hand and many felt it was time to fight back. The move came from the members of the Cheyenne Club. Like most of the established ranchers, Harry frequented the club. (He wore Selkirk's and Alexander's cast-off three-piece suits). His old Canadian friend Charlie Campbell, who had made it into the Wyoming legislature, was a member as well. They all formed the West's new "old boy" network, and they were fed up with the grip of fear on the state.

At a club meeting, Frank Wolcott, a neighbour of Harry, called for $100,000 to hire "regulators" and stop the rustling. It was a neat word for vigilante, and Wolcott specifically looked to Harry when he called for contributions and volunteers. As a victim of rustling, Harry sympathized with the group but had no wish to shoot his neighbours. He donated $50 to the cause but refused to ride with them. Wolcott accused Harry of letting his friends down. Harry stood firm. A few other ranchers joined his stance. Then more. In the end twenty-six Texan mercenaries had to be hired to meet the quota of fifty regulators.

To Harry's dismay, Charlie Campbell and one of the Dowling boys rode off to Johnson County with the regulators. The trigger-happy mercenaries who joined them were a dangerous lot. En route, two rustlers were killed and their cabin burned. A witness galloped into Buffalo to get Sheriff Red Angus. According to Harry's memoirs, Angus was the rustlers' ringleader hiding behind a badge. He and the ranchers hated each other. Angus handed out free guns and supplies to a volunteer posse of nearly six hundred. Fired with the scent of battle and with no Mounties to stop them, they thundered over the ground toward the regulators. Finding them at the TA Ranch, the posse captured two wagons full of ammunition, surrounded the regulators and fired two thousand rounds into the ranch. For three days bullets zinged through chinks and broken windows. They killed twenty-six horses trapped in a corral and shot Charlie Campbell's pipe out of his mouth.

Harry wrote that three nights later the Dowling boy slipped out of the ranch house and escaped to get help. An awakened President Harrison ordered the army at Fort McKinney to the TA Ranch. When the soldiers arrived, Angus's men were just pushing a wagon filled with dynamite toward the cabin. Charlie Campbell told Harry, "We were all so dirty and bedraggled it was difficult to find a white rag to hang out for surrender." They used an old grey dishcloth.

The army locked the regulators up at Fort McKinney, but Angus's men set fire to the barracks. The only hope for the prisoners' lives was to send them to Cheyenne. Immediately informed of the move by that mysterious "prairie telegraph," Harry grabbed a reporter and rode hard for a deserted Fort Fetterman where he knew the train would stop for water. He wrote, "It was bitterly cold, but during the train's brief stop, I boarded it and handed my old friend Charlie Campbell a jug. He had a bad cold and most of the others were coughing and looked worn from their ordeal. The gurgle of my gift in the gunny sack brought smiles from Billie Irvine and others. Frank Wolcott grabbed my hand and said, 'I knew you wouldn't let us down.'" Avoiding the approaching onslaught of newsmen and ranchers who had also figured on the Fetterman stop, Harry slipped out and rode for home. He had endeared himself to the regulators but disappeared before he became identified with them.

With the exception of the mercenaries, Harry considered them good men who had defended their way of life. People either sided for or against, with fist-fights often deciding arguments. School children fought amongst themselves depending upon who their Pa stood for. There was such a mixture of good men, bad men, responsible citizens and hired killers that they were too varied to convict. They were freed. The Cheyenne Club threw a celebration but feelings ran so high that even today people still get angry over what became known as the Johnson County War, or the Johnson County Massacre.

This was Harry Cross's era, and as with his Canadian family, history was swinging into another time frame which heralded the Wyoming politician. At the 1894 senatorial elections, Harry would be an overwhelming winner. The *Central Wyoming News* editorial said of Senator Cross's brief speech, "His remarks took in the whole situation ... in the most concise and clear manner we have yet heard. He is the best man that could have been selected for the Senate...." Wyoming, which had declared equal rights for women upon the occasion of its statehood in 1890, was a perfect home for Harry and his French wife. From Montreal, Alexander sent his love and congratulations, and refrained from offering any advice. He never got to Braehead.

Senator George H. Cross, as he became known, grew in stature with his state and was always known for his fairness. In 1896, following the Conservative government's suppression of French separate schools in Manitoba, he would write a furious letter to Ernest, referring to the British "curs" as having bought off all the Manitoba members and condemning the Canadian government as "the most corrupt in the world."

At the turn of the century when nominated by acclamation to stand as governor of the state of Wyoming, Harry declined, ever conscious of his father's admonitions to attend first to his family and business. He would continue in the Senate for another forty years and draft many of the ordinances of Wyoming. Léa would survive the lone, terrible birth of twin sons and go on to bear six more children (one delivered by Harry). The couple would watch their children grow into ranchers, lawyers, soldiers, writers, all with a deep conscience for public service. For three more generations Harry and Léa Cross's progeny would nurture the growth of their state, serving as lobbyists, councilmen and senators. Their list of personal accomplishments and of public service is prodigious.

Braehead, Wyoming, grew gradually. The Crosses built a large Georgian home not unlike Pine Avenue, Montreal, and furnished it with some of the finest furniture in Wyoming. Harry and Léa themselves were testimony to the folly of cultural and religious schisms. Their experiences both underscored some differences in settling the Canadian and American wests, and united both countries in their mutual battles over survival, peace, loneliness and grief. The very business of living superseded the political, socio-economic differences then and for generations to come.

North of the border, the Canadian government controlled land leases and homesteading, and the NWMP saw that the laws were kept. In

1888 Ernest threw himself into developing a broader, more formal stockgrowers' association than the original one in Pincher Creek circa 1882. Unlike the Wyoming vigilante groups, Albertans believed that the land-settling problems could be dealt with through an official association. The "sod-busters," or farmers, were considered worse than the wolves because they threw fences across watering holes and rendered hundreds of thousands of acres useless for cattle. Ernest believed that everyone could have a future in Alberta but contended that even smaller ranchers could not make a living under these conditions. On the other hand, the settlers argued that ranchers were unfair in hoarding vast tracts of land.

As secretary-treasurer of the High River Stockgrowers' Association, Ernest found the rancher/settler dispute to be only one of the issues. Just getting the ranchers to pay up their stock association membership fees, or their share in roundup costs, proved a time-consuming job. At the end of a hectic day, and by the light of coal oil in his shack, he would write each rancher a letter expecting the fees. Bills ranged from $1 to $14. He arranged for the tally and payment of mavericks. He helped fight for fair water rights. He wrote to Edgar Dewdney who, having moved from lieutenant-governor to Dominion minister of the interior, was the man responsible for cancelling huge government leases to make way for the settler.

In innumerable ways Ernest acted as den mother for the illiterate and for those who would rather be out in the saddle. His letter books would fill thousands of pages over the years as he pursued the most infinitesimal details, always remaining courteous yet resolute. In another fifteen years the educated, British-oriented men like Ernest Cross would be resented by huge numbers of working-class settlers, but at that time he was needed and appreciated.

The changes and growth in Alberta were phenomenal. Thousands of horses covered the territory in addition to cattle. A broken three-year-old might sell for as much as $125. Export to England was mushrooming, particularly through Ernest's old school chum, Edward ffolkes, and his brother Robert. The Calgary real estate market was booming. Prime land on Stephen Avenue was now worth $2,000 per front foot. The little wooden Church of the Redeemer, built with funds raised by Cyprian Pinkham, Ernest Cross and other Calgarians, graced Seventh Avenue and First Street S.E. The Grain Exchange and City Hall were either being designed or built. In 1889 Ernest reported the completion of a grist mill, a foundry, a branch of the Bank of Montreal and several new stores. Business was so good that he urged Willie Heber to give up his European travels and return to help firmly establish Cross Brothers Limited.

As fast as the West changed, Ernest kept pace or moved a little faster to create a space for the Crosses. He planted his own potatoes and vegetables, continued to break broncos for hours on end, then sold them to the police in High River. He organized roundups, writing, "Sometimes I am in the saddle 20 hours out of 24." He joined with James Lougheed to invest in Calgary buildings. That spring when a huge prairie fire roared across the land to within five miles of his homestead, he wrote only that it was on all sides save for the west, and that it was almost impossible to cross Mosquito Creek. His parents had no idea of what happened after that.

Ernest's letters came to reflect his frenetic pace. He soon reported in staccato as if he were firing off telegrams. "Have no time for more. Send map. Cattle and horses doing well. None dying. Have no more to say. Remember me kindly to all." He was forgetting to mention this and that, apologizing, "Please excuse so much. My love to all at home, I remain, yr. Aff. son, A.E. Cross." His abbreviated signature was the way he would be remembered. It was not as much the respectful nomenclature of a senior statesman as it was for a young man in a hurry. Somehow he found time to become engaged to a girl in Montreal, but it seemed he was too busy to attend to courting matters. Would his sister Maggie pick up an engagement ring for him? Continuing on in the very same line, he closed, "Will have by far the largest calf crop since I have been in the business."

In one letter to his mother, Ernest expressed gratitude for her weekly letters of family news, for it was something he could "reckon on for a certainty." In letters to Alexander, he repeatedly outlined his father's investments and his money-lending, which was competitive with the Bank of Montreal. He moved with a sense of conviction. Rather than ask permission of his father, he often wrote to report what he had done: "I have just arranged with a party here to lend him $1,500 at 12 per cent for one year on a mortgage on real estate in Calgary. It is almost the central block of the town and the two lots are valued at $3,000. The ... Bank of Montreal has loaned $1,400 on lots of the same value. I would be much obliged to you if you would send up the money as soon as possible. I could get a guarantee from the same party of 20 per cent on the money provided I bought the lots myself at the end of one year, but thought it better to take a mortgage. He is to pay all expenses on the transaction."

So enthusiastic did the Montreal Crosses become over Calgary investments and Ernest's belief that real estate could rise 100 per cent within the year that even Julia joined the frenzy. She sent her son $1,500 to invest on two lots in the block west of the Alberta Hotel. Selkirk sent $1,500 and Willie Heber $3,000. Ernest was happy to invest everyone's money in real estate, but personally clung to his vision of building a ranch with the best beef and horses in the West. He noted that he hoped to invest $450 in a two-year-old purebred Clydesdale horse. The risk in investing in a horse which might be killed by wolves or from a twisted gut was far greater in 1889 than investing in Calgary real estate.

Willie Heber's $3,000 went into eighty acres of land inside the town limit (the future Agricultural Exhibition and Stampede site). When the brothers asked Ernest to check out Vancouver investments, he replied that he was too busy and really couldn't afford the train fare. At the insistence of his father, Ernest kept meticulous books. Any monies which were sent out for personal investment were considered non-interest loans. When he could, Ernest repaid them to the penny. (Harry did the same.) At times Alexander would chide Ernest, saying that he really could have reinvested the money rather than sending it back to Montreal. Then to remind his son that while the reins may be in Ernest's hands, the curb chain was in the father's, Alexander would caution, "festina lente," or make haste slowly, and continue his polite demands, his gentle criticisms. Once he pointed out a $2.50 error in bookkeeping.

When Edmund returned to Montreal to live, the family noticed that he had improved in manner and person but had no desire to return west. He wanted his Alberta homestead sold for the quick profit of $400. The River Beaudette farm was not going well and Edmund suggested that Alexander sell it too. Ernest drew a huge breath of exasperation over Edmund, writing Selkirk the longest sentence in his lifetime of letters: "Edmund is foolish to desire to leave Beaudette as he ought in time to make a good living there without much anxiety if he will only look at it in the proper light and not imagine that he is able to be the governor of the state of California or something equally absurd."

Concerned over Edmund's lacklustre performance, Alexander broke a cardinal rule and gave his sixth son an early legacy, the River Beaudette farm. Conducting family business as formally as he would with strangers, Alexander oversaw the trading of River Beaudette with Edmund's Alberta homestead. Edmund drew up an official document relinquishing his entire share in the livestock and land in Mosquito

Creek and elsewhere in the district of Alberta. It was a move he would bitterly regret for a lifetime. Watching Ernest soar to success, he would blame his father, the church, the elements, and everyone but himself for his failures.

Despite the growing attractions of Calgary, Ernest remained at his sod shack. He watched the town become modernized and his colleagues such as George Lane make dramatic changes in their lifestyles. With the advent of the Calgary Electric Light Company in December of 1889, five hundred Calgarians blew out their kerosene lamps and switched on "hot hairpins in bottles," or sixteen candle-power lights. Calgary's first waterworks was completed that year. Elegant houses of pleasure provided the men with women of any race or nationality they might fancy. But apart from lusty forays into Calgary still remembered by Calgary's oldest cowboy, Harry Brayne, Ernest remained in his shack. He would move when he was ready.

The great victory for Ernest that year was to establish an ordinance through the stockmen's associations to punish rustlers with a $100 fine or forty days in jail. He continued working with his neighbours to revive and relocate the several stock associations from Pincher Creek to Calgary. This angered the individual associations, but for Ernest and his friends located further north, the move was one of expediency, and it made sense to develop a collective lobbying power.

Fascinated by the growth of Calgary, Alexander prepared for a safari into the wilds of Canada. He sent ahead a tent and a gun. Of specific interest, he wrote, were Sir Alexander Galt's coal mines near Lethbridge. Ernest replied that he was so busy he would hardly be ready for roundup. He really didn't believe for a moment that Alexander would come west and did not seem pleased at the thought of his father invading his territory. He also advised Alexander to stay away from Galt's investment, retorting, "From all I can find out, it is a humbug." Not long after, Galt lost his Montana smelting deal just as the last spike was driven into his railway. The North-West Coal and Navigation Company offered blocks of 40,000 acres of land for as little as $1.25.

Another bitter winter proved disastrous to a7 cattle, although the losses were not as severe as in 1886-87. But Ernest managed to sell culled (sub-standard) mares to the police, plus eighteen other horses, for a total of $1,800. This proved so successful that he met his losses and made a profit. Believing the business of calving was devastating in so harsh a climate, he imported two hundred yearling dogies – weaned, hardier calves – to fatten throughout the year. Finally, concluding that his present homestead was a failure, he took steps to relocate the a7.

Every time Ernest rode into the foothills he kept an eye out for a large range with good winter grazing and plenty of water unfenced by sod-busters. Available land was swiftly diminishing, yet the hills and valleys that stretched like endless ocean swells still hid virgin land. Riding out one day about twelve miles west of his flat homestead, he stumbled upon some rolling hills and, on the other side, a magnificent valley. Springs actually bubbled from the high ground. It was listed as Section #34, Township 15, Range 1 west of the first meridian. To the southeast, woods rose to 4,500 feet. The hills protected lush valleys with native grass that grew as tall as at Braehead, Wyoming. The upper slopes were either covered with woods or grazing land. Flowers sprinkled the grass in a kaleidoscope of colour. Incredibly, no one had claimed it. Compared to his first homestead Ernest must have felt like St. Peter casting his net on the other side of the boat.

Still, he had a problem. He already had a homestead so was ineligible for another. Enticing Willie Heber west from River Beaudette, where he was recuperating from a European jaunt, Ernest registered the new a7 in his brother's name. Then he began constructing a sod shack and moving over his cattle and horses. Ernest had barely completed the living quarters, with bugs and worms working their way through the roof, when Willie Heber drove up in a buckboard with their sister Maggie. Clad in silk and lace fineries complete with bustle and white gloves, the lovely debutante looked as if she'd just stepped from the cover of the *Canadian Illustrated News*. After all, Calgary boasted entertainment as gracious as any in Montreal.

Throughout that spring and summer, Alberta's gentry buggied to Senator Cochrane's ranch west of Calgary where they waltzed the nights away. By day, protected from the sun's ravages in gaily striped tents, beautifully dressed ladies applauded the men's horse races and polo matches. Everyone had a splendid time – everyone, that is, except Maggie. Ernest was always in demand both as a bachelor and polo player, but that summer he and Willie Heber were too busy to take their sister to the parties.

Filled with the excitement of their fledgling venture, the brothers cheerfully carried on as usual. When it rained they put the dishes outside for a washing, and they cleaned their shirts and underwear by anchoring them under a rock in the creek for two or three days. The current and stones scrubbed them like a washboard. Maggie was unaccustomed to domestic work and to the isolation. She felt helpless and trapped. Used only to her well-trained steed and the groomed paths of Mount Royal, she dared not ride a bronco. The broad horizons were insufficient to captivate any pioneering spirit within her and before long she returned to Montreal. Years later Maggie confided in her daughter that she had found her brothers' lifestyle "utterly vulgar."

Everything went right for the Cross brothers until the June roundup. One day during the confusion of milling cattle and loosely corralled horses, Ernest's pinto suddenly dropped its head between its legs and tried to throw him. It might have been better if he had been tossed into the spring mud. Instead, he flew out of his stirrups into the air, then jolted onto the saddle horn which in turn hooked onto his belt. The horse continued bucking, pummelling Ernest's gut until Billie Cochrane and another cowboy got control of the animal. So excruciating was Ernest's pain that Billie put him in a buckboard and drove him to High River and the doctor, the ex-surgeon general of India. The title said more than his operating powers. Ernest was diagnosed as having a twisted bowel or appendicitis, and frontier surgery could be lethal. Perhaps remembering Dr. Osler's pathology classes, the patient chose luck over surgery, but his prognosis was poor. He could outlast the cold that killed his cattle and the wolves that ate his colts but he couldn't fight primitive medicine. Seriously ill and suffering excruciating pain, he wrote to tell his father.

Alexander and Julia were still struggling with the pain of their granddaughters' deaths, and they would never stop grieving over Robert. It was both inconceivable and utterly unacceptable to Alexander that he might lose his beloved son and protégé. Geographically, he was too far removed to control events. Furthermore, at sixty-two with limbs that sometimes shook uncontrollably, he was no candidate for travelling over rugged rail beds into the frontier. He might have sent out a doctor for Ernest but Crosses did things themselves. Dispatching Julia to New Brunswick, Maggie to Scotland, Edmund to the River Beaudette farm and leaving Pine Avenue in the care of the servants, the patriarch boarded the CPR train for Calgary. A weakened, emaciated Ernest was probably as stupefied as anyone when his father stepped off the train. Alexander spirited his son off to Banff Hot Springs to bathe in the healing waters. There wasn't much else they could do but Ernest's condition improved sufficiently to return to the a7 homestead. Perhaps their collective will had wrought a temporary cure.

The opportunity to walk over his last grand frontier must have thrilled Alexander. Although the Cross grassland with its growing herds of cattle and horses were not yet large enough to be called a ranch, it had no visible boundaries. Its expanse of earth and sky encompassed all that Crosses had loved for hundreds of years. It was here at the a7 that Cross foundations would be rooted forever. Yet only one record of that moment remains. In the sod shack Alexander sat at the rough-hewn desk, took pen in shaking hand and scribbled one note. Addressing it to the Ministry of the Interior he relinquished the six sections of land granted to the Crosses one year earlier. Alexander described neither his experiences nor his feelings, perhaps waiting to return to Montreal and relate personally his adventure to Julia.

Leaving Willie Heber in charge of the homestead and the almost epidemic plague of wolves, Ernest showed his father around Calgary and introduced him to James Lougheed, William Pearce, T.S.C. Lee, and other prominent men of the times. It was an incredible opportunity for him to appeal to his father's entrepreneurial spirit. In the coming year Alexander would sell property in Quebec to release funds for Alberta land purchases, dealing through his son and James Lougheed.

Alexander noted that as Ernest's health improved, he became anxious to have him on his way. The father could no longer move at the pace of the son, and the elderly man's right arm and leg visibly shook. Months later Alexander remarked that he didn't think he would return to Calgary; he seemed to have been embarrassingly in the way. Twenty-nine-year-old Ernest was a courteous but callow fellow in a hurry. If Alexander's feelings were hurt, perhaps he recognized a replica of himself in his son. Nevertheless, he did prevail upon Ernest to return to Montreal for further diagnostic tests.

Ernest's acquiescence probably hinged on his getting further financing for business ventures. The great rumour of the West was that prohibition, such as it was, would soon be repealed and the Crosses envisioned a brewery venture for the West. As he would be in Montreal for months he wondered if Willie Heber would stay to run the a7. His brother had already spent more time than usual far from the enticements of city life. Nevertheless, Willie Heber was willing to run the a7 as long as he could return east before winter. Ernest agreed and took off for Montreal.

Throughout that summer, a 320-pound Willie Heber huffed and puffed about the a7, attending to his duties with a monkish dedication. Although skilled at training matched teams of geldings, he couldn't move fast enough to manage the untethered mares. Each evening he organized a roundup to protect the horses from attacking wolves, but the broncos easily dodged their keeper and galloped off through holes in the fences to the oat fields. Edmund the fence-builder had left and there was no one to replace him. The dog that had helped with the nightly roundups had taken to killing and eating the chickens. When Willie Heber did corral the horses, he would head in for a desperately needed drink only to hear the cattle crunch through a fence. By the time he lumbered out to repair the damage, the horses were cavorting in the oats again. By August, sixteen colts had been killed by wolves and Willie Heber had lost eighteen pounds. His mother was delighted, but Willie Heber was desperate. It rained incessantly yet the air was hot and heavy. A neighbour's sheep kept breaking through the fences onto a7 land. One day a hailstorm thundered down with what Willie Heber described as six-and-a-half inch stones. He concluded his August letter, "After this you needn't expect to hear from me regularly." Reading the letters in Montreal, Ernest recognized the signs of his brother slipping the reins, the lights of Montmartre glimmering more brilliantly than the candles of the a7.

Like Oscar Wilde, Willie Heber was a man of simple tastes; he was always satisfied with the very best. A homestead that suffered violent weather and ungrateful livestock was not his style. He took to his bed, complained of gum rot and begged Selkirk for a Bible, having lost his somewhere in the foothills. Willie Heber's Bibles and notebooks were more than reading material. He filled the margins with maxims to guide his peregrinations by rail or by heart. On this occasion he recorded Sydney Smith's, "Be what nature intended you for, and you will succeed: be anything else and you will be a thousand times worse than nothing." Willie Heber knew that he would realize fame and fortune but his route would not be through broken fences or stampeding horses.

His threat that he would not write again lasted for about five days. The next letter recorded his Armaggedon on the a7. The well water had become so foul to taste and smell that he stormed the hills to examine the springs. There he found rotting mice half-floating, tails down and mouths agape in silly grins.

In late September, Willie Heber was still bedridden and suffering bleeding gums. He blamed them on neuralgia and was utterly disgusted with everything. One day he watched a huge wolf waltz into the corral in full daylight and, before he could grab his gun, haul off a colt.

Hiring a herder to handle and protect the livestock, he arranged to move the main shack to higher ground, nearer the springs and with a more commanding view of the surrounding terrain. In the valley the wolves were able to sneak up too easily. First, he had to get back on his feet, and Ernest must come home. Fearing that his younger brother might never arrive, Willie Heber informed Ernest that his deadline was up.

But Ernest was not only still in pain, he was busy studying at the Montreal Brewing Academy. He was also being consoled by a Miss M. following a broken engagement to Miss R. Nevertheless, envisioning his fledgling ranch slipping away, he wrote to cheer Willie Heber up. He would return soon, and with some girls.

Probably for the one and only time in his life Willie Heber retorted: what did Ernest think he was doing sending girls? He'd be polite to them but they could stay at the lower ranch. He had bought his ticket to Montreal for October 13 and he intended to make that date. To ensure his departure, Willie Heber arranged to act as herdsman for none other than the ffolkes brothers, brokers for selling horses in England. Long-standing friendships with Haileybury and Guelph old boys remained strong. Letters of introduction were all one gentleman needed for immediate acceptance by another. Edward's brother Robert had visited the a7 Ranche, made a pick of geldings and mares and offered $80 a head for them.

With Willie Heber leaving, Ernest had no option but to return. Still suffering from recurring abdominal pain, he had refused surgery and arrived thinner and weaker in Calgary. He found the Calgary General Hospital filled with typhoid patients. Realizing that he was too weak to risk infection, he stayed one night at the Alberta Hotel, then returned to his ranch. He was shocked to discover that he had lost twenty colts to wolves, which were running in packs of up to thirty. He couldn't possibly protect his herd. A man had to sit up all night with several guns cocked by his knees, watching, listening for the rustling sounds, waiting for the attacks. Staggered by his losses and ill health, he must have wondered just how he would continue.

It was then that wild Billie Cochrane rode over from the Little Bow Cattle Company. Billie was small in stature but a giant in mischief and goodness. He had just returned from a jaunt to Paris and still sported a white silk scarf. Riding up to the far side of the flooded Mosquito River, Billie stripped off all his finery and swam the torrent naked. With a levity that belied his caring, he took over Ernest's a7 homestead and ran the show while his friend convalesced. No more colts were lost, fences were properly repaired and the dog even stopped eating the chickens. Billie was so enthusiastic in executing his duties that when he caught an Indian butchering a calf he jumped the rustler and ear-marked him. In the subsequent hearing, Justice Macleod not only sentenced the Indian but he also fined Billie $5. In his opinion, as one of Her Majesty's subjects, the Indian had deserved more civilized treatment.

Billie's generosity cemented their life-long friendship. Like Ernest's other neighbours, the Cochranes were monied gentry from the old country who established their Alberta ranch on the proviso that they winter in England or the Continent. They never really meant to suffer the rigours of the West. Still, Billie would put in faithful years of work establishing his Canadian ranch before spiriting away to a life of pleasure.

His ranch in hand, Ernest now faced another complication: his engagement to the young Montreal widow who had become a favourite at Pine Avenue. Ernest was a flaming romantic, the names of his fiancées changing with almost every trip. Perhaps overwhelmed by the vision of placing a Montreal socialite in a sod shack, by the urgency of preparing his homestead for winter, or just beating out the competition in the land game, Ernest broke the engagement. His mother and Maggie were furious with him.

Ernest's abdominal pain remained like a dull toothache, a constant warning that his final hope might be emergency surgery. Ultimately preferring hospital to death in the foothills, he hired a couple of hands and a cook to care for the ranch, packed up and moved permanently into Calgary. His address was the Alberta Hotel, but he spent more time with his friends in an old boxcar which they leased for a clubhouse. Men such as W. Pearce, Sir Francis A. McNaghten, and Ernest's original roundup pals joined him in the venture. They named their club the "Wolves' Den." There they could play a little poker and plan the future industrial West. For the work-conscious, duty-bound Ernest, those times were a crazy respite. One old cowboy remembered, "Cross could celebrate! By God, when he and Cochrane came to Calgary . . . they tore them Houses all apart!"

Billie Cochrane always made sure that an 80-gallon barrel of ten-year-old whiskey was on hand, prohibition or no. His personal friend was the Scottish distiller Glen Grant. One night the thoroughly squiffed friends left the boxcar and caroused through the streets of Calgary howling like a pack of wolves. Arrested and hauled before the magistrate, the recalcitrant bunch was defended by James Lougheed. Defence called the policeman to the witness stand and said, "Sir, could you please recreate this particular noise which you found so offensive?" Squirming before the court, the constable couldn't emit a squeak. The case was dismissed.

Eventually deciding an image of propriety was necessary, Ernest wrote Selkirk for the objectives, policies and cigars of Montreal's St. James Club. Selkirk complied and the members of the Wolves' Den incorporated themselves as the Ranchmen's Club. One founding member was Jermy Jephson, Christin Drever's husband, and as a judge, James Macleod was welcomed into this selective enclave of the gentlemen frontiersmen.

A year after Ernest's accident in 1892, he was again so consumed with pain that he telegraphed his parents to arrange a consultation with a Montreal doctor. Julia was sure his problem emanated from his refusal to give up polo. The eastward-bound Ernest again entrusted the a7 to a westbound Willie Heber, a man returned from the Continent filled with renewed religion and resolve.

In Montreal, Pine Avenue was undergoing a modernization program. Flowered wallpaper freshened the halls and bedrooms. While a new kitchen and plumbing system were being installed, the family dined at the gardener's cottage beside the lower garden. Ernest visited Edmund at the River Beaudette farm and was disturbed to find his younger brother dreaming of moving to brighter horizons out west. He thought he was in love with Hélène Sequine, a French-Canadian girl from a family of thirteen on the neighbouring farm. Edmund would never marry a Roman Catholic, he assured his family, but fortunately the Sequines had left that church, he explained, because the priest had made a pass at Hélène. A bright, bilingual girl, she had begun teaching school. What did Ernest think of her? At first Ernest encouraged Edmund to make his own decisions but upon meeting the pleasant Hélène, urged his younger brother to marry her. Edmund promptly complied.

The year 1892 was important for everyone. Alexander had spent four months as chief justice of Quebec following Dorion's death. It was an accolade that he only begrudgingly enjoyed, for it meant spending even more time in Quebec City. Renewed pressure was put on him to move. In turn, Alexander drafted rebuttals to the prime minister and to the secretary of state, then deleted his most irascible comments in the final copies.

Although he hated to admit it, Alexander was ill. His bearing, branded by his incisive if slightly cross-eyed gaze, his sound judgments and his white mutton-chop whiskers no longer hid his condition. In the spring of 1892, he climbed unsteadily into his cart to drive the goat around the gardens. It was a whimsy, the goat as rheumatic and shaky as its master. Signs of spring were well on the way, crocuses and snowdrops competing with robins and blue jays for the old man's attention. The hawthorne bush where the boys had built their forts still sprawled over the grounds, its thorny, gnarled branches hanging on through another year just as stubbornly as Alexander. Suddenly at a fork in the path the goat jolted to a stop. It knocked the cart off balance, ignominiously dumping Alexander into last year's holly-hock bed. A decade before the tumble would merely have annoyed the judge, but this time he suffered bruised and torn muscles. He was confined to bed for weeks. When he was able to write again, he noted to Harry, "I am not robust these days."

Alexander determined to take a six months' leave of absence from the Court of Queen's Bench with salary, a period which would bring him to his fifteen years' service and retirement pension. Having handed the reins of chief justice over to Sir Alexandre Lacoste, he felt that after fourteen years and six months of dedicated service, he was entitled to sick leave – with pay. The Privy Council thought differently. Ignoring the 1888 decree by Dorion and the governor general which had sanctioned Alexander's Montreal residency, the government renewed its efforts to force his move to Quebec City. That Alexander had not, claimed the government, had resulted in an accumulation of arrears and a disorganization in the Court of Appeal. Should Alexander retire six months early he would receive no pension.

It was the hint that he might have been responsible for poor administration that mobilized Alexander to seize his pen one more time. He wrote from one to four drafts, polishing his argument as a politician hones a campaign speech. A wonderful dramatist with a flair for statesmanship, he claimed of Montreal in a letter to Sir John Thompson, minister of justice and later that year prime minister of Canada, "I have grown old in its society and its surroundings, as well as in the execution of my duty." He listed his accomplishments, including his pre-Confederation contributions to framing the laws of Canada, and his self-perceived objective both as a lawyer and as a judge "to never merely interpret the law but to reform it when I saw inequities." To secure further attention for his case, Alexander also wrote to his old friend, senator and current prime minister, Sir John Abbott. He listed statistical evidence and problems such as lawyers' interminably lengthy arguments and the court's adoption of Saturday afternoon holidays as reasons why he could not have caused the cited confusion. Indeed, if there was mismanagement, he snapped, it was certainly not his fault. He concluded that the court "had long been presided over by an able chief (Dorion)." And therein, he left unsaid, so could lie the blame.

The chief justice and Queen's Bench justices conferred with Alexander's physician, then gave him six months' medical leave of absence, full salary and his dignity. Alexander wrote to Justice Wurtale: "Had you and the Chief Justice not concurred in the opinion of Dr. Star, my splendid physician, I might have felt bound to return to duty, but the matter is now decided. I have today mailed to Ottawa my resignation as Judge of the Queen's Bench."

The *Montreal Star* called for Her Majesty's "mark of recognition" of Alexander, for his innumerable contributions to such fields as private international law. Also, "his struggles for a liberal construction of the law of libel as it applied to the press were particularly noticeable and deserving the gratitude of publishers. . . . He proved himself to be a sound lawyer and safe guide . . . [and] as a whole his opinions were remarkably well sustained by the courts of final appeal. . . . His assiduity was incessant, and with no intermission from his labors for upwards of fourteen years [and six months]." Alexander was never knighted or otherwise recognized. He received a courteous letter of acknowledgment for his note of resignation, and from that time to his death, a monthly pension cheque of $277.77.

Whiskey traders had been amongst Alberta's first immigrants. In 1875 James Macleod and the NWMP claimed to have wiped them out and kept the country more or less dry until 1890. In fact, the original six hundred permits averaging two gallons each in 1880 had soared to endless permits for whites and 151,628 gallons a decade later. The traders' expertise in transporting illicit spirits to the whites had reached a plateau of creative art. They hid liquor in barrels of sugar, salt or oatmeal. They labelled bottles of it "Ginger Ale." They hollowed out Bibles for bottles of gin and injected fake eggs with whiskey. In Calgary, a man in the know could gain entrance to some of the most elegant drinking rooms in the country. When caught smuggling, settlers could usually cover the illicit amount through their permits, but as a kind of territorial pastime it was more fun to bootleg.

So frustrated were the NWMP, who enjoyed a snifter themselves, that Commissioner Herchmer recommended the abolition of the permit system. He advocated both the importation and manufacturer of lager beer. James Macleod was against the recommendation but Herchmer was exasperated with the embarrassment showered on the police and their mismanagement of liquor charges, when in fact few judges would levy convictions.

The harshest critics of liquor came from temperance groups and church leaders. One of these was Bishop Pinkham, who preached temperance from the pulpit but loved his whiskey as much as did his brother-in-law. And even James once suffered such a hangover that he moaned to Mary, "Would that liquor could be abolished from the world!" It was marvellous irony that while James rode west to stamp out the whiskey trade, his future son-in-law would become the beer baron of southern Alberta.

Ernest had remained in Montreal for part of 1891-92 to study the industrial side of brewing. A national plebiscite would soon decide the future of liquor in Canada, and he believed that the liquor laws in Alberta territory were obsolete if not little short of farcical. He was in luck. Although the nationwide plebiscite showed that a majority of voters favoured prohibition in 1892, the government decreed that as only 44 per cent of the electorate had voted, the plebiscite had not been an indicator of the Canadian public as a whole. The matter was dropped, the sale of liquor was wide open and Ernest returned west to build his brewery.

Three thousand people now lived in Calgary. The Calgary-Edmonton railway would soon be completed, narrowing the travelling time between Calgary and Strathcona to eighteen hours. Natural gas had just been found at 600 feet just south of the city. Optimism ran high as houses swiftly replaced tent villages. With such an influx of thirsty pioneers Ernest knew that if he moved fast enough, he could dominate the beer industry west of Winnipeg.

In Calgary, he had borrowed a total $50,000 from the Bank of Montreal and the Imperial Bank of Canada. Concurrently, he floated a company with five hundred shares, purchasing two hundred of them himself on December 2, 1891, and finding five other business friends to invest in the company. The shareholders put up another $50,000 and searched for land. Ernest was aware that Calgary had adopted a bonus policy to entice industry into the core area, but when he requested a tax exemption, it was refused. He subsequently bought land just outside the city limits from James Walker, William Pearce and W.F. Orr for $1,700. Situated directly above the confluence of the Bow and Elbow rivers, the site enjoyed a natural stream which would flow directly into the future brewery. The Calgary Brewing

& Malting Company was to be the first brewery in the North-West Territories. W.R. Hull, H. Samson, Billie Cochrane, H. Eckford, J. Lineham, D. MacPherson, and the president, Ernest Cross, held their first official meeting on March 7, 1892.

Wishing to insure his fledgling business with some failsafe product, Ernest approached Hiram Walker Distillers to be its agent for southern Alberta. At first they agreed, then, after he had spent a preliminary $500, reneged. In an angry outburst Ernest accused them of not standing behind their word. He wrote to Walker listing the considerable expense, inconvenience and time he had already put into the project, and urged Walker to reconsider, closing with, "Certainly you would be doing nothing more than you have already agreed to." He never got the agency.

Ernest then lobbied for a railway siding for the brewery. He argued that his Calgary Brewing & Malting Company would employ a dozen men year round, placing it among Calgary's most important industries. A great collector of statistics and blunt in his requests, Ernest argued that the CPR should encourage this type of growth as they would be marketing their product by rail. But the CPR retorted that the volume of business Ernest would do would not warrant constructing another line, "even if the whole of the expense of building the side track was borne by you." Smarting under this rebuff, Ernest accused the CPR of acting in a "mean way" for refusing to build the tracks or to reduce the freight rate from Calgary.

As Ernest was piecing together his business and serving as secretary to the new Stockmen's Committee, a Toronto friend warned him that Winnipeg businessmen were intending to establish a brewery in Calgary. Ernest reacted like a man defending his territory from an alien invasion. He went into debt to build. Understanding that all monies from Alexander were interest-free loans to be repaid when possible, he drew $2,000 from his own bank account and took a draft on his father for $1,500. When his cheque for $18.45 to the CPR bounced, as did one to the Alberta Hotel, he received stringent letters demanding payment. It was the only time in his life that he missed payments.

Throughout the fall a construction crew of twenty worked round the clock to house the giant vats. The company would also manufacture ale porter, aerated waters and malt. By late fall the buildings were shaping into gargantuan proportions on the Calgary skyline. Calgarians said there were three main areas of the city: West Calgary, East Calgary and the Brewery. Determined to have expert employees to start up,

Ernest lured Martin Broderick, head brewer from the Montreal Brewing Company, for $14 a week. Broderick offered to marry the cook and run the boarding house Ernest intended to build for the staff. This latter move would save Broderick the $5 room and board fee which would otherwise be deducted from his salary.

By March 9, 1893, the first brew was started. As March 17 approached a number of local Irishmen suggested they sample the brew on St. Patrick's Day. The beer was immature. But an impatient Calgary couldn't wait and neither could Ernest. Some claim the Irish employees dyed it green before turning on the taps. When the news was shouted throughout the Alberta Hotel, citizens jumped into carriages or onto horses and galloped out to the brewery. In an orgy of drink, Calgarians consumed the entire forty kegs of lager. There wasn't a sober man on the streets and the next morning a giant hangover enveloped the town. Alexander commended Ernest for completing his brewery within his estimated costs. Julia exalted, "So happy to hear your beer was such a success.... I'm sending your summer underclothing but be careful not to change too soon." The industrial era of the West was on its way.

15

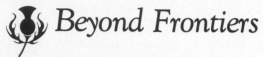 *Beyond Frontiers*

"May Heaven grant we may never be separated so long again."
James to Mary

Fort Macleod was incorporated as Macleod in 1892. Forsaken by the CPR in favour of the coal-mining centre of Lethbridge, the first NWMP outpost and agricultural centre of southern Alberta was doomed to small-town status. Mary found it a dismal place. She preferred the hunting at Pincher Creek, or the cities of Calgary, Winnipeg and Toronto to the town which was the centre of James's judicial district. She saw Macleod as a parochial society, composed of cowboys and largely uneducated settlers. It would never acquire the sophistication or the varied shopping of her favourite cities.

On the other hand, Mrs. Inderwick, a friend of Mary's and former Macleod resident, wrote that the town revolved around James and Mary. She recalled coming as a bride and sending her laundry to "that dignified coloured." It did not turn up for weeks because, she claimed, Auntie considered the Macleod home a kind of government house and was working to Mary's schedule. Indeed, "keeping up" was important to Mary. Like other women, she hunted in a formal riding habit and occasionally imported her clothes from England. Jean Pinkham remembered that one of her sister's outfits was a gorgeous primrose gown made with velvet ribbons of mignonette green. Although Mary had lost her teeth to the ravages of frontier living (Auntie had performed the dentistry while a dentist supplied the new teeth), her smile was still a masterpiece – of porcelain perfection.

Even with proper attire and appearance, status in the small community depended upon making the guest lists. To be cancelled from a soirée was a major insult; to receive an invitation and fail to attend was a blatant snub; to be eliminated from a major party bespoke disaster. The Macleods were thus shamed one New Year's Eve. A few days earlier, their own Christmas dinner party with James's brilliantly funny theatricals had been considered a thundering success. Then the Garnetts, who summered on their ranch near Macleod and wintered in California after the Christmas holidays, threw a New Year's Eve ball which excluded Mary and James. In a letter to Mrs. Inderwick, Mary complained, "It was terrible being deliberately put out of society that way. We gave great offence by not going there last summer as we had promised to do, so we were now to feel the weight of their displeasure."

Mary lamented in another letter to Mrs. Inderwick, "... tho' I would love to have you living here, there is no denying the fact that this is a sadly demoralising place." The wife of the supreme court justice secretly hoped that rumours of a move for James to Calgary might materialize.

By 1892, the oldest Macleod children were into their teens. In a letter to Mrs. Inderwick, Mary described eleven-year-old Norman at Trinity College in Port Hope as a "bright, manly fellow full of life and fun" and always ready with a helping hand. But she added that cricket and football were more to his liking than lessons. Rather than push Norman on to university, James wanted him to enlist into the navy to toughen him up and let him see the world, but Mary refused to let her only son go so far away. The younger children, Roma, Mary and Jean, remained in Macleod supplementing their regular studies with music and French. Nell was happy at Bishop Strachan's School, and at home her mother considered her "a dear, useful girl and the greatest comfort in the house." On occasion when she sensed her mother's unhappiness, Nell would write notes specifically to cheer her up.

The Macleods' expenses continued to mount and Mary's legacy dwindled. One day she was shocked to receive a letter from Norman explaining that his class position of twenty-ninth out of thirty in Greek and Latin was due to his lack of attendance rather than his intellect. His private school bills had not been paid, and he had been barred from classes altogether. One master asked permission to continue tutoring Norman privately but the headmaster insisted the cheque must first be in hand. When Mary fumed to James over Norman's fees he replied jauntily that he would pay the bill and closed with endless love.

As none of Mary's letters to James survive, it is sometimes difficult to document or fully appreciate her frontier contributions and her love of the West. And as letters were written only when one of them was travelling, it may appear as though she was rarely in Macleod. In fact, while James became the more visible historical figure, Mary played a pivotal role in maintaining the value systems established by the emigrating Rothney-Drever-Macleods. Years later a friend would write that Mary was a woman not only of humour and dignity, but that she seemed "a romantic figure who personified all the strength, courage and spirit of adventure that made the dear old West...."

By the end of the nineteenth century, many medical diagnoses remained vague. The fear of infectious disease racing across the country by railroad was omnipresent. If news of a diphtheria epidemic in Toronto reached Macleod, Mary was frantic with worry for Nell and Norman, as well as wondering how soon it might reach the West. "Throats" were still a threat to the lives of children, diphtheria and whooping cough being deadly killers. When a smallpox epidemic began in a Calgary Chinese laundry, buildings were put under police guard, patrols rode out to keep the Indians away from Calgary, train passengers were not allowed to disembark, and the governor of North Dakota placed police along the boundary line to stop any immigration. All NWMP were vaccinated, but not the entire citizenry. Although the Drever family was vaccinated in the Red River Settlement about 1850, quarantine was still the only real preventive medicine regularly practised.

Once, when Mary was in Calgary and James holding court in Macleod, their daughter Jean developed a sore throat which deepened into the dreaded sounds of croup. Immediately the judge left the bench and headed for home. The neighbours took the twins, quarantining Jean. James mixed a paste of mustard between two old, soft pieces of cotton, then placed it on Jean's chest. Kept on for the required twenty minutes, the spice grew increasingly hot, nature's own decongestant. Jean coughed repeatedly, then went to sleep. For the next few days James watched over her, finally writing Mary of the incident when the danger was past, and reporting, "She slept splendidly last night and this morning she is as bright as a cricket." Then he returned to court.

At fifty-four, James's own health was breaking down. He sported an expanding waistline, a receding hairline, and suffered from what he described as creeping rheumatism. Usually after seven-course official dinners, pains would shoot through his right side up into his shoulder. Today's diagnosis may have read classic gall bladder trouble but he rejected any affliction which might influence his diet. Regardless of weather he would walk off the heavy dinners, noting more frequently that "It was a pretty hard pull up the hill." When mysterious fevers began striking him he worked on, sweating in his shirt-sleeves and making passing reference to his discomfort.

Perhaps no one was more aware of the dearth of medical facilities than Jean Pinkham, who had nursed the sick alongside Cyprian in shacks and lodges about the country. Calgary was in dire need of a hospital. Too many babies and mothers still died alone in childbirth. In some cases the screams of a mother in labour brought a cowboy rushing to her door, only to be turned away if he was unmarried. So great were the socio-religious proprieties of the era that a woman would rather die or lose her child than be improperly exposed to a man who had guided hundreds of cows through safe deliveries. And for years ranch accidents or those on the trail went attended only by the cowboys riding herd. Broken backs from buckboard spills or Ernest Cross's terror of death from abdominal illness were common ailments. Worse, so many settlers arrived daily that it was impossible to keep track of communicable disease.

One day, a Chinese man died in a local hotel. Although Orientals were a race of people generally despised by westerners, this man's generosity inspired one of Calgary's all-time great community efforts. He had left a suit of clothes to a clergyman and $100 to start a hospital. The money was given to Jean Pinkham, who persuaded the mayor to challenge all Calgarians to help. She wrote that so many feared that the proposed Cottage Hospital might become an Anglican institution that they turned out in force. A great one for titles, Jean also organized the Women's Hospital Aid Society, enticing a number of women and bachelor ranchers to become involved in the project. Ernest Cross was one who rolled up his sleeves and pitched in to help. The town raised money by holding suppers and dances in Hull's Opera House. No one in the business community refused to help.

By fall Jean had found a small two-storey frame building with accommodation for eight patients at 9th Street West and 7th Avenue. The kitchen table became the surgery. Medical aid was voluntary, the Women's Aid agreeing to provide nursing care, bedding and bandages. Using his medical knowledge gained at McGill, and carefully researching the advances in medical technology, Ernest even advised the doctors on stocking their operating room. In October the board, which included Bishop Pinkham, James Lougheed, Ernest Cross and a number of his 1887 roundup pals, officially opened the hospital. Jean Pinkham was named president of the Women's Hospital Aid Society.

When the 1892 smallpox epidemic struck, infuriated mobs of Calgarians wanted to drive all Orientals away. Every night the beleaguered Chinese would make for the NWMP barracks and safety, the police riding patrol throughout the city. Some of their homes were burned, as racial hatred became entrenched in the frontier town. Jean Pinkham was incensed that the Chinese should be treated so poorly when one of them had willed his legacy to establish the Calgary General Hospital.

The tone of the West was altering from wholly agricultural to expanding industrial. Even some of the surviving Indians had adapted to an agrarian lifestyle combined with fledgling industry in the form of a coal mine on the Blackfoot reserve. Nevertheless, continuing his travels by stagecoach and rail, James never lost sight of the fact that nature, not progress, still ruled man's destiny on the prairies. He watched cinders from the smokestacks of trains ignite the worst fires he ever remembered. Floods derailed boxcars and washed out new bridges or smashed new ferries to pieces on river banks. For the first time in his life he suffered a terrible attack of snow blindness, even a shaft of light from a crack in a door setting off a thousand needles of pain in his eyes. Another time during a stormy buckboard trip to Moose Jaw, he wrote that a bolt of lightning killed a child on another man's knee.

As trains brought tens of thousands of settlers, more towns sprang up and the crime rate soared. The demands on James became greater than ever and he continued to seethe over the lengthy arguments of lawyers. Following one case which lasted two and a half days he wrote, "We have two Calgary lawyers here who talk and talk till I feel inclined to choke them." Yet he never hurried the proceedings along at the expense of the judgment, nor did he complain about being a public servant. He preferred long days to get the job done, holding court from ten in the morning until long after dark. Rather than join Justice Rouleau in his all-night poker games, James worked through to midnight. Ironically, when the religious holiday of the Immaculate Conception was first announced, it was the poker-playing Rouleau who got "religious scruples," as James put it, and refused to work. On the first Thanksgiving holiday, November 6, 1890, James worked through the day, trying to bring all the Supreme Court judges' duties to a close so that he could return home. A week later he wrote from council,"I have a very strong desire to resign. In fact my resignation is written out but I will sleep over it – would to Heaven it was to be with you. . . . There is a regular *ruction* going on around me."

A great joy to frontier Canada and the distances separating loved ones was the commercializing of photography. Just prior to Christmas, when Mary managed to visit Nell and Norman in Toronto, James wrote from Macleod, "I rec'd the photos all right and yours has almost done me. I never saw a more perfect picture of a perfect woman. How often have I seen you look just like that when I have drawn you into my arms. It is before me now and I feel an almost overwhelming desire to clasp it to me as I have so often done with the darling original. The children are simply perfect.

"Every time I come into the house I get these pictures and place them on the table as I walk up and down, but it is yours and yours only that catches my eye every time I pass, and not only my eye. . . ." He described Mary's figure as still shapely and beautiful, at thirty-eight years of age a truly regal woman.

In 1893 Calgarians sent a petition to the minister of justice complaining that it was impossible for three judges to cover the whole of the NWT judicial business. Calgary needed a Supreme Court judge for its own, and they wanted James Macleod. The petition was signed by "A.J. Hogg and *eighty-four others*." The petition argued that Calgary was the headquarters of mining, stock, agricultural and lumbering interests, as well as standing on the line of the CPR and the main distribution point for the NWT. They also argued that the only communication between Calgary and Macleod was a weekly stage, that the sittings were irregular and the arrears piled out of sight.

Macleod citizens were incensed at the request. They saw the demand as another in a long list of snubs by the government. They had lost a bid for the CPR, now they were in danger of losing their only natural resource, Colonel Macleod and his family. Unlike Justice Alexander Cross who fought his own move from Montreal to Quebec City for years, James had a whole district fighting against his. Yet he wrote only one letter to the minister of justice asking to remain in Macleod. The *Macleod Gazette* howled, "The removal of the Judge to Calgary at this time would be an act of the rankest kind of injustice and if there is any department in the government from which we expect to receive justice, it is the department which administers it."

The *Gazette* blamed the Alberta Bar Association for the petition.

The removal of the judge, it continued, "would no doubt increase the income of the Calgary lawyers [but] the administration of justice should not be regulated solely . . . to the convenience and incomes of lawyers." Macleod residents followed with a petition signed by "C. Kentes and *one hundred and forty six others*." Calgary citizens simply doubled their next petition.

The *Edmonton Bulletin* got into the fray, advocating that James be appointed lieutenant-governor of the North-West Territories in recognition that he had done more for Canada in the West than any man alive. Sir John A. Macdonald, James's old benefactor, had died in 1891, but the federal government was still Conservative, thus such a patronage appointment could materialize. But James was too valuable where he was. His brand of law – tough, incisive, fair – was widely respected by the lawyers about whom he grouched; he was still the man to get a bill through council even now that it was an elected assembly; and he was still the quickest at clearing the huge Calgary dockets. As lieutenant-governor he would be removed from many of those duties. Within three months his "soldiers" lost a battle he himself had never really fought. He dutifully accepted the decree to leave the town he had begun as a fort in 1873 and moved to Calgary, the fort he had named in 1876.

That October James and Mary presided as guests of honour at the Macleod Agricultural Fair. It was a huge farewell tribute to the town's most beloved citizens. A ball was held the night before and the *Gazette* published four straight days to provide a running report of the week's events. Ranchers, farmers, Indians, Americans and children turned up to compete in agricultural events, and in polo, horse-racing, cattle judging, calf-roping and horse-bucking. James and Mary drove their coach and four to start the fair and to present the Colonel Macleod Polo Cup. With so many policemen and British expatriates, the quality of polo was formidable and dangerous. The game purported few rules designed to maintain a semblance of propriety, but a stirrup jammed under an opponent's foot and hooked upwards, on the off side to the referee, was an effective method of sending an opponent to the turf. If lucky, other players of both teams would swerve in time to miss the downed man. Eventually the Oxley Ranche team beat Calgary to win the cup.

James presided over the half-mile races, standing on top of his coach to start them with a gun shot. The Macleod Turf Association would not be formed for another five years but citizens bet up to

$600 on a race that week. And they agreed that never again would a race be as exciting as that day in 1886 when an Indian boy and his pony had beaten an eastern thoroughbred.

The family was greeted by all as Alberta's most beloved and illustrious personages. Their home overflowed all week, with guests ranging from titled Englishmen to down-and-out cowboys. James was never more ebullient, never more generous, and it must have emptied his pockets completely to entertain in such a fashion.

Soon off to Regina, James sent Mary to Calgary to search for a home. James Lougheed offered to get a house built for them and ready for occupancy in two months, at $45 a month. Worried over receiving no news of a raise in pay, however, James declined. He would think about building the following year. Initially, Mary rented a seven-room sandstone house near the south entrance of Louise Bridge. The moving bill from Macleod to Calgary was sent to the Macleods.

In the 1880s Nell and Norman had seen James just as "Papa," but by the nineties they could see that their father exemplified the land in which they lived. If the newspapers lauded the NWMP for a chase well executed or an act of bravery, the incident reflected the moral tone of the force, originally moulded with the help of Commissioner Macleod. And while NWMP incidents no longer affected the family directly, James often tried the culprit. Rather than James reminding anyone of his association with the force, he simply embodied its credo, *Maintain le Droit*. With this awareness, and with the knowledge that they had a network of influential relatives and friends across the country, the Macleod children grew up with a sense of position and of public service.

In 1894 Nell was sixteen, Norman almost fifteen, Roma and Mary eleven, and Jean eight. With the exception of Norman, Mary insisted that all become proficient at cooking, sewing, outdoor duties and, in fact, at all tasks undertaken by any servants. Her demand for her children's resourcefulness was rooted in her own childhood. She used to remind them that she came from a log cabin in the Red River Settlement with an Indian encampment on one side. From her stories, it must have been hard for her children to imagine that the Indians they now saw in lodges or lying around the plains were the same race that once wore scalps on their belts and terrified the Drevers. Mary was only forty-one years old.

During her first summer in Calgary, Nell met so many people she could not possibly remember them all. She loved meeting her father on the Court House steps or at the Ranchmen's Club, then walking down the street where everyone knew him.

Calgary was a town of brouhaha and balls, of riders galloping horses or driving cattle along 8th Avenue as elegant guests headed for a formal dance held in the Opera House. The West was in Nell's blood. Years later she would write, "This is going to be a great country." And, "How great for the West!" At the time she may have imagined marrying a rancher or a lawyer but he would have to like horses, children and God. She might also have thought twice about ever marrying a judge like her father because he was rarely at home.

One day James emerged from the club with a black-haired man with brown eyes and a dark mustache that glinted auburn highlights in the sun. His three-piece suit was well made but baggy in the knees from riding, and his hat was as battered as that of a cowboy. Nevertheless, he was pleasant looking if not handsome. "My dear," smiled Nell's father, "this is Mr. Ernest Cross." Thirty-six-year-old Ernest smiled broadly, extended a charming greeting, then turned and walked toward the brewery.

A regular at the polo tournaments and influential on the hospital boards and other services in Calgary, Ernest Cross was well known and admired, particularly by James Macleod. Watching him stride off, Nell may have wondered why her father liked Mr. Cross so much when he had spent his life battling the whiskey traders. All that the NWMP and the brewery shared in common were their time-honoured trademarks of the buffalo, the NWMP buffalo gazing proudly from the crest, the Calgary Brewing & Malting Company's buffalo winking from their bottles.

Through the spring and summer of 1894, James's health deteriorated. From Regina he wrote of the pesky insects, the first time he had ever been bothered by them. He was out of sorts more often, losing weight and suffering fevers and tissue swellings. He could hardly stand the rigours of travel but, pressed for finances, kept his illness a carefully guarded secret. In August James was hard on the whistle-stops, sweating from fevers and the heat, slowing ever more for his walks as he coped with swelling in his legs. Photographed in his robes he appeared thin, intense. Mary watched his encroaching illness and dreaded their partings. He wrote to her from Dunmore, "My dearest Mary, I felt quite sad yesterday as the train moved out of the station, to see you following me with your handkerchief up to your eyes and I sat thinking for ever so long. My dear pet, it can't be helped.

The pot must be kept boiling and I can't keep it so, except out here." Then he asked Mary to send him the bundles of papers he left on her desk as well as a pile of typewritten papers entitled *Index to Civil Justice*. This note tells much of the modernization of the West: typewriters and registered mail, appeal books for Regina and even secretaries.

From Regina, James described a lengthy court hearing in sweltering weather. The room was full and all the windows closed up by men looking in: "There was no fresh air. It was war to the knife between the lawyers and I had to hold a tight rein over them."

At the end of the month, having taken no breaks, James returned from Regina to Calgary and rested a few days with his family. After church one Sunday morning, the children caught the stage for Pincher Creek. Compared to the heat and dust of Macleod, the gentle green hills surrounding Kyleakin farm were lush and cool and sprinkled as always with flowers. It was an invitation to any child like Nell to jump astride her horse and gallop off to heaven. None of them had any notion that their father was dying.

That evening a Mountie rode hard into Pincher Creek and strode up to Nell. He was breathing heavily, his face stricken. He said, "Please come with me at once. Your father is very ill." As they left Pincher Creek in a carriage and galloped through Macleod, people lined the streets in sorrow and some in fear. The Mounties escorted the children back to Calgary in record time, as if their speed might help save their former commissioner. Indians had wrapped themselves in blankets under James's window and were chanting night and day. No one sent them away. Mary explained to the children that they had done the same thing when her own father, William Drever, was ill in the Red River Settlement.

As the poisons built up in James, fluid amassed and pressured his heart. Throughout the next few days, his fever periodically abated and he would regain consciousness. Then the children came in one by one to see him. He smiled at little Jean and tried to put her at ease. If he gave any advice no one remembers; he never was a man to lecture.

James died in Mary's arms on September 5. Two days later his funeral befitted a statesman. Martin Macleod's black coffin on a farm wagon had been as simple as his son's would be regal. Shortly after two o'clock in the afternoon, the Church of the Redeemer bells began tolling over a silent Calgary. Twenty-three North West Mounted Police riding magnificently groomed horses led the procession in scarlet coats, polished brass buttons, and white helmets and gloves. Immediately behind them was James's coffin, resting on a gun carriage and covered with a flag, his helmet, sword and wreath. His own thoroughbred charger, draped in black with boots reversed in the stirrups, followed immediately behind. As the funeral cortège moved out from the Macleods' house, the NWMP band began a drum roll, leading into the slow "Dead March in Saul." Mary and the children followed immediately behind the gun carriage. Retired police officers backed them up, including some militia men from Wolseley's 1870 Red River Expedition. The cortège stretched for half a mile as friends, members of the Calgary bar, law students, groups representing city corporations, schools, representatives of government and the commissioner of police joined the procession. The silence was broken only by crunching footsteps, the drum roll and the Blackfoot's mournful cry.

After the service, the procession marched to Union Cemetery. The police formed a hollow square around the Macleod family, the last words of the blessing died away and James was lowered into the grave. The honour guard fired three volleys, each followed by a salute, then his bugler from the 1870 expedition played "Taps."

Letters showered upon the family, one from former Governor General Lord Lorne. He wrote to Mary from Kensington Gardens of his grief and admiration. And Colonel Sam Steele wrote, "As a soldier, a judge and a gentleman he had few equals. From the time he arrived, in everything for the well-being of the people of the North West Territory his hand was to be seen. No one was jealous of him; he was the admired of all, and kind to a fault.... The Blackfeet regarded him as the personification of truth and honour."

Soon, along with letters of condolence, came the bills, and a banker who had the unhappy task of informing Mary that James had left a savings account of exactly $8. Letters from boot-makers and clothing shops arrived expressing deep regret at the colonel's death but reminding Mary of his outstanding accounts. Mary paid them all from her own diminishing funds. The list seemed endless: insurance policies, school bills, the moving invoice from Macleod for $115.15. After all the entertaining, the horses, the eastern schools, the trips to Drynoch, Masquoteh and Winnipeg, Mary Macleod's life had ground to a shocking halt.

The newspapers from Alberta to Manitoba wrote pleas to the federal government for a substantial pension for the family in honour of the man who had achieved "peace with honour" in the northwest.

But it seemed as if Ottawa had never heard of him. The Conservative government, which had awarded General Middleton $20,000 and a knighthood following the short-lived if bloody 1885 Riel Rebellion, remained silent on the matter of Justice Macleod. Lord Lorne sent a petition to the government, signed as well by Governor General Lord Dufferin, also requesting that Mary be granted a pension. Reviewing James's association with the chiefs of the Blackfoot nation, the governors general wrote,

> ... It is not too much to say that Lt. Col. Macleod's influence with his Indian friends has time and again averted bloodshed. ... Not in this public capacity alone did this late servant of the government deserve well of his country; as guide, philosopher and friend to the early settlers in Alberta, his experience, tact and judgement were of inestimable advantage.

Nothing happened. Jean Pinkham took the Macleod family into her home, selling her diamond ring to meet the cost of feeding six more people. She insisted that the only jewellery she ever cared about was her wedding ring made by the Winnipeg tinsmith. Grocery hampers mysteriously appeared on their doorstep.

Frederick W. Haultain, who had been a close friend of the Macleods, called the government's behaviour shameful. Then, waiting no longer, he and others gathered to help. A little black book quickly became filled with names of citizens willing to donate anything from $2 to $150 for the Macleods. Haultain took Norman to live with him in Regina and raised enough money from ranchers to send the boy to his father's old school, Upper Canada College. Calgarians raised sufficient funds to buy a two-storey house near the corner of Fourth Street and Twelfth Avenue S.W. for the family.

For sixteen-year-old Nell, Bishop Strachan School in Toronto was not only out of the question but further schooling of any kind was impossible. In an era when children of prominent families did volunteer work but never took a job, Nell became a cashier at the Hudson's Bay Company for $25 a month. Her salary paid the food and clothing bills for the family. One day she left a dollar gold piece in the cash register and went for her tea break. Upon returning, she found that a clerk had mistakenly given it as a 5 cent piece in change. Nell had to make up the difference out of her salary.

For a time Mary gratefully accepted the kindness of Calgarians but she was not one to depend upon charity. Perhaps with thoughts of the tailor, Stuttaford, a man once considered beneath the Macleods' station, Mary took up her needle to become one of Calgary's leading dressmakers. The wives of wealthy remittance men loved her skills, honed in the Red River as she and her sisters had whipped up homespun cloth for an evening's dance. Now in Calgary in 1894, Mary sewed constantly for the numerous balls, training her daughters Mary, Roma and Jean as her assistants. Young Mary later vowed that she never wanted to see another basting stitch in her life. As Nell became older, Calgary doyennes would quietly slip a twice-worn, imported ball gown into her closet. Under her mother's guidance, Nell would then remake it into something smashing and, to all eyes, original.

After graduation from Central School, young Jean Macleod also worked as a cashier for the Hudson's Bay Company. Roma worked as a receptionist at the city hall while twin sister Mary stayed home with her mother. Despite their near poverty, the Macleod girls were sought out by society. Position was what the matriarch of Drynoch had sought for her children, and now in the reputation of her son and daughter-in-law, it was firmly rooted in another generation and a new frontier. Because of this status, the children were invited to the balls and the hunts, hostesses lending them habits to wear and horses to jump.

Mary Macleod gradually stitched together the pieces of her torn life, staying involved in church work and the Women's Auxiliary of the hospital. Her large and loving family was a comfort, but part of her soul had slipped away with James. Grandchildren would remember her watching a sunset or a violent storm with a faraway look of longing. She had saved all her husband's letters, and would read them in quiet times in his favourite rocking chair.

One of his last letters is thumb-worn and stained at the creases, as if it had been carried in the garden or on horseback. In it James wrote to Mary that he had found "a perfect bed of wild roses. I plucked them to send to you. . . . They are all in a jumble now but still retain some fragrance. Darling, it made me so happy to go back to this place but still I felt lonely. . . . I do so long to see you, and may Heaven grant we may never be separated so long again. With endless love . . . Jim."

16

The Industrial Frontier

"You are the hope for the family."
Alexander to Ernest

Alexander hardly glanced at his vanishing bench career as he mobilized, in absentia, the construction of his western empire. He fired off daily, sometimes twice-daily letters, querying and advising Ernest on everything from financial investments to bookkeeping. At times his tone was so paternalistic that Ernest must have felt like a boy in short pants; yet when he was ill and depressed by the growing competition, his father wrote, "Hope you will not lose [faith] but revive your courage." In 1890 the Wall Street market had crashed, and when the western Canadian market fell off in January of 1893, Alexander sent a volley of advice to Ernest: " ... press the government for favorable terms for the land. I suppose you have not failed to charge all disbursements made for the brewery. I have sent you a memo.... Let us hear from you at least once a week."

When Ernest told his father that he planned to aid the Alberta farmer by organizing a barley-seed lease plan, Alexander researched that grain with the thoroughness of a scientist investigating a newly discovered bacterium. He wrote pages of his findings, comparing optimum kernels with seasonal influences, methods of shipping and so on. He also advised Ernest to get his lager plant going as soon as possible. Referring to his father as "the Governor" (a name which stuck with all the brothers), Ernest responded to Alexander's barrages by growing more circumspect. He knew that his father's faith in Calgary speculation was diminishing, but his own spirits remained high and he had managed to secure from his father a verbal promise for a loan of $7,000 to his friend T.S.C. Lee. Despite his reservations,

Alexander had given Lee his word and honoured the loan.

In Alberta, the drought and the plunging market signalled a coming time of economic fluctuations as drastic as the climate. Land investors increasingly defaulted in their payments to the Crosses. Lamenting that Ernest and Willie Heber did not seem able to call in their debts, Alexander advanced Lougheed $2,371.96, partly due to him for the Calgary Gas and Water Works Company, and sent several $2,000 notes for interim coverage on other commitments. Over the first six months of 1893, money shuttled back and forth between Montreal and Calgary. In closing one deal, Alexander claimed that Lougheed agreed to pay the exchange premium of $5. It seems he never did so, despite nagging notes for another thirty years. For the Crosses, it made for untidy bookkeeping. According to Alexander's papers, the Lougheeds still owe the Crosses $5.

It was out of character for Alexander to continue investing capital in the face of falling markets. His old adversary, the cresting wave, was curling with a force he recognized. Noting that property values had plunged to as low as $50 per front foot on Eighth Avenue, he grumbled, "I don't relish furnishing capital for others' defaults. I would rather avoid all unnecessary liability at the start and stress moderation and economy in everything. . . . Many enterprises are wrecked for want of the heedful at the critical beginning." But when Ernest assured him it was an excellent time to buy, for the market would turn around and they "would reap great dividends," Alexander agreed to continue helping but warned that further investments would be minimal. He added that the brewery should pay Ernest no salary that year and that he should not promote the local growth of barley. He followed with point form advice for Ernest and Willie Heber:

1. Make yourself strong by calling in all the subscribed capital.

2. Incur no liabilities that cannot be dispensed with and do not be tempted by any projects, however flattering, not strictly within the lines of your undertaking.

3. Limit your output as to proportion of the capital you can readily command. [Any profit could be used to induce more capital from the original stockholders.] Shareholders should be required to pay up. I suppose you will say that all this will be done. The difficulty is to put this into practice.

Ernest continued buying land at $1.25 an acre for his father, who wanted only waterfront property for future resale. On the leases relinquished around the a7 the previous year, Alexander reneged, informing the minister of the interior that he had furnished Ernest with blank cheques to expedite land purchases instead. His moves reflected the constant game of trying to out-guess the government's ill-conceived land policy. He then admonished his son that the money was but a loan and to use sage judgment in its use. Changing his mind about the lager plant, Alexander told Ernest not to build. Too late. Ernest had already completed it, a new ice house for 900 tons, a barrel shed and a cooper shop for $12,000, borrowed from the Bank of Montreal at 7 per cent.

As if he hadn't read his father's cautionary tales, Ernest added that the CB&M would require all of $10,000 additional capital. As for their Dominion land lease, he was hoping to purchase some of it adjacent to his new a7 homestead. In his reply, Alexander advised Ernest to raise new capital through the shareholders pro rata on their present subscriptions. Warning that government policy on land was still shaky, he cautioned, "Pay [for land] by installment with a balance unpaid." "Festina lente," Alexander periodically reminded him, or "make haste slowly." Once he closed with, "My money is going fast."

All the signs of a downturn in the economy were there to see, but it was not until August 1894 that Ernest finally acknowledged, "The depression in Calgary is great just now and outside lots are unsaleable. Whether they will ever recover enough to get out what they cost is hard to say. In my opinion, it depends entirely on whether irrigation is successful. So far it has gone on very slowly."

Up to this period of his life, Ernest had seen land only appreciate in value. Now he watched men ruined and he finally appreciated his father's warnings. He realized that whereas land had meant speculative profit, it would come to mean longevity. Rarely would he ever again buy property to make a quick profit. He came to deplore the get-rich-quick scheme so often instigated at the expense of those less fortunate. To him, land became a precious commodity, something which did not transform into currency. Long after Ernest Cross had gone, he intended his progeny to remain on his a7 Ranche.

Alexander requested Ernest to complete an account of each Cross asset in Alberta. The inventory included several lots, the Glen estate and the Calgary Gas and Water Works in Alexander's name. Willie Heber's investments included shares in the Lougheed block, Alberta Hotel, the future Stampede grounds, and three mortgages to individual businessmen. Julia and Selkirk held two lots each. Ernest held twenty-six city lots and a mortgage in the Lougheed block. His capital investment in the brewery was $20,000 and the a7 Ranche was now valued, both land and cattle, at $22,687. It was a large investment for a family depending upon the adolescent brewery to cover costs through sales. Problems at the CB&M abounded. Perhaps it was the brewer's recipe rather than the depression, but people weren't drinking much beer. That year the sales remained almost static and outlets repeatedly reneged on their payments. Despite Ernest's meticulous research and long hours, he had made errors in construction, materials purchased and beer recipes. Green, cloudy beer, leaky vats and broken machinery kept him going twenty hours of the day. He rushed about like the Sorcerer's Apprentice dancing one step ahead of the roaring flood. But he remained ever confident that if he improved the recipe, despite war, pestilence, depression or temperance groups, people would still drink beer.

One night, while returning from a party with Billie Cochrane and mining speculator Randolph Bruce, Ernest was thrown from the buckboard into a roadside ditch and knocked unconscious. Billie thought he was dead. The bruised and scratched pair delivered Ernest to the Calgary General Hospital. He was still unconscious, had suffered a concussion and had a bad gash across his forehead. At first, Willie Heber did not inform Julia and Alexander of the seriousness of his injury. Eventually Ernest regained consciousness. During his two-week convalescence he threw one nurse (at least) into a twitter as she struggled with her conscience and strove to do her duty to God. Ernest promised his parents he would make it to Montreal in time for his sister Maggie's wedding.

Willie Heber again took over the a7 homestead, dashing about with the intensity and effectiveness of chain lightning. Although he had realized sales of some $4,020.97 (or a respectable $48.44 per head) during his previous visit and ploughed considerable land, he soon took his old familiar slide.

As in previous years, he offered to oversee the transport of 196 horses from several Calgary ranches as far as Winnipeg for the company, ffolkes & Hodgens. It was Willie Heber's understanding that ffolkes was responsible for the in-transit insurance, and that upon arrival of the horses in Bothwell, Ontario, ffolkes would break them for sale in England. As a7 horses were already trained, there was no need for them to be detained and it seemed like a good deal. Accompanying the horses as far as Winnipeg, the family story goes that only Willie Heber arrived well-quaffed and fed. He allegedly careened off the train followed by a carload of horses whimpering for water. Another herdsman took the horses to Bothwell, where ffolkes refused to take them off the CPR until the transportation fee of $2,000 was paid. Then, instead of sending any off to England, he kept the entire 196 horses throughout the winter, running down their deteriorated condition while running up huge boarding costs.

Some witnesses claimed that ffolkes had purposely corralled the horses to run up expenses. Word would later come from England that he had quadrupled his profits and that the horses hadn't been so badly off after all. Willie Heber wrote that in Bothwell ffolkes was considered a fraud. ffolkes claimed differently and launched a damage suit against the various Alberta ranches for his fees. Alexander knew Willie Heber well and, learning that the horses of five other ranches were also involved, scolded Ernest: "I should judge him to be the least suitable person to have in charge of disposing of horses and the risk too great to have been ventured in." The issue was shelved until the spring. Willie Heber was never again assigned to transport anything other than himself.

On his 1894 Christmas visit home, Senator Harry Cross was astonished to find electric light brightening every room of Pine Avenue. He hardly recognized the heavily built-up Sherbrooke Street. Sleighing was diminishing as streets were kept clear of snow for the electric cars which ran on tracks down the main streets. Harry was also saddened at how his father had aged in the five years since he had last seen him. In turn, his parents were disturbed by the lonely hardships Léa still faced with the twins on their Braehead ranch. Alexander and Julia insisted that Harry return to Wyoming with a French servant for his wife. They couldn't imagine how she continued to cope.

Following a swirl of Christmas balls and glitter, Maggie Cross was married to William Robinson MacInnes, son of a major CPR shareholder, Senator Donald MacInnes (the owner of Dundurn castle and president of the Bank of Hamilton), and grandson of former Chief Justice John Beverley Robinson. As personal secretary to CPR president William Van Horne, William MacInnes was en route to a vice-presidency in the great company. Alexander described the handsome groom as a gentle, manly young man, and a recuperating Ernest was no doubt delighted with the merger. In the interest of the Crosses' western land holdings, Senator MacInnes had already spoken privately with the powerful mandarin, A.M. Burgess, deputy minister of the interior. Alexander built a brick home for the young couple in the lower garden overlooking Pine Avenue and the city.

In February Ernest cautioned his brewery manager, C.W. Macmillan, to say nothing of his whereabouts. Then he headed for the Brewer's Academy, New York, and a four-month master brewer's course. Within weeks everyone out west knew that he had gone back to school. For laughs Randolph Bruce circulated a rumour that he was actually married and subsequently reported that the "nurses at the Calgary General Hospital were indignant." Upon his return, Ernest would be dubbed the "Jolly, Jolly Brewer."

Macmillan was less than amused, reporting to Ernest that the economy was devastated, collections were impossible, the ale house smelled from leaking beer which had soaked into the dirt floor, and the load of beer barged downriver to Battleford was so terrible that he had dumped fifty gallons onto the ground. CB&M beer in the Crow's Nest Pass was as bad. It just didn't travel. Ernest responded by inviting young Herbert Molson to join the CB&M as brewer. Molson replied that he really knew so little about brewing that he did not consider himself qualified for the job. Reports to Ernest in New York grew worse. Liabilities were growing. The CB&M was just scraping along. Some of the directors threatened to sell their shares if the beer recipe wasn't improved.

By spring, the ffolkes case had grown into a nightmare of furious ranchers, witnesses scattered from Maine to England, accusations and counter-accusations criss-crossing the country. As one of the ranches had declared bankruptcy, then relocated in England, the mounting costs fell onto Cross Brothers Limited. From New York Ernest wrote in favour of settling out of court, concluding, "[it is] . . . the most reasonable way out of this horrible mess I seem to have got into through a worthless scalywag." No old boys' friendship between the blithe Edward ffolkes and the puckish Ernest Cross could mollify their differences. Instead of a settlement, the case went to the Supreme Court of the NWT.

Throughout the spring Alexander requested all the information on the development of the case and suggested the use of Quebec defence lawyers. Instead, Ernest arranged for a young Calgary lawyer, D'Alton McCarthy, to prepare the defence. In Alexander's opinion, McCarthy was careless in his preparation, failing even to use correct legal terminology. A harassed McCarthy ran up his bills while trying to appease Alexander and work with the furious, independent-minded ranchers. Confusion over litigation and legal fees ensued.

In bed with a chest cold and frustrated with the distance separating him from his investments, Alexander fired his directives through Julia's pen. With the urgency of an old man whose vicarious hopes lay in the success of his son, Alexander could not – would not – see his son fail. In repeated letters he advised Ernest to argue this or to try that in court. Finally, when it looked as though the evidence was piling inexorably against Cross Brothers Limited, Alexander decreed that all friendly witnesses should be brought out from England on an expense-paid trip to testify, and to have the brewery bookkeeper deal with the receipts.

The ranchers lost the case. The expense for Cross Brothers Limited alone came to $3,600. McCarthy was forced to reduce his three-year-old fees to $860, one-third of which was paid by Ernest. The decision was a staggering blow to both Ernest's wallet and his morale. He lost everything on those horses and determined to get out of the business. Snorted Willie Heber, "What an awful swindle that ffolkes affair is."

During the summer Alexander added an iron-clad codicil to his will, which was written in entirety in his shaky longhand. Unbeknownst to his children, he established six corporations. Each had a holding company for a portion of their father's securities, which would remain indissoluable until the death of his last living child. Far more important than money, however, he had already given, or forced upon, his children the legacy of education. In review, they were doing well. Harry was a Wyoming senator and against the odds had made it solely in ranching. Braehead was steadily growing and its future was ensured for generations to come. Nearby Casper built its first oil refinery that year, and the scent of drilling was in the air.

In Montreal, Selkirk Cross, QC, a full partner of Hall, Cross, Brown and Sharp, counsel for the Royal Bank, was competently juggling the multifarious family estates. In Paris, Cannes, Switzerland or wherever, Willie Heber proved a sound if unconventional financier. Handling other people's investments particularly in Mexico, he made scads of money while dallying in restaurants and clubs. He must have been one of the first entrepreneurs to venture into the Mexican market. At the River Beaudette farm, Edmund proved a kind man and the most handsome of the sons, but he lacked "get" as Willie Heber put it. His ploughing was always late, he bought too much seed, he let the farm run down. While Edmund felt a compassion for others, he couldn't get on with the business of living. The brothers would watch out for him, which he resented but eternally sought. In Chicago, Maggie MacInnes's William was rising swiftly through the CPR ranks. And in Alexander's eye, Ernest was his alter ego.

Alexander's health improved once his affairs were in order. By midsummer he felt sufficiently strong to spend a little time at the River Beaudette farm. He packed an overnight bag intending to leave in the morning, but during the night suffered a bladder stoppage. Bedridden for two weeks, he was stricken by pneumonia. Often called the "old man's friend," the condition claimed many a tired life in the pre-antibiotic days. Maggie returned from Chicago to Pine Avenue to help her mother nurse her father. He needed round the clock care as he lay with poultices on his chest, lapsing into unconsciousness and feverishly moaning about the brewery.

Maggie wrote Ernest to come east immediately. But their seventy-five-year-old father fought back and amazed the doctor with a recovery. Alexander joked that his strength was a quality curious to all Crosses, but his constant tremor both annoyed and pained him and he confided to Julia, "I have a strong desire to leave this world." His words shattered Julia and he promised he wouldn't mention it again. Upon receiving Maggie's more hopeful letter, Ernest remained in Calgary. He would come east for Christmas and wrote his father not to worry, that brewery accounts were being paid and sales were improving.

Julia read Ernest's letter repeatedly to Alexander but he had relapsed again and did not seem to hear the words. She wrote daily to their sons, recounting their father's deep love and concern for each of them. In one letter she feared, "I don't know how we can live without your father, home will be desolate." In their forty-four years together, Alexander's and Julia's letters had remained as poetic as in their courting days of 1849. It pained her to watch the once alert face with its twinkling eyes grow expressionless, but she noted that he looked so peaceful and bore an uncanny resemblance to Ernest. Just before 9:30 p.m. on October 17, a deeply unconscious Alexander suddenly whispered, "The brewery is rising . . ." Then, peacefully, he died.

Following a service at Pine Avenue and one at St. Gabriel's Church, Alexander was buried at the Cross obelisk in the Mount Royal Cemetery along with his youngsters, Charles, Julia and Robert. A devastated Ernest wrote to Julia that he and his father had had an especially affectionate parting in June, as if they had feared it might be their last meeting. The front page of the *Montreal Star* reported of Alexander and his bench duties: "As a judge he was patient with excited lawyers and witnesses, and by a kind, well-placed word healed many a rough blow given in the heat of discussion. His judgements were plain, matter-of-fact ones, standing squarely on the law, without any ornate style of language. They were given after careful sifting of evidence and mature reflection and deliberation."

Upon the reading of the will the sons learned that their father had forgiven each of the loans he had made. Each child received the equivalent of $12,000 in their respective corporations. Willie Heber got free title to the a7 Ranche and fifty volumes from Alexander's library. Ernest received free title to the brewery. Harry received Bank of Montreal capital stock and was forgiven any outstanding loans to Braehead, Wyoming. Edmund received clear title to the River Beaudette farm. Maggie received twenty-seven shares in the capital stock, Bank of Montreal, a large portion of his precious leather-bound library, and the brick house at the foot of the garden. Selkirk received fifty capital shares of Bank of Montreal, a number of properties and the vast library of law books. Following a bequest to the Montreal General Hospital, and succession duty payments of 3 per cent on any estate over $200,000, Julia was given full use of the estate during her lifetime. For the next half-century, each child would receive quarterly interest on it, which for years remained at $473.72, and which would remain impregnable during the life of Julia. No capital windfall would befall Cross sons. It was as they had wished, and they intended to keep Pine Avenue for future generations.

PART THREE

1896–1932

Dear Brewer

"Grass is the forgiveness of nature, her constant benefaction. Forests decay, harvests perish, flowers vanish, but grass is immortal . . . its tenacious fibres hold the earth in its place and prevent its soluable components from washing into the wasting sea. It invades the solitudes of deserts, climbs the inaccessible slopes and forbidding pinnacles of mountains, modifies climates and determines the history, character and destination of nations. Unobtrusive and patient, it has immortal vigor and aggression. Banished from the thoroughfare and the field, it abides its time to return and when vigilance is relaxed, or the dynasty has perished, it silently resumes the throne from which it has been expelled, but which it never abdicates. It bares no blazonery or bloom to charm the senses with fragrance of splendor, but its wholly hue is more enchanting than the lily or the rose. It yields no fruit in earth or air, and yet, should harvest it fail for a single year, famine would depopulate the world. . . ."

Ernest Cross Papers

17

The Sorcerer's Apprentice

"Our Canadians are as usual, slow, and the cream of the business will be picked up by the Americans."

Stephens to Cross, 1897

In 1896 the depression-battered central Canadian economy was cautiously recovering, but in Alberta three years of dry weather and crop failures had driven many farmers to the United States. On the abandoned homesteads, cattle tumbled into wells and half-completed buildings stood deserted, their frames rattling in the wind like skeletons. Ernest wrote that barbed wire from untended fences was strewn about the prairie. In five years the population had grown by less than one thousand people and real estate investments were practically valueless.

Despite the disastrous market, Cross Brothers Limited had prospered more than other investors, thanks to Alexander's 1893 infusion of cash. Ernest's brewery inventory included eight acres of land adjacent to the city of Calgary surrounded by roads on three sides, with frontage on the Calgary and Edmonton Railway from which they had their own siding. The buildings included a malt-house, a four-storey building with stone on three sides and one side frame to allow for extension, a cooper shop and ice houses, stable and carriage shed, a brick office, and dwelling houses for brewery employees. Another CB&M parcel of four lots with the mineral water business and housed in a wooden frame building was located within the city limits.

In British Columbia the CB&M owned cold-storage buildings in Kaslo, Ferguson and Trout Lake. Business connections extended four hundred miles east, three hundred west, two hundred north and one hundred south, besides east and west Kootenay. (Harry wrote from Wyoming to say the Canadian government probably didn't even know the Kootenays were in Canada.) Ernest remarked of CB&M sales, "Our prices are high and . . . the profits should be from ten percent, increasing rapidly with increase in output which I am perfectly satisfied should triple in five years." But profits failed to materialize that year.

By January 1897 settlers were flooding into Alberta again and the economy was on the upswing. That spring, gold rush fever hit the West. Unconcerned with geographical trivia, the Board of Trade touted Calgary as the jumping-off spot for the Klondike gold mines. Beer sales soared as thousands of festive fortune hunters poured into the city. Nell Macleod watched some men so green they didn't even know they were walking on ice, and they bought wild broncos which were passed off as docile pack horses.

Ernest wrote to Selkirk telling him the depression was over and would he like to invest in mines? Selkirk's reply was immediate and blunt. The East had no confidence in mining. The stock was flat. There was no money to be found.

Selkirk's reply disappointed Ernest. He knew that in the Crow's Nest Pass five hundred men were digging for coke and hollering for the coal miners' champagne to slake their thirst. In response, Ernest sent his manager, C.W. Macmillan, to wrest control from the American competition, to build a beer monopoly, to oversee transport and to stake claims. In the rough-and-tumble coal towns of the pass, it was no task for the faint of heart. With a little help from Randolph Bruce, who captured five claims for the CB&M, the roving Macmillan secured nine of eleven British Columbian beer outlets and bonded a dozen or so mining claims. Some he began shoring up immediately.

It was then that Ernest's friend Stephens wrote of the American hustlers and urged Ernest to become involved in Kootenay mining. Having staked land in Rossland, British Columbia, Stephens wrote that his assay of black sand showed gold, silver and platinum, "but the real money is further north. Will head there soon." Ernest couldn't resist. He purchased a British Columbia miner's licence for $5, then for $2,000 bought into a mine called the Aberdeen, and three-quarters of an interest in the Kootenay Ore Company. By late spring, Ernest and the CB&M had "invested themselves broke."

Left alone to run the a7 Ranche while Ernest put in twelve-hour days at the brewery, Willie Heber slipped into one of his escape passions. One thousand head now roamed the Cross ranchlands, and it was Willie Heber upon whom the burden had fallen. True, it had always been his homestead but only because Ernest already owned one. He had been pressed into a hands-on role which to him was anathema. He began drinking heavily and making strange speeches while sleepwalking.

That summer Willie Heber told Ernest he wanted out of the a7 Ranche and wouldn't be back. He was going to live in the south of France. Ernest could buy him out or he would sell it to William MacInnes, or if necessary, put it on the open market. Inherited the previous year at a value of $12,000, Willie Heber figured the ranch was worth $15,000. He suggested payments of $2,000 per annum and 5 per cent interest on the outstanding balance.

Ernest was dismayed. His heart was in beef, not beer, but the brewery had proved the more difficult child. Although he had helped incorporate the Western Stockgrowers' Association that year, he had neglected the ranch, which was being choked by settlement. As he had no capital to pay Willie Heber, he stood to lose what he had come west for in the first place. He even considered putting his brewery shares up for sale at $110,000. Shortly thereafter, he managed to raise $2,000 for a down payment on the ranch and accepted Willie Heber's deal. There was no ill will between them. The brothers had been trained by their father to conduct business matters amongst themselves as they would with strangers. Willie Heber had struck a hard deal but it was what he believed the market would have stood.

Ernest then purchased land from the Calgary and Edmonton Land Company, substantially increasing the size of his debts. He also hired a number of men to dig irrigation ditches at the ranch. Billie Cochrane oversaw the job and fired one gentleman who "handled dirt like putting sugar into a tea cup with a spoon."

Simultaneously, two brewery directors, Hull and McNaghten, threatened to put their shares on the open market. As the business had been started as a kind of private club, Billie Cochrane was furious. He wrote Ernest encouraging him to hang in with the brewery and added, "I won't raise a cent for the Hull and the Jew. . . . Hull would be a good riddance . . . and he is certainly most offensive in his remarks toward you. . . . I have implicit faith in a brilliant future for the brewery. . . . I will assist you with my credit and cash and if necessary take up his shares."

English concerns were buying up Canadian breweries, and selling the CB&M was tempting, but Ernest hung in. The Klondike boom had ended as abruptly as it had begun. Most men were broke. Prospectors were holding up to thirty claims each and had no cash to even quench their thirst. As gambling had been suppressed as well, it was no fun for anyone to frequent the saloons. Macmillan wrote from the West Kootenay, "Houses selling a keg a day three weeks ago are not selling one keg every three days." He wasn't even able to collect payment for goods he'd supplied during the rush even though Ernest wrote, "Get it any way you can." Then another CB&M shareholder, Herbert Eckford, became nervous and wanted out for $5,000. Ernest told him he couldn't afford to buy up his shares. He had managed to repay the bank $12,500 since the beginning of the year but still owed $1,500.

As the banks demanded the CB&M keep to its payment schedule, Ernest chased after his losses and near disasters as he had once pounded after his disappearing broncos. No sooner did he get partial control of one facet than another broke loose. Later in the year he received a letter from Willie Heber in Nice. Short of cash, he asked that the annual payments for the ranch be increased by $500. Ernest couldn't spare a cent. Willie replied that he was sorry Ernest was having worries but then everybody did. He proposed that Ernest buy the a7 outright in six years' time instead of the current 5 per cent interest on monthly instalments. But Ernest couldn't see having that kind of capital in the near future and held Willie to the original deal.

With all his juggling, Ernest couldn't keep pace with the book-keeping. He wired Montreal for help. Selkirk sent out what he described as "a hustler," a man both "dirty and untidy ... [who] probably got his appearance from his former job in newspaper work." The man proved brilliant at balancing the books of an increasingly complex structure. By hiring others to deal with such thorny trivia, Ernest was freed to deal with more immediate disasters. Corks blew, kegs leaked, second-hand bottles proved faulty, shipments to British Columbia arrived incomplete. Some shipments never arrived at all, having been side-tracked en route or even during night-time loading at the CB&M rail yard. Often those cars that did reach their destination were insufficiently cooled. Warm beer that tasted like soap disgusted the consumers.

Once when the frazzled Macmillan snarled at Ernest to hurry and send ice, 120,000 pounds arrived by rail only to melt on a siding before being discovered. A Hudson's Bay Company agent complained from the Kootenays, "I am sorry to say the last beer you shipped into this country has done your firm a great deal of harm and has had the effect of stopping the sale of your goods entirely. I am not aware of a single instance where your beer has not been returned. It is simply a dead loss."

Brewery headaches aside, Ernest was actively involved in almost every committee and association engaged in ranching conditions, and in boosting the industrial development of the West. He helped lobby for a huge government-sponsored irrigation scheme and he argued over the best method of installing a sewage system in Calgary. He believed the hotelkeepers were a much abused and misjudged class of men that should be better protected under the law; inherent in this belief was the move for fairer liquor laws. The exclusivity of ranchers also slipped in while incorporating the Western Stockgrowers' Association that year: as organizational chairman, Ernest wrote the influential government agent, William Pearce, that tickets would be sold for their meetings "to keep outsiders away." The government had announced that all leases not providing for homesteading would end by December 31, 1896.

As Clifford Sifton's immigration campaign proved increasingly successful and Europeans flooded the land, Ernest wrote letters to the Dominion Lands Office begging them to disallow settlement on one of his leased quarter sections. He did believe that with government-assisted irrigation and agricultural experimentation there would be a rightful place for farming in Alberta, but if his springs were fenced in, the a7 Ranche would be ruined. Yet another bugaboo he complained about was the inequitable freight rates on the prairies. It was cheaper to send equipment such as beer bottles through Vancouver, then back to Alberta.

Overall, Ernest saw a place in the West for everyone and everything as long as major changes were implemented. The West was so heavily administered by the federal government and it was so dependent upon Ottawa for most of its revenue that the only real influence a westerner could exert was through politics. So Ernest secretly agreed to stand as candidate for Calgary East in the NWT government if his friends really believed he could win. He had no intention of investing his money or his time without the certainty of a seat in Regina. Billie Cochrane wrote of the legislature, "They are a very harmless assembly ... will deal you plenty of work & trouble. But if you think you can do any good, give the time. . . . Your election would be certain." Billie's comments were perceptive. With no distinct power in the territorial administration, the MLAs of the 1890s were less aligned to party politics than they were to a coalition of individualists. In 1897 Ernest's friend, F.W. Haultain, had again been appointed leader of the assembly and was referred to as the "acting premier."

While mulling over the possibility of a political win, Ernest watched the beer sales rise with summer temperatures. All of a sudden the plant wasn't big enough to meet the demand. In the Crows Nest Pass, Macmillan had done his job too well, convincing consumers that the brew and storage facilities were improved. The CB&M manager griped, "I think I must have been crazy to undertake what I have here when I knew so well your inability to produce the goods." Their profit that year of $5,469.84 would mark brewery capacity. Ernest would have to expand or relinquish his market monopoly.

At age thirty-seven, Ernest still confessed to a "restless, roving craze over women." Once when Randolph Bruce heard Aunt Emma extolling his virtues he wrote, "Is this the Ernest Cross that I know? Verily each man in his time plays many parts!" Ernest was either a confirmed bachelor like Selkirk and Willie Heber, or he had simply not found the woman with whom he wanted to spend his life. Three defunct engagements lay in his wake, all romances with Montreal women, so well-bred, so well-educated, so well-everything like his sister Maggie.

During that summer of 1898, Ernest entered the same barrel race as nineteen-year-old Nell Macleod. The race was a tough challenge for the skirt-clad women riders, and all competitors stuffed newspaper into their high boots while they waited. In a properly executed roll over the top of a CB&M oak barrel, a rider's leg could get badly bruised if unprotected. But Nell Macleod could ride as well as any man. Bolting with the starting gunshot, she galloped her pony flat out, low to the ground, dodging round the three barrels spaced sixty feet apart like runaway heifers. Then, swivelling her pony, its haunches tight to its belly, Nell charged back to race for the finish. An excellent horse and rider could execute the race in eight plus seconds. Today, no one can agree whether it was Nell Macleod or Ernest Cross who won. One of them did.

Ernest was caught off guard. To be smitten on horseback by someone he had met as a girl was hardly the Jolly Brewer's style. Yet even in a barrel race, Nell's style was both regal and captivating. The daughter of James and Mary Macleod embodied the best of Upper Canada schooling with the toughest of frontier fibre.

Usually cavalier in his way with women, Ernest shyly took to shopping at the Hudson's Bay Company where Nell had graduated upstairs from clerk to accountant. Perhaps he hoped she might descend from her second-floor cubicle and bump into him. He seemed to have lost his courage; no one ever remembers him trying to sweep Nell off her feet. In his frequent visits to the department store, he always carried a list, except for the day he mounted the grand spiral staircase to the upper gallery and sought her out. That time he proposed marriage. Nell used to say it was because he had gotten flustered without his list, but she knew what she wanted. Without a moment's hesitation she left the cubicle and walked down the street with Ernest, who intended to ask Mary Macleod for her daughter's hand. Nell was gloriously happy, yet wrote that she was fearful of what might lie in her future. After her delighted mother gave her consent, they agreed to keep the engagement a secret throughout the coming year.

In the fall, not knowing the immediate future of the brewery but intending to hang on to the a7 Ranche whatever happened, Ernest declared his intention to run for the 1899 elections for the Legislative Assembly of the North-West Territories. A visiting Englishman, eighteen-year-old Max Aitken, agreed to handle both Ernest's campaign in Calgary East and that of lawyer R.B. Bennett in Calgary West. Aitken, who had never run a campaign, would later become Lord Beaverbrook, one of the wealthiest men in the British Empire, and campaign manager for Andrew Bonar Law, the only Canadian prime minister of England.

This was an era in the West in which educated men could go far politically. R.B. Bennett would reach the prime minister's chair. But Ernest entertained no such ambitions. Rather than seek personal promotion or enduring power, he would remain free from political affiliation. When writing to the federal government, he would refer to himself as a "prominent liberal," but in the West he disassociated himself from the aggressive Sifton label and ran as an independent. The changes he wished to effect were for his ranch, for Alberta, for the future of the West. Once achieved, he intended to return to private business. In the meantime, instead of freeing himself to manage his ranch, he had complicated his life tenfold.

While he considered the sale of his brewery shares, Billie Cochrane wrote one of his many letters inspiring Ernest to hang in with the CB&M. He said, "It seems hard that you should chuck up now, after bearing all the expense and trouble and considerable wear and tear.... I am quite willing to stay with the brewery as long as you do and as long as you control the management. I would have no confidence in strangers." Billie had the backing of the two other absentee shareholders, men who had participated in the 1887 Mosquito Creek roundup: H.B. Alexander, who was shooting wild boar on the Continent, and T.S.C. Lee, who was stalking pheasant through his turnip fields in Scotland. For them, nothing could be more unpalatable than to have Ernest sell out and leave them without the prospect of dividends.

Ernest complied. It helped that the economy was on a solid upswing and westerners were quaffing beer again. Barely pausing to put the ranch in the hands of his foreman, J. Blake, and the CB&M onto the back of Macmillan, he launched into his election campaign. East Calgary included all the farming country as far as Gleichen and was considered one of the largest and most important districts in the territories. Announcing in the *Calgary Herald* his confidence in the farmers to grow more grain, Ernest was building a new 30,000-bushel barley elevator and would buy all the barley that was for sale. With three other men running against him, he campaigned around his constituency in a buckboard filled with Irish rye whiskey. The main difference in his opponents' political platforms concerned the status of Alberta Territory. Without provincial status, some argued, Albertans were but half citizens of the Dominion. At that time Ernest was still a central Canadian at heart and favoured federal control; and his visions extended far beyond the borders of Alberta Territory.

With a keen eye for Canadian potential in the international markets of the world, he corresponded with Ottawa and published articles encouraging economic expansion. He was particularly interested in a political and economic relationship between Canada and the Hawaiian Islands. Noting that the Americans were vying with the British over annexation, to say nothing of Asian interests which could soon absorb the islands, he recommended a joint British-American protectorate for Hawaii, with Canada having a reciprocity treaty with the islands. He also believed an agreement could be made allowing a Canadian-Australian telegraphic cable to land at Honolulu. In another article, Ernest proposed the international export of Canadian produce and even eggs by implementing sophisticated cold storage systems. Once, while in New York, he wrote to chide the Americans for their antagonism towards the British. All his articles he signed "Bovis."

In October the candidates' debate in Hull's Opera House, Calgary, promised great sport for the cooks, cowboys, blacksmiths and farmers who jammed the theatre along with eastern speculators and American prospectors. When the chairman banged the gavel through the noise of the cheers and jeers, the crowd was quiet just long enough to hear the rules. Each of the four candidates would get a half hour to speak, then four minutes to rebutt. The *Calgary Herald* recorded almost every word and breath of the entire evening, appropriately punctuating each speech with audience reaction.

As the second speaker, Ernest began nervously, flubbing his brewery's name as the "Calgary Malting and Brewing Company." He reviewed his fourteen years of hardships beginning in a sod shack during the winter of 1886-87. Then he launched into his platform. "I'd like to see Calgary made the capital of the Territories. (Cheers) ... I'd like to get CPR rates that would allow this city to compete with Winnipeg and Vancouver. This country needs as many railways as it can possibly get! (Loud Cheers)." Ernest relaxed and became adept at the pause for applause. His words were soon punctuated by cheering as he shouted, "We must create a market for our own beef.... We must create, ladies and gentlemen, a Chicago of the Canadian West! (Louder Cheers)."

He forgot no one, arguing in favour of a brand ordinance, more agricultural experimental stations for the farmer, and government-assisted irrigation systems. "In conclusion," he yelled over the din, "I will represent this district in a forward and businesslike way! (Loud Cheers)." Ernest jumped to the floor and made his way to his seat, shaking hands and perhaps tasting victory.

The next speaker, former NWMP constable S.J. Clarke, boomed, "Mr. Cross pretends to be a friend of the farmer. But tell me this: what does the farmer want with Calgary overseeing the Territories? What the farmer needs ... will be three provinces: Manitoba, the Territories and British Columbia." Clarke charged that instead of paying the farmers 40 cents a bushel for their barley, Cross had refused it, claiming it was frozen. He fleetingly switched to another subject before accusing Ernest of leaving the ranch because there was more money in brewing than in raising beef. "(Loud Laughter)."

Accusing the brewery of being a monopoly, Clarke explained, "The Toronto brewers charge 80c a dozen for beer and make millions, but Cross charges two dollars a dozen and pays less for his barley and less to his laborers. (Renewed Laughter)." Clarke charged that Cross "would never fight to reduce freight rates because if kept high, it would hold the eastern beer competitors at bay." Finally, he stated that Cross was running as an independent but was "really a personal friend of acting premier F.W. Haultain." As such, "Cross would support the existing elitist government which had its own rules for its special members." As an example Clarke referred to the Ranchmen's Club, which was "running wild open seven days a week – a disgrace to the Territories." S.J. Clarke figured it would be "in the best interest of the district to elect anyone other than Ernest Cross."

The next speaker, MLA veteran Joe Bannerman, also attacked Ernest. He claimed that rather than opening up the country, Cross had arrived only after the rest of them had "made this place solid." He charged that Ernest had asked council for a bonus and exemption from taxation when building the brewery. When council refused, he claimed, Ernest took his industry outside the city to escape paying taxes.

Ernest's rebuttal was one his father would have loved. He claimed that he trusted that both his employees and business associates would not only absolve him from any accusations of wrong-doing, but salute him as a fair and businesslike man. He emphatically denied that he ever asked for a bonus from council, although he did ask for an exemption, explaining, "It is difficult to start up a new industry in a new country, and I had every hope that the brewery, given half a chance, could ... repay the city many times over. Our monthly payroll is currently twelve hundred dollars. We provide employment and utilize most of the city's services and utilities.... The reason I chose to build the brewery outside the city limits was not to escape taxation but to obtain a side track from the railroad.... CB&M utilizes most of the city's services and utilities, [and] I pay more taxes than the average Calgarian."

As a final shot to Clarke and the farmers he pretended to represent, Ernest claimed that he had always paid 30 per cent more for barley than Winnipeg paid, and he would continue to do so, election year or not. He would prove in time that he fought for equitable freight rates as hard as any man in the West. Then he strode from the stage. Those were gentlemanly times. Bannerman stood and withdrew his comment about the bonus. The chairman was thanked and the speeches were over.

As voting day drew closer, Ernest found himself in the unenviable position of a private man forced into public recognition – on the streets, in the hotels, about the town. His only refuge was the impregnable Ranchmen's Club. The bookmakers put Ernest at seven to six, giving him neither the certainty of defeat nor victory. Bannerman and Reilly were also even money but Clarke was figured a winner ten to one.

On the night of November 4 Ernest and his followers gathered at city hall, site of No. 1 polling booth. As the ballots arrived, officials squinted into the flickering kerosene light and counted the coloured votes. Ernest's were blue, Reilly's green. Near midnight and the final tally, money flew around the room in a betting frenzy. One man stood to gain $1,400 if he won. Suddenly with a roar from his partisans, Reilly's green papers captured an incredible ninety-one votes while Ernest was the big loser with nineteen. As he had had sixty-three of his own men at the poll, Max Aitken knew something was wrong. The total ballots nowhere near balanced with the number of voters. The next day the *Herald* announced R.B. Bennett's win for West Calgary and Reilly for East Calgary. It was a glorious time for Reilly until the officials discovered by daylight that Ernest's blue votes had been undiscernible from Reilly's greens. They were all mixed up together. Aitken demanded and got a recount.

On November 10, Ernest rode out to Billie Cochrane's ranch to while away the last two days before the count. He returned Saturday afternoon for the announcement. A large crowd had gathered in front of city hall, many of them Ernest's friends. The returning officer droned the results across the street, "The official election returns for East Calgary ... Reilly 117 ... Bannerman 118 ... Clarke 127 ... Cross 180."

An exuberant crowd swept Ernest up in an impromptu parade of barking dogs, backslapping, hollering and gun-firing. Shopkeepers and residents poured out of their homes to join in and to shake the hand of Ernest Cross, MLA. Ranching friends rode their horses up and down the steps of buildings and private homes. By dark a massive crowd had collected on Stephen Avenue. Cross supporters dipped brewery brooms into coal oil and fired them as torches for the revelry which continued until midnight. Fireworks blasted from one end of town to the other. With typical spontaneity Calgarians flowed in and out of buildings, laughing and drinking Cross beer. Finished with depression, everyone felt the turn-of-the-century mood of change and growth. Rich harvests and a good crop of calves that year had buoyed many a westerner's spirits. The market was on an upswing, Alberta was entering a new age of economic prosperity and, hopefully, political recognition.

Ernest threw himself into the work of the North-West Territories legislature in Regina. Like Haultain, he labelled himself a western conservative with progressive ideas. As such he became a public target for any and all opposition. When elected vice-president of Calgary's Sir J.A. Macdonald Club by acclamation, he refused, explaining that partisan politics "has a tendency to divide the North West Legislature. Such a division I consider disastrous." He incurred the wrath of his own ranching colleagues by fighting the government inspection bill sanctioned by the WSGA. The president wrote Ernest, "Surely the Assembly will look upon our Association as being rather an insignificant affair when one of our longest members come out in this manner and virtually ridicules our act."

Ernest continued acting as a separate entity while attempting to draw central Canada and the North-West Territories together. Today his memory provides a touchstone to the individualistic character of Calgarians. Increasingly frustrated by the federal government's lack of understanding, by Clifford Sifton's bold settlement policies which snatched land away from the rancher and fenced in their water, Ernest was imbued with the seeds of regionalism by the turn of the century. While he constantly challenged both the federal government and western citizens to match each others' contributions, he embodied the independent, do-it-yourself spirit so prevalent in Alberta today.

During Ernest's four years in the legislature, wells would be dug, schools constructed, roads built, irrigation systems designed, regulations developed, railway routes examined. With an eye to endangered big game he wrote the minister of the interior to recommend the expansion of Banff National Park. He was always a scrapper concerning the liquor laws, and protected the hoteliers by describing them as a much abused and misjudged class of men earning their living under the law. Nevertheless, for a long time, only one hotel per three hundred citizens was allowed.

His political tasks completed, Ernest would return to private life, venturing into grain, oil, minerals and motion pictures. Alexander's fifth son seemed forever driven. Political spheres, public benefits and financial successes were only segments of his master plan. Each pursuit seemed but a tool not to compete with other men's achievements, as much as to measure himself against his father's timeless challenge.

In making his maiden speech in the legislature, Ernest urged, "We should take steps which might be termed speculative. We should aspire to what will be more dangerous and less secure because the prospects warrant that risk. There is no such thing as standing still. We must either progress or retrograde!" Referring to the intolerable CPR railway rates, Ernest warned that unless the federal government dictated a fair rate, the Territories would find other railroad competitors.

In farming matters, he was not in the least shy over taking credit for the idea of an agricultural experimental station, having spent $600 of his own funds on a trial irrigation system. He complimented the government for its initial support as well as that of private citizens. "It would be damned!!" hollered R.B. Bennett. Ernest was stunned into silence as the opposition jumped to his feet. Pounding the desk with his fists, Bennett attacked the proposed experimental site, saying the land offered for it by an incompetent farmer was cropped out, worn out and all the soil was blown off.

As if he were an agronomist describing the nitrogen components in the soil, Ernest calmly rose again and expressed the importance of actually using faulty soil. If the experiment succeeded, it would prove beyond reasonable doubt that a scientific approach to farming would work. Citing his own education at Guelph (but not his exam results), Ernest suggested that he spoke with authority and closed with his "splendid hopes for the success of the project." *The Leader* credited his "calm and dispassionate statement of facts [as] never surpassed in the North-West Legislature." Later, R.B. Bennett rose, commended Ernest for his impartial presentation, and concluded, "Though I will not withdraw my opposition to it . . . I sincerely hope that the scheme will enjoy the very best results." The experimental station was subsequently established.

Ernest had one personal matter to raise in the Assembly: the question of a pension for his future mother-in-law, Mary Macleod. Believing it would be improper to speak himself, he asked Haultain if he would bring the matter forward. Haultain gladly reviewed the historical contribution made by James and the steps taken upon his death to procure his pension. James's only error was not surviving long enough to take his allowed sick leave. His reputation, continued Haultain, extended deep into the free-wheeling United States where the Indians knew the Mountie in the north who had always spoken the truth and kept his promises. Haultain went further, saying, "I believe that in all probability Canada has saved millions of dollars by the tact . . . with which Colonel Macleod performed [his] duties." He added that Ottawa had told him public sentiment was necessary before any recompense was possible. But even in James Macleod's home province of Ontario, his name was forgotten. Haultain was unsuccessful in getting the federal government to recognize a man who made "the most important and most valuable services ever rendered by any man to the Dominion of Canada." He concluded, "As there was no memory, no recollection, no gratitude on the part of the Government of Canada, then the people of the Territories

... should show a small amount of gratitude ... by not allowing the widow and family of one of Canada's most distinguished men to suffer from penury and want."

A Mr. McKay retorted that many men before James had arrived had already done the same kind of work without a military force at their back. "There were scores of widows and orphans of men who were advance of Colonel Macleod and made his work possible, yet these were not provided for by the country. . . ." Then he conceded, "It *is* a crying shame that any Federal government whether Liberal or Conservative should not have recognized Macleod's services by providing for his family." But he stressed that the responsibility rested in Ottawa, not Regina. A motion to award Mary a one-time grant of $600 was passed. The issue was ended, save for a letter to Ernest from Mary, who had suffered enough from public indignity.

My dear Ernest,

You little thought when you asked for Nell that you would have to marry the whole family. I never thought I'd allow it to be so. . . . With all my heart, I thank and bless you for what you are doing for me. I wanted to say something to you in person but my feelings have a nasty way of getting the better of me when I try to talk. May God bless and prosper you and yours, dear Ernest.

Always affectionately yours, Mary I. Macleod

Nell's June wedding was approaching. Unable to afford a wedding gown for Nell, Mary offered to design a grey dress lined with pale rose satin, something which could be sensibly remade for future wear. Grey was a widow's colour and Nell was dismayed. When Ernest learned of her disappointment, he purchased an ivory satin gown from a Toronto dress shop. In Montreal Selkirk purchased an engagement ring from Birks for her long slender hands, and advised Ernest on engraving. Selkirk researched all the gifts for the ladies in the wedding party and when his mother could not find anything to her taste in Montreal arranged through Birks to import satin dress-bags from London. Selkirk then drew up a marriage contract, giving Nell one-third of the ranch or 750 head of cattle at $30 each, a total of $22,500; thirty head of horses at $40 each worth $1,240; 2,560 acres of land at $3 an acre, worth $7,936 and improvements for $2,000. The total contract was valued at $33,676 and would prevent something like a brewery bankruptcy from decimating the couple.

The legislature had prorogued in mid-May 1899, enabling Ernest to turn to his wedding plans and complete a few deals. He wrote to the traffic manager of the CPR, R. Kerr, outlining his plans to honeymoon in Montreal, then requested a drawing room from Calgary to Fort William and a good cabin on the boat to Owen Sound. In recognition of what the Macleods and Crosses had done for the West, including for the revenue of the CPR, wrote Ernest, "I think it only due to us that you give us both round trip passes." Ernest made it clear that he didn't want them for political reasons or for any business his company or ranch might do in the future with the CPR. In style, the request was typical of Ernest's brevity rather than arrogance. He had been raised in central Canada where patronage was considered sensible and expedient.

Just four days before the wedding, Kerr replied that the CPR would authorize round trip passage only from Calgary to Fort William. He could not guarantee a drawing room as they were all booked for a Chinese contingent boarding in Vancouver. Perhaps some would disembark in Banff. Thanking Kerr for the partial recognition, Ernest retorted that the refusal was understandable, he and Nell being "essentially western people."

For $2,305 Ernest purchased the roomy, two-storey wood house at 1240 8th Avenue S.E., Calgary. Its bevel siding was painted grey and he added white gingerbread scallops to set off the gabled roof and a widow's walk. Surrounded by fruit trees and acres of land stretching down to the river, the house was within walking distance of the brewery. The land provided ample space for many a future picnic and polo match.

Ernest chose as his best man D.H. Andrews, the manager of Sir Horace Plunkett's Powder River Cattle Company, Wyoming. Then he celebrated with a western custom. Buying an entire ensemble, he pitched his old wardrobe out the Alberta Hotel window to the waiting rag man. After wiring a Winnipeg florist to send bouquets of roses, carnations and orange blossoms for the bridal party, he wrote Billie Cochrane the day before his wedding, "Tomorrow is the big day, and I suppose I shall not know whether to stand on my head or heels."

Neither did Nell. The ceremony had already been postponed once, and her wedding dress did not arrive until the evening of that day. On her last day at work when she submitted her addition of the day's receipts the store accountant discovered an error of one million dollars. She framed her last pay cheque, a farewell to the life of a working woman, 1899. Her mother had saved for this event, and gave to "my Nellie" a wedding gift of $20. It was this precious daughter who had, without a word of complaint or a backward look at the age of sixteen, given up her education and gone to work to help support the family.

On the sunny evening of June 8, 1899, Helen Rothney "Nell" Macleod, the first white child born in southern Alberta, entered the packed Church of the Redeemer. A frantic search for a volunteer organ pumper just before the service began would have delighted James Macleod. Suddenly the church reverberated with Mendelssohn's Wedding March as bridesmaid Mary Pinkham began moving down the aisle. Nell followed, much taller than her Uncle Jermy Jephson, QC, on whose arm she gracefully floated. Her high-necked dress fell in satiny folds into a long train upon which, some claim, a cowboy tossed his hat. Watching Nell approach were Mary Macleod and her Drever sisters, Mrs. Cyprian Pinkham and Mrs. Jermy Jephson. Across the aisle stood the Montreal Crosses, Selkirk and Willie Heber, quite possibly with their sister Margaret and William MacInnes. Nell's "Uncle Cyp" waited at the head of the aisle, resplendent in dazzling white robes and the pectoral cross symbolic of a bishop. Beside him stood a curate, the best man, and the groom. Ernest Cross waited, the cowboy's trademark of a whitened brow and sun-tanned features setting his intense eyes and dark mustache in relief above his white wing collar and formal attire.

The ceremony uniting Ernest Cross and Nell Macleod marked the union of three influential Scottish families from three geographically and politically disparate regions of Canada. Honed and humbled by three generations of bitter climate, the families had never forgotten who they were. At the time, it was the royal marriage of the West.

The reception was held at 210 Second Avenue S.W., in the garden of the sandstone home Calgarians had given to Mary Macleod. Following the speeches and toasts, Nell and Ernest headed for the station and the CPR's "No. 1." They spent five days (and $52.95) at the Banff Springs Hotel. Congratulatory telegrams and letters poured in from all over the country as they waited for the appropriate CPR accommodations to travel on to Montreal. Heading east on June 13, they stopped briefly in Winnipeg to receive the good wishes of friends and, in particular, of the MacInneses. The CPR had promoted William to Winnipeg, the hub of the country's shipments of grain, beef and beer. Some seventy-three trains shunted through its station every day.

In Montreal Ernest and Nell spent three weeks at Pine Avenue and shopped for furnishings for their Calgary home. While Julia described her new daughter-in-law as tall, slight, stylish and good-looking, Nell found she had to win over her reserved mother-in-law. Julia was still smarting over her son's rejection of the family favourite three years earlier. Ernest was able to catch up with all the news of his family. Edmund and Hélène at the River Beaudette farm had six-month-old twins. Selkirk had been made a QC and (like Ernest) enjoyed an open-door relationship with Prime Minister Sir Wilfrid Laurier – particularly in the interests of his client and long-time friend, Senator Ogilvie. Harry wrote from Wyoming that he had been elected a second time to the Senate. His wins were always marked by an overwhelming majority and his colleagues always understood when he had to return to Braehead to fence the land or to deal with incompetent help.

Ernest frequented the St. James Club with Selkirk and observed firsthand yet again the cultural wounds tearing at the soul of a magnificent city. The French-English issue was festering anew as Sir Wilfrid Laurier had sanctioned Canadian troops to fight in the Boer War. The French accused British Colonial Secretary Joseph Chamberlain of promoting English imperialism. As a supporter of Chamberlain's policies, Ernest revealed why he could never have lived in Quebec despite his bilingualism and his father's conciliatory example. Writing to Chamberlain as a friend, he warned him of the dangers of allowing the official use of the Dutch language in South Africa. As an example he cited his own family living amongst the French Canadians for three generations and explained,

> The dual system of language has been a positive curse to both French and English. A smouldering hatred has always existed. . . . The constant rivalry and friction between the two languages . . . does nothing to benefit business . . . which, in Quebec, is inconvenient and expensive.
>
> Should the Dutch language be allowed in South Africa, I predict in due course South Africa will be a Dutch republic with very little English spoken at all. I further predict those English that remain in that country will curse their ancestors for being thick-headed Englishmen, as we Canadians do today in looking on the language dualty in Quebec. Make almost any concession but not the language!

Upon returning to Calgary from his honeymoon, Ernest found his mail piled high with personal problems and political issues. A note from Billie Cochrane listed a7 Ranche business and the latest lurid gossip. Other correspondence reported that the Gleichen ferry needed maintaining. Worst, mange was epidemic throughout southern Alberta. Cattle stood miserably about the range, scratching themselves on the barbed wire and their fur falling out around ugly, oozing sores. The federal inspector presented a mandate that all stock be quarantined and dipped.

In late March 1900 Ernest left Nell pregnant with their first child and returned to Regina. He served on the Public Accounts and the Agriculture and Municipal Law committees but the liquor licence question was the most controversial of the session. For once Ernest agreed with R.B. Bennett that it needed to be restructured.

Even the Ranchmen's Club fell under attack over the liquor laws. Annoyed by a motion that every incorporated club, society and corporation be required to have a licence to sell liquor, Ernest jumped to his feet to denounce it. To him, a gentleman's club was his fortress and should be sacrosanct from public scrutiny:

I find it objectionable and insulting. It is not the fact that a club would have to pay a revenue, but the fact that it would be placed in a position nearly akin to having to have a licence to drink liquor in one's own house. I consider it more due to ignorance than anything else that such a resolution should be presented. Having myself enjoyed for years the privileges of a club, I could not realize the position of being subject to the insults of the law under a system by which a licence inspector could come in at any moment of the day or night.

The motion failed.

In Ernest's personal business, the Aberdeen mine claim looked good and there was talk of incorporating it into a company capitalized for $1.5 million. A few weeks later he was shocked to learn that the manager had committed suicide. Stephens wrote shortly afterwards that he was broke and needed a loan. So much for that mine. Ernest invested in another called the Burton. He never lost his optimism for the future of mining exploration.

In the midst of the legislative session, Ernest received word of the birth of their first child. He wired Nell his heartfelt love and wrote Selkirk in Montreal appointing him godfather to little "Helen Macleod Cross." He sent pictures of Helen to his ranching friends and in time told his mother that his first-born was just like himself.

During their courtship, Nell had begun the first of hundreds of letters she would write to Ernest over the coming fifteen years. She had no idea that she was marrying a man almost wedded to his business creations, one from whom she would be separated almost as much as Mary Macleod had been from James. In her writing, she related each experience of her life to her husband, with nature forming the link between them: "Last evening we had a thunder storm. After the rain and just as the sun was setting, a beautiful bow appeared in the sky. It formed a perfect arch across the heavens, and appeared to touch the earth between here and the brewery."

Nell was thrilled with Ernest's hurried notes yet disappointed by their brevity. A passionate woman, she once wrote, "I go nearly wild when I think of your return and how we can show the joy we shall feel." And Ernest once tore himself away from the business at hand to reply that he missed her particularly in the morning, for it was then that he longed for her sweet, quiet talk before entering the cares of the day.

In 1901 Ernest doubled the CB&M malt-house capacity and by June 30 had made a record 159 brewings. His greatly improved beer had captured 90 per cent of the Brandon market and much of the business at all points along the CPR west of Winnipeg. He was selling all over the Kootenays and boundary country. Esmonde Clarke, a Montreal friend and owner of a barley, malt and hop establishment, wrote that CB&M beer was "superior to any Canadian beer . . . or other imported beers. . . . This beer should sell in the Windsor Hotel. I don't see how it can be improved in any way." Ernest replied that he could never lead himself to accept that anything was perfect but that his beer was not far short of it.

With his shareholders hollering again for dividends, Ernest moved to procure CB&M stock above his 20 per cent control. Eckford and Samson wanted to sell, H.B. Alexander wanted to buy more. Offering the latter some of Eckford's shares, Ernest intended to pick up all of Samson's himself. He tossed H.B. Alexander a red herring offer to invest in a different part of the country, hoping it would soften his anger at not getting Samson's proffered shares. Then, without consulting his partners, Ernest borrowed $20,000 from the bank to cover production expenses, expansion and the purchase of new machinery. There would be no dividends that year.

From July to December of 1901, CB&M made two hundred brewings. As company taxes amounted to $2.50, Ernest reported that the shareholders could look forward to a small dividend in 1902 if things kept up so favourably. On the other hand, said he, closing his annual report with his perennial caveat, should he expand the plant to keep pace with the demand, such a dividend would be postponed. With assets totalling $183,588 and the CB&M net worth at $171,860, Ernest ploughed the earnings back into the company. The CB&M owed the Bank of Montreal $8,236. Having not claimed a salary for the first six years of operation, Ernest paid himself $5,538.93 for 1902. He also bought two more acres of land with a railway spur and space to build a badly needed stables. Just how big the CB&M might have become if Ernest had borrowed against his assets for capital expansion would remain a conjecture for a time. His father's advice to hasten slowly remained ever within him.

18

The Rancher and the Settler

"Grass is the forgiveness of nature. . . . should it fail for a single year, famine would depopulate the world."

Ernest Cross Papers

Perhaps no issue divided the West as bitterly as the conflict between settler and rancher. At the time, settlers from the United States were arriving in Alberta on trains with banners, "Another trainload of settlers for the last best west!" Their foreign and American tongues diluted the tone of the imperial West and infuriated the ranchers. Many settlers knew only that 160-acre homesteads were being offered for free, and built their shacks on someone else's land. Since James Macleod's arrival in 1873, 73,000 people had settled or been born in the district of Alberta.

Ernest was a renegade rancher in believing that there was a future for farmers in southern Alberta, but he wanted, as he put it to one friend, "the least objectionable settler." Such a person was an eighteen-year-old Shropshire lad named Harry Brayne. In 1897 Brayne arrived in Calgary after months of travelling in a fetid immigrant ship, then on board a stripped-down CPR colonist car which had received the railway's lowest priority in crossing Canada – even cattle cars had been placed before those of the immigrants. Brayne had come to join his brother Joe, an engineer at the CB&M.

At first Ernest set young Brayne to work with the predominantly German staff labelling bottles. He was paid $36 a month, $15 of which went for board. Two months later Ernest offered Brayne the position of cook at the a7 Ranche. The youth hesitated, for he enjoyed

303

Calgary's wild town life. But Ernest counselled, "Harry, there's no future for you here. But there are prospects ranching." Brayne went. After taking the train to Nanton he walked westward into the foothills. At one point he had stopped off for a drink at a spring, and knew that it was where he'd eventually homestead. "It just felt right," he remembered years later. Seventeen miles west of Nanton he found the a7 Ranche.

Brayne received $15 a month for cooking breakfast, shovelling manure, digging forty post-holes a day (he claimed), then dashing in to bake bread and heat the evening stew. In return the boys taught him how to brand, how to make sourdough starter, how to chew tobacco instead of lighting cigarettes on range land, how to wash away the inevitable lice with coal oil and soap, then how to drape his clothes over an ant hill, leaving the ants to nitpick the lice. Brayne survived his first, terrifying night-time cattle stampede through the camp, when "the ground shook and their horns rattled like chains of death"; and he had his first experience of watching really good poker cheaters.

One of Brayne's most important duties was to learn how to operate on animals. Giving him the scalpel and sutures, Ernest verbally guided the youth through reducing a cow's fungal disease known as Big Jaw (sometimes infectious to man). Later that day under Ernest's supervision, he performed oopherectomy and a castration. Continuing on his own, Brayne had trouble with another castration and the bull died. After losing another bull he devised his own fool-proof surgery. Curious, Ernest asked for details. Brayne replied, "Well, basically, it's a string." Some of the newest procedures and indeed the best vets in the country were cowboys who learned their skills out of necessity. In all things, Ernest guided Brayne as he grew from a Shropshire greenhorn into an Albertan rancher.

When he was twenty-two, Brayne was appointed as the a7 Ranche foreman. He was the youngest and still the most naive in the country. Skilled at cow-punching and brewing roundup coffee, he yet had to understand that a rancher's destiny depended upon the grassland. One day, just after Brayne's promotion, Ernest rode out to the a7 Ranche to find him ploughing up twenty acres of oats destined for winter fodder. At the age of 106 in 1984, Brayne still remembered that his boss went cold with anger; a man could tell that only by the look in his eye. Ernest explained: "Harry, each day you can see another settler coming into these foothills. If that settler sees us breaking good land like you've just ploughed, what will keep them from doing the same? The plough could be the ruin of ranching. Each acre it turns under will never hold active grass again. It's the grass that gives us our living, Harry. If it goes, we go."

Homesteading rules required that a man plough thirty of his 160 acres and reside on that acreage for six months a year for three years before he would gain title. To meet these requirements, many just put a lantern in a shack each night. Then near the end of the three years they'd plough a circle around a thirty-acre plot and with hand on a Bible tell the Dominion Lands officer. "I ploughed around thirty acres."

But Harry Brayne was not of that ilk. After working as a7 Ranche foreman for three years, he left in March 1902 to establish his own homestead. He had neither tools nor animals with which to begin, and he had to seed his thirty acres of land. A year earlier Ernest had asked Brayne to do him a favour without warning – head out on a four-day roundup. Brayne had done so without asking any recompense. "That was very decent of you, Harry," was all Ernest had said. Brayne thought nothing more about it. Then as he was building his sod shack in 1902, an a7 Ranche hand appeared over the hills driving a plough and four horses. The man stayed for one week making sure Brayne got established. "Cross was a good man, who always kept his word," remembered Brayne. And Harry Brayne was the right kind of settler.

As the settlers quickly filled up the rangeland, the federal government gave little hope for change. It considered the erection of fences and range division an evolution of western development. From Ernest's view it caused incalculable harm. He predicted massive ecological and economic damage perpetrated through a carelessly controlled immigration program. It wasn't just a question of power over water rights. Cattle immunity depended upon it as well; Ernest blamed anthrax and mange on the indiscriminate proliferation of settlers and their livestock.

Each new piece of legislation made it harder for the rancher to prosper. Soon, the government even levied a tax of $4 per mile of road allowance under all border fences. Grazing rental of a section cost $12.80, while grazing on either side of a road allowance cost an additional $8. Overshadowing these problems was a poor buying market. Ernest wrote his friend, T.S.C. Lee: "Cattlemen [do] not fully realize what a weak position they are in. . . . [They] have to make certain the range cannot be taken up ... by owning as much land as possible. Your suggestion of joint ownership is probably the only remedy."

Regional discontent had begun when James Macleod and his NWMP struggled through their first winter with no word from Ottawa. It mushroomed with the arbitrary moves of the CPR, then blossomed with Sifton's immigration policies. Although differing in content from the French-English issue in Quebec, the rift showed similar potential for damage to Confederation. Once central Canadians, men such as Ernest Cross increasingly viewed Ottawa as a heavy-handed parent imposing unfair restrictions upon its infant frontier.

In February 1902 George Lane headed for Ottawa to lobby for legislation more favourable to ranchmen. He personally presented Ernest Cross's plea written to Clifford Sifton. In it, Ernest warned that due to vast fencing of grazing land, "hundreds of thousands of breeding cattle and horses have been forced onto the market at ridiculously low prices." The result was a dearth of breeding stock and a glut of feed. Both farmer and rancher lost. Ernest claimed:

> This condition has been brought about by the disregard of the Government in any way to foster the condition of growing cattle or horses. Original lease-holders had their leases cancelled, their water rights sold, their range settled and fenced by wire. They found themselves with more stick than feed and in most cases were obliged either to reduce their herd or get out of the business. ... This condition of affairs should have been anticipated. Provisions should have been made for the good, bona fide stock raiser to continue in the stock business under suitable and profitable conditions.

Frustrated by the deaf ear, Ernest turned to the United States and the Chicago beef brokers, Clay Robinson and Company. They had first written in 1901, urging him to sell a7 beef through them. In turn, Ernest urged them to start a packing house in Canada, suggesting Winnipeg, Fort William, Toronto, Ottawa or Montreal as the most profitable places. He believed it imperative that the rancher offer all classes of cattle and get exactly what each was worth. In Calgary, however, P. Burns Limited was the only firm to handle rough cattle. Unchallenged, it stated its rates regardless of quality.

At that time Chicago was not interested: their business was strictly one of commission on the market. Ernest could not entice a potential competitor and the ranchers had not won Ottawa's help in dealing with settlers. Fed up, he sold his original homestead, by then 320 acres, for $1,340, then wrote Selkirk of his intent to sell the a7 Ranche. This time Selkirk agreed. But Billie Cochrane didn't; he swore at the immigrants and wanted a good fight. Following a roaring drunk, he wrote Ernest, "These d_____d sod fuckers have driven me to drink." As usual, he brought Ernest around.

Ernest's change of heart may have been due to a change in conditions for beef sales. At the time there was still no overall grading of cattle. Herds were sent willy-nilly to Burns's slaughterhouse. Everyone was wheeling and dealing on a different level and the ranchers were tired of asking for government help in finding alternative Canadian markets. Billie wanted to see a fixed price. Was there anything Ernest could do about it?

There was. Ernest convinced Burns to buy the cattle for 3 cents per pound and 3 per cent shrink. As most were over 1,400 pounds, it was a good price. A few days later he received a wire from Billie, "Thanks for yours. Have seen Pat [Burns] this morning. Everything most satisfactory – it means $1000 to me." Quick to get in on the deal, Ernest had Harry Brayne drive his cattle into Burns's corral for the night. Upon examining them the following morning, Burns said they were too full, too heavy and thus too expensive. He told Ernest to weigh them in at four o'clock that afternoon. Readily agreeing, Ernest then instructed Brayne to drive them back to pasture where they grazed all day, staggering back to the weigh scales with overloaded bellies. Ernest did all right that year.

Trying to block settlement again, Ernest sent Clifford Sifton a list of his townships and a diagram of the a7 Ranche. He reviewed the history of the country since he had arrived and noted that he was now totally surrounded by settlers. He listed his cattle and his land requirements, keeping in mind that each cow required a minimum of ten acres of grassland in order to survive. One particular section, he pointed out, was erroneously listed as a water reserve. Ernest made his point with, "I do not think the country will be benefitted by being split up as it is being done. It will be only a question of a few years before the grass is eaten, forcing the weaker settlers to leave." He offered to buy the surrounding lands and concluded, "I have done a good deal for this part of the country. I have started a good number of people who are now prosperous settlers and citizens. I feel I should have consideration." He signed the letter, "From a prominent Liberal."

This time Selkirk delivered the letter to Sifton. He was greeted cordially and one month later the lands in question were withdrawn from settlement. Nevertheless, one of the last to grade a road into his ranch, Ernest was frustrated to watch settlers use it to make deep inroads into his own grazing land. In a letter to H.B. Alexander, he noted that his only hope to preserve land was to buy it. His key to his family's survival lay in the land. If it was chipped away, so would be his destiny.

In 1901 Ernest introduced a bill in the House to amend the legislation for incorporating Calgary. His bill proposed using water power from the Bow and Elbow rivers and extending the waterworks system to the city-owned agricultural grounds. It also called for raising debentures to lay sewers and changed the procedure for voting for mayor and council. The bill passed. When a motion was raised against the annexation of territorial land to Manitoba, Ernest supported it, pointing out that as Manitoba was financially independent, "it would ... be an unjust step to force that province into a union which it so opposed."

While he juggled ranch, beer and legislative duties, the 1901 elections loomed again. Attorney General F.W. Haultain wrote to Ernest on the prickly matter of their feisty opponent R.B. Bennett, acknowledging, "Without him, the Opposition must degenerate into a perfect farce and that will reflect on the whole institution.... Could you suggest an independent who might have a shot at Bennett?"

Ernest replied, "There is no one in sight that can beat Bennett.... Capt. Gordon is a conservative but without knowledge, brains or character. J. Hayes, a farmer, is a gas bag; A.P. Patrick, a surveyor, never pays his debts unless he has to. My opinion is to allow Bennett to get in by acclamation. He is really the only opposition in Regina and I think it would be better for both sides to have him there." Ernest and Bennett ran and won again.

Ernest, Nell and baby Helen returned to Montreal for Christmas. As scarlet fever and typhoid were endemic in Quebec, the family remained close to home. One of Edmund's children had tonsillitis, so the Pine Avenue nurse and Willie Heber went out to help in Beaudette. For Julia the holiday was one of gaiety and exhaustion with the influx of her grandchildren. She considered herself too old to enjoy the little ones permanently underfoot, and although she did not know it, it would be her last Christmas.

The 1901 visit to Calgary of Lieutenant-Governor Forget and the entire North-West Legislature was the brain child of the Calgary Board of Trade. The idea was to impress upon the government that Calgary was a better site for the Territorial capital than Regina, and to get some national press. Furthermore, Ottawa seemed to be taking more notice of its feisty frontier and may have reasoned that an official visit would appease the adolescent territory of the Canadian family.

The visit was a great excuse for an Albertan party, an important factor of which was always the weather. No one ever paid any attention to it. At one o'clock in the morning in the spring of 1901, a howling snowstorm pelted forty MLAs happily chatting on the Regina platform. When the lieutenant-governor's train pulled into the station, the group hopped aboard for a two a.m. Medicine Hat reception. Then they shunted through the night toward Calgary. Arriving at three in the morning, the formal welcome was immediately held. Everyone made what the *Calgary Herald* called witty speeches before Lieutenant-Governor Forget headed for the Alberta Hotel and Ernest Cross went home to Nell. At dawn, Calgary's Mayor Mackie was so stunned to learn that he had slept through the festivities that he insisted the welcome be restaged at the depot. Back everyone cheerfully went to welcome the lieutenant-governor and make their witty speeches all over again.

During the day, storm clouds merely served as a dramatic backdrop to the colourful parade and decorations that stretched down Stephen Street. Sixty-five Mounties patrolled the crowds, six bands, floats and a mass of riders hallooing from horseback. The CB&M float was a grandiose display of barrels and bottles topped by a huge banner boasting "Calgary's Chief Industry." The firemen clanged their bells and squirted water on a squealing crowd from their horse-drawn engine. Following a mock fire call in which men, horses and engines galloped off at breakneck speed, a banquet was given at Hull's Opera House in tribute to the survivors of the Boer War. Female spectators were allowed to watch from the balcony as the men feasted and toasted. A Major Sanders was cheered when he said, "Western men do not go into hysterics over trifles. They go to war as western men." The *Calgary Herald* reported that during the rainy afternoon fifty sporting events, from football, horse races, squaw races and bicycling, were held. That evening a concert was followed by a formal ball at the Alexandra room.

The following morning twenty rigs reconvened to drive the entourage to Calgary's main industrial bases – the brewery and the abattoir. Ernest guided the lieutenant-governor and the legislative party among the huge brewery vats, explaining every aspect of the operations from the art of brewing to bottling and drinking beer. From the hundreds of brewings per year, it appeared that beer matured in the wagons en route to the consumer. Nevertheless, the overall operations had improved. Floors were scrubbed, leaks and breakdowns were reduced to manageable proportions. Power corking machines, crown seal stopper machines, a power filter washing machine, power filter press and a wiring machine modernized the processes. Imported beer bottles were so perfectly formed it was said a man could shoot a .22 bullet through the bull's eye and not shatter the glass. The CB&M's only major problem was getting its empty fifty-gallon kegs back from the customers. Outside, the yard was a jumble of sleighs, carts, harnesses and as Ernest wrote, "horses tied up all over the place." Inadequate stable facilities created a traffic jam of kegs and Clydesdale horses mixed up with the MLAs' twenty rigs.

After moving on to Pat Burns's abattoir, the legislature broke from the smell of hops and cattle innards to drive out to W.R. Hull's pristine ranch. Following a magnificent buffet, Lieutenant-Governor Forget rose to speak. He boomed, "You are a progressive people. A determined people. You make things happen!" He paused for the expected cheers, after which Haultain rose to make his pitch for Calgary as the new territorial capital. Only half joking, he said, "When one considers the sixteen places between here and Regina, I have come to the conclusion that a suitable place for the future capital of the Territories would be halfway between Mr. Hull's magnificent ranch and Mr. Cross's brewery. Do I hear a motion to that effect?!"

While Ernest was travelling on to Banff with the MLAs, Nell was preparing for the birth of their second child. She had written often to her husband that spring, praying that he would be home for the event. She also wrote of the lilacs and maples beginning to leaf out and the gooseberry bush already in flower, admiring such courage to grow despite cold, windy nights. One time, she lamented that Ernest's dear letters seemed so short although his words spoke such calm. And she touched on his inscrutable nature when she added, "I look at your photograph with its sweet expression. I am only concerned with the eyes. They won't turn toward your loved one."

Upon leaving Banff, Ernest detoured for a visit with an overdue and unusually heavy Nell before immediately catching another train to Montreal. From her nearby home, Mary Macleod believed that Ernest or the housekeeper was still with Nell. But labour pangs struck while she was alone. Staggering to her bed, she might as well have been in a log cabin in the frontier. Without the comfort of another woman or the assistance of a doctor, Nell suffered the terrifying and violent delivery of a ten-pound boy. Mary arrived shortly after, the doctor an hour later. Mary's subsequent note to Ernest contained a thinly veiled rebuke, "It seems cruel you should have to be away from her again. The boy, Selkirk [Macleod], is very big and strong. The poor mother has suffered a good deal, but is as sweet and brave as can be. Everything is as right as can be under the circumstances. . . . In very great haste, M.I. Macleod."

The letter caught up with Ernest in Winnipeg. He rushed to a florist to wire Nell roses, and wrote to her of his happiness. He would return to Calgary in a few weeks, he promised, before returning to Regina, and he would be home for the summer. On this last comment, Nell replied that she was thrilled with the idea of Ernest gardening, building a fence around the garden and playing with the children.

That summer in an attempt to curb his activities, he wrote his friend Samson: "Polo isn't flourishing this year as Oswald Critchley is not well and Rodgers went off his head. I am not keen on participating either as I have settled down to a quiet married life and have a fine girl and boy to look after." He spent his spare time with Nell, playing solitaire in the evenings when he couldn't shake his business problems. However, when the Millarville Polo Team announced the upcoming Sheep Creek Challenge Cup to be played in August, Ernest couldn't resist. The Ranchmen's Club reputation was at stake. Brewery shareholder Sir Francis McNaghten appointed himself captain and gathered his team of Wolley-Dod, Ross and Cross. Harry Brayne remembered, "Cross was a reckless devil but a high scorer."

A huge crowd gathered for the two-day event. It was a wonderful opportunity to shake out picnic cloths and to unpack homemade breads, pickled beef and pies. Women in large straw hats shaded their eyes and gazed over the polo fields at the omnipresent CB&M wagons on the side lines. The riders galloped about the polo pitch, manoeuvring, darting, racing, swinging their mallets at the ball. The first chukker of the match saw no score thanks to what the *Calgary Herald* described as "brilliant defensive riding." In the second and third chukkers Millarville pressed Calgary. In the final chukker Millarville's Freeman and Calgary's Cross thundered down the field neck and neck after the ball. In a gigantic swing, Freeman swung wide and slammed his mallet into Ernest's forehead. Dazed, Ernest slowed to a trot, shaking his head and wondering why his vision was blurred. Hearing the two teams pound toward him and skid to a halt, Ernest realized that blood, not sweat, was pouring into his eyes. Jamming a hat firmly onto his forehead as a tourniquet for his wound, he wiped the blood away from his eyes with the back of his shirt, and roared, "We won't quit 'til we've won!" Then he raced far down the field after the motionless ball. Wheeling their mounts, both teams thundered in pursuit. Ernest reached the ball first, swinging at it for the goal that secured a Calgary win and the Sheep Creek Challenge Cup. Only then was he carried off to a kitchen table to have his head sewn up. A scar across his forehead was his lifetime badge of honour.

Shortly after, Ernest wrote to the territorial treasurer, Arthur Sifton, asking him if Calgary could get a $500 allowance to entertain the Duke and Duchess of York, who were planning to visit Calgary in September. Sifton agreed, if Calgary would meet the gift dollar for dollar. That proviso was easy to meet. The *Calgary Herald* reported that nowhere in the British Empire could greater loyalty to the crown be found. Innumerable entertainment committees sprouted up.

By sunrise on Saturday September 28, 1901, thousands had already gathered at the station to welcome the two royal trains. In a city already dubbed "cow town" by the Canadian establishment, the Drever women showed that while the veneer may be wild west, Calgary roots were solidly British. Mary Macleod, Jean Pinkham and Christin Jephson joined Nell Cross (in a full-length fur coat) to lead the formal welcoming committee for the royal party. Standing with their husbands, aldermen, judges and senators, far more than feminine beauty graced the platform. The Drever women embodied the history of the frontier while their men personified its opportunity.

Just before nine, the first train arrived and disgorged a large press contingent. They scrambled off to photograph the disembarking Countess of Minto (wrapped in a full-length mink coat), Governor General Lord Minto, Prime Minister Sir Wilfrid Laurier, and Lieutenant-Governor Forget. No sooner had the Calgary committee greeted this group, than they hurried down to the east end of the platform where a red carpet was being unrolled for the royal train. Out of the distance the circular-nosed engine belched and hooted, screeching to a halt in a shower of soot. The first to appear was the wife of the future King George V, the Duchess of York – the Princess Mary, or "May." Not quite as tall as Nell, the duchess wore her hair low on her brow, coiled behind. The duke was resplendent with naval decorations. After each member of the welcoming committee was presented to His Royal Highness, a parade immediately took place down Stephen Street in a town filled to capacity. The *Calgary Herald* wrote that the citizens "demonstrated their unqualified loyalty with unprecedented enthusiasm."

While Ernest was preoccupied with the royal tour, a CB&M floor swabber slipped over to a huge lager tank and turned on the spigot for a sip. A few other men joined him, then more. Pretty soon the CB&M had their own sensational party going. The head brewer first watched, then shrugged his shoulders and joined them. The tap was just left running for speedier refills. When no sober hand could lift its mug to the faucet, the beer drained onto the floor. By late morning some four hundred gallons were either drunk or gurgling down the sewer en route to the river.

Meanwhile, to the accompaniment of brass bands the duke presented medals to Boer War veterans, then met Indian chiefs resplendent in their buckskin dress. With boundless courtesy, the chiefs expressed gratitude for the peace and prosperity the deceased Great Mother and now the Great Father brought to them. In reply the duke said, "The Great King, my father, makes promises that last as long as the sun shall shine and the waters flow," and presented each chief with a silver medal to commemorate the day. The Indian children sang "God Save the King" and the royal party departed for a military lunch.

During the afternoon rodeo, Ernest and Nell sat with the royal couple, laughing as they shrugged off a sleet storm, then grimacing over one of the events. Thinking it would be fun to stage an old-time buffalo hunt, the rodeo committee had rounded up what tattered buffalo were left on the range and driven them before the royal party. White men dressed as Indians raced into the ring and began shooting bows and arrows at the animals. The ill-aimed weapons of the masquerading Indians either bounced off buffalo hides or wounded without killing. Fired up for one last angry roar, the buffalo refused to stand still and die. They stampeded. Fiasco rather than finesse unfolded before the royal visitors. Distracting the press with free beer in the CB&M tent, organizers hastily rounded up real Indians. They leaped on the white men's horses and, whooping and hollering, finished the job. Reporters agreed not to publish the bloody incident and shame the West.

All in all the visit had been a show unparalleled for local panache and international publicity. Calgary really knew how to put a place on the map. It also gave Ernest and his colleagues a promotional idea to be stored up for future use.

Upon returning to his brewery, Ernest discovered a drunken staff and floors awash in lager. He also noticed a tiny pipe leading to the malting tank. Pointing to it he asked his head brewer, "Eli, what's this?" The intoxicated brewer reddened but swore he had no idea. Eli had long been downing beer like Earl Grey tea. Ernest dumped him onto the train for Nanton, sending orders to Harry Brayne to dry him out. This meant that the CB&M was without a brewer at a time when it was brewing twice daily and bursting to capacity. In Billie Cochrane's view, Ernest was not spending enough time at the CB&M: "If you would terminate that tomfoolery at Regina and return to Calgary, we'll talk beer. We need to talk."

Knowing Eli might never dry out, Ernest hired Montreal brewmaster Percy Barton for the princely sum of $2,000 annually. He then enticed two Montreal businessmen to help raise $250,000 for a malt plant at Lethbridge. Sir Francis McNaghten was so intrigued at the idea that he agreed to invest $10,000 and offered to run it. Ernest's rival in the business, Fritz Sick, was simultaneously starting up a brewery in Lethbridge with $8,000 cash. A survivor of the British Columbian mining boom, Sick would be a formidable opponent. Nevertheless, they temporarily joined forces. Ernest wrote the mayor of Lethbridge indicating that he would erect a plant within the coming year if he was guaranteed a water supply, and if both he and Sick were exempted from taxes for twenty years. Explaining that his outlay would be $100,000, Ernest argued, "I am not asking anything more than I should. You know very well new industries in a new country are a gamble . . . first businesses should be encouraged."

Ernest also wrote to Elliott Galt, president of the Alberta Railway and Coal Company in Lethbridge, asking him for a free site for the proposed plant. It might have worked twenty years earlier but the folksy frontier atmosphere had already given way to a suspicion of the industrialists. Galt's reply was curt. "The Alberta Railway is the owner of the land in question. Its ownership is vested in the names of Trustees who would, under no circumstances, consent to a free grant." A year and a half later, in 1903, a bylaw exempting both brewers from taxes was drafted, but the supply of high-quality water remained uncertain. As this was critical to the brewing recipe, the Lethbridge venture was delayed. No water, no beer. Fritz Sick went on to control the Lethbridge market.

Ernest was also embroiled in a customs suit with the federal government that year. He had declared imported American machinery at a value of $750. Examining the goods, the customs officer valued them at a resale price of $1,263.70. "Swindle!" roared Ernest, writing Selkirk to fight the suit in Ottawa. Selkirk warned his brother that the customs commissioner would "insist on his pound of flesh." Ignoring the fact that Ernest had installed the machinery in the CB&M, the government justified its position by claiming that the goods could have been sold in Canada for up to $4,000. Following a year's battle and several trips to Ottawa, Selkirk got the assessment reduced to $900. Ernest swallowed his principles and paid up to be rid of the case. He found it almost impossible to take on the Dominion government, particularly when too busy to attend to matters himself. The customs case removed himself that much further from his dealings with central Canada.

By 1903 Calgary real estate values had improved. Ernest paid the last $2,000 to Willie Heber and transferred the a7 brand from Cross Brothers Limited to his own name. He also received title to three Calgary lots and dealt with payments owed to him by the Water Works Company. Prices were rising steadily and more sanely than in 1890 and Ernest found himself on a more solid footing.

Despite ten-hour days at the brewery when he was in Calgary, the business suffered from Ernest's time in Regina. Nell was lonely, the children were growing quickly, and ranch problems were mushrooming. He could no longer handle the load of public office. After writing to Haultain of his intention not to run for another term, he returned for a last speech in the legislature. It concerned the issue of territorial division.

In Alberta's drive for territorial independence, Ottawa had repeatedly shelved discussions in what the *Regina Leader* termed "a cavalier fashion." The attitude had affected Ernest. Once an unabashed federalist, the former Montrealer had undergone a metamorphosis. In 1899 as a fledgling politician he had not been keen to see western provinces formed. Now, he saw federal attitudes as unreasonable and stifling. Nevertheless, for a man who would be remembered mainly for beef and beer, Ernest demonstrated a remarkable statesmanship. He cared about the West but not to the exclusion of Canada.

Delivering an impassioned speech for the creation of two provinces to be equally divided east-west and not north-south, he explained his point of view. "Americans have aggressive ideas and look down on our country." A north-south division would encourage massive

American immigration and "introduce a wedge of discord right in the heart of Western Canada." Ernest sketched a scenario of future disagreements causing agitation between Ottawa and Washington, commenting, "before we knew it we would have an international question on our hands."

He received a standing ovation even from R.B. Bennett when he stated that the proposed provinces should be divided equally in area. He described future markets and outlined how the arable land could support a population larger than other provinces and eventually larger than any in the Dominion. Over the table-thumping of approval Ernest shouted, "I have *that* much confidence in the West, gentlemen. The outcome of this reconstruction will be the formation of the nation's greatest and most powerful provinces. Most importantly, the people will be in the front rank!" With that Ernest left politics.

As a family man, Ernest assumed Alexander's role of patriarch, and as such inherited the problems of his youngest brother. Edmund was both burdened by his lowly position compared to his brothers' prestige and puzzled by the processes leading to success. He mistakenly perceived his father's pursuit of accomplishment solely as making money, a factor which eluded him. Edmund still believed that his brothers were always pushing him around although he relied heavily on their judgment. He had developed a strong distaste for his farm. His mill had burned to the ground and some of his cattle had died. Although French was the household language, he hated living in a Catholic community. Edmund also had grown to resent his mother's patronizing; each week she sent the horses' feed down from Montreal in the family carriage, gold crest on the side and all.

In 1902 Edmund had just noticed in the newspapers that there were great opportunities for settlers moving westward. He decided to sell the River Beaudette farm and join them. Writing Ernest that he would appreciate any advice about Manitoba, the northwest, and anything about British Columbia fruit farms, he ended his letter with family news: Willie Heber was growing fatter every day; he had a special servant to put on his socks and tie his boot laces.

Warning Edmund to clarify his priorities, Ernest posed some questions: Was he aiming at farming or ranching? Did he plan to raise his children to do the same? If the latter were true, they would receive little formal education and they would experience a good deal of hardship.

Captivated by images of success without the bother of a master plan, Edmund sent to Ernest the Sifton advertisements on the West's great land buys. Ernest replied as cautiously as might have his father. "I do not think much of this as it has the characteristic ring of the western land boomer who is to be avoided." He advised Edmund to take a trip west and see what suited him best, privately worrying to Selkirk that their young brother was still careless in his appearance and lacked ambition.

Ernest advised Edmund to get Maggie MacInnes to introduce him to the right people in Winnipeg and that he would look after him in Calgary. He added, "Get Selkirk to get you a decent outfit of clothes as it pays to appear well. By so doing you meet the influential people who can give you reliable information and help." Extending kindest regards to Hélène and the children, Ernest closed with, "Do not hesitate to write about anything you want to know, as you must bear in mind you are making an important move and should not take any chances on making a mistake."

Shortly afterwards, Willie Heber accompanied Edmund with two carloads of animals and effects to Manitoba to look for land. No decisions were made and Willie Heber returned to Montreal. Left alone, Edmund promptly bought 650 acres of land six miles west of Virden, Manitoba, for the inflated sum of $9,000. Then he wired Hélène to bring out their four children. Surprised, Willie Heber assisted in closing down River Beaudette, packing and entraining for the remote farm. Just as they had departed from Montreal, Edmund wired from Winnipeg that he had changed his mind and wanted to return to Quebec. It was too late. Edmund would have to face his new life.

In a panic at what he had done, Edmund sent a spate of telegrams begging for $500 to take him out of the country. Before he could escape, Willie Heber and the family arrived. A furious Edmund blamed his brother for having bought the place. Two days later he cooled down and with the help of neighbours settled in. During his two-week stay Willie Heber wrote Ernest:

The country is all under wheat and slightly rolling with poplar bluffs. [The Crosses] are a mile from Church and school and six miles from Virden, [a town of] 1,500 people. The settlers thereabout seem a respectable lot of Ontario farmers. Of the three wells, one worked while I was there but only after a great deal of priming.

The water is more or less alkali. If Edmund would only take an interest in his affairs. . . .

For the next few years Edmund and Hélène would live in the tiny house, produce nine children and dream of success.

Another family concern for Ernest was Nell's twenty-three-year-old brother Norman, a ticket agent with the CPR. Unhappy with the demands on railway employees, Norman had joined the union. William MacInnes warned Ernest that Norman's job was in jeopardy. Alarmed that such potential executive material as a son of Colonel Macleod would join "the association," the general freight agent, W.B. Lanigan, agreed that the men had been overworked but so had the officials. Lanigan explained to Ernest that joining a union was "a handicap to a boy's career, especially if he aspires to anything beyond a mere clerkship." He urged Ernest to encourage Norman to withdraw, claiming that the uneducated freight handlers, the "6 o'clock men," rarely got promoted. "Council Norman to join in no rash project of the union. That would certainly mean disaster. We can man every post on the line if they all left." Ernest reminded Norman that his mother was dependent upon him and he could not afford to risk losing his position. But Norman stood by his principles and his union. Despite his Upper Canada College education and his influential name, he would never be promoted beyond ticket agent of the CPR.

In Montreal, Julia Cross slipped in and out of a coma. Edmund had already returned home. Harry had just left Montreal and wrote how wonderful it had been to go home to his mother and the "Old Homestead" as he often called Pine Avenue. In moments of clarity, Julia knew she was dying. She asked for Maggie, who immediately caught a train from Winnipeg while Julia's doctor administered stimulants. Mother and daughter were reunited on May 18; Julia died six hours later. Edmund was so shattered he could not stay in the house and that night slept in the stable. Ernest was heartbroken that he had missed seeing his mother for the last time.

Julia's role in life had been one of wife, mother and family helpmate, conveying the warmth of Pine Avenue to her energetic family. She had been the eye in the hurricane of activities, scandals and expectations of her husband, Uncle James Hutchison and her father William Lunn. She had had a good eye for finance, encouraged her children's horsemanship, and joined the Lunns in volunteer work at the church, the Montreal General Hospital and the Protestant Orphans' Home. Hers had been a time-consuming and demanding job and she had done it well – perhaps too well after the death of Robert, showering her grief, love and protection on Edmund. She was buried in the family plot with Alexander and their children, Charles, Julia and Robert.

When Julia had married Alexander and signed their marriage contract, she had identified some $2,600 as her own. Upon reading her will in 1902, Selkirk and Willie Heber learned that she had left her children $200,000, by today's measure a value of around $2 million and, by anyone's measure, not a bad capitalization of investments.

19

🌿 The Visionary

"God damn it, Cross! Things are never going to be in perfect running order because you'll never be satisfied with the present. . . !"

Billie to Ernest, 1903

Addressed as either "X" or "Dear Brewer" by Billie Cochrane, Alexander's fifth son remained as mysterious as his pseudonyms. His decisions were arbitrary and based on his own private deductions. Determined that the CB&M would grow and operate with its own cash flow, he kept bank loans to an absolute minimum. The CB&M had assets of $183,588 and it owed the bank $3,492. Ernest had yet to declare a dividend.

In 1903 it looked like a good time to sell the brewery again. Economic events in the West fluctuated as violently as squalls in an ocean. No sooner were a man's sails set than he was forced to tack, beat, or sometimes to turn tail and run before a gale. Ernest was good at the game. Probably more than any other factor in the West, he enjoyed the elements of change. He offered his 40 per cent of the CB&M to Calgary businessman W.R. Hull for $175,000, and agreed to be legally bound not to start up the brewing or malting business in the West for a given number of years. But Hull wanted the Lethbridge plans thrown in as well. Ernest countered that the $175,000 wouldn't begin to cover the expansion program, that the price took into consideration his personal knowledge and the years he put into developing the beer industry. Miffed at Hull's response, he called the deal off.

Tired of battling Clifford Sifton, Ernest considered the sale of his a7 Ranche as well. Claiming the best quality of beef in the country, he calculated the ranch's value as 17,000 acres for $170,000; 7,000 cattle at $30 for a total of $210,000; 500 horses at $35 for $16,500; for a total valuation of $396,500. Then he wrote Selkirk, "I would rather hate selling it, as it ... will be one of the best properties in the West."

That same year the British government put an embargo on imported Argentine cattle due to hoof-and-mouth disease. Cross, Cochrane, Hull, Eckford and a few others immediately formed a combine which they delicately called a "small union." They announced their arbitrary prices depending upon the age, weight and the time of year. They agreed to 5 per cent shrinkage on gross weight with no cattle delivered after November 1. Buyers came from everywhere. The group sold 3,500 steers and 1,750 cows, 555 head going to England. Everything had worked – climate, restricted importation, the game plan. It was a very good year but the next might be disastrous. Beef was a risky business.

As Ernest considered the 1903 sales of his ranch and brewery, the economy rose strongly. He immediately changed tack, sailing swiftly on a broad reach. Billie Cochrane celebrated the good times by driving the first Locomobile car into Alberta. Oil was discovered west of the Blood reserve and 100,000 shares were put on the market at 50 cents a share. Nine hotels served the expanding community. Ernest wrote Maggie, "There are no houses to be had in Calgary. The builders are building as rapidly as possible but cannot keep up with the requirements." Thanks to local donations and the efforts of men like Bishop Pinkham, who raised money in England for schools, some considered the education in Calgary comparable to that of Ontario. The Ranchmen's Club membership had cautiously increased from forty-five to seventy-eight, including every prominent WASP businessman, judicial personage or wealthy landowner west of Winnipeg.

From time to time Ernest travelled to Montreal, always including a stop in Winnipeg to do business or to visit the race track. During these trips Nell kept him informed of all and sundry, in particular the activities of Helen, Selkirk and baby Jim, born May 13, 1903, and christened James Braehead. She continued to refuse full-time help. Despite a difficult pregnancy and a sore knee, she had limped about baking as many as eleven loaves of bread in a day while caring for the children and maintaining the house.

In 1904 Ernest wrote to Selkirk suggesting that instead of selling the a7 Ranche or the brewery, they pool resources with Hull and buy the Oxley Ranche. Its 8,000 head were valued at $250,000, the land at $50,000. Seeking a loan from the Bank of Montreal for the venture and making clear his needs would be above and beyond the $25,000 worth of shares he would need if the Lethbridge malting plant materialized, Ernest was in for a surprise.

Montreal banks refused such huge monies because Ernest's security – his share in his father's estate – was unseizable by creditors. Selkirk advised Ernest to forget his proposal: "It seems a risky venture. One bad winter or cattle disease could wreck the prospect of profit." He closed with the complaint that he was sick of looking after their father's and Uncle James Hutchison's complicated estates, as well as all the other family investments. Ernest relinquished the Oxley Ranche and stuck with the brewery. Later he would thank Selkirk for his advice.

Several of Ernest's original roundup pals had sold their interests in Alberta and returned to Europe. Alexander, Skrine and Samson were gone. In a rare expression of feeling Ernest wrote to the latter, "I shall be very glad to hear from you as I miss my old friends terribly." He noted that they were spending a great deal expanding the CB&M, in expectation that the country north of Calgary was going to be filled with railroads and a new influx of settlers from the mid-western United States. On the other hand, across the mountains, British Columbia was in bad shape with labour troubles and strikes.

Internal problems expanded with the growing brewery and Ernest became more circumspect. His staff considered their Montreal brewmaster, Percy Barton, "a crook." One loyal employee who quit because of him told Ernest that Barton was responsible for mismanagement and that the place was knee-deep in dirt. With yet another alcoholic brewmaster on the decline, the position seemed to entail a perennial occupational hazard. Like most other aspects of his businesses, Ernest concluded that the only way to ensure a continuity of standards was to do it himself. So in the spring of 1904, he returned to school. He enrolled at the Wahl-Henius Institute, Chicago, for a two-month postgraduate course in pure yeast culture. The tuition of $200 was far less costly than his time away from the business or from Nell and the children. Just before he left Calgary, he was offered a substantial price for his lots across from Pat Burns's house. He owned the entire block and needed to make the decision whether or not to sell as a unit or as individual lots. He left for Chicago anyway, knowing that each hour of every day would bring new opportunities or fresh headaches.

Having implored Macmillan not to divulge his whereabouts, Ernest became enthralled by the academic atmosphere and the opportunity to improve his beer. Daily CB&M samples mailed to Chicago were scientifically tested and changes suggested. So striking was the improvement that R. Labatt wrote to Ernest, "anxious to introduce your most excellent beer at the Hamilton Club as I consider it better than Milwaukee."

Young Jim was not quite a year old when his father was attending the Wahl-Henius Institute. Nell wrote of their son, "Dear Jim is a wild one indeed, and has such a hearty laugh. He makes quite an audience for the other two. They often make me laugh too. Selkirk came running into the house bawling the other day with Helen on his heels, smiling. Selkirk's face was covered with mud and snow. They had been in a scrap and I'm afraid our dear boy got the short end of it. In the end they both began laughing. They do enjoy life so."

Ernest wrote from Chicago to ask Nell what colour of silk she would like for sewing. Mauve was her choice but she cautioned her husband, "Please don't buy anything too extravagant for me. We can't afford that." He must have expressed some frustration with being a student again, for Nell comforted, "Don't get disheartened my darling. Just stay with it and you will succeed. Your desire for knowledge will ultimately take a more practical turn which should greatly please you."

With his multifarious challenges, it must have seemed a bit bizarre even to Ernest to be back in class. One person it did not amuse was Billie Cochrane. Ernest had pushed his shareholders to the wall, moving ahead with expansion programs and other plans without informing his board of directors. When Billie learned Ernest was studying in Chicago he couldn't believe it and exploded with his, "God damn it, Cross! You're not aiming to give dividends. You're aiming to be one of the largest concerns in Canada and compete with the world's best!" Too many issues had built up, not the least of which was Billie's belief that Samson was selling his brewery shares to Ernest without sharing with the others. No dividends and the boss playing hooky finished Billie. The two old friends had a falling out.

Upon Ernest's return and a visit to Billie's Mosquito Creek Ranch one night, the two consumed a few bottles of wine and got into a row. Billie worked himself up into a drunken rage over Ernest's modus operandi. He accused the brewer of "keeping hungry shareholders at bay by dangling a live rabbit" of forever promising them large dividends when everything was in running order but never delivering. Ernest stormed off.

A few days later Billie wrote an apology. He acknowledged Ernest's October 12 circular announcing that Samson's shares, originally amounting to $7,800 and now valued at $15,600, would be divided amongst the shareholders proportionate to their initial investment. Ernest retorted that never again would the two be partners in future business, especially the proposed Lethbridge malting venture. In return Billie growled, "You should remember the suggestion of partnership came from you and was not of my seeking." Guessing that Ernest might be suffering from combat fatigue while the rest of the shareholders caroused in their global playing fields, Billie closed his note, "You deserve a vote of thanks from the shareholders for your excellent work and personal attention and time you have given to the business for small remuneration. Hoping you will forgive me for any expressions I used last Friday in the heat of wine and discussion, I am yours as ever, Bill Cochrane."

Ignoring the hand of friendship, Ernest steamed about for another three months, angered and frustrated by his directors' lack of vision. Then he cooled down and drowned his feud with Billie in a bottle of Johnny Walker. He even paid dividends for the first time in the brewery's eleven-year history: a total of $15,000.

As for the Lethbridge malt-house, nature once again stepped in. Excessive rain and early frost killed the barley crops. Not even the undersized CB&M malt-house could be filled. Montrealers cancelled the proposition of investing in the venture. In a last-ditch effort Ernest suggested that another malt-house based in Calgary could supply all of Alberta and British Columbia. That bid failed also and he determined to do it himself.

In the fall of 1904 mange swept through the cattle. Compulsory dipping in a brew of hot sulphur and lime, or sulphur and oil of tar, was enforced by the federal government. The cure sounded worse than the ailment, and the mammoth project was expensive. The vats and corrals would cost $1,000 each. On behalf of the ranchers, Ernest wrote to Dr. Rutherford, the veterinary director-general of the Department of Agriculture, to request financial help. As Ernest was overworked at the brewery, Billie Cochrane volunteered to oversee the dipping for the Mosquito Creek ranges. Building a huge 7,000-gallon vat connected with 500 feet of piping to the spring, he wrote Ernest, "We are all in the dark about this dipping racket and I am one of the few that is in anyway prepared."

In September a smallpox fear sent Calgary into a frenzy. Carried by an American visitor to the Imperial Hotel, the disease forced the hotel's entire guest list and workers to be quarantined. On September 19 Ernest was preparing to drive out to the a7 Ranche to examine the dipping setup when four-year-old Helen, three-year-old Selkirk and sixteen-month-old Jim all awoke with severe colds. Their throats were sore and they had difficulty swallowing. Ernest stayed behind. The following morning they were running high fevers. Ernest walked to the brewery as usual and worried in a letter to Selkirk that he suspected tonsillitis, although the children had improved slightly. But later in that day when the dreaded bluish-black membrane darkened on their tonsils, and they developed excessive thirsts and little choking swallows, he and Nell knew they faced the horror of diphtheria. Ernest wired to Winnipeg for a new diphtheria anti-toxin. It had been discovered and used in the Boer War but was not yet stabilized and available to the public. Cultured in the blood of horses, the anti-toxin itself could be as lethal as the disease. But the Crosses had little choice. Complications of diphtheria included convulsions, paralysis, meningitis and heart attacks; anything that might help had to be tried.

As Jim was the youngest and the sickest, Nell isolated him from the others, even hanging blankets around the air spaces of his door. With the help of Mary Macleod, she ran from infant to infant, steaming their rooms to thin the phlegm, then sponging their bodies to lower their fevers.

It took Ernest a series of wires to locate the serum and arrange to have it loaded onto a CPR freight train due to arrive on the morning of September 25. Throughout that night he and Harry Brayne paced the station platform in case it came on an earlier train. Brayne remembered that Ernest was nearly crazy with worry. When the expected train pulled in at dawn, no serum was aboard. Knowing that the next train wouldn't be there for hours, Ernest wired again, then strode for home. There, he was horrified to find Nell frozen with shock at the foot of their hall stairs, Helen dead in her arms. Suddenly Nell cried out and rushed up to Selkirk, reaching for him as he, too, choked and died. She stumbled back down the stairs with Selkirk, crumpling momentarily on the bottom step at Ernest's feet. Then with a deep shriek, Nell thrust Selkirk into Ernest's arms, gathered her skirts and raced back up the stairs. She tore the blankets from Jim's door, swept her baby into her arms, rushed down the stairs and out of the contaminated house. Ernest found her in a garden shed, crouched in a corner as if hiding. She was nursing her fevered Jim, believing that antibodies in mother's milk could save her baby. Within twenty minutes two of their children had died, and the third now struggled for his life. Ernest picked up Nell and Jim and took them to hospital. The *Calgary Herald* immediately reported the tragedy and added that unfortunately, the baby, Jim, was not expected to live.

Ernest insisted the funeral be in the morning. That evening Mary Macleod stayed up late, sewing a white pillow to place under Helen's and Selkirk's heads. Nell remained in shock in the hospital watching Jim struggle for his life.

Just before the funeral service, Ernest telephoned Billie Cochrane and tried to tell him what had happened. He could only sob, and Billie knew only that some dreadful tragedy had struck his friend. After the funeral, Ernest walked home with Harry Brayne. He stood outside his empty house which only days before was filled with laughter and said tightly, "Harry, for two cents I'd burn down the house."

Whether from personal sorrow, economic opportunity, or a sense of regional isolation, Ernest threw himself into a hectic round of economic growth and political change. He lobbied for Edmonton to be the capital of Alberta if Calgary could have the university. He invested in Metals Limited, a company established by Hull and Lougheed. He renewed his interest in British Columbian mines. He wrote the gold commissioner in Kaslo making sure his dues were paid up. He started new storage facilities in Humboldt, Saskatchewan, and revamped the entire beer distributorship. He repeatedly wrote the Wahl-Henius Institute for advice. He planned a new $30,000 elevator for 50,000 more bushels of barley. He opened a CB&M outlet in Vancouver to better service the coastal towns and the Yukon. He examined a prospectus for installing a pneumatic bottling system in the brewery.

He looked at purchasing a glass manufacturing company near Medicine Hat, a move to make the CB&M totally independent of central Canada. He wanted no Canada Malting Company in Toronto, no foreign glass company, no outside investor. Businessman L.H. Clarke of Toronto tried to discourage Ernest from isolation but he persisted in raising western money to better his own facilities. And whenever he had a few extra dollars, instead of indulging in a motor car or some luxury, Ernest added another quarter section to the a7 Ranche, encroaching on the surrounding townships like some prolific weed spreading across the land. Instead of dividends, he sent his shareholders brewery calendars.

In late 1904 Billie Cochrane renewed his efforts to get a decent dividend for the shareholders. Ernest retorted that he had already started construction of badly needed buildings and there would be no dissipating of profits at this stage. Auditors who examined the books reported a lack of security in the accounting department and payments that were vague in nature. Ernest replied that he was concerned with results more than internal accounting. No one seemed able to reason with the man by then referred to most frequently as "the Brewer," or "A.E. Cross." Not even his polo mates could reach him, for Ernest had hung up his mallet for ever.

In November, while in this frenzy of activity, Ernest received a letter from a poor German immigrant whose baggage had gone astray. He and his family were destitute. Although long gone from any politicking and holding only a desperate wish for privacy, Ernest spent a month tracking down and finding the family's belongings through the minister of immigration, then arranged for the items to be delivered from eastern Canada to Calgary.

Jim lived, but Nell's handwriting remained wobbly with grief for months. For a time they visited a favourite haven from the snow-bound prairies, Victoria, British Columbia: perhaps they hoped that distance would ease the pain. Twice, Ernest began letters to Selkirk but couldn't finish. He sent them anyway, along with a photograph of Selkirk's deceased goddaughter, Helen.

Billie Cochrane sent myriad letters to the Brewer describing his jaunts through Montreal where the MacInneses entertained him and where he and his pal, John Auld, "went out and drank eighty-three glasses of beer every night." One night Auld took a whole orchestra home. Billie quipped that "the impromptu concert of drums, fiddles, brass etc. woke old Mary the housekeeper up." He reported Selkirk as being wilder than ever, Willie Heber as not having lost any weight, and he graded the most voluptuous ladies of pleasure in Montreal.

On December 10, 1904, just before that first dreaded Christmas following any bereavement, the a7 Ranche house mysteriously burned to the ground. Destroyed in the fire was Ernest's framed diploma signed by Dr. Osler and Dr. McEachran. The Montreal Veterinarian College had closed down and he had wanted the irreplaceable document for his grandchildren. Ernest was devastated. Perhaps the fire unleashed his terrible grief over the loss of Helen and Selkirk.

Harry Brayne remembered, "Cross took it very bad." Again, Ernest and Nell left Alberta for Victoria, waiting for the frozen winter to drag into a sluggish spring. Finally, the temperature began to rise steadily. Jack Blake, the a7 Ranche foreman, scribbled a note in pencil: "Dear Ernest, the creeks ar running, Blake." That brief, misspelt sentence heralded new life. The sunshine coaxed green shoots from the river bank's frozen mud; chunks of ice cracked up, allowing the river to burst through and race cheerfully down the valley into the spring of 1905. In time, warmth and life would also break through the numbed souls of Ernest and Nell. Over the next year Ernest built a two-storey ranch house and named it Braehead.

On July 1, 1905, when Alberta became a province and Edmonton got both the capital and the university, the Crosses fourth child, Mary Julia, was born. Once again, the delivery had been a dangerous one for Nell, and for a time doctors feared for her life. Not until July 17 did Ernest write that she was able to sit up. Selkirk expressed his relief that her acute danger was past and that she was on the road to recovery. Nell's subsequent children would all be born in Victoria, in the mild coastal climate under the supervision of her trusted obstetrician.

That spring, for the first time ever, the Brewer wrote each of his colleagues proposing an expansion program. He secretly informed McNaghten that "The CB&M showed a profit of nearly $97,000," and assured him that after the new building completions, he should be able to pay considerable dividends. It all sounded good to Billie, who had his humour back over the CB&M, and who was tiring of Alberta's hardships. Like Willie Heber, he increasingly sought the good life. On one occasion, following an early snowfall, Billie told his wife that he was heading into Calgary for supplies. Upon arrival he picked up his mistress and just kept going all the way to England.

By the summer of 1906, Albertans had become over-confident with successes in cattle breeding, growth and ranching in general. Like numerous ranches in southern Alberta, Ernest believed the a7 to be dangerously over-stocked, blaming a complacency born of steady growth and kind winters. Worried about the coming winter, he and Billie requested from Frank Oliver, Ottawa's new minister of the interior, an additional 32,160 acres of leased land for grazing.

Nearly three weeks later they had received no reply. Ernest wrote again, "I have *got* to make some provision for grazing cattle or get out of the business." Desperate for land, he offered to buy out existing squatters or take them on as partners. Then he went ahead and leased two undesirable townships (46,043 acres) from the CPR south of the Red Deer River near Bassano. Although it gave him an extra twenty miles of river frontage, Ernest worried that the hay would be of poor quality. He wrote his foreman, Archie McCallum, "It was this or nothing. I have run chances on it." Advising his men to drive all the steers and yearling heifers up, he cautioned them not to start out too early as the country seemed all burnt up and dry. It was August. Besides being over-stocked and under-ranged, there was something Ernest didn't like about this summer. In no other correspondence did he fuss so over an approaching winter.

By mid-August, Nell was tiring under the strain of caring for her youngsters, Jim and Mary. Calgary was hot and dusty and she still felt the dreadful ennui of bereavement. It was also a time of soaring beer production, and although the Brewer was needed everywhere, he arranged to take his family to Lake Louise for two weeks. It was hardly a holiday. Ernest seemed possessed by an inner barometer forecasting a bad winter. Again he wrote Archie McCallum to put up plenty of hay and as fast as possible. He also wanted more cattle run north to the Red Deer area after the fall roundup, and told Archie to complete the new ranch house, to speed up the ploughing and fencing and, as always, to cut down expenses.

As the snows began to fall, the minister of the interior finally replied to Ernest's request for land. Instead of receiving more leases, two sections or some 1,280 acres would officially be opened to settlers. It was a terrible blow, for Ernest owned the land on both sides and had been "personally assured that the land would *not* be opened for settlement." He stressed, "Give me a fair chance to prevent my place from being spoiled." The bigger he got in the free enterprise system, the more his competitor became not other ranchers or breweries, but the government itself.

As there was nothing more Ernest could do, he and Nell sailed for a five-week trip to Hawaii. Even there he could not escape news of the dismal winter. Worst hit was the Red Deer area, exactly where he had driven so many head. A ranching colleague, Charles Douglass, wrote from the Bassano district that hauling hay was a nightmare. Constant blizzards and winds created huge drifts which buried the hay stacks. The snow was belly-deep to a horse and the cattle were eating brush. The cold winds were so terrible that cattle driven to patches of sage simply fought the wranglers back to the gullies and shelter. The cowboys did what they could but the cattle kept dying.

Old ranchers still talk about the winter of 1906-7. Chilling blizzards and freezing rains brought stock deaths in the Calgary area alone to 60 per cent. When Ernest returned from Hawaii he rode a train through the lands to witness the endless carcasses littered around the tracks. Some a7 strays ended up in Chicago. Over fifty years later Ernest's son Sandy would recall, "Daddy lost 2,000 steers. I think the brewery saved the ranch." Always a fighter, Ernest wrote to Clay Robinson & Company Stockyards in Chicago that instead of the usual trainload of a7 cattle, there would only be a few carloads arriving. Nevertheless, he still expected good prices, for during the past twelve years he had used nothing but pedigreed Shorthorn and Hereford bulls and "I have as good a bunch of range steers you can find anywhere in the West."

While the subsequent 1907 recession from poor beef prices and bad crops affected the merchants and general public, the CB&M thrived. Just a year earlier Ernest had borrowed $60,000 from the Bank of Montreal to enlarge the brew, boiler, and bottle houses to five times their present capacity. The result would be five carloads of beer daily. Enlarging the barley storage would cost an additional $30,000 but the shareholders wanted to pay that in as additional capital. In the spring of 1907, Ernest reduced the bank loan by $50,000 in two months. He also doubled the company's malting capacity.

Some Calgarians seemed less than pleased that A.E. Cross survived the general economic disasters. The editor of Calgary's *Eye Opener*, Bob Edwards, resigned from the Board of Trade because he claimed that incumbent Calgarians were getting rich forming combines. In a five-page letter to the editor, himself, Edwards referred to "the beer atrocity," citing, "one glass of thin slop actually cost the brewery *one cent* while the public was charged fifteen cents for one, twenty-five for two." He also attacked Calgary merchants in general for not lowering prices on their goods following reduced freight rates, and berated the industry combines and the "mutual arrangement amongst the grocers, landlords, hotel men and others who make their living off the public." He concluded, "There is a great future ahead for this country, but if the businessmen of Alberta don't change their methods, they will kill it."

During the first decade of the twentieth century Willie Heber frolicked through restaurants from Paris to Nice, then on to Switzerland and the Lausanne country. He loved the festivals, the opera and the theatre, and indulged in all with a seemingly endless supply of funds. As his enormous weight kept pace with his growing wealth, it simply attracted more feminine companions. He was grateful for this, for as the doors of Parisian cabs were narrower than anywhere else on the Continent, giggling ladies had to push or pull their three-hundred-pound escort in and out of conveyances. Open carriages were obviously preferred, as were two ladies for an evening rather than one.

Everyone loved Willie Heber. On Julia's death, he had assumed a maternal concern for his brothers. He sent Selkirk's old suits and new long johns to Harry, clothes to the Wyoming children and pictures to Léa. From Europe, he annually sent sailor uniforms of scratchy serge to Edmund's nine children in Virden. Edmund's children, Annie, Bill and Jack, would recall fifty years later, "How we hated those sailor suits. They were just awful. We had to wear them for years and years."

Tragedy in Edmund's life brought Willie Heber home to Canada. One day Edmund's two-year-old Julia fell ill with the dreaded "throat" and died in her father's arms. In a fit of grief, Edmund blamed his daughter's death on the harsh Virden life and vowed he would head further west. Not knowing that his farm was sitting on top of Manitoba's richest oil field, he left his grieving wife and eight children behind, venturing to seek his utopia in Saskatchewan. He wrote Ernest en route, "We made a mistake in buying a wheat farm in Manitoba as well as paying too much for it. I believe you when you say that there are great prospects in the future for the west, but I am afraid that I'm too far gone in life to take advantage of them." Edmund was forty years old.

Before long Willie Heber lumbered into the diminutive Virden home to help Hélène and the children. For the first time Edmund's offspring would know the leather belt of discipline, at least until they realized that they were more fleet of foot. The only time one of them had to venture near their uncle was to tie or untie his boot laces and even then they could escape his hand. One day young Jack snitched the leather belt and hid it in a wheat field, thus ending the threatened punishment. Willie Heber wrote in his notebook, "How sharper than a serpent's tooth it is to have a thankless child!"

That summer Edmund contemplated homesteading in the Carrot River Country of Saskatchewan, changed his mind several times, then sold the Virden farm and purchased 6,000 acres near Battleford, Saskatchewan. Not knowing if he could afford it, he wrote Willie Heber for advice. Talk of finance mystified Edmund. His expertise was fences and he was forever designing a better post-hole, a better method of preserving the wood, a better method of stringing wire. Although he lived off Alexander's, Julia's, and Uncle James's quarterly income, and in fact became adept at playing the stock market, Edmund's coffers would never fill from self-initiated effort.

Exhausted with foster parenting, Willie Heber performed one more task. He moved the family to Battleford and their new homestead. Edmund's daughter Annie remembered the rattling, sweaty train ride only too well. "Two of my sisters had to share a bunk with Uncle Willie. He was so fat. It was awful for them." It was pretty awful for Willie Heber, too. After safely delivering his brother's family, he escaped to Europe to find Edmund and Hélène a maid.

In Switzerland, Willie Heber found a French maid but fell in love with her. Marguerite Françoise Burnat was a twenty-two-year-old beauty from Lausanne. Instead of sending her to Edmund, he brought her back to Montreal and offered her to Maggie MacInnes at Pine Avenue. Maggie sniffed a conspiracy and refused to hire Marguerite. She knew her gallivanting brother only too well. A few years earlier Willie Heber had compromised another mistress but got a friend to marry her instead. In Billie Cochrane's words, Willie Heber had "got off easy, paying his best friend only $3,500 for the wedding party including $100 for drinks, plus a silk dress and orange blossoms." The consummate Victorian gentleman, Willie Heber held singular ideas on women and had clearly outlined them in his notebook:

Who marries for love takes a wife; who marries for fortune takes a mistress. Who marries for position takes a lady. You are loved by your wife, regarded by your mistress, tolerated by your lady. You have a wife for yourself, a mistress for your house and friends, a lady for the world and society.

Your wife will agree with you, your mistress will rule you, your lady will manage you. Your wife will take care of your household, your mistress of your house, your lady of your appearance. If you are sick your wife will nurse you, your mistress will visit you, your lady will enquire after your health. You take a walk with your wife, a ride with your mistress and go to a party with your lady. Your wife will share your grief, your mistress your money, your lady your debt. If you are dead your wife will weep, your mistress will lament and your lady will wear mourning. Which will you have?

Willie Heber chose Marguerite. His blood lines were British, his lifestyle was French. Disregarding the shaking heads of his Protestant friends, he married Marguerite in a Roman Catholic ceremony in the Shrine of Reparation, Point-aux-Trembles, Quebec. Following the formal wedding ceremony, he threw a fabulous outdoor reception in the aspen grove. His friends were very polite to his bride, who could speak not one word of English, but a credo had been broken – a French servant might be accepted at certain soirées but a man wasn't supposed to marry her. Subsequently, with the exception of Billie Cochrane, who thought Willie Heber was hilarious in French or English, Montrealers dropped the couple. Willie Heber lamented that "the Montreal crowd won't have anything to do with her."

They moved to Montreaux, Switzerland, where their first child, Fleurange, was born. She was followed by Yvette, Simone and Willie. The children had no idea that to be of French and English parentage was fine as long as it wasn't in Canada, and as long as their mother had never been a maid. As they spoke only French at home, they would eventually learn English only through trial by fire at a thoroughly British private school on Vancouver Island, British Columbia.

In Montreal, Maggie and William MacInnes cared for the Pine Avenue estate and welcomed the western relatives whenever they passed through. Maggie remained active in the "In His Name" society repairing clothes for the poor, and one year acted as president for the Women's Canadian Club. William rose quickly through the ranks of the CPR to the position of vice-president of traffic. Given the task of opening hotels and purchasing CPR ships, he and Maggie travelled frequently to England and made several trips around the world. Even in North America the MacInneses used leather, gold-embossed tickets for every railway from the Chicago lines to the Atchison, Topeka and the Santa Fe. Trips to Europe were first class all the way. In 1912 William would take his family along when he presided at the highly publicized opening ceremonies of the Ritz Carlton Hotel – built by wealthy Montrealers and the CPR.

The MacInneses summered at Kedgemakoogee in Nova Scotia, and in Europe the extended family shared their itineraries. Selkirk, Willie Heber and Maggie co-ordinated their jaunts at such resorts as Carolles, opposite Mont San Michel. Selkirk continued to escort Aunt Emma Lunn and the widowed Mrs. Daniel (Vanderbilt) Torrance about Europe. The latter, noted Aunt Emma, enjoyed annual pin money of $100,000.

In the West, the year 1908 and onward was a significant period to be involved in any club or voluntary organization. Alberta was exploding with growth again and volunteers in every field had opportunities to help shape its routes. When Bishop Pinkham established Calgary's St. Hilda's school for girls, Nell promptly enrolled Jim into kindergarten along with two other boys. They proved unmanageable and the school soon reverted to girls only. Nell served as Calgary's first president of the Women's Canadian Club, as well as helping to found the Women's Hospital Aid group and the IODE. Surrounded by electricity and other modern conveniences at home, she still preferred firing up her old wood stove. It was kept in a kind of lean-to kitchen attached to the house and was actually set onto the floor without legs. One morning Nell smelt smoke and discovered the floor on fire under the belching stove. Hailing Calgary No. 3 firehall, who got the blaze under control, Nell demonstrated her gratitude for the next fifty years by baking them an annual Christmas pudding.

As president of the Calgary Board of Trade in 1908, Ernest spoke out in favour of government bonds to expand the railway system. At stake, in particular, was the future development of the Canadian National Railway. The network, he stressed, was vital to Calgary's progress – and to his own master plan. During those years he moved about as president, first vice-president and secretary of the Western Stock Growers' Association, the Ranchmen's Club, the Canadian Manufacturers' Association (Alberta branch). He was on the board of the Calgary General Hospital, the Western Canada Polo Association, the Prairie Thoroughbred Breeders and Racing Association, and the Chinook Jockey Club. His honorary presidencies included the Calgary Gun Club, the Winnipeg Turf Club and the Calgary Board of Trade. One thing members knew, the Crosses were never simply titular members of any voluntary organization.

By 1908 almost a million acres of land were under cultivation and there were as many cattle, 250,000 horses and 185,000 people. New Buicks which ran up to forty miles per hour could be bought in Calgary for $1,800. An automatic telephone system was proposed for the city in 1907. The first hot-air balloon floated above the city, drifting in the breezes and like everyone and everything else, seeking new horizons.

Ernest continued to expand his enterprises, thus maintaining a perpetual risk status with the brewery. Needing immediate cash for more Calgary Natural Gas Company shares, he offered to sell the entire Calgary block No. 89 to Pat Burns, and sold $3,000 worth of property to R.B. Bennett. It was a frenzied era in the oil and gas business, with secrets and speculations running amok. Ernest was once accused by his friend Stephens of leaking information. Hurt, for he was known as a man who kept his word, Ernest wrote of their long friendship. He emphasized, "I value old friends more than all the gas companies and I certainly trust you will think of me in the same way as I always will of you."

Operating the brewery with a permanent staff of over one hundred men, Ernest began buying the odd hotel throughout Alberta and Saskatchewan, then locking out the competition. This was common practice in England but illegal in Alberta. Ernest solved the problem by instructing R.B. Bennett to incorporate a holding company known as the Ranchmen's Trust. Future hotels would all be bought under this name. Not intending to make money from the hoteliers, Ernest explained that the CB&M charged no more than 7 to 8 per cent interest on loans made to the hotels, as "we are not a money-loaning business but simply an accommodation in order to get their business."

Labour dissension in Ernest's world was escalating for the first time. At the ranch, foreman Archie McCallum had fired some men and trouble was afoot. Billie Cochrane checked up, subsequently explaining that whereas the workers were strictly eight-hour men, the foreman wanted them to work sixteen hours a day. For Billie and Ernest, who had once spent twenty-three hours of the day in the saddle, such labour gripes were anathema. Nevertheless, Ernest compromised with the ranch hands and hired three hay-makers at $35 dollars per month plus fare. Then in June 1908 the CB&M officially joined its first labour union. Much of the pressure had come from the Crow's Nest Pass railway workers who threatened to stop drinking CB&M beer unless the union became a reality.

To the close of the decade Ernest's annual reports would commend his partners for their patience, then express disappointment that there could be no dividend. He would remind them once more of their policy to expand where they could, promising large dividends when "everything is in running order." As no written policy of anything, let alone expansion, was ever found, his statements exasperated his four colleagues. New ideas, such as advancing money to hotelkeepers and thus tying down beer sales, were those of Ernest himself and not of his sporting shareholders. He purchased the Grand Union, Imperial and Emperor hotels, valued around $100,000 each, then announced that he was sorry, but there would be no dividends that year.

Following the death of his wife in 1908, Billie Cochrane sold his Alberta lands and more or less permanently repaired to Scotland with his two children. It was during this period that he increased his "Dear Brewer" letters. He wrote of his continental trips with ribald humour, and he dispensed sound advice to Ernest, who was cranking out twelve-hour work days at the CB&M. Billie's missives hailed from Tahiti, Europe, South America, and often from castles in Scotland, in particular, Lewis Castle, Stornoway. As Ernest's absentee watchdog over brewery expansion, Billie would amuse the Brewer with his tales, then in the next sentence fire tough questions at him on the CB&M.

Billie bought a Mercedes and spent his time unsuccessfully outrunning the police who frequently chased him for "furious driving." Lewis Castle proved an excellent place for hunting and fishing and he often reported killing fifty salmon in a day and as many snipe or grouse the next. Except for reunions, CB&M directors' meetings and keeping tabs on the Brewer, he was finished with Alberta. A letter sent care of the Constitutional Club, London, would always find him wherever he was in the world.

Ernest may have missed Billie's companionship but his absence probably suited the Brewer just fine. Eyeing the market, the increasing population and drilling operations, he was free to launch another expansion. He had mentioned to Billie a plan for reorganizing the capital stock of the brewery, but said no more when Billie warned, "If we cannot pay a dividend on a capital of $52,000, I cannot see that a larger capital on paper would help us." For once he said, "I have no doubt our partners are howling for cash, Hull, Eckford, and MacDirty. I hope you won't give them any. I wish you would come over here. You have slaved for that company long enough and deserve a holiday.... You could take one when you get the beer running right and uniform in colour, quality etc." As Billie added that uniform quality was impossible with the current steam kettle, Ernest would have to stay on the job.

In the coming three years Calgary's population would grow by 30,000. Public houses mushroomed and beer sales proliferated. Seven Alberta breweries competed against the CB&M. Wishing to expand again, Ernest requested and received from the Bank of Montreal an increase of credit to $300,000. In the fall the CB&M bought the Grand Central Hotel and the Golden West Brewery. Billie learned of the purchase only when he read it in The Albertan, mailed to him in England. When he complained, Ernest sent him a picture of the Walker Well, a Calgary Natural Gas Company strike just east of the brewery; he had run the first pipeline to the CB&M.

As Ernest increased CB&M investments in hotel and wholesale liquor licence houses and extended operations to the Pacific coast and up to Dawson City, cries for prohibition bounced about the country from New Brunswick to Victoria. The breweries countered the growing temperance armies by forming a Canadian Western Brewers Association "for mutual protection" and for doing business in a more "friendly way." Ernest would serve as president. As an organized group for lobbying against prohibition, the association also provided a civilized facade for the brewers to keep an eye on each other.

By June of 1909 Ernest announced CB&M liquid assets of $286,073, total assets over one million, surplus $771,000. It was a conservative evaluation, as was that of the a7 Ranche holdings. Its Calgary Natural Gas Company stock was worth ten times what it had originally paid for it. Constraining friends and dividend-seekers be damned. The Brewer was about to make his first major move.

20

 Boom Times

"My dear Ernest . . . so you are a millionaire!"
Nell to Ernest, 1912

Shored up by a facade of conservatism, Ernest launched out into new enterprises. He had recovered from his entrenched views of 1904-5, and was again encouraging Quebec financing in Alberta. Sending Nell and the children to Victoria for the winter, he took the train to Montreal, convinced the Bank of Montreal to extend his line of credit to $500,000, then sent notice of CB&M's annual meeting too late for his gallivanting directors to attend. Their collective mood emulated Billie's, who wrote from Ballyduff, Ireland, on May 29, 1910, "My dear Brewer, Your notice of May 9 announcing [that] the Annual Meeting of the CB & M will be held on June 7th, does not give me possible time to get there." Billie's complaints or critiques rarely extended beyond one-liners. He respected the only man to struggle with overflowing vats and threatened labour strikes while the rest of them killed salmon and shot elephants.

Brewings soared into the hundreds that year. Few would know how Ernest built his operations, for his private annual reports depicted him as a master of the non-statement. In 1909 his balance sheet had referred to "some doubtful debts, costs due to wear and tear of buildings etc., leaving a net profit of $152,149.75." Outlining the CB&M sales empire throughout four western provinces and beer on nearly all boats sailing out of Pacific ports in Canada, Ernest vaguely referred to some improvements which could be financed in "terms of a private nature" through a bond to the bank. End of report. Later clarifications never materialized.

Securing the $500,000 loan with a one-line agreement, Ernest purchased specially made bottles, upgraded machinery, explored the world of rice beer, added huge glass-enamelled steel tanks for beer storage, extended the engine room and built a cellar tunnel connecting the wash house. He built four new cold storages at Vernon, British Columbia, Melville, Saskatchewan, Lacombe and Camrose, Alberta, with a cold cellar at Kamloops. These enabled CB&M to move entire carloads at controlled temperatures. Macmillan's nightmares of rushing melting ice by train and delivering warm, cloudy beer were ended.

As the Ranchmen's Trust purchased each hotel, CB&M beer would be almost exclusively sold from that outlet. Ernest kept a weather eye on the temperance groups but saw them as no real threat for the coming year. His collection of information on them ranged from western Canada to Europe.

During his annual visits to Montreal over the New Year, Ernest stayed at Pine Avenue. He spent hours at Alexander's desk developing a family tree, and explaining to young Evelynn MacInnes, "It is important to know who our people were." Seventy-three years later, Evelynn would recall, "There were drawers full of these papers. They were all tattered and peculiar looking. I can remember Uncle Ernest sitting there copying them off, and as a child I was thrilled because someone was called Elizabeth Wotherspoon and I used to think that was a lovely name."

Pine Avenue, the Homestead, or whatever the family called it, rollicked with action as the MacInnes children, Donald, Evelynn, Judy and Emma, grew up. When the Calgary Cross children began attending the bilingual Miss Edgar's and Miss Cramp's School for Girls, just down the street, they would stay at the Pine Avenue estate on weekends. Although the stables of Clydesdale horses and carriages gradually gave way to the motor car, Maggie MacInnes still kept a hunter and rode in Mount Royal Park with the Van Hornes. The MacInnes children remember the wonderful home where the wallpaper was changed once a year; where the Irish cook, Mrs. Flower, and the French sewing maid, Philomene, kept things in order, and where the ancient parrot in the upstairs bathroom still squawked out the window in chorus to the church bells pealing below. It was just the way Alexander and Julia had envisioned the home for their grandchildren.

The closest Montreal friends of Ernest were the Robert Refords, who had bought the Allan shipping lines. The Refords lived more elegantly than the Crosses and were frequently featured in the news with either their magnificent sailing ship, the *Thermopylae*, or their famous botanical parklands and thirty-room mansion established in Grand Métis, Quebec.

Mrs. Reford, formerly Elsie Meighen and favourite niece of Lord Mount Stephen, was both an accomplished gardener and an armchair politician. She was a staunch Conservative who wasn't the least intimidated by any man when expounding her political theories. She was also an avid promoter of improved French-English relations. Ernest would delight in visiting the Refords with his young daughter Mary when she was a teen-ager attending school in Montreal.

In 1907 Selkirk, often called Montreal's most eligible bachelor, married a maid he had placed in the Windsor Hotel. The girl's father was the Cross's blacksmith. Aunt Emma did not approve.

During this time, Alberta growth soared as never before. Bank clearings nearly tripled from $98.8 million to $275.5 million. Land was at a premium. The Royal Bank paid $4,000 a foot for the old Hudson's Bay property on Centre Street and 8th Avenue. The Hudson's Bay paid $750,000 for a 7th Avenue site. Bordellos boomed between four-storey office buildings, a strip of hotels sprang up and the Alberta Hotel boasted the longest bar in Canada. Calgary streets hummed with white-collar easterners scrambling to establish their territory alongside sweat-stained cowboys.

While some investors plunged into high-risk land deals for sensational profits, Ernest never forgot his father's admonitions. He held a tight rein on his ventures and a cynical eye toward the speculative frenzy. He invested in industry, irrigation and agriculture, but never again the quick-flip real estate deal. Land to Ernest no longer meant speculation but longevity. Referring to soaring values in his annual report, he hoped the "real estate curse will not get too far to injure the people."

He kept a frenetic pace, pushing his brewery holdings throughout British Columbia and barely producing beer fast enough to meet the needs. With the leap into big business, he inherited all the ramifications of growth, such as rewriting his union contract to meet tougher demands from his men. At least seven other breweries were competing for the market share, the temperance crusaders were crowding, the CB&M was expanding its hook-up to natural gas, and the Canadian National Railway had chosen a station in Calgary. In June 1910 he rebuilt the wooden section of the brewery. In July, cloudy beer and failed crops kept him chained to Alberta. As a backroom Conservative he campaigned against Arthur Sifton in Wetaskiwin. Ernest enjoyed the battles, and like a doting, worried parent he could not bear to miss out on any segment of growth in the adolescent province.

Nell had gone to Victoria with the children and Ernest promised to join them whenever he could, but the visits rarely materialized. The Brewer dared not holiday in Victoria when his workers were rumbling "strike." Just getting there took days on the railway, then an overnight ferry ride from Vancouver. Once trapped on the island without interprovincial telephones, he couldn't even make a deal. When he did make it west it was for only a few days of pacing the beach, the waves lapping the shore with maddening repetition to remind him that he was on an island. He would soon be off, once stopping long enough to check out the Nelson Brewing Company up for sale at $100,000, then to visit a dozen different outlets – whose managers were guilty of unpaid bills – before continuing home to Alberta.

Dutifully awaiting her husband's pleasure for her to return to Calgary, Nell's life became the opposite of his explosive pace. It appears that living in the milder coastal climate was a mutual choice, for she often wrote that before she could bring the little ones back, it was necessary to insulate their Calgary home against the bitter winter drafts. Also, she was frequently under the care of her Victoria doctor and suffering from debilitating anemia. But at the same time, Nell was removed from Ernest and from the action of Alberta. In earlier years she had been Ernest's confidante in running the CB&M. Her comments on labour problems and the annual reports indicate a working knowledge of the company. She recalled the time when she had shared in Ernest's political excitements, and another when he had laughed so hard as she hurried through the chicken yard pushing the wheelbarrow between herself and the curious cow. Then there was the summer when they had built Braehead house and counted the calves. As the months dragged on, Nell wrote, "I like you to work and love to see you succeed, but, OH! How I want you ... before business cares have had all of the best." Jim and Mary each drew pictures of their activities and pleaded, "Please Daddy, when are you coming to see me?"

Without Ernest at her side, Nell was unable to enjoy the elegance and gaiety that was 1910-11 Victoria. Women rarely went anywhere other than church without an escort and she did not know how to meet people unless properly introduced. Once she attended a performance of the famous German soprano, Johanna Gadski, but felt apart from other theatre patrons joyfully arriving as couples in their Model T Fords. Most evenings after putting the children to bed, she just sat in the living room with the servants. Her maid Polly, aware of her mistress's unhappiness, sat stiff-backed, reddened hands folded, staring in silence and occasionally snickering at Nell. In turn, Nell "listened to the clock tick and tock," the emptiness a painful contrast to the hard work and inspiring aloneness she had known in the foothills.

When Ernest wrote of crushing demands, Nell replied with, "There [was] a great old electrical disturbance last night. The sky was quite wonderful and the moon a vivid green. . . . It is cooler this afternoon and I wish I could send you a great whiff of sea air." Into each of her daily letters she placed violets and primroses, vignettes of spring – or roses and daisies, blooms of summer. And she gathered in Ernest's postcards and telegrams like bouquets, knowing that his soul was consumed by the energy of an increasingly complex frontier. As tenaciously as she clung to her husband and their children, she watched Ernest cling to the earth and his fledgling province.

In the early summer of 1910, Nell eventually learnt that a fire had roared across four sections of high land on the a7 Ranche, then wheeled westward through tinder-dry grass toward Braehead. Rushing southward, Ernest had found his men ploughing a deep ditch around the house, fighting to control the terrified horses as smoke and heat swirled around them. The Nanton volunteer fire department was joined by neighbours who rode along the edge of the flames coughing, their squinting eyes loosely protected by scarves. They dragged sacks and disemboweled cattle along the edge of the fire line to soak the ground, their horses' legs wrapped in wet rags to ease the pain of scorching-hot earth. With the help of a water-pail brigade the fire was brought under control and the house saved. Old-timer Jim Ryan remembered, "the whole mountain was burning up."

In September when Nell was hospitalized in Victoria from a violent miscarriage, Mary Macleod headed for her daughter's side. The white-haired matriarch threw herself into the Cross's Oak Bay Avenue household, creating the same buzz of activity that she had in Rothney cottage some forty years earlier. There was no doubt in anyone's mind who commanded Nell's home. Even Ernest was awed by his mother-in-law. When Lucy, the Cross nannie, fell in love with a drifter called Curlie, Mary ordered Ernest to return the girl to Calgary immediately. "We don't want any heartbroken farewells. . . . You know what brutes men are. . . . Please write to me at once. Lovingly yours, Grannie.''

In Paris, Willie Heber had celebrated himself up to 320 pounds and one evening suffered a stroke. Partially paralysed down his left side and far from home, he sought Ernest's advice. He wanted to move to the Canadian West for the children's sake, but Marguerite wanted to run a Parisian hotel. Blessing the skill of the French doctors for saving his life, Willie Heber regretted the cost of his illness: ''I shall have to live the rest of my days on a starvation diet or I shall immediately fall ill again. . . . I often think of the time you were laid up at the Ranche. It was always the Ranche that saved me in years gone by, as it prevented me making a fools' errand of a voyage to Europe . . . .''

In Calgary, Ernest built the Mountain Spring Brewery, writing in haste to Nell that he was always rushed and tired. She replied by personifying the magnificent Mount Baker, which ''looked grander last night than I have seen him. The sun was setting and the huge mountain and surrounding peaks were flooded with glorious colours. . . .'' She said of Ernest's long, long days, ''You have a brave heart and I trust you will someday have your reward.'' Nell's quiet steadfastness would bequeath to her children a strength of character which would endure throughout the ensuing generations.

By October 1910, Nell was fussing over the a7 cattle, the shortage of hay, the dreadful fire and the prairie flowers which she had missed. As Ernest had installed gas heating in their Calgary home and Mary Macleod had chosen and hung yellow wallpaper in the dining room, Nell anticipated a cosy, draftless household and soon headed for Calgary.

This was a golden era. A natural gas seepage on Sheep River sparked more speculation and drilling. The CPR completed its major irrigation system, which meant more barley could be grown; the CB&M's yawning machinery already consumed over 800,000 bushels annually. As president of the Ranchmen's Club, Ernest oversaw its land sale for $300,000, relocating to its present site at 13th Avenue and 6th Street. On May 4, 1911, the Calgary Power Company's project at Kananaskis was completed, lighting up Calgary with its first major hydro-electric power.

The summer of 1911 proved a glorious one. In July the family rode the streetcar out to an old building on the corner of 12th Street on the CPR tracks where Ernest would wave at the engineer to stop the train. The Crosses, or anyone else, would climb on one of the eight coaches which Mary Cross remembered smelling of oranges. Upon reaching Nanton they switched to democrats, teetering just above the rumps of a team of horses as they bumped along the rutted tracks. As they climbed above the timber line some 4,500 feet high, the sight of the rolling hills of heather and wildflowers was reminiscent of stories they had heard of their ancestors' homes in Scotland. Upon reaching the a7, they continued on to their cottage at Willow Springs, located eight miles south of the home ranch.

Nell never tired of the Alberta foothills. Some believe that the ocean and the prairies share a kinship in the endless flowing of their elements. But for her, nothing would ever take the place of the foothills, and she would instill in her daughters Mary and "Marmo" that same sense of freedom they gave to her. She also taught Mary the Latin names of the wildflowers. After all, if one had to learn a name at all, the Latin version was just as easy, more informative, and it was correct.

For the Cross children, much of their lives were not matters of choice. They did what they were told. Like their mother and grandmother, the daughters were expected to learn domestic skills. Nell taught Mary to sew when she was four, encouraging her, "try and do it as well as possible." The upstairs maid taught the children how to make a proper bed and tidy their rooms. Jim spent hours tinkering with machines and building gadgetry, once nearly blowing the house up with a kerosene engine. When sent to boarding school at a young age, the children neither questioned nor thought about it. "We just did what we were told."

At bedtime Nell read the youngsters Scott, Dickens, Henty, Defoe and Beatrix Potter. Children's books were beautifully illustrated and for a lifetime Mary and Jim would marvel at the pictures in their books. Of his mother, Jim recalled, "She was just one of the nicest people I ever met in my life. She was a quiet disciplinarian, gentle. Of course if you were doing something wrong she'd give you hell."

As a woman reprieved from exile, Nell's 1911 letters conveyed the joy of completeness. She wrote of the children so full of mischief when riding their ponies, of baking twenty-seven loaves of wonderful bread in the wood stove, of Billie Cochrane and "Old [Sam] Steele" dropping in for a visit and how glad she was to give the verandah a good sweeping afterwards. It threatened rain after a very hot morning. It was so very pretty outside. It was so good inside. She and the children worked in the hay field and fixed the chicken house and they had music and tea and long stories every night. Nell's letters soared with happiness. Ernest's visits sent her into rapture, and following one of their trysts she sketched a metaphor from nature, "The feeling you put in me keeps me green."

On June 22, 1911, Cyprian and Jean Pinkham had attended the coronation of King George V. Travelling by third class and arriving late in London, they were avalanched by invitations. Cyprian was prominent in England, where his preaching had generated funds for churches and schools in the Canadian West. In 1909 he had raised $15,000 in England for the new Bishop Pinkham College in Calgary, where entrance exams to Cambridge University were written and recognized.

For a couple with diminutive personal funds, the expenses had been frightening, but Jean was determined to attend. She was instructed to appear for the coronation in court dress topped by a hairdo coiffed by the court hairdresser. The resourceful woman bought an inexpensive, outsized gown which was almost a cast-off; Cyprian bunched it around her and fastened it with handfuls of safety pins. Wrestling her long, white hair into an upsweep, she tossed a cloak over her shoulders and glided out the door with the bishop, a smashing looking couple from Calgary via the Red River Settlement. After the unforgettable four-hour ceremony at Westminster Abbey, then the Buckingham Palace garden party, Jean wrote, "It was a great time to be in England and the English people seemed to vie with each other in doing honour to Canadians."

In December a pregnant Nell returned to Victoria where Ernest joined her for the 1911 Christmas at the Beach Hotel. Although they owned several lots – bought for $1,200 and now worth $1,500 each – Ernest did not wish to build. In the first week of 1912, he hastily purchased a house at 1113 Fairfield Road, not hearing Nell's comment that it was so far from the sea. His mind and soon his body were already rushing back to Alberta.

On the board of, and financially committed to, almost every major company and event, Ernest was pivotal to the province's growth: a syndicate was formed for Calgary Petroleum Products Limited, which was already drilling for oil in Turner Valley; the Canadian Western Natural Gas, Light, Heat and Power Company laid a 170-mile pipeline from Bow Island, then bought the Calgary Natural Gas Company. In his notebook Ernest reminded himself to write Lougheed a warning that Calgary could go ahead or be left behind on the whims of the railway commission. In staccato notations typical of his movements, he urged Lougheed "not to let personal or political inferences outweigh your judgement. What we have for guaranteeing [brewery] bonds: railway and business."

This was also the year in which Ernest joined with Pat Burns, George Lane and Archie McLean, each of whom contributed $20,000 to establish Calgary's first Stampede. Wyoming cowboy and showman Guy Weadick had captured the entrepreneurial spirit of these men who were dubbed "the Big Four" to stage North America's biggest rodeo. Over $15,000 in cash prizes were offered. Even women would be allowed to ride broncos but ladies were discouraged from attending. Calgary bashes, polished since royalty began visiting in the 1890s, had reached stellar proportions. The promotional hype was as immense as the financial gamble.

On May 25, with plans fully launched for the Prince of Wales and other international notables to attend what would become one of the most popular events in North America, Nell was still pacing the Pacific beaches and beginning to hear that something big was in the wind. She wrote to Ernest, "Your talk at Pat Burns was the first I had heard of the 'Western Stampede.' I should like to know more about it if you are taking an interest in it."

In the spectrum of Ernest's priorities, the Stampede paled in comparison to his plans for the brewery. Gathering his board for once, he proposed that it launch a public bond issue through the Bank of Montreal of £250,000 sterling, or $1,500,000 at 6 per cent per annum with semi-annual dividends. Already having a credit line of $750,000 on loan to the Ranchmen's Trust Company, Ernest offered to secure the new loan by continuing his personal guarantee for $100,000. By using the bond issue to pay off all debts and to purchase the controlling interest in Alberta hotels, the CB&M would control the western beer market.

In outlining his proposal to the Bank of Montreal in Calgary on February 4, 1911, Ernest presented a blueprint of how the CB&M established itself in an agent's territory – by building cold storages and shipping only in carloads on the essential railways. If the agent was unsuccessful, the Ranchmen's Trust would buy one or more hotels at the best points in his district. Claiming the CB&M could supply the best quality, temperature-controlled beer in this manner, Ernest explained, "It is not long before most of the other hotel men are obliged to buy their beer from our agent. Examples of the success of this method we can give all over this country." To illustrate, he described the Crow's Nest Pass rail line where a proliferation of coal mines within a radius of ten miles gave them at least five carloads of business per month for most of the year. The CB&M had already procured three of the best beer hotels in the area, although lack of cash had forced them to delay cold storage plans.

Their rapidly increasing business, continued Ernest, necessitated an expenditure of $100,000 in expansion of the brewery, now showing an investment of over $800,000 exclusive of their hotel investments. Reviewing the reason why their capital stock of $52,000 must remain in the hands of the five shareholders, Ernest wrote, "... We can conduct our business to the best advantage in the most private way, free from the criticisms of the public who are filled with municipal and government ownership." Claiming that the CB&M already had the bulk of all beer business, Ernest concluded, "We want the Bank of Montreal to allow us to continue ... in the same way as we have done with them the last nineteen years, [and] to carefully extend our investments in loans on mortgages and purchases of hotels until we are firmly established over this country.... We know our account is a good one ... and feel that if your Bank wants to do business in Western Canada and lay their future banking business on a good foundation, they should grant such requests."

The directors objected to the confrontational tone of Ernest's letter but it was delivered to the bank in that form. Despite the growing threat of prohibition, and annual interest payments of $118,000, the banks felt secure with Ernest Cross. The CB&M got the loan.

As each and every bond had to be signed by hand, the task placed on the carousing directors was poetic justice. It took them months. Billie snorted from Scotland that they were harder to tally than calves. No computers or copying machines eased his aching wrist. He signed thousands of them, admired the beautiful engraving and reported, "I can do them clean at rate of 200 per hour. It curtailed knocking off for a drink now and again, but am very glad to render any assistance towards the Brewery." He grumbled that shareholder Eckford signed three in the wrong place, omitted to sign one and "covered them all with blots and scratches."

The company then sold its first and second issues, signed a new labour agreement for one year, bought the Golden West Brewery and paid up its debts. Over the coming months, the Ranchmen's Trust acquired a total of fifty hotels, all of which were renovated, with the emphasis on small bedrooms and big bars.

Ernest then made a move that overjoyed his directors. The five hundred original shares issued at $100 were now worth $3,000 apiece. He split the stock thirty times by taking $1,448,000 out of his surplus account to create 14,500 new $100 shares. In March, he announced a stock dividend to the shareholders of $1,448,000 and a cash dividend of $81,380, or 5 per cent paid out of the profit and loss account. The move still left a reserve of $250,000. By locking up the directors' original investments for twenty years, Ernest was able to revalue the assets of the company at $2,700,000, and most of the bond issue would be used to pay down Bank of Montreal loans.

The CB&M buildings smoked and screeched with production. Vats worked overtime and beer sold faster than it could be brewed. Net profits of $179,000 in 1910-11 more than doubled to $396,564.56 in 1911-12. The Golden West Brewery, run as an independent, paid a dividend of 15 per cent to its shareholders. In a subsequent CB&M meeting, the five directors – Cochrane, Hull, MacNaghten, Eckford and Cross – paid themselves a 4 per cent dividend on the new capital stock of $1,500,000.

Nell wrote from Victoria, "My darling Ernest, So you are a millionaire! Congratulations!" Rather than build a flamboyant home or take a trip around the world, her husband continued to sink his profits back into the a7 Ranche. Usually he bought a quarter section at a time but that year he purchased the McIntosh Ranch bordering his own. The 827 acres of deeded lands, leases of 4,901 acres, and about three hundred head of cattle cost Ernest $9,000. Seventy years later Jim Cross would say, "Alexander Cross and Daddy were always putting their money in the land. They loved land."

Had Nell realized that she would be in Victoria for almost an entire year with no one to talk to but the servants, she may have, as she put it, "gone off my head." She attended Christ Church Cathedral frequently, and spent more time on her painting, the limpid water-colours a gentle reflection of the artist. Her spirits soared each time Ernest wrote, and once she answered, "Your dear letters come like a breath of the freedom the hills give one." But as time dragged on, with Ernest visiting only two weeks in the spring, Nell's desperate longing for Alberta and home grew. In turn, he mailed his children knives and books on their birthdays, while continuing to build an empire on the other side of the mountains.

That spring Ernest had visited Montreal to reorganize financing and to meet with other brewers. Of greatest concern to the business as a whole were the temperance organizers, who were launching an all-out attack. In turn, anonymous letters aimed against temperance leaders may well have been the resurrection of "Bovis." In one, found amongst Ernest's private papers, the writer illustrated a knowledge of biology and chemistry, skilfully uniting the influence of God and fermenting bacilli with grapes ripening into wine on the vine. In the future Stampede parade, the inevitable and ostentatious CB&M float would be followed by a temperance wagon loaded with women crying, "Help us! We would close the Saloons!" Ernest stopped buying up competitive breweries that encroached on his territory and diversified into oil exploration and natural gas.

In the spring of 1912 Nell returned to Calgary for a couple of months. She discovered that Ernest had bought a large piece of land on the bald Mount Royal hill just west of downtown Calgary and had hired an architect to design a mansion. He had wanted to surprise Nell, for their house on 8th Avenue was now in the centre of the industrial area known as Brewery Flats. The opportunity to build on this hill overlooking Calgary must have seemed thrilling. Their contemporaries, such as R.B. Bennett and gas magnate E. Coste, would establish their sandstone mansions in this Mount Royal enclave of exclusivity, success and power. The CPR-owned site was Calgary's counterpart to Montreal's Mount Royal.

Ernest drove Nell up the hill in an open carriage on a day when the wind whipped the top soil of the prairie into mini-tornadoes. Dust and grime whooshed under skirts and up pant legs. Suddenly a gust whipped Nell's hat off her head and spun it away. A woman of nature, Nell was also practical. Climbing back into the buggy she said that she really preferred the more sheltered and unpretentious wood home near the brewery. Probably to Ernest's confusion over the enigma of women combined with delight over the fiscal savings, they shelved the mansion plans. Nell Cross had no need of grand statements. They remained at the other end of town. Jim Cross commented of his father, "He didn't splash money around. He did things quietly. A lot of people were building palaces. He didn't."

Nell and Billie Cochrane both missed the first Calgary Stampede. Nell because she was back in Victoria having given birth to her seventh baby, Margaret "Marmo" Victoria, and Billie because he was having too much fun. At Lake Temagami, Ontario, he had outfitted himself with a two-room tent, two canoes, a guide from Gaspé, and a French bistro cook who specialized in clams capolin. He reported of the remote area, "Booze scarce but plenty of fish and damned little else to eat."

Nell's absence was less jovial. She wrote to Ernest on August 21, "Everything sounds fine for the Stampede and I wish the 'Big Four' and all the others every success, but one of the oldest 'Old Timers'

... is missing it." Of her mother's absence Mary Cross Dover would comment in 1981, "It was better that wives and nice young things not go to the Stampede. My first Stampede was after the First World War." On the other hand, nine-year-old Jim Cross travelled to Calgary to ride beside his father in the parade, establishing what would become a seventy-one-year tradition for himself. And many of the old roundup pals of 1887 came, although H.B. Alexander was off organizing an expedition to the North Pole. Selkirk, John Auld and other Montrealers also showed up in Calgary to laud the greatest show ever staged in the Canadian West.

Octogenarian cow-puncher Jim Ryan remembered the Stampede's opening day:

> Thousands came on trains from the east, the west, the north, the south. The governor general of Canada came. It had been raining that afternoon. The first guy out of the shutes was Powder River Thompson of Wyoming and he got bucked off and he got up and said, "Howdy Duke and howdy Princess" and he bowed.
>
> There were about a half a dozen lady barbers that came over from Spokane Washington and God Almighty, every cowboy wanted his hair cut every other day and a shave at least twice a day. They'd pay 'em two or three dollars and never pick up any change. There was a marquis where you could drink and a marquis where you could dine and dance. We had a hell of a time!

As Christmas approached, Ernest hoped to reach Victoria, but he had to attend the annual brewery meeting en route. It was scheduled in Revelstoke on December 21. If snowslides blocked the Crow's Nest Pass, he would never make it to the island by December 25. Nell's determination to bring her family together was reminiscent of her father's lonely Christmas of 1883. With her encouragement, letters from the children poured forth from Victoria to Calgary. "My dear Daddy, I wish you would come out here for Christmas and bring me a book. Our school closes on the 20th. I wish you could come on the 20th.... With love from Mary." Jim and Mary filled the remaining days before Christmas screaming through the house brandishing Jim's self-made swords and riding in his home-made ambulance wagon. Nell wrote that night-time gales rattled the windows and doors in the drafty house. She sank into a sitting room chair while Jim took after Mary with a broom. The servants called each other names. Selkirk sent thirty dollars for gifts and a fur from

Montreal's Holt Renfrew, but without Ernest, the festivities fell flat for Nell. She adopted a bright facade to humour the children. Christmas Eve tea at the richly decorated Empress Hotel and a tour around the twinkling Victoria harbour failed to cheer her. Somehow Ernest made his Revelstoke meeting, and on December 24 his ferry connections in Vancouver. He arrived in Victoria for a jubilant Christmas Day, Ulysses welcomed home from the wars.

In January 1913, Calgary Petroleum Products – founded by ten men including R.B. Bennett, Ernest Cross and James Lougheed, with $40,000 cash on a bank loan of up to $50,000 – spudded its first well. The founders had pulled it off with expenses of $25,000, which also financed a second well. A speculation frenzy fuelled oil exploration and immigration reminiscent of the Klondike gold rush. Calgary's population swelled by the tens of thousands. Tent cities and oil companies sprang up like desert flowers after a rain shower. Real estate changed ownership with a shot of whiskey and a handshake. An alarmed government warned of the instability of such investing but no one paid any attention. A tone of optimism pervaded almost every aspect of society, from the mechanized farmer expanding his fields with new threshing machines and binders, to the coal miner's frenetic productivity, to the lumber worker in the proliferating sawmills. Exporters able to choose from a spiderweb of railway lines enjoyed an extension of trade hitherto unrealized.

When Nell returned to Calgary Ernest hired an army of workmen to build a three-storey, six-bedroom, a7 Ranche house with a massive porch wrapping the outside. The house was situated just below the spring where Willie Heber had found the mice. The water still ran by gravity and pumped forcefully through winter or summer. Ernest and Nell built their home together and, like its predecessor, named it Braehead. In 1982, Mary Cross Dover would remember:

The house down there was built for five servants. They never had five servants. The vegetable garden supplied everything, the ranch supplied all the meat. They made their own butter. People would talk of mother's flower arranging – you see she grew sweet peas and peonies in enormous profusion. There was always the most beautiful arrangements, bouquets of flowers everywhere all through that house, and the vases were all lovely and the silver was always shining. Just lovely. She loved Calgary and her affiliation with the Church of the Redeemer but she loved the ranch and its nearby country church too. She was a very elegant woman and graced both worlds.

An aura of optimism and anticipation spun through the province, and the proliferation of industry created a cornucopia of fledgling investments. Keeping a weather eye on the horizon, Ernest joined the speculation. In February he turned down a land offer of 1,466 acres at $15 per share but bought a lot with James Lougheed in downtown Calgary and a Medicine Hat property for $35,000 with Sir Max Aitken (knighted in 1911) and R.B. Bennett. Buying more Calgary Petroleum Products stock for $12 a share, he declined an offer of stock participation in a New York company, explaining, "There are so many investment opportunities out here that I cannot begin to meet them."

Had Ernest been more adventuresome he might have used the brewery and ranch assets as collateral, gambling tens of millions that the drilling would soon strike oil. Save for Willie Heber, who became inordinately rich apparently through the stock market, that was never the Cross style. Ernest moved carefully but inexorably forward, never getting so deeply in debt that he would endanger his empire. Like his father, he established a solid estate and unlike so many families who epitomized the cliché, "shirt-sleeves to shirt-sleeves in three generations," this philosophy would strengthen the Cross holdings through six generations of wealth. Of the other Big Four, Pat Burns would realize a fortune but George Lane and Archie McLean would be bankrupt within one generation.

It was a time of insatiable thirst in the bars of Alberta. CB&M burned out an engine but managed to ship to outside points two hundred more carloads than in the preceding year. By 1913 the company had realized a 200 per cent increase over the past five years.

Always one to capture a deal, Ernest wired William MacInnes asking for a special CPR freight rate, as he had heard the Winnipeg Breweries were getting one. A man of propriety, MacInnes wired, "MacInnes out of town, MacInnes." Then he faced up to Ernest with, "Could not get what you ask for my own personal friends, therefore absolutely impossible meet request made." Nevertheless, MacInnes was also swept up in the excitement of the West. He enthused to his brother-in-law, "My dear Ernest, What do you think of 'Alberta's Beer without a Peer' for your labels?"

Even Nell, ensconced once more in Victoria with Mary attending St. Margaret's private school, Jim at St. Michael's Boys' School, and

Marmo toddling about, was caught up in the gaiety of the era. At the age of thirty-four, she began to rely upon herself for her source of fun and often had a driver take the car out to Oak Bay to see her lots before walking to the sea. She also took tentative steps into the community. First, she accompanied the servants to see *Naughty Marietta*, then took the children to a carnival and a moving picture called *African Hunt*. On her snowbound birthday, a phenomenon for Victoria, Nell hired a driver to tour the family around the magical city before seeing Sarah Bernhardt in *Camille*. Afterwards, a friend of the great actress took Nell, Jim and Mary around to the side door to meet her. Nell wrote that Bernhardt "was indeed a fright in daylight. You could have scraped the paint off. It was so red and all over her face. But she was wonderful, very gracious." That spring Ernest swept Nell off for a trip to Montreal and New York. From then on they would often take trips to the East or to San Francisco, Ernest always managing to do a little business on the side.

Of Mary and James Macleod's children, Jean, only seven when her father had died in 1894, married Calgary lawyer John Montgomerie-Bell. Of all the beautiful Drever/Macleod women, Jean was reputed to be the loveliest. She had two children, Helen Rothney and Roma Macleod. Following Jean's wedding, Mary Macleod returned to Winnipeg, taking her thirty-four-year-old son, Norman, as her companion. Captive son of a legend, Norman served his father's memory well. He was always the considerate gentleman, speaking at historical association meetings and representing the family at memorial functions in honour of Colonel J.F. Macleod.

Mary Macleod vied with Jean Pinkham as the undisputed duchess of the family if not the city. With the passage of time, her humour bordered on the ascerbic. Friends in Winnipeg and Calgary remembered her as a beautiful, imperious, chain-smoking old lady who entertained everyone with tales of the frontier. Her grandchildren remembered that she would use a hatpin to skewer the stub of each cigarette, then puff away until it disappeared. When one was seventy-nine years old, he would exclaim, "I was so damn scared of my grandmother. She was like the Queen. She was a tall woman, severe. She was the matriarch." A brother would add, "I was scared to death of her. She was a Drever."

In France, Willie Heber Cross found the nutritional restrictions imposed by his doctors unbearable and the political unrest threatening.

Consequently he made three major decisions. He converted to Christian Science, gave up his diet, and decided to move home "to find a castle in Canada." But Marguerite loved their Paris home. Once when the landlord threatened to raise the rent and Willie Heber refused to pay, prospective tenants toured through the glamorously appointed rooms but turned their noses up and walked away. A smiling Marguerite had placed Gorgonzola cheese on all the heating elements and whispered about dead mice. The landlord gave up.

Willie Heber wrote to Ernest: "If anything were to happen to me I would like my family to be left in an English country. I have been talking English to the wife for the last few months and it is wonderful how she has picked it up. She is a good business woman and an excellent cook with lots of fire. She is 29 and I am 55!"

The summer of 1913 was a grand one for the Cross clan. Selkirk, Maggie MacInnes and Billie Cochrane spent wonderful months travelling around Europe before visiting Willie Heber's summer home in a small village called Carob, near St. Michel. They found their brother dieting happily on champagne.

Of Willie Heber's subsequent visit to Montreal, the MacInnes children recalled, "When he came to visit us on Pine Avenue, he would see ghosts on the driveway at night. It was probably the birch trees weaving in the wind. He said they were beckoning him to the Windsor Hotel, so he would go off." Eccentric or no, Willie Heber possessed an uncanny talent for making successful deals. One of his purchases was a $25,000 share in Uplands Limited, the bankrupt Montreal company owning the most exclusive residential land in Victoria. Along with other Montrealers Willie Heber refinanced Uplands and would sanction the building of sidewalks and underground lighting.

From Victoria, Nell wrote that the city was full of scarlet fever, measles and whooping cough and she intended to return to Calgary to live. Crosses, Pinkhams, Jephsons and Macleods were the pillars of the Calgary community. Calgary Hunt Club members enjoyed hunt breakfasts before riding to hounds in formal pinks. They chased prairie coyotes instead of foxes. Formal horse shows were popular; Ernest bred polo ponies and Irish wolfhounds (Sophie was his favourite), and to perpetuate a good shoot he imported pheasant and Hungarian partridge. A tour of the CB&M or a trip to the a7 Ranche was a main attraction for distinguished visitors to Calgary. It was a man's world and ladies were seldom invited. Nevertheless, to Nell it mattered not that Victoria was considered more civilized and genuinely more elegant with its shiny convertibles and top-hatted drivers gracing the streets instead of cattle and cowboys. She wrote that the cold weather would be a small price to pay for the prairies, old friendships and home.

Ernest did not immediately receive Nell's letter, for he had already left for the north country. He believed that the great, untapped future of Alberta lay in a land whose frozen ground held mineral resources vast beyond dreams. Returning to Calgary, he launched another issue of CB&M bonds, then sent out a rash of queries on mining ventures.

Towards the end of 1913 Billie Cochrane began his "Dear Brewer" letters again with, "I have heard nothing of the Dividend which you promised to pay to the shareholders in August. I hope it has not been sunk in more bonds. I am overdrawn on both sides of the Atlantic and could use some cash." A.H. Eckford was also hard up and offered, yet once again, his entire High River ranchland and stock to Ernest for $155,000. Ernest declined as usual but requested that the directors sign more bonds. In turn they demanded dividends in that form. They kept the bonds tightly controlled amongst the old guard. Despite the directors' entreaties, Ernest refused to pay the 1913 dividend.

The autumn of 1913 and a bounteous harvest paid final tribute to the good times. Farmers drove wagon after wagon off to the grain elevators, then bought themselves the latest motor cars. The chugging gas guzzlers increased in number from 3,000 to over 10,000 in one year. Beef on the hoof from a7 bawled their way to another successful Chicago market, and young Jim Cross delighted in a ranching summer with Ernest and his explorer-godfather, H.B. Alexander.

Further afield, a crisis of global proportions was building. The CB&M directors living in Europe were the first to warn Ernest of war, and Billie was more suspicious than ever of prohibition and a falling economy. But with the exception of Willie Heber, who was still in Paris for the summer, the Crosses and other Albertans seemed unaware of the European crisis. They were insulated from the world by bumper wheat harvests and drilling speculation. Then chinks appeared in the economy and the market softened. Thousands of Calgarians caught in the real estate slide left the city and relocated on farms. In Montreal, William MacInnes wrote, "I hear all your real estate boomsters have folded their tents like the arabs."

In Scotland, Billie sniffed trouble with the pending Irish Home Rule. He intended to return to his three miles of Slaney river bank with a gun and fight for the Orangemen in Ulster. "Write me about the oil, commercial quality and quantity. . . . I went to Montmorency Falls and tried to shoot an old Buffalo bull with a camera. He was in heat with a balling cow. As soon as he got my wind, Alcoholic, he charged me twice. . . . It was the closest call I ever had. But absence of body is better than presence of mind."

21

Prohibition

"It must be dull times, and 8th Ave. a long street to travel without a drink."
Billie Cochrane, 1918

In the spring of 1914 Ernest and Selkirk sailed for England aboard the *Lusitania*. Selkirk's marriage was not working out, and while Ernest probably felt he was doing his brother a favour, Selkirk was the only one to lure the Brewer away for a vacation.

In England, Ernest and Selkirk met up with Billie Cochrane to learn that Turner Valley drilling reports promised success and that Nell in Victoria had delivered her sixth child, Alexander "Sandy" Rothney. Ernest immediately wrote:

> My dearest Nell, I cannot express my joy and surprise when I opened the cable saying "son born both well." No other four words could mean so much to me; how I wish I was near you. It makes me feel angry with myself ... but I am sure I would be very much in the road and all the women would wish I was a thousand miles away. On such occasions men are not wanted.... A good doctor, a good nurse and old Mrs. Brumby will do best. It is a great comfort to hear my own dearest is well.... How I wish I could be with you all.

Ernest visited the Guinness Brewery, where he was loaded up with stout, then taken to the races. Willie Heber and Marguerite came over from Paris, he saw Sir Max Aitken and Walter Skrine, and he lunched with T.S.C. Lee. Assuring Nell that he would soon start for home to "see my lovely family," Ernest first planned to detour via Chicago and buy bulls.

Selkirk's improvement was a reprieve. He returned to Pine Avenue and passed on the complex estate duties to William MacInnes, who would be the new custodian of the Pine Avenue property for the next thirty-five years. On December 28, 1915, he smiled at his adored niece Evelynn, went upstairs to his old room and died. The *Montreal Evening News* described Selkirk as "one of the city's most distinguished barristers. He was considered a somewhat secretive, albeit generous philanthropist and generous with his time." Selkirk's funeral was conducted like those of all the other Crosses – at Pine Avenue in the drawing room. His estate of $185,000 was modest. Selkirk was not an empire-builder.

Ernest arrived home as the Calgary Petroleum Products well struck high-grade oil at a depth of 2,718 feet. He joined the frenzy of thousands of people who flocked to Turner Valley, northwest of the a7 Ranche, to see the Dingman well gush forth the future. Calgary Petroleum Products stock shot up from $12 to $200 before midnight. Buyers ran through the streets with waste baskets filled with money. Land sales skyrocketed again and within one week newly incorporated oil companies boasted a capitalization of $35,820,000. The Calgary Petroleum well ran the deepest, followed quickly by other strikes in a dozen companies. While some crowed that they were the "Rockefellers of Alberta," and that "Coal is going, oil has come," the Calgary Petroleum Products' Dingman well just kept pumping quietly away.

An air of festivity again pervaded the province, and elaborate plans for the Stampede were made. Then in the spring Billie wrote to Ernest that war was imminent in Europe and that it would soon affect Canada. He added that his recent visit in Montreal had been quiet except for a panicky stock market. Billie hoped that at least in Ireland the war would divert the attention of Britain away from home rule, thus reducing the danger to his favourite fishing hole on the Slaney River.

When England declared war against Germany in August 1914, forty-six-year-old Billie enlisted in the British army, citing his age as "44 yrs, 39 days." The Brewer's wild friend possessed a sense of duty which infiltrated his jocular letters like a spy sneaking through enemy lines. Every CB&M director who enlisted in the First World War had experienced the unpredictable hardships of ranching, underscored by the relentlessness of a vicious climate. Trained to resourcefulness, their current battles, although bloodier, simply took place in different arenas of the world. T.S.C. Lee joined the French Red Cross and throughout the war repeatedly returned to Europe, allegedly to rescue his £1,000 of pocket money locked up in France. H.B. Alexander drove a motor ambulance for the French army from the field hospitals to the base. H.B. Eckford worked in a munitions plant for a period, then left because, Billie suspected, he fought with everyone. The crazy Howard flew reconnaisance planes behind the German lines for French intelligence, was shot down, imprisoned in Germany, then escaped to rejoin the RAF.

As summer slipped into fall young Ernest Pinkham, Jermy Jephson, Cecil Townshend (married to Roma Macleod), Jack Montgomery-Bell (married to Jean Macleod), and Robert Cross (Harry and Léa's son) all signed up with battalions heading overseas. An entire corps from Bishop Pinkham College enlisted and went off to war. A few months later, at the battle of Courcellette, Ernest Pinkham was killed; Jermy was also killed in France; Robert Cross was killed fighting alongside other students from the University of Wyoming.

On August 30, when the first German air raid struck Paris, Willie Heber was still entrenched in his apartment. He wrote to Ernest, "In this war, England is in with two blackguard nations, Russia and Japan, who will skin her of everything worth having. The Slav Yoke will be infinitely worse that the Teuton Yoke." When German guns were heard on the outskirts of Paris and occupation appeared imminent, he wrote Ernest a final letter as packers crated his Louis XV furniture. Hastily signing off with, "Thousands upon thousands of the first picked men going off to get slaughtered; a horrible disgrace," Willie Heber moved with astonishing alacrity and escaped with his family and his furniture to London.

In Calgary, R.B. Bennett called a meeting in his office with Jean Pinkham and her daughters to form the Canadian Red Cross. Jean was later awarded the Order of the British Empire and two foreign decorations for outstanding community service. She founded a women's volunteer army which established Red Cross branches throughout the province, rolled bandages and sent the packages overseas. Nell's children may have been too young to fight, but they also rolled bandages and helped in many capacities.

The onset of the war coincided with the death of Willie Drever in Saskatchewan. Like James Macleod, he had enjoyed his life each day as it came, and ended it in Prince Albert as postmaster. Trader, loyalist supporter in the first Riel rebellion, scout par excellence, Willie had experienced an adventurous life. With a stable of horses and a postillion at his gate, he had also enjoyed the fruits of civilization while trying to escape it.

Many Albertans found themselves reluctantly drawn into the war.

For the mixture of Europeans who had settled there, thousands of their sons were trooping off to fight against their own nationalities in their own homelands. Almost as much German was spoken in the West as English. The British subjects, however, marched off without question, and Ernest's 142 brewery workers diminished as they enlisted for service overseas. He found he could not train women for the jobs because they kept leaving to marry the soldiers.

While the war raged in Europe, Alberta reported a bumper crop of wheat and doubled coal production, while the oil wells often ran dry within weeks of strikes, and real estate values plummeted. On the latter, owners relinquished their lots in lieu of newly levied taxes. Some of the railway companies went bankrupt, and hundreds of tiny communities soon became ghost towns.

With an eye to the world market, Ernest bought 17,000 rubles or $5,000 worth of Russian bonds. To support this venture he argued that Russia had reached the high tide of her imports, and that the vast country occupying about one-sixth of the globe and having a population in excess of 170 million people would soon begin exporting her agricultural and mineral wealth to other countries. He believed the value of the ruble would skyrocket. His war revolved around the prevention of prohibition in Canada, the survival of CB&M and, most important, the survival and expansion of beef and farming as part of the bread basket of the West. If the CB&M went bankrupt, it was possible that the a7 Ranche would not survive on its own.

Closer to the theatre of war, Billie Cochrane observed developing events and advised Ernest accordingly. To Billie, whatever happened in England would soon reach Canada. Two factors deeply concerned him. First, prohibition seemed imminent, and second, chemical warfare was being used in France. Billie advised Ernest to close down the brewery operation and manufacture noxious gasses. In 1915, over lunch at London's Savoy Hotel with teetotaller R.B. Bennett and Prime Minister Sir Robert Borden, Billie was given little encouragement over the avoidance of prohibition. Instead, they discussed the possibility of converting the CB&M into an acetone plant, and Billie subsequently gleaned information from head British chemist Sir Frederick Mattearn on chemical warfare.

Ernest launched an expensive, collective brewery lobby against the prohibitionists. Had he to contend solely with the male voter, his and other breweries of the day may well have won their fight. With the exception of a few professed alcoholics such as the editor of Calgary's *Eye Opener*, Bob Edwards, who roared in print on July 17, 1915, "For God's Sake, let's vote for it!" thousands of men wanted the hateful bill to be defeated. But concomitant with the brewery lobby was the emergence of the Nelly McClungs and the Emily Murphys of the feminist cause. Had Mary Drever Macleod lived in a later era, or had Ernest's own daughter Mary Cross come of age in an earlier generation, the Drever women might well have shortened their skirts and made history as suffragettes. They possessed the same characteristics of drive, individuality, and passion for a cause that would bring women into an influential position on the prohibition issue.

In the Crosses' domestic life, Ernest fussed over twelve-year-old Jim's mediocre marks at St. Michael's School in Victoria. In the Easter term he sent the teen-ager to Appleby School in Ontario with the hopes of producing a tougher-minded, more academic son to inherit the threatened dynasty.

In Victoria, a pregnant Nell survived a serious throat infection and tonsillectomy, saying nothing to Ernest of the painful surgery and recuperation until it was over. Ernest responded with a grateful, touching letter. He was being "hounded by the income people" and had much on his mind. He wished he could head for Victoria immediately but unfortunately, he first had to attend the bull sale. It was all right with Nell. Her poignant letters of 1910-13 had ceased. Never relinquishing her gentle demeanour, her innate Drever toughness had emerged. Questioning her function and value in life as might a woman of the 1980s, she stood taller, wrote stronger, looked more for fulfilment in community service. That fall Nell did not wait for Ernest to summons her. Just before returning to Calgary, she dashed a note to him giving simply the date and "Home!"

For the Cross family, "home" was still 1240 8th Avenue S.E., Calgary. It was not a huge house like Pine Avenue, but it was full of the same mysteries and a back stairs that allowed the children to rush in unseen from all angles. Whenever they heard the ice man's horses clump their great hooves by the fence, they could dash from any one of the four bedrooms, past the two servants' rooms, down through the pantry, into the kitchen and out to the water pump just beyond the washing shed. The ice man stomped through the gate, giant tongs slung over his shoulder clenching a huge block of ice on his back. He would swing the ice off his leather shoulder pad, dumping it into the wooden, galvanized iron icebox just outside the kitchen door. After taking a playful swing at the children, he would return to his wagon and drive the Percherons across the fields to the next home.

The children spent their days playing in the garden or visiting the firemen and their horses just one block away. Clydesdales and Percherons were a common sight ploughing snow from the roads in winter and grading the ruts in spring. Horses and wagons hauled the CB&M kegs, and a great outing was to visit the brewery stables and blacksmith shop. Once a year Ernest would perform a solemn ritual: he would measure Jim and Mary on the door near the anvil. Then they would stand on the weigh scale, a structure so delicately balanced it wiggled under their feet. At the end of a working day, the children would run to an upstairs bedroom to watch their father leave his office, knowing he could walk home in minutes.

In Europe, Billie Cochrane made it his mission to pull a good near-beer recipe out of drunken brewmasters, and entertained Ernest with tales of the latest diversions in his life. He had joined the Royal Fusiliers, Sportsman's Battalion, and was considered the best shanghai expert in the British army. He accomplished this feat by enlisting the help of friendly bartenders. Parking army trucks outside the pubs, Billie offered free drinks to everyone, then dumped the drunks into the lorries which promptly roared off to camp. The men hardly knew where they were when Billie's piper twilled them into camp with, "Hey Johnnie Cope are you walking yet?" Most stayed and joined up. Billie kept score as if he was playing a game of skittles: "I was up here before Xmas and got 5 game keepers, a piper and a miller and turned up on time early in the morning." His regiment's ranks swelled to 1,600 men before the overflow was sent to others.

In June 1915 Billie wrote to the Brewer, "I am surprised you defaulted in the payment of the 5 per cent dividend of $75,000 for the year 1913. You paid only one third in Dec. 1914, six months overdue, then promised the balance in March 1915. What does the Horrible Francis A. Macnaghten say on this matter? The failure to pay it needs no explanation. It should be paid. R.B. Bennett is of the same opinion." In reply Ernest wrote Billie a polite letter explaining very little of anything and hoping that all the Germans would fall that ever came before him. He did say, "We had a hard and costly fight [against prohibition] ... we cannot pay any more dividends now." He had travelled to Ottawa and spent $75,000 of the CB&M would-be dividends lobbying for a 4 per cent beer licence. It was all in vain. He couldn't even get support from his own family. One Sunday, whiskey-connoisseur Bishop Pinkham stood in the pulpit directly in front of his furious brother-in-law and preached for prohibition. Ernest informed Billie that Alberta voted to go dry in July 1916, and while he would continue to lobby with Saskatchewan,

British Columbia and Manitoba, all would probably follow suit.

Although Billie was not in active combat, he often wrote of slogging through British mud on manoeuvres and watching his friends returning more dead than alive from Europe. Their lungs were burned by the same noxious gasses he was advising Ernest to manufacture. In reply, the Brewer wrote to Billie of happier scenes, "The crops never were as good. Wheat and oats as high as the fences. You would be surprised to see old Mosquito Creek. Cattle and horses have a great bloom on, fresh long green grass everywhere and I never saw so many springs as there are in the hills with splendid hay if weather keeps fine."

By November, even Billie advised Ernest to sell the brewery, take his losses and call it a day. It was a surprising letter for the scrappy Billie, but he could see no way around the prohibition stalemate. He began his letter, "My dear Brewer, I was glad to get another ⅓ dividend for year 1913, only 2½ years overdue. . . . I much doubt if you will be able to carry on business after 1st July 1916. The Publicans will . . . nearly all go out of business with no bar profits. Their hotels and the Brewery will look like last years birds' nests." But Ernest would not give up. He informed Billie of his decision to hang in with the brewery, queried him on munitions matters, then headed to British Columbia with a mining delegation. He had extended CB&M investment to copper mines in Greenwood, coal resources in the Queen Charlottes, and researched a gold-separating machine.

In mid-war Willie Heber somehow brought his family across the Atlantic and travelled through the Panama Canal en route to the west coast. He was enthralled by the $500,000 canal and considered it a marvel of the world. Travelling via Mexico, San Diego and San Francisco, the Crosses arrived in the "pretty, sleepy English town" of Victoria, British Columbia, in late spring. They had seen the Russian ballet dancer Pavlova twice in California, then again in Victoria. Willie Heber considered her the greatest dancer in the world.

During the war years and throughout prohibition, Willie Heber grew richer, his parties never lacking for the finest imported champagne on the market. In 1982 a Victoria resident, A. Helmcken, guessed that Willie Heber may have indulged in prohibition's national pastime and reminisced: "We had wonderful rum-running from Port Angeles and back. . . . They would dress up in black and go out in row boats at midnight. Then they would bring it ashore and someone would deliver it straight to your house. I had a friend who had boats shot out from under him twice. Oh heck, it was great!"

Before the war, Willie Heber and Marguerite had built "Val Rose," a wooden mansion which they promptly encased in brick from foundations to chimney. The Crosses were not only the second family in Uplands but the first French-speaking one to invade the imperial stronghold. Surrounded by a forest of oaks and positioned on the highest rise in Uplands, their estate resembled an impenetrable fortress. Tudor-loving Victorians had laughed at the edifice and called it "Frog Factory." Shortly afterwards a third family (British) had moved into the exclusive area. One day the children were out walking in crocodile style with their grey-uniformed governess, when five-year-old Willie broke ranks and dashed for the trees. He had espied a child in the woods. Delighted at first to find a friend, Willie was soon astonished to hear the newcomer speaking English. He rushed home to Marguerite yelling, "Maman! Maman! Il y a un étranger dans la region!"

On July 1, 1916, the advent of prohibition pulled the plugs from CB&M vats. Hundreds of people were affected: farmers sold their barley to the company; truckers drove kegs to the hotel managers who ran their businesses and paid their staff almost exclusively on the profits from CB&M beer. The union staff agreed to work a full month without pay to see if the Brewer could restructure the business. The CB&M scooped up the remaining mortgages on the hotels, then turned them back to the previous owners to manage. Ernest struggled to stay afloat legally by exporting his product. But he watched the Silver Spray Brewery across the street produce full strength beer round the clock. One of his sons would comment on his father's frustration during this time: "Did you ever hear about these guys in politics where you slide something under the table? Well. The Silver Spray and Lethbridge too, day and night turned out the real stuff. We couldn't sell this damn near beer. So the CB&M sat there."

Hotel managers, distillers and brewers developed a network of payoffs for government agents. An inspector would inform a brewery when he was planning a "visit." After a few beers the inspector would repair to the men's room where he knew $100 bills would be already tucked into the toilet paper roll. That brewery was never charged with brewing full-strength beer. Jim Ryan would comment of the real beer, "It was winked at, if you know what I mean. You could get it damn near anywhere."

Most harmful to the brewery, James Macleod's whiskey traders were back, a more sophisticated, more determined bunch than those of 1873. They ran their illicit booze across the borders in souped-up Fords, while whiskey and ale were sold openly as prescription drugs. The government reported that in 1915 there had been 321 hotels, clubs and wholesale houses entitled to sell liquor; in 1919 there were 498 physicians and 224 druggists entitled to dispense "prescriptions."

Ernest considered bootlegging offensive, and in the beginning tried to avoid it. Eschewing government payoffs, he wrote to Sir Max Aitken of the law-breakers, "I am afraid . . . it's only a matter of time when the Prohibition people will get after them if they allow this state of affairs to go on." Although the British Columbian authorities were turning a blind eye to their own provincial operations, Ernest feared that the CB&M would be made the scapegoat if ever caught breaking the law in that province. The CB&M sold real beer by shipping orders destined for Alberta markets in a legal, if novel, way. It sent the beer into Saskatchewan by just a few feet, then imported it back to Alberta. In Lloydminster, where the boundary line ran down the main street of town, men unloaded carloads of beer from one side of the train into Saskatchewan, then simply transferred it over the tracks to the other side and back into Alberta.

When the United States, Saskatchewan and British Columbia went dry, Ernest began to bootleg. He never considered, let alone attempted, to realize the massive profits made in the Bronfman or Reifel whiskey empires. Such a move would be impossible, for the bulky hops could hardly be hidden under Chrysler floorboards. Abhorring the idea, Ernest turned the plant over to one of his managers to run. One of his sons would explain of his father, "He had to get into the business or go broke. Daddy never wanted to do it. But he had to do it, to survive."

In the pre-dawn hours during prohibition years, a drama was constantly replayed at the network of sidings and back roads throughout the wilds of Saskatchewan, Alberta and British Columbia – particularly through the crossing at the Crow's Nest Pass. CB&M boxcars slated for Mexico whistled their way toward the American border only to be "short-circuited." Trucks and cars mysteriously appeared, the kegs were reloaded, and full-strength beer was distributed throughout the province.

Even Billie Cochrane and Sir Max Aitken dining together at the Savoy in London had no idea that 3,600 bottles per hour were being turned out of the CB&M and that the carloads rarely got further than one hundred miles south of Calgary before being distributed over the countryside. Frowning on the export to Mexico, Billie wrote, "Mexico seems a long way to ship beer. Being so low in strength,

I would think it would go rotten before it got there." Billie spent the remainder of the war filling various British brewers full of Glen Grant, trying to get their secret near-beer recipes for the CB&M and never realizing that the Brewer was already playing the roughest game of survival.

In that year of 1917, Billie saw his last days of soldiering. At fifty-four he faced a dozen medical boards to obtain an honourable discharge, dug up all his unrationed Glen Grant and headed for the hills. Unaware that income tax had just been levied in Canada, he was astonished to receive a 14 per cent dividend from Ernest.

For the next two years CB&M sales would register practically nil, the highest annual sum showing $22,016. Of the ranching operations Ernest showed a loss of $24,000. He submitted his deductions at $34,157, making him one of the early pioneers in skilful tax assessment.

Nell spent the latter part of the war years partly in Victoria in their new hillside mansion, "Rappahannock" at 1595 Rockland Avenue. It was just a few doors down from the palatial Government House. The three-storey shingle and half-timbered structure commanded an expansive if distant view of Georgia Strait. It was a marvel of attic, basement and exploratory nooks and crannies for the growing family. Nell decorated the sunny drawing room all in white with lilac chintz and magnificent white roses. Both the back and front doors opened onto a circular driveway and Rockland Avenue. The south gardens, surrounded by granite walls, were filled with roses and the children used to sit on a stone fountain eating nectarines and peaches from the trees.

During 1918 Ernest visited British Columbia frequently to oversee his mining interests and continue on to Victoria. Nell loved to dine with him at elegant parties in private homes. Mary Cross Dover described the Nell of that era:

Mother was very beautiful, with lovely eyes and a straight nose. She had big, soft dark curls that fell into great curves when brushed. She used to do it up neatly. I remember once, when we were little before they went out to dinner – they were quite popular – they came in in their evening clothes. Daddy wore a tail coat with white tie, white westcoat, mother of pearl studs. Mother wore a long black satin dress. The skirt had swirls of black satin pulled to the back, and tucked in at the waist was a magnificent red silk rose. She wore elegant slippers, and the appropriate jewels, and lovely kid gloves with buttons. I remember doing them up for her before she went out of the house. She was just a vision.

Willie Heber's move to Victoria proved more imprudent than living in Quebec. Marguerite's fractured English was as unacceptable in the drawing rooms of the imperial outpost as it had been in the Square Mile, Montreal. Long-time Victorian and friend of the Crosses, Mrs. Dodie Watney would explain that while they were very well known, they were never accepted:

> The British had a sort of thing against French people. Even our policemen had proper Bobby helmets. Do you realize that up until the first world war Victoria still drove on the left side of the road? The Americans used to come up here and raised havoc, of course.
> Many of the girls living from Victoria to Duncan on these fabulous estates were daughters of remittance men. You know, usually second sons of titled families who blotted their copy-books at Cambridge, or been cashiered out of their regiments or something. They were quite proud to be the black sheep.... You see, people were so frightfully British and Marguerite was so French.

In 1981 John Munklands Cross, youngest son of Nell and Ernest, recalled his first visit to Willie Heber's Uplands home. The little boy was stunned when Ernest threw an arm around his Uncle Willie Heber and spoke in a strange tongue. He had never before realized that another language existed, let alone that his father could speak it. John laughed, "I was horrified!" in a tone which conveyed utter delight. But in those days the visits to Val Rose were infrequent. The upright Nell had little in common with the boisterous Marguerite, and she did not approve of the spoiled, undisciplined children of the continental Crosses.

Periodically Yvette, Simone and Fleurange would attend Victoria's exclusive girls' school, St. Margaret's, with Marmo and Mary Cross. Mrs. Watney recalled the British-oriented institution: "St. Margaret's in those days was quite the nicest school I ever went to. All the English girls whose parents were bankers and lawyers and business men in Hong Kong, Shanghai, and all those places, couldn't get back to school in England. They all came to St. Margaret's." But Willie Heber's children were never accepted in that school's milieu. A fellow student remembered: "We thought of Simone as definitely being French. She had dark hair and eyes. I wasn't a bit friendly with her."

They wore the school uniform sporadically, disappearing on European jaunts at the whim of Willie Heber, and eventually they remained in France to complete their education. Willie Junior was kept at home near his father. After all, he was the male heir of the family.

One classmate of Mary Cross and Dodie Watney was Dola Dunsmuir, a coal baron's daughter who lived in Hatley Castle, Sooke. The castle was a favourite weekend home for Mary and Dodie. There, elegance shone as if estate and servants had been transplanted from Sussex, England. The girls played tennis, rode fine steeds and had tea parties with the best of titled personages. When the lethal influenza raged throughout the world from Europe to Victoria in 1919 and struck down Mary Cross, Dodie and nearly the whole of St. Margaret's school, Dola was safely quarantined in her famous castle. She dispatched the servants with food packages and bunches of grapes for her friends at St. Margaret's School.

The education of the boys differed. Ernest hoped that Jim would earn a spot at Royal Military College, Kingston, but it would be young Sandy who was accepted. Their father's reason for sending a son to the military college was intriguing. He explained to the headmaster of Appleby College: "Many difficulties may arise in future in this part of the country where it will be hard to enforce law and order, and a military training should put him in a good position to uphold them."

In the summer of 1919 Nell returned to Calgary with the children and stayed through Christmas. She would return to Victoria annually, and upon occasion to visit her children in school, but she would never again leave Alberta for long. Their Calgary home was filled with the comfort and memorabilia of generations – the silver soup tureen brought by Helen Rothney in 1839, the medicine chest which had accompanied James Macleod about the prairies, the iron door stops from Dunvegan Castle, Scotland. It was where Nell felt she belonged.

Friends remembered Ernest as a quiet man who was devoted to Nell, and who did things rather than talked about them. He encouraged his children to become involved, and to learn all they could about every endeavour. He impressed upon them the importance of understanding Canadian history and, as Mary put it years later, "he felt that we should take our place." His recognition that children needed to experience the self-respect of earning something rather than just receiving was seen in his church donations. For example, at Christ Church near the a7 Ranche, Ernest donated heifers instead of funds.

It was up to the children to feed, groom and care for the animals. After the eventual sale, the proceeds would then be donated to the church. As in previous generations, the children were taught the Bible and each Sunday walked with their parents up to the Holy Church of the Redeemer Cathedral in Calgary. While at St. Margaret's in Victoria they attended Christ Church Cathedral, and at Miss Edgar's and Miss Cramp's School for Girls in Montreal, the Crosses had their own pew at St. James the Apostle.

The end of the war marked the beginning of staggering social upheaval in Canada. Returning veterans and dissatisfied workers found outrageous inflation and few jobs. Strikes raged throughout the country, the worst being the general strike in Winnipeg with 35,000 men shutting down the city. In Calgary, 1,900 workers staged a sympathy strike but the CB&M brewed on. When strikers closed the Winnipeg breweries, Ernest and his men launched into overdrive and supplied (legally) the entire province of Manitoba. For some, the loyalty of Ernest's staff was not entirely without personal gain, for along with the surreptitious nature of prohibition, midnight black-marketing in the brewery was also flourishing. With the added production, some of the staff just stepped up their nocturnal pace. The Brewer had preferred to know as little as possible and to a fault he believed that a man's word was as good as his bond. It would take another ten years before Jim went into the business and discovered that some of the staff were "robbing Daddy blind."

Nineteen-nineteen was a bad year all around. Terrible droughts rendered ranching as dry as the liquor business. Thirsty, mange-infected cattle endured through long months with practically no hay. Horses died and shades of 1896 returned. In these roughest of times, and with the thinnest capital backing ever, Ernest joined in a flour mill venture with R.B. Bennett, George Lane and American and British financiers. He reasoned that Alberta wheat was the lowest price anywhere in America, that as a livestock centre the by-products could be sold at a high price, and that the flour could be produced at the lowest cost. All ensured that the mill would be competitive with world markets. With an unlimited supply of coal, natural gas and water power, Ernest believed it was a winner. It proved a disaster. Jim Cross would remember that the freight costs in moving flour were so astronomical that it was cheaper to ship the wheat out and buy back the finished product. Over the coming four years, the investors would lose 60 cents on every dollar.

Ernest rarely viewed tough financial times or even disasters in a strictly personal manner. Recognizing that individual success depended upon the health of the whole, he wrote to Eckford, "The country is in worse shape than I ever have seen it. The old grass is pretty well eaten off and the hay crop practically nil. If it's a hard winter I don't know what is going to become of the livestock owners. It is too bad when we want a good crop to pay off the liabilities of the country."

The Brewer's financial situation appeared desperate, testimony to his soft bootlegging principles. Unable to meet the $500 each for continued mining ventures in British Columbia, he and partner Pat Burns ordered an immediate work stoppage. Alexander Cross's legacy, now worth $1,076 quarterly, was insufficient to save the brewery from bankruptcy. The patriarch's influence lived on, his capital still tied up in bonds, Bank of Montreal stock, and in the Pine Avenue estate. For once, Ernest wrote candid letters to each of his directors. He claimed that the CB&M was not meeting its running expenses and would neither be able to meet its interest nor sinking fund on the bonds. Their only hope was to borrow money which the bank would ask the directors to guarantee. With the soldiers' return, he foresaw a petition forcing the repeal of prohibition and predicted:

If beer is allowed to be sold the concern should very soon get on its feet again and the paid up capital stock be worth considerable money. I feel that it is worth the effort to keep the business going as there is a strong feeling all over the country in favour of allowing the sale of beer.... If it comes in force before next spring, we should probably be able to pay the Bond Interest and Sinking Fund. Please consider this carefully as it is a vital crisis in the history of this institution and requires everybody's best judgement to decide what is to be done.

This was the first time in thirty years that Ernest had collectively asked the directors for advice. Billie's reply was characteristic of the partners' mood when he expressed sorrow that business was so bad, but he felt strongly against making any bank loans. If Ernest could not pay running expenses and pay the shareholders a dividend, he advised him to let the bond holders take over the brewery. Billie also suggested they sue the federal and provincial governments for destroying the brewing industry. Foreseeing the nationalization of breweries and distilleries in the old country and subsequent prohibition, Billie panicked, "I'm down to my last two gallons of Glen Grant."

The Brewer responded by eliciting the help of Hull and other directors to make the interest payments themselves. He could not know that prohibition would drag on another five years before being rescinded. Instead of despairing, he stated his faith in the future by moving into a new venture of moving pictures, buying thirty $10 dollar shares of Canadian Photoplays Limited.

One tough decision to make in 1919 was whether or not to have a Stampede. No one had any money. While debating the Stampede's future in the depressed aftermath of war, Ernest received the following letter:

Deer Sir, I am hear in Calgary an figger on stayen heer till this stampead is puled off I been follerin cowmens gatherins from el Paso to Heare from 83 till now An this un is Shure gonta bee a plum humdinger,
    Yore Old Longhorn friend Shorty

The Brewer promptly signed the contracts for a Victory Stampede and Shorty got his show. Ernest knew that in times of recession and tribulation, the human spirit turns to diversion and levity. Cash from sugar bowls and mattress stuffings suddenly surfaced. The Calgary Annual Exhibition was the most successful ever held. It cleared over $25,000, and the following month the biggest Stampede to date was attended by the Prince of Wales and the dukes of Devonshire and Connaught. The profits went to the Great War Veterans' Association, the YMCA and the Salvation Army.

Mary Cross, then fourteen and home in Calgary for the summer, remembered, "It was my first Stampede, and the first time I ever saw a barbecue. Daddy took me over there, and they were roasting a whole steer in a pit filled with hot stones, right in front of what is the present grandstand. Everybody was given a sandwich – anybody who came by."

Even the Brewer's friends came from Europe. Jim's godfather, H.B. Alexander, hitched a ride to Canada on a battleship and eventually reached the a7 Ranche. The Prince of Wales, often referred to as "the P of W," bought the Bar U and renamed it the EP Ranche. Nell turned a deaf ear to the wild stories of the ranching community of 1919. Rumour has it that Ernest entertained the Prince of Wales at the a7 Ranche with Mary Macleod sitting out the party in an upstairs bedroom with a tippling of gin.

Jim Ryan remembered, "My friend, Jimmy Farqueson and I were in the G&B Garage in Nanton. The owner of the garage was the police magistrate. Well, we decided to get out a bottle of Scotch. Just after we'd unwrapped it, those big doors of the garage swung open and in drove this huge mudspattered car. Cross got out, so I offered him a drink. He said, 'I can't. I have the Governor with me.'

"Well, I thought he was kidding. Then out of the car got this huge man – six foot four at least. And he said, 'By Jove! That's an excellent idea!' And at that he took a helluva slug. It was the governor general of Canada! So, the bottle got passed and eventually it ended back with my friend and me. The police magistrate didn't give a damn."

In late October Ernest accompanied his cattle to Chicago and earned the highest price in North America for his beef. It had been his dream since 1886 when he had requested a brand of "A1." Nell had returned to Calgary and her letters to him in Chicago were exuberant. She wondered how he was getting on, and described her "splendid, mischievous Marmo." Ernest returned to joyous Christmas celebrations. Harry Brayne was pleased that Cross took the day to travel to the a7 Ranche with a carload of turkeys for his men.

Upon reading the press releases of the Stampede, Billie Cochrane hollered, "Dear Brewer, You should have sold the P of W the Brewery!"

22

Shifting Fortunes

"We are [still] doing business contrary to the law."
Ernest to McNaghten, 1924

Out of the stock of three families, the Macleods, the Crosses and
the Drevers, the generations had proliferated and diversified like
streams flowing down a single mountainside. By 1920 the three
founding families had funnelled into the name of Cross. The Macleods
and Drevers had propelled the nineteenth-century generations through
the age of survival and settlement. Combined with the collective
heritage of Alexander and Julia, it was the Crosses who would guide
them through an industrial age of wealth, gaiety and the Depression.
As much as any other generation, Ernest and Nell's children illum-
inated the work ethic, the religious dedication, the love of land and
the hopes for opportunity which had brought the Drevers, Crosses
and Macleods across the Atlantic in the first place.

In Wyoming, Harry and Léa's Braehead Ranch blanketed the
mountain range which he had coveted in 1883. Their several thousand
head of Shorthorns and Durhams were reputed by the turn of the
century to be the largest herd north of Argentina. The progenitors
of these blue-ribbon winners were the motley Longhorns bought by
Harry at Fort Bent, Colorado, in 1875. Harry had served five terms
in the legislature and loved being president of the Wyoming Pioneer
Association, president of the Converse County Bank, and a member
of the Old Boys' Association of Upper Canada College. In his letters
to his Canadian brothers he continued to deride the attitude of the
English in Quebec and frequently warned of the need to give French
Canadians a greater say in government. The Crosses summered at
Braehead and wintered in their spacious San Francisco home.

Edmund Cross made a permanent commitment at the age of forty-five. A few years earlier, he had moved the family to Edmonton to provide schooling for his eight children, but continued to drift off alone to his Saskatchewan homestead. In 1920 he purchased farmland in Vermillion, 140 miles east of Edmonton, and once again moved his family to virgin territory. His children explained: "Father never bought convenient land. He bought wilderness. He'd buy a place where the roads were no good. He was always seeking untouched land." Little of Alexander's Montreal remained within Edmund save for his three-piece suit. He and Hélène grew increasingly remote from the Calgary Crosses, their life on the isolated farm reminiscent of the first struggling homesteaders. It would be Edmund's children, offspring of the earth rather than of Montreal's Pine Avenue, who would establish a farm with award-winning cattle.

In Montreal, the Cross links to prominent Canadians still resembled the network of railway connections presided over by CPR vice-president William MacInnes. Maggie and William's daughter Evelynn joined two prominent families with her marriage to Robert Reford of the steamship lines. Evelynn's mother-in-law, the former Elsie Meighen and favourite niece of Lord Mount Stephen, gave to Evelynn two of the fulgent iron and diamond brooches made from the original Last Spike. Driven into the CPR railway by Donald Smith at Craigellachie, British Columbia, it had bent and been discarded.

Maggie MacInnes wrote newsy letters to Ernest and co-ordinated the young cousins through Montreal on their jaunts to Victoria or Europe. It was she who spun a tenuous thread from Pine Avenue amongst the travelling Crosses as they drifted further and further away from their roots. The MacInneses cared for the estate at great personal expense, fighting inflationary costs for maintenance and land taxes. Nevertheless, they managed to keep the estate as it had been some sixty years earlier, with stables, chicken houses and a milking cow.

By 1920, the most prominent Cross other than Ernest was Willie Heber in Victoria. In 1982 Willie Heber's nephews would remember their uncle as a Santa Claus-sized character who built a successful career while sitting in a chair. They reasoned that he never got out of it because he was too fat. If Uncle Willie suspected his relatives' opinions, he continued on his merry way, speculating at the stock exchange. In 1880 he had written his credo in his notebook: "The best of me is diligence."

Marguerite ran a household as free, breezy and undisciplined as

Nell's was clean, ordered and defined. She was described as a charming, excitable woman who employed the best Swiss housekeeper, Chinese houseboys and Chinese gardeners. One Victorian remembered that "Margaret had birds in cages in every room in the house and they stank to high heaven. She had parrots and finches and heaven knows what. They chirped. I suppose they had a maid to look after them."

Oblivious at first that being French made her different, Marguerite adored Victoria, to her reminiscent of a market village in the Cotswolds. Victorian accents ranged from Oxonian to Cockney and thickened over the years in a contest of cultural survival. At least that was in the good old days when Victoria was truly British. Mrs. Merston, original owner of Victoria's Beach Hotel, explained, "Before the War you'd hear all the different English accents. After the war, *Canadians* moved west."

Each winter Willie Heber sailed with his family and his shoelace maid to Europe via the Panama Canal. They stayed in Switzerland, Paris or in their fabulous pied-à-terre in Nice. Summers were spent in Victoria at Val Rose. For a city that boasted eccentrics, it was some kind of distinction that Victorians marked the Crosses as Continental sybarites. Willie Heber had finally succumbed wholly to Marguerite's French cuisine. Dodie Watney recalled, "Willie was absolutely rotund. They had the most gorgeous, great lovely long dining room table with twelve beautiful chairs each side. It was probably Chippendale. And at Willie's end they had sawn a piece out so that he could get his tummy in. Cut out a mahogany table for his bulge!"

The word went out when Willie Heber came to town. Just how he would extricate himself from his beige and chocolate-brown, custom-made Aubern roadster became a favourite puzzle for strolling Victorians. One day he drove to the Pacific Club for lunch only to find himself so immobilized between wheel and seat that onlookers were stymied. A watching construction worker finally drove his derrick over and, before the eyes of the delighted crowd, swung the crane and plucked Willie Heber out.

He became a familiar sight striding down Government Street in his full-length black cape and top hat, reminiscent of his namesake, Grandfather William Lunn. Upon reaching the brokerage firm of C.M. Oliver & Company, Willie Heber would storm through the glass doors and roar, "Buy Bell!" or "Sell the cotton!" As he about-faced and headed out, his cape would sweep the floor and his over-proof breath made the boys on the chalk-boards snicker. But skeptical brokers soon passed his hunches on to other customers. One old-timer shook his head, "I met an old stockbroker once who said he had never seen a man as lucky as Willie was."

Willie Heber continued grappling with his paradox of worlds, clinging to his British foundations as tenaciously as to his French lifestyle. It made him an unwilling participant in the religious-cultural conflict uniquely Canadian. Victorians drank the Crosses' champagne but would not accept the mixed marriage. By the 1920s his health was failing and he was increasingly confined to Victoria instead of the amiable Continent. He sent Fleurange, Yvette and Simone to school in Paris, noting that although it cost thousands of dollars it was worth it. Suffering from obesity, high blood pressure and mini-strokes, Willie Heber would frequently predict his demise before uncorking a medicinal bottle of gin.

While the Cross youths from Montreal to Victoria partied through the postwar era of flapper dresses, slicked hair and the Charleston, Ernest juggled mangy cattle, a rash of rustling, labour unrest and dry hotels. Among other setbacks for the Brewer, George Lane suddenly demanded the $25,000 cash he had invested in the collapsing Alberta Flour Mills Limited. Over-extending his debt load, Ernest gambled his future stability on explorations by Calgary Petroleum Products. Another $15,000 and a third well was already under way for a total investment by the original ten men of $40,000. Ernest had also leased some a7 land to Dingman for future exploration. With the absorption plant in Turner Valley functioning smoothly and prospects of yet another oil strike, the debts must have seemed a reasonable risk.

In September 1920 an accident occurred that changed the status of the original shareholders of Calgary Petroleum Products. "Skunk gas," an oil-well waste of hydrogen sulphide gas, was ill-controlled in those days. The highly flammable poison seeped out of the primitive fittings of the absorption plant and into the air. Whether a worker lit a cigarette or a careless welder flipped on his torch in an unventilated area, fire broke out and raged through the CPP plant. The entire complex exploded and burned to the ground.

Scrambling to save their empires, Ernest and R.B. Bennett negotiated a deal with Imperial Oil to refinance Calgary Petroleum Products. Cross, Bennett, Lougheed and the seven other shareholders required at least $1 million to pay off creditors, rebuild the plant and continue exploration. Imperial Oil reacted swiftly. By early December it had agreed on all points, providing an immediate $400,000 capital to continue drilling No.3 Well and sink No. 4 Well.

In the deal, Imperial Oil offered Calgary Petroleum Products fully paid shares to the par value of $200,000, or 20 per cent of a new company named Royalite, with the authorized capital of $1 million – in return for all assets. Thus, the company which would launch Alberta into the international world of oil had been founded by ten men on $40,000 of a $50,000 loan, and was refinanced for $800,000. Had the absorption plant not burned down, the controlling percentage of No. 4 Well, known as one of the greatest strikes in Turner Valley history and for years the largest naptha producer in the Empire, may still have been safely tucked in the pockets of the original ten shareholders.

Maintaining his percentage of the CPP company, Ernest served on the Royalite board for the remainder of his life. In 1923 Royalite would begin paying dividends, beginning at $64,006. When Sir James Lougheed died in 1926, leaving a $1,500,000 worthless paper estate, his Royalite shares would be sold off to pay his taxes. It would be too soon to realize the mind-boggling windfall of Turner Valley fame.

Despite the bail-out, Ernest's empire remained unstable because the CB&M was still locked in the grip of prohibition. He had become so tight-lipped that his directors renewed their complaints with a vengeance. No dividends had been declared for five years. Two wondered if the brewery had disappeared. From Britain H.B. Eckford and "Sir Francis McDirty," as Billie Cochrane called McNaghten, demanded disclosures. Although still on the CB&M board, they had turned "guano," as Billie put it, by investing in the Lethbridge Brewery. McNaghten informed Ernest that he had received the staggering sums of 25 and 35 per cent dividends from the Lethbridge Brewery in the previous two years. Jim Cross explained of the competition's dividends, "Let's just say they were better bootleggers than we were."

Someone in the CB&M was keeping McNaghten informed of all figures, and he in turn pressured Ernest, "I notice that the profit and loss is practically even, but that is really a matter of juggling with figures. You clearly earned enough for a dividend last year and why not this?" The Brewer stayed silent, not bothering to compare the enormous scale of the Lethbridge production to the modest survival policy of the CB&M.

McNaghten would continue firing his criticisms over a period of three and a half years. He did not know that not only was Ernest struggling to keep the brewery solvent but he had made a disastrous attempt to ship his cattle to England and still had not succeeded in dumping the flour mill. Ernest and R.B. Bennett were secretly negotiating with W. Sifton and Spillers of Minneapolis to sell the mill at a loss of 60 cents on the dollar.

Today, brewers across the country from Alberta to New Brunswick agree that the rules were bent, broken and winked at throughout the eight dry years. For example, at a Calgary Golf and Country Club tournament attended by about a thousand spectators, the CB&M beer arrived in an old white truck with a chain drive and solid tires. Some innocuous name was emblazoned on the side. Jim Cross remembered, "Everybody cheered – judges, players, spectators. Nobody prosecuted for that one." In 1922 Ernest would take out a full-page CB&M ad with his picture in the *Financial Times*.

Although no longer in politics, Ernest would speak up when he thought it necessary. He never wasted his time but went straight to the top. In a letter to Prime Minister Arthur Meighen in November 1920, he showed that while he was regional in some aspects, he in fact remained a federalist. The issue about which he wrote concerned the government's consideration of turning over the natural resources to the provinces. With Alberta on the threshold of massive oil strikes, Ernest believed such action would be a mistake:

> The Provincial Government . . . would be almost obliged to make extravagant expenditures which has been the case ever since the Province was created, with result that we have got heavily into debt and our taxes are mounting . . . I feel tht [*sic*] the real thinking country and town people do not want the Province to administer the Natural Resources just now. This agitation has been [perpetrated] principally by office seekers and newspapers who think they are going to get . . . more money. . . .
>
> The people and the newspapers have got into the habit of abusing the Government for everything . . . and it is largely due to their ignorance in not being told what really has taken place and what is going to take place. Please excuse me if you think I have gone out of my way to interfere in Politics, which I have not taken any active part in for many years, nor do I intend to, and have no axes to grind.

Pain returned to nag the sixty-year-old Brewer. It felt like appendicitis, the surgery for which still claimed the lives of 25 per cent of patients. He lost weight, and wondered often if it was the old twisted bowel suffered on the saddle horn in 1891. Holding little faith in the ability of western surgeons, and preoccupied with his shaky business ventures, he put off having it attended to. He continued to work sixteen-hour days, juggling profits and loss to maintain a holding pattern on most investments.

In the spring of 1921 Ernest collapsed from abdominal pain and left for Johns Hopkins Hospital, Baltimore, finally succumbing to the first of several exploratory operations. When surgeons removed gall stones, reports of his serious condition prompted another spate of letters from CB&M directors. Billie lamented Ernest's illness in the first line, then requested dividends in the next: "You and I have no business to be alive. We can thank our parents for having lead a decent life.... Your Annual Report as usual gives ... very little information."

Billie needed cash in a hurry. This time he had altered his theatre of war from the Germans to the Irish Republican Army. One night he was served a death warrant by the IRA. They had just burned out the Walter Skrines, now neighbours of Billie, forcing them to walk six miles for help in their nightshirts. Unaware of this, Billie noted of the IRA, "I talked to them like a YMCA captain and asked them if they were ashamed of their faces as they wore masks and why they did not ring the bell instead of knocking the paint off my door with the butt end of their rifles." His bluff worked but the IRA left a warning, "Your grave is dug." At daylight Billie hired two trucks, loaded his furniture, circumvented the trenched roads and blown bridges, caught the train for Belfast, and then a boat for Scotland. He noted, "There will be a bloody war in Ireland before it is settled."

Ernest survived his operation and sent Billie a private account sheet of the CB&M. Billie replied "I am glad to hear the Brewery has done so well. The Statement, which is good enough for the Bond Holders, was a gloomy account. I hope you will be able to pay a dividend to the shareholders in the near future. Prohibition is such a fiasco." Billie blamed Britain's "labour unrest, red flags and Bolshiviki" on diluted beer and quipped, "If they could get drunk occasionally they would feel good natured and more inclined to do an honest day's work."

During Ernest's convalescence, Billie continued to entertain him. Whether hunting for gold mines or extricating themselves from the IRA, Ernest's friends provided him with a kind of international theatre in which to escape the confines of the brewery vats.

Near the end of 1921 Ernest's own papers suggest that his tight-lipped policy and elusive reports disguised a healthy business. Certainly he had recuperated from the disasters of 1919, redeemed half a million in bonds, and had invested over $1 million in hotels. On the down side, he was resigned to a prolonged prohibition under the United Farmers' Association, which had formed the government that July. For years the UFA had preached the philosophy of two classes in Alberta: the capitalistic plutocrats versus the poor, democratic farmers, many of whom were temperance-oriented. Ernest Cross had no friends in government.

Sir Francis McNaghten continued to query Ernest's management while commending his diligence and reaffirming their friendship. In a form of blackmail, McNaghten again listed his astonishing dividends from the Lethbridge Brewery, yet never questioned their business procedures. Ernest did not reply to the last salvo. He was battling a new round of abdominal pain. It drove him to the Montreal General Hospital for another operation just as Billie Cochrane was heading for the Scottish hills with the flu and twelve gallons of Glen Grant. Unable to resist the lure of the Slaney River, Billie had returned to Ireland. He was raided and shuddered, "It is not nice looking down the muzzle of a colt full of flat-nosed bullets, especially when the gunner is crazy drunk." Billie had talked them out of murder whereupon they stole his Mercedes. He groused, "The IRA generals are joy riding in my car. If I had a Winchester I could have wiped out the bunch."

Ernest could not reply. He was seriously ill. For the first time ever the man who had kept everything in his head had scribbled notes on ranch management to his nineteen-year-old son, Jim. In retrospect, the Cross sons mused, "He must have thought he was going to die. That's why he wrote it all down." He listed his cattle, some 2,057 including 540 calves – at his Bob's Creek Ranch, and the McIntosh Ranch, both amalgamated into the a7 Ranche – and explained how they were watered, fenced and fed, including the amount of supplement feeding required for the coming winter. He cautioned Jim to watch for the day when every discount could be taken, and on taxes to always protest those he considered unfair: "they are still too high, but the government has very heavy obligations to meet. They should curb their expenditures." No one seems to ever have diagnosed the nature of Ernest's illnesses, although surgery ran the gamut from gall bladder, prostate, appendix to exploratory. Billie wrote from London that a doctor there was curing a great many growths with the use of radium but no connection was made to Ernest's condition.

Young Jim proved an excellent wrangler and, with Ernest ill, was heavily involved in the workings of the ranch. He planned to make it his career. Like his father, he attended agricultural school at Guelph. His younger brother Sandy, aged ten, shared Ernest's dream of prospecting the untapped mining resources of the north. Sandy would later attend Appleby School in Ontario, showing both academic and gymnastic abilities, then continue on to Royal Military College and the University of Alberta to study mining engineering. John Munklands would attend Shawnigan Lake School on Vancouver Island and Guelph College. He, too, would rather be ranching. Each son was finding a niche within their father's empire, but no one wanted the brewery. As usual, Ernest survived and returned to preside at a huge Calgary Stampede.

That November, 1923, saw the repeal of the eight-year prohibition law, though it was enacted until the spring of 1924. Instead of writing about future dividends, Ernest wrote a long, entertaining article for the *Calgary Daily Herald* on the roundup of 1887. With unusual emotion he said of his Wolves' Den days, "I always look back with great joy to those far too few days of exquisite pleasure spent with such dear, hospitable people."

Totally fed up with the Brewer by the early spring of 1924, Sir Francis McNaghten appointed chartered accountant Frank Harvey to investigate the CB&M, particularly the cursory accounting systems which existed mostly in Ernest's head. McNaghten's list ran from staff salaries, production costs, the lack of invoices or records concerning cash expenditures, to petty cash which was disappearing by thousands of dollars a month. McNaghten acknowledged that prohibition conditions over the past years had not lent themselves to satisfactory auditing of the company and he stressed that the investigation had nothing to do with their personal friendship. In no way was he inferring that Ernest was dipping his hand into the till; rather, his questioning was directed toward which government officials were being rewarded for turning blind eyes to the distribution of beer. Fed up with McNaghten, Ernest replied with a surprisingly candid, "It always must be remembered that the Brewery is travelling on thin, floating ice, or in other words, doing business contrary to the law. Care must be exercised in making any radical moves that might interfere with this." Then he declared a 3 per cent dividend.

Grand times began as the end of prohibition heralded a new era of profits and quenched thirsts. Even the cattle market soared, and in the fall word reached Ernest that Royalite No. 4 was close to a strike. Fifty-eight years later John and Sandy Cross would remember their father driving them down to see the great well. They were eight and ten years old at the time. Sandy's eyes lit up as he related the event:

> When Daddy took us down to Turner Valley we'd rented a car from a guy called Ready. The only car Daddy ever drove was an old 1916 brass-fronted Model T Ford ... I don't know how many hours it took us to get down there. We had to cross Shit Creek – I can remember it was all mud and we slithered around. There was no gravel, just mud.
>
> Number 4 sizzled on the site and then she blew! My God, I was never so impressed with anything so much in my whole life. It was on fire! It lifted the gosh-darn pipe – the casing – way up in the air at least thirty feet. Between the top of the pipe and the bottom of the flame was another thirty feet and then flame on top of that. I remember Daddy was keenly interested in that. The air was on fire. It burnt the barrack down. Don't know if anyone was killed or not. And it was still firing away six months later.

No. 4 Royalite gushed twenty-two million cubic feet a day, two years later still producing 646 barrels of naptha a day, one of the greatest strikes of all time. Sandy mused, "Daddy knew what kind of an impact this would have on Canada, especially on Alberta. That was the sort of thing he was interested in. Not just ranching and brewing." Nevertheless, Ernest was finally free to coast on the crested wave of his own achievements.

Those were happy years for Nell too, involved as she was in the hubbub of a youthful family and an active social life in Calgary, which always included the names of Macleod and Pinkham. Although no gadabout, Nell was never lovelier, nor more involved with her church, her community and her children. She had grown into a woman of dignity, serenity and influence. In her speeches to the church diocese she even urged women to take their places equally alongside men.

By 1924, Marmo, John and Sandy Cross were still at private school. They continually tested their teachers' patience with their exuberant spirits and sense of fun. Like their most famous grandfather, James Macleod, action rather than scholarship was their credo. At the same time, the two oldest Calgary Cross children stood on the threshold of their own careers. Jim, twenty-one, tall, lean and dark with Nell's fine features, showed managerial abilities as well as skills in running the ranch. He had never worked in the brewery even as a boy. Dodie Watney would remember of the laconic Jim, "What is that famous movie actor – cowboy star – Gary Cooper. Yes. That was Jim. He was always laughing and cheerful, but you don't get terribly pally with a Gary Cooper. And of course he was dark – because the Cross family ancestry goes back to the Indians. The Macleods down in Fort Macleod – my family were insistent that somewhere along the line. . . . Well, anyway Jim was well liked." Possessing the gentle voice and clipped diction of his mother, the polite Jim Cross would present an image of friendly distance throughout his career. In this way he disguised a remarkable ability to run the business on his own, and to block out the encroaching eastern breweries.

Mary Cross, aged nineteen, possessed the same qualities which marked the Drever women as outstanding over four generations. A superb horsewoman, she was determined in personality and aristocratic in deportment. She combined the toughness of Ernest with the playfulness of James Macleod. Referring to Mary's "endless tall tales," Dodie Watney explained, "Mary's flair for dramatizing things was wonderful when she was speaking. She could bring ideas alive and really put things across." Perhaps her personality was best described in the paradoxical assessment of the headmistress at her private school in Montreal: "Mary has a high sense of honour and is trustworthy whenever it is a question of right and wrong. She is eager to be helpful, so should take a very high place in the school when she learns to be consistently law abiding."

Mary's coming-out party coincided with the end of prohibition. Champagne gushed as legally, as cheerfully and almost as powerfully as No. 4 Royalite. It was an era of magic. At one masquerade, look-alikes Mary and Jim dressed in shapeless clown costumes and made their faces up in identical expressions. Mary recalled, "We did acrobatics around the dancers . . . behaving awfully badly and having an awful lot of fun." Late in the evening a well-known Calgarian grabbed a clown and said, "Mary, you think you are fooling me," and kissed Jim. The red-faced clown broke loose, grabbed Mary and said, "C'mon, we're going home!"

Dodie Watney remembered one royal ball in Calgary for the Prince of Wales. She was escorted to the Palliser Hotel, Calgary, by a blue-blooded polo player named Pocklington who held together his formal attire with picture wire. She recalled, "Mary was there. And Jim. The Prince of Wales was very drunk – he'd come and dance, then disappear. He'd got very hard looking – rather dissipated. When the orchestra played God Save the King the Prince came in and stood at attention with everyone. At the end while there was still silence he said in a very loud voice, 'Well, now we've put father to bed, let's get on with the party.' "

Throughout that year and into the next, weekend parties at Banff with black-tie dinners were de rigeur, with the magnificent Banff Springs Hotel looming over a village that Dodie Watney remembered as "one greasy-spoon Chinese restaurant after the other. It had wooden sidewalks, mud streets . . . and one old fashioned, charming, English-run hotel."

A rheumatic Billie Cochrane tried to make the Stampede that festive year. Surviving an illness and the IRA, he gave witness in an Irish court over two poachers and his pilfered auto. He got the judge laughing whilst being interrogated in the "sweat box" and was awarded £695. In early August he arrived at the a7 Ranche to find Ernest was home from hospital. The pair were getting a little crotchety.

After visiting Ernest, Billie took the CPR through the mountains to the hot springs in Banff and Radium. It became one of his favourite haunts as he searched for an elixir to dilute his alcoholic blood. With a hint of melancholy, Billie wished the Brewer was with him. They would get a car and visit their old Wolves' Den pal, Randolph Bruce. The founder of Consolidated Mining and Smelting, Bruce had built a magnificent home on Lake Windermere named "Pynelogs." Possibly as further enticement for Ernest to visit Radium, the internationally spirited Billie ended with, "I like this place much better than Banff. . . . There are lots of interesting old stiffs to have a crack with of all nationalities – Scots, Poles, Jews, Greeks, Scandinavians." The only kind of man Billie Cochrane really disliked was one whose self-opinion and disdain for work were as inflated as his title or wealth.

Billie's descriptions of Banff in the twenties bring alive the smells and tastes of the era. "Banff is one whirl of Stink wagons and the worst type of American trippers. The baths are full of them. On Saturday there were over 600 in the Bath and no less than twenty-six people fainted. They are too crowded with dirty people and the constant whirl of dust and stink of petrol . . . noise is a terror. We saw Lougheed, Sir James and his Lady. Little H.B. Alexander runs around like a piss Ant full of energy. Come up if you can."

But the Brewer never came. He was studying an amalgamation offer from other Alberta breweries. They wished to strengthen their ranks against central Canadian brewers eyeing the prairie market. Billie was appalled that Ernest would even consider it. He wrote, "I am dead against it. . . . Our $900,000 bonded debt being a big handicap, also the valuation of our hotels and tied houses. It would also entail an enormous amount of work . . . and I doubt if you would pull well in any team composed of some of our competition in the brewing industry of Alberta. You have got the weight of the Big Flour Mill off your chest and should not look for another load to carry." (The flour mill issue had finally ended in 1925 with the sale to Spillers. Ernest wrote fellow shareholder and London financier J. Albert Burgess of the latter's $100,000 investment, "We have a salvage proposition and we have got to take our medicine and grin over it." Ernest served on the board of the Spillers, Alberta Flour Mills for the remainder of his life.)

Ernest stubbornly continued negotiations for amalgamating the breweries. One day in the middle of a meeting, the telephone rang with the news that a7 cattle once again got the highest price in Chicago. Jim recalled, "Daddy just hung up the phone, closed the door on the negotiators and headed for the Ranchmen's Club." That was the end of the merger, but Ernest did purchase the Silver Spray Brewery, the one across the street which had given them such trouble during prohibition. He renamed it the Big Horn.

By the end of August Billie had returned to Montreal, which he considered Canada's "most civilized city and by far the best one to live in." He wrote that the St. Lawrence River was beautiful, the restuarants were superb, as were the Windsor Hotel and 751 Pine Avenue where he was enjoying "all the abdominal felicity possible." Some Montreal stocks, such as Ogilvies, had gone up twenty-five points since Billie had purchased them only a month earlier. He found Bob Reford in great form, and Maggie and William's daughter Judy had married lawyer Philip Durnford, a nephew of Sir Alexander Galt. The Durnfords would live in the brick home which Alexander had built for the MacInneses at the foot of the Pine Avenue estate. The only drawback Billie saw to a perfect city was the noisy American tourists pouring in.

Billie sailed back to Europe on the CPR's *Montreal* from Quebec City. In a letter to Ernest he reminisced over their last meeting: "How much I enjoyed the trip west and my trip south to the old Range with you." The two had ridden down to Mosquito Creek to Ernest's first homesteading failure, then off to Billie's ranch where they had worked so hard in the 1880s and 1890s. They continued on to the a7 Ranche, which had grown so large that chinook winds could melt snows in the north with a freeze still gripping the land to the south. The a7 beef was sure to top the Chicago market in another record year. With the West's transformation from fenceless land to an industrial era unparalleled in Canadian history, the pair had plenty to reminisce about. But they had probably ridden mostly in silence, Ernest in his baggy three-piece suit, Billie in worn western. The Brewer would always be looking for a new deal, Billie would always be searching for a new fishing hole. They were two old friends gazing over their land whose horizons, each hoped, would never be reached.

23

The Fourth Generation

"You should see the photos of the old days. You should see the photos! Tons of them – white gloves, elbow length white gloves, gowns from Paris – and oh, the parties!"

Dodie Watney, 1982

No two brothers could have had more divergent families than those of Willie Heber and Ernest Cross. Willie Heber's children waltzed through the 1920s with a fatalistic fervour. Dodie Watney remarked of them, "They never rode. They were very French, you know. All they thought of was clothes and dithering." On the other hand, the Crosses had spent two generations establishing a frontier society in Alberta with little time to play in the drawing-room sense of the word. They were driven with a settling instinct where survival and opportunity were often dependent upon the weather and where time or conditions could seldom be manipulated.

The Calgary Crosses, "the proper Crosses," as Victorians came to call them – Jim, Mary, Marmo, Sandy and John – knew what was expected of them. They attended boarding schools either on Vancouver Island or in central Canada, becoming versed in religion, French and Canadian history. The girls' free time was properly regimented and chaperoned either at Rockland Avenue, Victoria, or Pine Avenue, Montreal. Jim neither questioned nor rebelled when sent off that year to brewers' school in Birmingham, England. He reminisced, "The ranch was the thing I really wanted. But when I was in third year of agriculture, Guelph University, Daddy asked me – told me – that I was going into the brewery. I had never thought about it at all. It was just a place where Daddy worked. I had never worked [there] as a boy – no mopping floors, no capping bottles, nothing. But I said,

'If you want me to go into the brewery, I'll go.' " That summer before attending Birmingham, Jim worked in the dark, yeast-smelling brewery, light years from the windy freedom of the a7 Ranche.

On the other hand, Willie Heber Cross lavished on his children every luxury they desired. He considered the girls' European schooling a kind of globe-trotting scholarship. Theirs was a life of exposure to countries, languages and cultures which could have been a superb education. But Fleurange, Willie, Simone and Yvette had no cattle to fuss over in winter, no stalls to muck out, no spouting wells to amaze them. Their father's lucrative stocks were understood only in that they produced dividends. The girls made all the guest lists but they were never wholly accepted by either Montreal's Square Milers or Victoria's Uplanders. They responded to the snub by speaking French or German at parties from Government House to Maple Bay. Later, Fleurange touted her Swiss passport while living in Victoria, then switched to Canadian citizenship when she eventually moved to Paris.

Willie Heber had been openly disappointed at the birth of his daughters, wishing five sons like his own father. It was boys who perpetuated the family name. He showered young Willie with attention and money, turning his room into a slot-machine haven, giving him flying lessons, and paying him $100 every time he managed to pass an exam. Willie grew into a blond six-footer and became Oak Bay High School's Don Juan. When sober, the teen-ager was as charming as any Cross, but he had quick fists and no one teased him when he was drunk. An old friend, Stan Williams, remembered Willie's lifestyle, "When we had a bike with no fenders Willie Jr. had a brand new bike. When we had a Model T Ford with no hood on it, he had a brand new Model T. If we had a row boat, he'd have a power boat. We had maybe one suit, Willie had three. . . . He was a darn lucky fellow you would say in those days."

Marguerite yearned for France, for the gossipy street corners where she once bargained for her bread and fresh vegetables, where her flat was surrounded by friends chatting noisily over laundry lines. Isolated in one of five Uplands homes in 450 acres of Victoria parkland, Marguerite had only her canaries, the nannie, her Chinese gardeners and her semi-invalid husband for company. Once a tee-totaller, she began lacing her tea with gin.

In Calgary, British Canadian Pictures, founded by Ernest, Pat Burns and J.I. McFarland, took off when Hollywood moved north to Calgary to film *His Destiny*. Staged at the Calgary Stampede and the Prince of Wales's EP Ranche, the story promised everything from broncos and bad guys to Indians swathed in Hudson's Bay blankets. Hero-director Neal Hart arrived in a cream-coloured stetson with stove-pipe crown to direct the film. They made up the plot as they went along. Men in knickers, white shirts with rolled up sleeves, tweed caps perched backwards above squinting eyes, ground their cameras for the great chase. Everyone's eyes followed a lone girl galloping amongst thousands of wild horses rounded up for this scene. It was Mary Cross, stunt rider for film star Barbara Kent, and billed as second female lead. For Grandmother Mary Macleod, aged seventy-five, it might well have been a reflection of herself at nineteen, riding messages through Riel's lines in the Red River Settlement. Now she witnessed her granddaughter racing through a cinematic rendition of times faded into history.

Ernest was having fun with his new venture and his daughter's participation. In commemoration of the event, he bought a car and a horse which he called Moonshine. He preferred the latter, and he ignored Billie's grouchy, "I am surprised to hear you have gone in for the movies. These Charlie Chaplin and cowboy stunts are very violent." *His Destiny* would finally premier in December 1928 at Calgary's Palace Theatre, billed, "Action! Thrills and Spills!" Not exactly a hit, the film was sold to Warner Brothers for export to England. By 1929 Ernest would still not realize his production cost of $25,000 but Neal Hart was optimistic that would make $30,000. In 1930 Ernest would try to interest Hart in making a movie of the north, his horizons firmly placed in the mining future of the North-West Territories. But Hart would decline, reasoning that a film of frozen wastelands would not sell.

When Randolph Bruce was made lieutenant-governor of British Columbia in August 1926, the founding member of the Wolves' Den did not forget his Calgary beginnings. Billie Cochrane lunched with "the Bruce" shortly afterwards and had typically levelling words of his friend: "He is suffering badly from swelled head. The lower orders of Scots cannot stand prosperity and are the very worst of snobs. He looks like an old bald headed boor, is drinking cocktails and digging his grave with his teeth." Billie surmised that Bruce's true ambition was to be knighted and made governor general of Canada.

The stately Government House on Rockland Avenue in Victoria became a home away from home for John Cross attending Shawnigan Lake School or for whatever Calgary Cross was passing through the city. Ernest's and Nell's own home at 1595 Rockland was almost as close as the Government House coach house. With Lieutenant-Governor Bruce in Victoria, the Crosses and Pinkhams in Alberta, CPR's vice-president W. MacInnes in Montreal, and R.B. Bennett now minister of mines in Ottawa, the Calgary Crosses moved about the country in an atmosphere of distinction and fun. Montreal friends remember a vivacious Mary snipe-shooting in a white fur coat, and fabulous black-tie dinner parties at Pine Avenue in honour of the western Crosses.

As in any other era, civic pride flourished in the 1920s. Montrealers claimed that no other city in Canada really counted and called Toronto "hog town." Out west Calgarians breathed their oil- and beef-scented air or skied in Banff and felt sorry for central Canadians. But today, titled octogenarians argue that the twenties were grand times to be nowhere else but somewhere between Victoria and Duncan, B.C. One Victorian sighed of the twenties, "No one ever went to bed. It was just one party after another."

Swiss-born Helmuth Preiswerk epitomized the eligible Victorian bachelor of the day. Grandson of the Count Maggi of concentrated soup fame and fluently trilingual, Helmuth's credentials were impeccable. Destined to inherit his father's Swiss sanitariums, the nineteen-year-old Helmuth had been struggling through his third year of medicine in Davos, when he saw a Canadian Pacific Railway advertisement in the newspaper. It assured the reader that farmers on the Canadian prairies worked for a few months in the summer, then spent their winters either in California or in Victoria, the Monte Carlo of Canada. The revelation coincided with Helmuth's realization that his future lay other than in medicine. "Whenever I saw blood I fainted." He showed the advertisement to his father and announced that he had decided to become a Canadian farmer.

Dr. Preiswerk decided medicine was too rigorous for him, too, sold the sanitariums and moved the entire family to this extraordinary land of sunshine and sophistication. In December 1925 the Preiswerks detrained in Winnipeg to a prairie temperature of 25 degrees below zero. Dr. Preiswerk packed everyone back on the next train for the salubrious climate of Vancouver Island. Upon arrival, sheets of rain drenched the doctor's tweeds and his only gambling was sneaked in over pinochle. The Preiswerk family was about to return to Switzerland, when Helmuth noticed a "For Sale" sign on the Columbia theatre on Government Street. It had both a legitimate stage and film facilities. Helmuth's parents raised their eyebrows over their son's lowered ambitions but with rumours of talking movies about to infuse the fledgling industry, Dr. Preiswerk gave his blessing. They unpacked their bags, bought four theatres and learned how to work the projection machines.

Crucial was the title of Count in Helmuth's family tree. Invitations flooded his mailbox. At seventy-eight, still graced with the dignity and charm of Swiss nobility, Preiswerk explained his introduction to Victoria society: "The title was important. Everyone in Duncan was either an admiral or a general. The Yacht Club in Maple Bay was the most snobbish yacht club. The only reason I got in was because my grandfather was a Count. My older brother Kurt had a right to the title but he said, 'What is the sense of taking it when we can't afford it?' So we never used it. But we were always called the Counts."

The dashing Preiswerk brothers sported bowler hats and canes by day, black capes with white silk lining for evening. They cut elegant figures about the city in their new Chevy car, and before long met the French-speaking Crosses through mutual Swiss friends. It must have overjoyed Fleurange, Simone and Yvette to share the company of Continental gentlemen. Preiswerk sighed in memory, "Those were wonderful days." Parties ran non-stop for entire weekends. In those days the E&N Railroad disgorged dozens of sybarites either coming down from Duncan to Government House, or going up to Maple Bay for formal parties. Most of the debutantes came from the exclusive private school, St. Margaret's. The Old Girls' network, which includes Mary Cross Dover of Calgary, runs strong today. An impeccable Victoria gentleman remembered Mary Cross, Dodie Watney and Dola Dunsmuir of Hatley Park days and all the St. Margaret's young ladies who kept Victoria hopping throughout the twenties: "Mary Cross was at Hatley Park but I don't remember much about her because Dola Dunsmuir played tennis without any panties and we hardly noticed anyone else. And our tennis wasn't very good either."

One beauty squired about by the Preiswerks and competed for by Willie Cross was dark-haired Edie Gore-Langton, daughter of a wealthy Englishman married to a Creole. It would be Willie whom Edie eventually married, but in early 1925 he was merely a provocative fifteen years of age and nudging his father for a Cadillac. The Gore-Langtons lived at Maple Bay and entertained lavishly. Their guest lists included the Willie Heber Cross family and actresses Sarah Bernhardt and Tallulah Bankhead. At one Gore-Langton tea party the massive British actor James Robertson Justice, clad in thirty yards of Highland kilt, fell out of a rowboat and sank. Horrified guests held their breath and scanned the surface from a waterside gazebo. Suddenly, to great cheering and charging of champagne glasses, a bearded, kilted leviathan lumbered up and out of the lake, expelling water like a broken dam. Upon hitting the bottom, James Robertson Justice had simply held his breath and walked uphill.

Fleurange was considered the most beautiful of Willie Heber's daughters. Invitations flowed through her mailbox but she knew that some doors were permanently closed to her. While the titled, Swiss-born Preiswerks possessed an alluring aura of internationalism, Fleurange's sin was speaking French with a Canadian birthright. Like Willie Heber struggling with his tormented soul and his Bible, Fleurange filled her journals with religious entreaties while cruising through wine and lovers at a pace that kept Victoria gasping.

In early 1925 Willie Heber wrote, "My dear Ernest, the Crosses seem to be decreasing." Suffering from high blood pressure, mini-strokes and visions of ghosts in his Val Rose home, he presided infrequently at his scooped out table. Surgeons discovered a cirrhosed liver and put him on the wagon, which made him even more miserable. Stripped of his Montreal credentials he wrote to Harry in Wyoming, "We all hate this place [Victoria], and I am sorry I bought here. I have to watch myself as I may have an attack which would carry me off."

On June 18, 1925, at the age of sixty-seven, Ernest's favourite brother, sometime rancher when the Brewer needed him, surrogate father to Edmund's children and beloved uncle to Harry's, suffered a massive stroke and died.

Willie Heber's past immediately returned to haunt Marguerite. Unable to read the will written in English, she called Helmuth Preiswerk over, who read that her husband had left $50,000 to his mistress and child of 1903. Had Marguerite but read his notebook she would have been prepared: "Your wife will share your grief, your mistress your money...." Willie Heber also haunted Ernest. When their mother Julia died in 1902, he had carefully listed and packed a large amount of her Lunn silverware into an oak chest and sent it off to the Royal Trust in Montreal. Upon his death, the Royal Trust promptly sent the silver to Marguerite in Victoria. Harry, Maggie, Edmund and Ernest laid claim to the silver, but Marguerite clung to the box.

Marguerite need not have worried about her future, for Willie Heber had adored her, and he forgot no one. The family would receive an annual income that allowed them to keep their European flats and winter on the Mediterranean even throughout the years of Depression. He was buried in Montreal with his father and mother, and his sister and brothers in Mount Royal Cemetery. In death, the city had accepted William Heber Cross home.

Helmuth Preiswerk's favourite Cross was Jim. He remembered, "Jim's mother thought he was such an angel. He and the Prince of Wales were friends. The Prince had parties on his [Calgary] ranch and he always imported the women from the States. Jim would always say to me, 'Come on over and stay with us the next time the Prince is in town. We'll have a ball!' "

On the surface, the pleasant if inscrutable Jim may have seemed to lack his father's entrepreneurial potential but his fighting instinct emerged in the propriety of a boxing ring. Representing the University of Birmingham in 1925, he reached the finals with Billie Cochrane cheering from the side lines. Jim got knocked out in two rounds by a boy from Sandhurst Military College but he loved the sport.

Billie and the Brewer fussed over Jim's education like parents watching their child take his first steps. They worried that his curriculum was comprised of excessive theory, especially on the manufacture of ale of which they believed the British knew nothing. In the spring of 1926 Nell, Ernest and Mary sailed for Europe, meeting with Billie in London before checking out Jim in Birmingham.

While Ernest and Billie plotted, Jim took off for the Alfred Jorgensen Institute in Copenhagen and a course in pure yeast culture. He travelled via Paris and the Moulin Rouge and was not seen again until he showed up in Scotland for Christmas at the Eckfords. Invited to Boswell Castle for a famous hunt, Jim had never before used a flat English saddle or double bridle. A groom led over a huge Irish hunter and, pointing towards the master of the hounds, gave Jim but one tip, "follow that man." Resplendent in tweeds and jodphurs, the Calgary cowboy spent the next few hours pounding over the frozen countryside, leaping stone walls and hedgerows. He managed to stay mounted during the entire hunt.

For New Year's Jim joined the Cochrane family at Ravenstone Castle. Billie's bash was predictable. The guests were drunk, his daughter-in-law was sniffing cocaine and the pianist vomited onto the bass fiddler. During the remainder of the holiday Billie managed Jim's fights in smoky pubs. While he took the bets, Jim fought the toughs in makeshift rings built by tables and chairs or just by a group of pubsters. He won enough to keep himself and Billie in drink, and for the customers it was more fun than skittles and darts.

When Jim returned to Birmingham he found it locked in a strike. Crowds of desperate coal miners roamed the city in an ugly mood. The police could not handle them if rioting broke out and requested volunteers to join their forces. Jim joined the night patrol, not sure if the men would help him or fight him as they travelled in threes throughout the darkened streets. Armed only with a billy up his sleeve and his own bravado, Jim helped maintain a kind of peace for a fortnight until the strike ended.

At the time, Ernest was ill again and had gone to Baltimore to seek a cure. It must have frustrated the Brewer no end, for he had left behind a province thriving with oil production, mining development, burgeoning grain markets and a stock market that was soaring out of sight. He was also leaving behind furious directors. McNaghten had expressed anger that Sicks (Lethbridge) and Edmonton breweries had again approached CB&M for a merger. Ernest was considering the offer, prompting a frantic letter from Billie: "We are better on our own with all our interest in Hotels. . . . Keep your eye on the McDirty. He is not brainy but hungry for dollars." A further problem was that, with W.R. Hull's death that year, the remaining directors would be hard pressed to buy out both men. During this time Jim returned to Alberta to drive the cattle to Chicago. He stuffed four bottles of the best whiskey in his bag and rode in the caboose to avoid detection.

In Ireland, Billie Cochrane's Slaney River ran dry and the fish went on strike so he and Howard headed off for Palma de Majorca. There, they bought a ranch, stocked it with cattle and learned to speak Spanish. At the age of sixty-nine, Billie claimed he had never laughed so much in his life although he worried, "Howard seems a trifle alcoholic."

Nineteen twenty-seven was a banner year for the Calgary Crosses. Nell and Ernest's annual New Year's Day party had swelled to gargantuan proportions and they celebrated R.B. Bennett becoming the first western leader of the national Conservative party.

Mary Drever Macleod was guest of honour at a ceremony marking the fiftieth anniversary of the Blackfoot Treaty. A modernized NWMP, which had changed its name to the Royal Canadian Mounted Police, brought tears to her eyes when they presented her with a bouquet and made her an honorary member of the NWMP Veterans' Association. Following the ceremony, which included the Blackfoot Indians,

Mary visited James's grave at Union cemetery. She laid her entire bouquet of flowers on his grave save for one rose, which she plucked and kept.

Jim Cross returned to Calgary and at age twenty-three was installed in the newly created position of director and secretary of CB&M. He was now able to observe and report to his father on internal problems which had been developing for years. The brewmaster was a drunk, neglect was rampant. Jim could see that the business had grown in such giant leaps that management had lost touch with the staff. He showed a quiet leadership, waiting, learning as much as he could about the working of the plant.

Some long-time employees were displeased to see Jim. Too busy travelling the CB&M hotel circuit to worry about balancing books, Macmillan had long entrusted entire signed, blank cheque books to other employees. Jim explained, "My father was an extremely trusting person. He always believed everybody and thought they were absolutely honest by their word. He didn't think it was necessary to keep stock of what was going on around the brewery itself." Jim periodically changed what he could before the brewmaster came out of his stupor and complained. Unwilling to rock the boat, Ernest would say each time, "Jim, we'd better keep the peace, so don't interfere too much." But he did follow Jim's suggestion that endorsed cheque books be abolished.

Jim had humoured his father's wish that he learn the brewery business, but he still harboured a dream of running the a7 Ranche. He rose early, visited his feisty Grandmother Mary Macleod en route to the office, worked hard in the brewery during the week and played hard on the weekends. He remembered, "I wasn't any blooming saint." During this time Jim met the beautiful, vivacious blonde, Eileen Russell, who would become his wife.

All other family excitement that year paled in importance to the news that Mary Cross had been nominated as a candidate for Queen of the Banff Winter Carnival. The February event drew holiday-makers from across the nation. They arrived in special trains, loaded down with skates, skis, whiskey, heaps of giggles and an endless supply of fur coats. They were met by bands and pennants and brilliantly costumed Indians. Hudson's Bay blankets brightened every corner of the mountain village as spectators stamped in the cold and cheered on the dogsled races. Ski-joring behind dogs and horses, ice skating, sled races, all started right on Main Street. New Brunswick's Irene and Louis B. Mayer of Metro-Goldwyn Mayer joined international newsmen with their cameras. To be named queen of the carnival meant international recognition. With Americans competing as well, Mary's win became a matter of national honour – a Miss Universe contest in mukluks. The Calgary Crosses attended in full force, with the Brewer fussing over Mary's candidacy.

Another beauty from the United States was the obvious contender to beat, especially when a member of the carnival committee whispered to Ernest that one dollar bought so many tickets, or votes, and that someone was buying masses of tickets for the American girl. One of Mary's brothers who begs anonymity laughed, "It was that same old gag. One was working the same deal on the American. Daddy fell for it." So calm and calculating in all his business ventures, the Brewer rushed around buying up tickets as if he was snaring controlling shares in an oil well. "While this was going on the Chrysler people got a big limousine to drive Mary all over with the idea of selling it to Daddy. I remember him walking around it and nudging it with his foot as if it was a steer or a cow. He said it was well-balanced. That's all he said. Mary did everything she could to get Daddy to buy that thing. He never did." Mary soon forgot about the car and proved her eligibility as a woman of the mountains by displaying expertise in riding, shooting, skating and in packing against the best of Banff guides. She won the horse-packing contest. Later she teamed up with a Robin Stronach to win the toboggan race in fifty-one seconds.

Chosen Queen of the Banff Winter Carnival on her own merit, Mary Cross was feted for days, given rare gifts by the Stony Indians in recognition of the esteem she held for them, awarded the keys to the city and honoured in a special parade with cheers and speeches. Following a gala dinner held by the Manitoba contingent in her honour, the *Winnipeg Evening Tribune* cheered, "One may question if there is another girl in Canada who is as competent in so many forms of outdoor life. And with all this she has not neglected the more usual accomplishments of the well-educated Canadian girl." The *Tribune* went on to describe the accomplishments of her father and her grandfather, James Macleod, but the Winnipeg paper failed to mention that her maternal great-grandparents were their own Helen Rothney and William Drever, the original residents of Portage and Main. The Drevers had long faded from memory.

It was in Calgary that the Drevers had become so prominent through the near octogenarian sisters, Jean Pinkham, Christin Jephson and Mary Macleod. Cyprian Pinkham had retired there in 1926. Once the youngest consecrated Anglican clergyman in Rupert's Land, the eighty-one-year-old cleric, who had built churches and schools in the belief that religion and education formed the foundation of any civilization, was now the oldest bishop in the British Empire. Gradually he had slipped into senility. Affectionately called "Old Man" by the Indians (who had also made him a chief of the Bloods), Cyprian began wandering out into the darkness in his nightshirt. He couldn't understand why houses and buildings had come between him and the wilderness. Each time Jean found him, his eyes glowed as he softly explained, "I want to go home."

No one knew where "home" was and Cyprian didn't say. Jean would throw a cape over shoulders still squared with dignity, then hand-in-hand and oblivious to stares they would turn back toward Bishop's Court. When they stopped at street corners for motor cars and trucks to pass by, Cyprian would shuffle impatiently in his slippers and wonder where his dogsled was. He would remain settled for a short time before disappearing on another quest. Calgary's Church of the Redeemer Cathedral was not Cyprian's home, and Bishop's Court was not what he sought. Most likely it was the nomadic Indian villages and the northern cabins spread across 300,000 square miles of prairie. The frontier itself was Cyprian's home and his cathedral. On July 18, 1928, the curate who had arrived in the Red River Settlement through a chain of errors sixty years earlier would die in a city of 75,000 people.

In Victoria, Helmuth Preiswerk had fallen in love with Fleurange. He remembered, "I was twenty-one, she was twenty. She was just under five feet with long blonde hair, a very beautiful woman and we were very much in love. Dinner parties in the Willie Heber Cross home were just beautiful." Like many other men, Helmuth found Fleurange a terrific challenge, especially when the Prince of Wales' yacht steamed into Victoria Harbour. Helmuth roared, "The prince wanted to sleep with Fleurange but I said to him, 'If you do I'll knock your bloody teeth out!' "

On June 10, 1927, Helmuth and Fleurange were married at Val Rose, 3125 Uplands Road, with Ernest giving the bride away. The groom remembered of the wedding reception, "It was in the garden and we had beautiful marquis all around. Champagne flowed like water. Imported. It was always imported. People dressed in morning coats and top hats. The lieutenant-governor was there, and Admiral Mainguay, even Auntie Helen. I was very disappointed that Jim couldn't attend."

Following a brief honeymoon in California, the Preiswerks returned to live for a time at Val Rose. If Helmuth had won the hand of the most desirable Fleurange, he had unwittingly become the inheritor of a bizarre household and parent to the increasingly wild young Willie. The youth was so unpredictable his friends could never guess what he would do next. Always short of cash, Willie complained that the estate monies of his father and his grandfather were badly invested by the Royal Trust in long-term, low-yielding bonds. One day he took all his available money and disappeared to the Polynesian islands in the South Pacific.

Running his theatre business left Helmuth little time to spend with Fleurange. She frequently left Victoria to shop in Seattle, and soon begged Helmuth to give up his job and live in Paris on her inheritance. He refused and bought a house for them outside of Uplands. In the following year Fleurange gave birth to a son, Paul. She remained with her baby through the first few months of life, then in 1928 left for Europe with her mother and a lover. Fleurange never returned. Despite her huge income, she lived frugally at the foot of Montmartre in Paris, clinging to an earthy reality and acceptance from artists and *la populace*. It was something which had eluded her in Canada.

Marguerite returned from Europe without Fleurange and offered to give the family nannie to Helmuth as Paul's governess. The young father refused, reasoning that Nannie had spoiled enough Crosses. For a time, however, Helmuth remained at Val Rose with Marguerite and raised a French-speaking Paul. The boy struggled through kindergarten in English-speaking Victoria with the same agony as had Willie Junior and Fleurange.

The year 1928 continued in an air of prosperity. Ernest was thrilled when Senator Harry Cross agreed to be the guest of honour at the Calgary Stampede. The last time the brothers had seen each other was at Cacouna, forty-three years earlier at Harry and Léa's wedding. Harry drove to Calgary with his son Bill, also serving in the Wyoming state legislature. The brothers met on the steps of the Palliser Hotel. Three-piece suits hung on slimmed down frames. Receding hairlines hid under battered hats. Black eyes glimmered from fissured, suntanned features. Underneath slightly hawkish noses, black moustaches were flecked with grey. Harry was a few inches taller, but they might have been twins.

Mary Cross Dover recalled of the moment: "They stood on the steps in silence. For a whole two minutes. Just staring at each other." For nearly half a century the brothers had settled in opposite frontiers, Harry in lawless American territory, Ernest in NWMP-controlled

Canada. Politics had made their settling differ, nature had kept them the same. Shaking his head years later, Jim Cross would wonder, "I don't know what they were thinking . . . but Daddy and Uncle Harry had the best time you ever saw in your life."

Edmund was invited to the family reunion and lunch at Nell and Ernest's 8th Avenue home but missed the rendezvous with his two famous brothers. After waiting on the Palliser steps alone for an hour, he returned to Edmonton, subsequently refusing to answer two of Harry's letters of apology. Harry and Léa invited Edmund and Hélène to visit them in Wyoming, then motor en famille for a California holiday, but no correspondence from Edmund appears again. It would be his children, Robbie, Bill, Maggie, Jack, Annie and Janet, businessmen and ranchers, who would reconnect with the Calgary Crosses through cattle sales during the decades to come. Edmund's daughter Maggie would display the business acumen of her Grandfather Alexander by parlaying his quarterly incomes into a fortune (only later, her brothers say, marrying W. Attenborough, vice-president of the Bank of America).

At the age of forty-nine, Mary Macleod's son Norman surprised everyone by marrying "Dodo" Banfield of Winnipeg. Yet he continued to care for his mother. For Mary, a life of dependency upon others had gnawed at her spirit. Even memories of James were hard to gather. Once when she had written to Sam Steele for more information he suggested she read the Indian treaties in the library and added, "It is a great pity that the Col. did not keep a diary." In 1920 Mary's house had been sold at a tax sale. Norman had to ask his Uncle Jock Jephson to mortgage their lot on Second Avenue in order to redeem the house for $641.25 back taxes. The accountant responded that no one would take out a mortgage on the land. The outcome is not explained, but the incident must have been demeaning for Mary.

In 1981 Dodo Macleod recalled that Mary was unable to relinquish her title of matriarch; hanging a picture of Queen Victoria in their Winnipeg living room, she ruled the household. Eventually, Norman and Dodo headed for a dairy farm in Ontario while Mary returned to live in Calgary with her daughter, Jean Montgomery-Bell. There, Rothnie Montgomery-Bell would remember her grandmother as an imperious but marvellous woman with a closet full of lightly perfumed dresses and a host of stories to tell.

24

🌿 Alexander's Cresting Wave

"The Old Homestead is the only link in a wandering family."
Ernest to Maggie, 1929

Toward the close of 1928 and the winter of 1929, a rash of western reflections arrived from Billie to the Brewer. From Marseilles he recalled the terrible winter of 1886-87 "when we only put up enough hay for a saddle horse." From Barcelona he reminisced over how they used to watch and pray for the life-saving chinooks. From Paris he wrote of his high opinion of Jim, and of his interest in the prosperity of Alberta and Canada. For the first time one of Billie's postmarks hailed from South America. The seventy-year-old adventurer had discovered an uncle who had been "one of Brazil's most distinguished pirates of the first class . . . and a blackguard of no small repute." The governor and president of Rio welcomed the pirate's grand-nephew and saw that his martinis were mixed just the way he liked them, dry with a dash of absinthe. Billie wrote, "The bathing is fine . . . and all class and colours meet here and we dive under the heavy surf breakers. You would enjoy it . . . I am taking to the mountains where . . . they want me to get up early shoot crockodillos. . . . Wishing you all the very best . . . I never had five aces dropt on me until I came here."

Billie would have been delighted with the Brewer's March 31 announcement of a 5 per cent dividend for 1928 and a 6 per cent dividend predicted for 1929, but he never knew about it. On April 4, 1929, H.B. Alexander wrote to Ernest, "Dear Brewer, Billie went off very suddenly. . . . We Mosquito Ck oldtimers are getting scarce." Ernest did not receive H.B. Alexander's letter. He and Nell had sailed to England to meet with Billie. The Brewer had missed his closest friend by a couple of weeks. For the next three years, Ernest would endeavour to settle an estate in which the British government, two children, a mistress-housekeeper and two illegitimate children all contested the will.

Following the complicated court battles over Billie Cochrane's estate, Ernest and Sir F.A. McNaghten bought out his shares valued at 40 cents on the dollar. It was a windfall and for the first time Ernest personally borrowed $119,000 for a three-month period in order to meet expenses. His worth in brewery shares had grown from $20,000 to over $1.5 million.

While Ernest was in Ireland, Jim assumed the responsibility of the a7 Ranche and the family finances. He purchased bulls, sold calves, repaired dams, built a barn and wrote to all his brothers and sisters. His letters to Ernest were long and thorough, at first giving the brewery only a cursory, "P.S. The beer is alright." Heavily into polo, Jim convinced the riders to buy stock in a Calgary company named Polo Limited because he felt the players should take an interest in their grounds. As the weeks went by, Jim's letters changed. Revelling in brewery profits of 40 per cent, he got the CB&M staff to sign up for a sickness and accident policy, convinced the brewmaster to change the malt recipe and to move ahead with the Ginger Ale Lager. He reported that problems seemed ironed out at the Big Horn Brewery and beer sales were doubled over the previous fall. Ernest's oldest son possessed an ability to present all options in a proposition, then cleverly justify his own decision. The Brewer could not fault his son, who had learned his lessons well at the feet of his father.

In the fall of 1929, Ernest returned to load his cattle for Chicago. The Crosses were anticipating at least $13.50 per head when the market plummeted into the Great Depression and a7 cattle were rendered almost valueless. George Lane and McLean of the Big Four were destroyed.

At the brewery, Ernest found that his men hadn't liked Jim's alert attention to the business in the boss's absence. They accused Jim of firing union workers and then hiring non-union men. It looked rough for the Brewer's son, but Jim suspected an internal black-market operation and convinced his father that he had fired with good reason. Seeking proof, Jim hid in the brewery one night and watched truckloads of beer being shipped out the back. He slipped out and headed for the Edmonton brewery, where he found similar practices.

He reported to C.W. Macmillan, whereupon the old manager wrote to Ernest, in January 1930:

Personal

Dear Mr. Cross, 'Tis just midnight and for two hours I have been listening to information that staggers me. In a word it is this. Beer to the value of $750 is going out of the brewery each weekend for bootlegging purposes. There is an impression in official quarters that someone in whom you have absolute confidence is double crossing you. . . . I will try and be in Calgary on Saturday morning to talk this over.

Back in Calgary that Saturday night, Jim again watched employees load under cover of dark, their movements silhouetted against the winter background and their silence broken only by boots squeaking in the snow. An unspoken code in the beer business demanded internal control; only cowards called the police. With a bravado born of youth and of skills honed in the pubs of Ireland, the Brewer's son stepped out alone and confronted the bootleggers. There were no witnesses. If he feared winding up a corpse in the Elbow River, Jim never said. Neither did he pass judgment. He ordered the men to report to his father the following day. Every one showed up. Rather than place criminal charges against them, a terribly disappointed A.E. Cross fired them all. Recalled Jim, "They were mad as hell." One wife of a CB&M employee subsequently wrote to Ernest:

Everybody is interested now in the Calgary Brewery's affairs. Fred White has information that young Jim gave orders to employ extra gang of scab and then laid off union men. You sacked some, but there are still men who work against your interest at good salary in the Brewery. You have them as shippers, truck drivers, office cleaners. . . .

There are men in Brewery today who were unjustly laid off. They can't keep payments on houses, others are dropping insurance, their wives losing washing machines, and others cancelling children's music lessons, while others get all the extras. But it is only fair that you should fight the gang who robbed you for years, whom you treated too well.

Through the shake-up, employees realized that a new generation of Crosses was moving in to build tighter operations and block the freewheeling practices spawned in prohibition. CB&M manager Clive Betts, long suspected of keeping McNaghten informed of the inner workings of the CB&M as it competed against the Lethbridge Brewery, resigned to establish his own brokerage business.

In 1930 Jim married Eileen Russell and Mary married ex-fighter pilot and Ford dealer Mel Dover. While Jim remained at the brewery, the Dovers went to Bombay to run the Ford dealership. India was perfect for Mary, who had already travelled around the world in first-class style with William MacInnes in 1928. The daughter of Nell and Ernest loved the international flavours. Mary wrote lively letters of dinners with the British high commissioner, and of racing through the streets of Bombay in her yellow convertible, the terrified driver relegated to the back seat. It was in India that she first searched out orchids and other exotic plants to create the lush gardens which would become a lifelong pursuit. Mary's letters also conveyed a subconscious hint that she held aspirations in a broader sphere of service than usual for an upper middle class Canadian lady of 1930.

At the end of the twenties and beginning of the thirties, three of Alexander and Julia's children, Harry, Ernest and Maggie, drew closer together. Correspondence over the box of silver, finally relinquished by Marguerite, had sparked renewed connections. Deciding the silver should go to Harry as the oldest living son, the Crosses had packed it off to the border where it was stopped by the United States customs. They refused to pass it duty free, judging that only one-quarter was over one hundred years old. Sent back to the Royal Trust in Montreal, the box was sorted and the oldest silver sent back to Wyoming. That time the United States customs judged that only half could legitimately pass as antique. Six months later Harry agreed to pay the full duty on the one-quarter-full oak box. Ernest actually purchased the remainder, whereupon it was sent to Braehead, Calgary.

In 1930, Nell and Ernest left Braehead, Alberta, and motored southward to visit Harry and Léa in Braehead, Wyoming. It was their first visit to the vast foothills of Red Canyon Valley where stirrup-high grassland rippled towards the craggy peaks of Tomahawk Bluffs. In 1876 the terrain had reminded Harry of Scotland and much of it was similar to the a7 Ranche in Alberta. Seventy-eight years old and recovering from a heart attack, Harry said he wanted to return to Montreal and Pine Avenue, or the Old Homestead as he called it, once more before "passing over the Great Divide." He wanted to visit the familiar haunts of his boyhood days, the St. Pierre Creek where he and his friends had sent their homemade boats into uncharted seas, and the Chateauguay River farm of his grandmother. He wanted to walk down St. Lawrence and St. Paul streets where, for him, two languages blended in joyous tribute to two great cultures.

Toward the end of 1931, Willie Cross from Victoria suddenly turned up at Harry and Léa's San Francisco home with a French-speaking Tahitian princess called Reri. He had married her in a Polynesian ceremony in which a holy man had broken a stick over their heads. The sultry native stunned Harry and Léa by shrieking that the telephone was the messenger of the devil. Taking the young couple back to Braehead, Wyoming, Harry wrote that Willie and Reri stayed for "six long weeks." One day Willie wired for money from his mother. Marguerite always complied, for he would threaten to commit suicide if he didn't get his way. Then he whisked Reri off to New York to make her a movie star. He actually made good his promise, introducing her to Ziegfeld who hired her first in his Follies, then as female lead in the movie classic, *Tabu*. Reri promptly dumped Willie for the producer, literally leaving her benefactor behind the scenes.

Enraged, penniless and threatening suicide, Willie caught a train for Montreal and Pine Avenue. The last thing the MacInneses needed around at that time was wild Willie. Maggie was terminally ill with cancer and Ernest, suffering severe pain again, was planning to head east.

Following a raucous Christmas and New Year, Willie solved the problem himself. Perhaps feeling caged in by the gentility of Pine Avenue he decided to move on and wired his mother for a large sum of cash. Upon receiving it, he bought a Fairchild plane, stocked it with Johnny Walker, then bade farewell to the MacInneses. Promising to follow the CPR railway tracks, Willie and a young Swedish flyer, Jarl Grubbstrom, took off on Canada's first mid-winter, cross-country flight. Rumour has it that Willie's substandard eyesight precluded him from doing much of the piloting. Newspapers picked up the progress of the intrepid aviators as they hopped across the country. They winged it through snowstorms, fog and rain, bending props in three forced landings and within hours of victory crashing into a slough in the Crow's Nest Pass. For three weeks they fuelled freezing limbs with bonfires and Johnny Walker, waiting for another propeller to arrive from Montreal.

While Willie was more or less airborne, his Uncle Ernest was helping to ease Depression hunger by establishing a downtown soup kitchen for the destitute of Calgary. John Cross remembered:

> It was a time when starving cattle really did nibble at rusting tractors
> and died of "hardware disease." And it was a terrible thing if we
> had to fire a man. My father had two game roosters; some young
> men crawled in under some boards down by the river bank. They
> stole these roosters and ate them. They were caught and jailed
> in October, I think, for six months. It meant they got good food,
> heat and everything all winter. My father knew what he was doing,
> and he hired as many men as he could afford to.

Those were the times when Ernest enjoyed visiting Jim and Eileen
for long afternoons and reminiscing about his life. Jim wished they
had had a tape recorder. "If we had just taken notes of some kind.
But Daddy was a shy sort of person. He would ask me about certain
things, talk about certain things. I should remember them but I don't,
or maybe some of them I could but I won't."

Suffering constantly and suspecting impending surgery, Ernest
elected to return to the Montreal surgeons. Nell wished to accompany
him, but she was immobilized in traction with a painful, degenerating
hip and would follow a week later. After selling his steers for 2½
cents a pound, Ernest headed east on the train with his eighteen-
year-old son Sandy. At the time, Sandy was like any other teen-ager
with an eye to the fun of tomorrows, oblivious to aging or illness.
To him, his father was invincible. In 1981, he wished quietly, "If
I could just remember a tenth or a hundredth of what Daddy tried
to tell me on the way down there. He was looking ahead. He wanted
me to be a mining engineer, to go north. He tried to give me advice
and I didn't realize it until it was too late."

As father and son sped eastward on the CPR, wild Willie's Fairchild
swooped and veered its way westward through the Crow's Nest Pass
and crashed into the slough. One of Alexander Cross's grandsons
was winging his way into stardom while the other was shunting
eastward to study at the Royal Military College, Kingston. It was
late January 1932.

On February 23, Willie landed at Victoria's Saanich airport to
a hero's welcome. He postponed his threatened demise. On the same
day, Ernest was admitted to the Montreal General Hospital for
abdominal surgery. Ernest's pilgrimage east to Montreal had been
much quicker than Willie's flight west, but a pilgrimage it was. After

a lifetime of either loving or berating Quebec and once in frustration over a refused loan referring to Montreal as "the worst place on earth," he had returned. He had even sent Mary and Marmo to school there. Pine Avenue, its forest, noisy Sherbrooke Avenue, the energy of two languages, all were his roots and, combined with the West, his Canada.

Two weeks later Jim arrived to find his father post-operative and shaded with the dusky pallor of advanced pneumonia. He found the hospital "a dirty, dingy old place down in the suburbs of Montreal. Daddy had got an infection in there. It had never dawned on me that he might not be coming back until I saw him. He was able to talk to me just a little, and said, 'If anything happens to me, well, you're in charge.' And that was that."

Although Nell and Marmo were with him, it seemed that the Brewer had waited for Jim, for he died the next morning, March 10, 1932. He would never know that two weeks later Jim's wife Eileen would give birth to his longed-for grandson Donald, the first of the fifth generation since Janet Cross had settled her family in the Chateauguay.

Jim wired Mary in Bombay before arranging three separate funeral services. The first was at Pine Avenue, after which Ernest's body was brought back to the West. Following a private family ceremony, the main service was held at the Church of the Redeemer. Calgarians crowded into the pews and spilled out onto the street. It was probably the only time in the forty-one-year history of the CB&M that production closed down for two hours, for most of the staff attended. Hundreds of condolences poured in, ranging from ranch hands to royalty.

Soon afterwards, the impact of "You're in charge" fully struck Jim. With two brothers still in their teens at school, it was he who had inherited the responsibility of his father's empire, much of which Ernest had carried in his head. It was in Jim's hands whether or not the CB&M, its fifty-odd hotels and hundreds of staff would survive the Depression. There would be no life on the a7 Ranche. The new, unfailingly courteous chairman soon punctuated his speech with frequent, "And that's that." He kept his own counsel. No one was better suited to carry on the Brewer's business.

Ernest's estate was publicly evaluated at a Depression (and succession duty) adjusted level of $902,603.02. It was written up as "One of the largest fortunes ever bequeathed by a resident of Calgary." Still untouched was Alexander's estate of stocks, bonds and land. Ernest deeded to Nell the Calgary house with a lifetime allowance of $600 per month. Both daughters received $50,000 and one-eighth of the estate upon turning twenty-five. The sons were each left $8,300 in cash and would share the brewery and the ranch. In the thirties, it was a windfall for the girls but a dubious inheritance for the boys, aged sixteen, eighteen and twenty-nine. Like Alexander's estate, Ernest's was land rich. With stock values and thirsts both diminished by hard times, the Cross brothers began a precarious trip through the Depression. Alexander probably would have delighted in the challenge to his grandsons to succeed through skill rather than by wealth.

Jim wheeled his wagons into a circle. Intending Cross Brothers Limited to control every facet of the CB&M and for the brewery to maintain its western monopoly, he sailed for England and bought out the widow, Lady McNaghten. To finance the venture and to ease pressure on depleted cash flows, he let all the downtown Calgary lots go in lieu of paying taxes, then sold the Saskatchewan lands and Royalite stock. In hindsight, he believed the latter two moves were the only mistakes he made, although at the time there were few options to gain control of the brewery and to pay the succession duties. His cash flow was nil. What would save Cross Brothers Limited was hard work and beer at 10 cents a glass.

Jim advised Sandy to switch from mining to chemical engineering at the University of Alberta, Edmonton, then to study brewing at the Wahl-Henius Institute. Sandy complied, realizing that he would never fulfil his father's dream of mining the north. When John failed his last year at Shawnigan Lake School, shocked by his father's death and specializing more in the school horses than in mathematics, Jim admonished him to return and complete his education. He did so. After graduation and a stint at the Ontario Agricultural College, John returned to the foothills to run the a7 Ranche. Looking back on that time, he would muse, "We were left an awful thing when Daddy died and I was only sixteen. We had so little money. Then we lost our shirts when we shipped cattle to England and the British pound dropped to about one dollar and fifty. After that we sold prime steers for 3 cents a pound. We survived because we were dedicated, and you know, we did a damn good job."

Nell advised Jim to sell 1595 Rockland Avenue and the Oak Bay lots. Crippled by her degenerating hip, she saw no reason to return to the lovely city which had never been her home. As soon as the Alberta winter faded and the roads were solid, she returned to the a7 Ranche with her eighty-year-old mother, Mary Macleod. The two

had shared a lifetime of change, of love and of tragedy. Both had
spent much of their marriages separated from the frontiersmen they
loved.

Although too heartbroken to attend her grandson's christening,
Nell's grief began to heal through her communion with God and
the land. She began writing again in June, gazing at her foothills over
which she could no longer walk. She clung to the sight of each storm
cloud and each blade of grass as she had en route to the Victoria
seaside twenty years earlier. In willing her spirit to carry on through
nature and in drawing on her own deep reserves of courage, Helen
Rothney Macleod Cross epitomized that spirit which has ensured
this family's survival over six generations.

On June 3, 1932, from Braehead on the a7 Ranche, Nell wrote
to Jim:

> It is a perfect growing day, dull and warm and everything getting
> green. Some of my flower seeds are up. . . . What a splendid rain
> it has been although we hear that High River has suffered heavily. . . .
> Joe is busy hauling wood as it is too wet to work on the land.
> They seem to be plowing. . . .
>
> Dear Daddy would have enjoyed all this moisture and the prospect
> of a good growing year. It is . . . such a comfort to be surrounded
> by so much that he loved and for which he worked so hard. We
> are getting this place into good shape and the work is such a
> blessing. . . .

It might have eased Nell's pain to know that half a century later,
even after her own passing, Martin and Jane Macleod's Drynoch would
still grace its Oak Ridges hill. The family living there still race up
the same stairways and fish for the evening rise in the same lake
as did young James Macleod. The hundreds of saplings planted by
Martin in 1848 loom as giant maples, their silver leaves shading his
carriage way and their roots reaching as deeply into the earth as the
Macleods' heritage.

It might also have warmed Nell's heart to know as she headed
for Braehead that spring, and as her children and grandchildren would
do some fifty years later, that on the banks of the Chateauguay River
in Quebec, the 1827 farm where Alexander was raised was still sturdy
and beautiful in age. It is cared for today by Janet's great-grand-
daughter, sprightly nonogenarian Bessie Cross. The attic with its
wasp's nest and leather traces can still be reached by ladder and the

willow trees still dip their branches toward the river as it races by house and outbuildings.

The massive Chateauguay hay barn, fifty feet north of the stables, is a silent, welcoming place. It stands almost empty. Soft hay from yesteryear lies underfoot. Above, a vast space soars in cathedral proportions. Sunbeams filter through cracks in the walls, illuminating prisms of dust particles floating lazily in the air. A rope and pulley dangle from the rafters to swing hay from loft to floor, or perhaps after the harvest long ago, to fling a child through the air before he fell into huge gentle mounds. On a lower level a buggy stands waiting, a whetstone nearby. Suddenly storm clouds blot out the sun, and wind whistles through the knotholes of the west wall. The sound is eerie yet gentle, an omniscient flautist blending past and present in perfect harmony. Like the Macleods and the Drevers, Janet Cross had built her farm and her family for permanency, and all had formed a continuum through time.

Epilogue

Only one request was made by the family in the writing of this book: that I end with the death of Ernest Cross in 1932. So many questions were left unanswered, however, that the epilogue serves to bring the reader up to date both on characters who were still alive at that time, and on subsequent events which help to complete the story.

The Drevers and the Macleods
In Winnipeg, William and Helen Drever's Portage and Main intersection is hailed as Canada's widest, never altered from the days when William fought for his home on the southwest corner. It might amuse the couple to know that some claim it is also Canada's coldest and windiest. Notre Dame Street still jogs around the former site of William's store.

Adam Drever, Calgary businessman and a grandson of the Red River scout, Willie Drever, died in August 1985 at the age of seventy-nine. He had researched the experiences of his great-grandparents, William and Helen Drever, and the life of those times with scholarly intent.

Jean Drever Pinkham, OBE, mother of seven children, died in Calgary at ninety, still a powerful matriarch. Her only living grandchild, Nancy Pinkham Walton, lives in Vancouver. Christin Jephson, youngest daughter of William and Helen Drever, died in Calgary in 1949 at the age of ninety-four.

Mary Drever Macleod died in Calgary on April 5, 1933. Three days later, as six red-coated Mounties carried Mary to her grave, a blizzard blanketed the earth with snow. Like James, she had been a living legend. The Macleod home is preserved in Calgary's Heritage Park. During the summer months it is open for tours.

In Macleod, the NWMP fort has been reconstructed. In 1956, Christ Church, erected in 1886, dedicated a stained-glass window of James Macleod in memoriam. His Order of St. Michael and St. George is in the RCMP museum, Regina Barracks.

James and Mary Macleod's daughter-in-law, Dodo, died at the age of ninety in Victoria in June 1984. Her sons Norrie and Jim Macleod live in Calgary. Norrie, an artistically oriented man, has filled his apartment with the furniture and memorabilia of his grandparents' life in Fort Macleod. Jim, married with four children, is president of a German oil company based in Calgary.

The living children of Jean Montgomery-Bell, James's youngest daughter, are Helen Rothney Montgomery-Bell, who lives in Calgary, and Roma Macleod "Biddy" Lawrence, Red Deer, Alberta. Elizabeth Townshend, a writer living in Calgary, is the daughter-in-law of Roma Macleod, one of the James and Mary's twins.

In the area now called Aurora, Ontario, Martin and Jane Macleod's 1846 Upper Canada estate, Drynoch, is owned by Gordon Gray, chairman and chief executive officer of Royal LePage Real Estate Limited, and his wife Pat. The house is expanded into a stately brick manor, but the Grays have restored the home as closely as possible to Martin Macleod's design. Even the original window glass remains. The Grays continue to live there in the spirit of enthusiasm and fun established by Martin and Jane Macleod 150 years ago. The active parish church of St. John's stands just across from the Drynoch gates.

The Crosses

Braehead, Scotland, burned to the ground. No records were found in the local libraries or the major archival centres of Scotland.

In Montreal in 1948, with the death of William MacInnes and shortly thereafter of Alexander and Julia's last child, Edmund, the Calgary Crosses liquidated Alexander's holdings and generously sold the eighty-six-year-old Pine Avenue estate for a specific purpose. The buildings and forest were razed in order to build the new Montreal General Hospital. Only the brick house at the foot of the lower garden was preserved. It was donated as the nurses' residence by Alexander's granddaughter, Judy MacInnes Durnford.

The other children of Maggie Cross MacInnes have left Montreal. Evelynn Reford Duke lives in Victoria, British Columbia. Her sister, Emma Creery, lives in Calgary. Donald MacInnes is deceased, but his wife, Jane Leggat MacInnes (a cousin of Eleanor Leggat Cross of the a7 Ranche), lives today in Mississauga, Ontario. Judy Durnford is deceased. Her son John, former dean of law, McGill University, and great-grandson of both Alexander Cross and Sir Alexander Galt, lives today with his family in Montreal at the end of Lexington Avenue.

In Wyoming, Léa Levasseur Cross died in 1940 at the age of seventy-eight. Harry died in 1946, aged ninety-two. Today, drilling rigs are moving about Braehead Ranch among the cattle, and Harry and Léa's grandchildren still serve in the Wyoming state legislature.

Edmund and Hélène Cross's children live in Alberta and British Columbia. The Vermillion farm is run by their son Bill, his daughter and his son-in-law. Their Herefords are national prize winners. In Edmund and Hélène's farmhouse, one of Alexander and Julia's eight-holder silver candelabra from Pine Avenue graces the formica kitchen table in anachronistic splendour.

On returning home to Victoria following his cross-Canada flight in 1932, Willie Cross joined the army. Marrying Edie Gore-Langton, he continued rolling motorcycles and heading his thirty-two-foot single-engine cruiser across the Strait of Georgia in gale-force winds. One morning in April 1940, after threatening to commit suicide yet again, Willie was found dead in his Val Rose garage, the car running and carbon monoxide oozing out the door cracks. He was given a military funeral. His stepson, Bevan Gore-Langton, is a musician who lives with his family in a beautiful log home in Sidney, north of Victoria.

Simone Cross married a Parisian pilot. During World War II they both served in the French Resistance. They settled in Nice with Willie Heber's widow Marguerite, who was reluctant to return to Canada.

Fleurange never returned to Vancouver Island, dying in Paris in August 1965. Helmuth Preiswerk remarried. He and his wife Inez live in Sidney, north of Victoria.

Yvette Cross married a Dutch baron in Victoria. In 1939 Baron and Baroness Semeyn had a son named, of course, Willie. William Heber "Willie" Semeyn recalled a bizarre childhood in which he often joined his mother and Fleurange for Mediterranean visits to be squired around by his fun-loving aunts. Yvette became a Victoria landmark in her yellow convertible and hats the size of giant chanterelles. One evening at Cherry Point, Baron Semeyn rowed out with Yvette and a few bottles of beer for a moonlight fish. Holding his rod in one hand and reaching for a beer with the other, the baron plunged backward over the stern and was never seen again. Inheriting his father's title at age seventeen, another wild Willie changed his address cards to read, "Baron Semeyn."

Willie raced through his youth with the Victoria police and the Royal Trust wringing their hands in pursuit. Then he moved to Montreal, learned to fly, established a charter airlines and married a French girl called Annette. He dropped the "Baron," settled down and made his venture successful. In 1980 the Semeyns returned to Victoria. It would probably delight Alexander Cross to know that Willie Semeyn and the Royal Trust continue to spar. He has re-established his flying business in Victoria as Skycom of Canada Limited. Annette is an active business partner in Mex-Dev, the managing company for the Crosses' nine villas and land holdings in Puerto Vallerta, Mexico. For Willie and Annette, the British bastion of the 1920s has matured. They find Victoria a wonderful place in which to live and to raise their French-English children.

Val Rose was sold after Marguerite's death in 1954. The brick home at 3125 Uplands is hidden by a huge laurel hedge planted by Helmuth Preiswerk in the 1920s. The current dwellers, Ron and Isabelle Mackenzie, assure that the ghosts Willie Heber saw in his basement have never returned.

From Calgary in 1936, Nell Cross accompanied her daughter Marmo on a trip to visit Mary Dover in Ceylon. Marmo tried to interest Nell in meeting other passengers on the ocean voyage, but her mind was elsewhere. In letters Nell fussed over seedlings and worried to Jim at home in Alberta that the winter wouldn't leave them with enough water on Braehead. Like her father, the gentle-woman's departure from home merely marked the beginning of her return. Nell remained active throughout her life on the executives of Calgary's IODE, the Women's Auxiliary of the Church of the Redeemer, and later as diocesan head of the Women's Auxiliary to the Missionary Society of the Church of England in Canada. Like her mother, Nell was known for her kindnesses to the wives of RCMP officers. On January 30, 1959, at age eighty, Helen Rothney Macleod Cross died in her Calgary 8th Avenue home. Her children subsequently gave the house and grounds to the city to use in whatever capacity it wished. Today it is used mainly by the Calgary Horticultural Society, something which would have delighted Nell.

"Rappahannock," Nell and Ernest's mansion at 1595 Rockland Avenue, Victoria, is an eleven-home apartment building.

Today in Alberta, the children of Nell and Ernest Cross, synthesis of the heritage which inspired this book, remain united in their dedication to the West and to Canada. Their widespread, and often anonymous, philanthropies are weighted toward education, and they continue to act as Stampede presidents and as hospital, church and education board members in Calgary, and in the ranching communities of Midnapore, Okotoks, Nanton and Millarville. They are the quintessential westerners, and although media accounts have referred to them as "Alberta's aristocrats," the Crosses keep their profiles as low as the foothills over which their vast lands sprawl.

Following the liquidation of Alexander's estate, Jim traded his Willow Springs property and deeded the a7 Ranche to John in return for purebred cattle. Purchasing his own Bar Pipe ranch in Okotoks south of Calgary, he then donated more land to the Calgary Polo Club and to an independent school named Strathcona. Originally founded in 1932, the latter is known today as Strathcona-Tweedsmuir. It is a school dedicated to excellence in academics and in leadership, with extra-curricular pursuits emphasizing outdoor sports and survival techniques.

The Calgary Stampede, founded by Burns, Cross, Lane and McLean in 1912, remains a vital institution in the West. Far from depicting Calgarians as stetson-swaggering cowboys, it reinforces a dignity inherent in the self-reliant community. Like the citizens who quietly supported a bereaved Mary Macleod in 1894, newcomers sense this special kinship through the Stampede. Besides the three thousand volunteers who set aside boardroom deals or construction hats to make Stampede week a resounding success, a waiting list of at least one thousand volunteers grows each year.

Jim's polo pony, wandering in a field just beyond his Bar Pipe golf course, is named "No Answer." Refusing to give up the game in his late sixties in spite of a spectacular accident, Jim continued playing into his seventies. Today, the Calgary Polo Club of some thirty-two skilful players and up to two hundred ponies, is arguably the first or second club in Canada, unofficially started by Ernest Cross and his friends in 1884-86.

It was Jim, Nell and Ernest's third child, who guided the family fortunes through the Depression onward. Upon taking control in 1932, he established a profit-sharing plan and kept his staff occupied by improving the brewery parklands. He also built on the site the largest inland trout hatchery in North America, the Calgary Aquarium, and founded the museum called the Horseman's Hall of Fame. The CB&M name remained synonymous with the Calgary community, and in recognition, Jim was awarded an honorary doctorate from the University of Calgary.

As late as the 1950s, eastern breweries had yet to break the Alberta brewery stronghold. Even CB&M ginger ale outsold Canada Dry. In 1952 Senator H. Molson of Molson's Brewery Limited made an offer to buy the company. Jim refused to sell, both men remembering that he could not bear to part with his father's creation nor open up the Alberta market. A few months later Toronto tycoon Eddie Plunkett Taylor of Canadian Breweries took a run at Alberta. He targeted a publicly owned company, North West Breweries and Malting in Edmonton. With the secret help of its president, J. Paterson, Taylor picked up 30,000 of NWB's 170,000 scattered shares. Before long, Bill Wilkin, the son of the original founder, discovered Paterson's deceit and informed Jim Cross. Jim didn't want another brewery but when told that the purchaser was E.P. Taylor, Wilkin remembered, "It was the east against the west."

Wilkin and three Royal Trust brokers spent the next two weeks dodging E.P. Taylor's army as convoys of Buicks and Dodges roared about the dusty backroads of northern Alberta in a stock-bidding war. Farmers held out on their $4 shares until the price reached $16. Then they started coming in to see the Cross team. Within two weeks Jim Cross had millions invested in the little brewery, a symbol of western supremacy. He won it with a purchase of $25 a share for a total of 51.9 per cent, and renamed the company Bohemian Maid.

In 1955 E.P. Taylor tried to purchase the CB&M but failed. Jim still wasn't interested, although he was becoming disenchanted over increased government pressure. The beer business had become a continual game of outsmarting the Alberta Liquor Control Board's taxes, quotas and advertising restrictions. In 1957, the board passed the harshest ruling since prohibition: no hotels could be owned by breweries. The luck had run out for the Ranchmen's Trust Company. Breweries were given ten years to get out of the hotel business, plenty of time for most, but a nightmare for the CB&M monopoly which included from forty-seven to fifty hotels. The sudden market glut enabled purchasers to offer ridiculous prices.

Jim elected to sell to Canadian Breweries. In a Calgary hotel room he appeared alone to negotiate for the CB&M, with Ian Dowie, E.P. Taylor and Wallace McCutcheon representing Canadian Breweries. One of them acknowledged, "We paid too much for it.... Taylor tended to throw money around if he really wanted something." Jim chuckled, "McCutcheon got drunk. If there is anything a brewer has to do, it's hold his liquor. It cost them an extra million."

In the $18 million sale, Cross Brothers Limited received $8 million in cash and $10 million in Canadian Brewery stock. Jim was also appointed a vice-president and director of the company. E.P. Taylor had not even examined the company books but he had finally got the Bohemian Maid Brewery over which he and Jim had fought a decade earlier. The most stunning recollection of the deal came from a Canadian Breweries vice-president: "Jim was a real loner. . . . Not even Jim Kerr [CB&M president] knew the earnings on the shares. He knew the sales, but not the earnings." The comment was reminiscent of 1849 when F.W. Torrance had written to Alexander Cross, "You must do it all yourself."

Canadian Breweries asked Jim to handle the hotel divestiture, arranging for him to buy his own string in the North-West Territories. Getting rid of the rest proved so difficult that eventually the mortgages were sold through the Alberta-based investment company, Principal Group Limited. Two years later Jim Cross had a falling out with the Taylor group. His son Donald, MBA, University of Western Ontario, returned from his Canadian Brewery position in Toronto, Jim resigned from the board and Cross Brothers Limited sold off all its shares.

The finest Cross hotel today is the twenty-five-acre Hastings House estate on Saltspring Island, British Columbia. A Sussex farmhouse and out-buildings remodelled for historical accuracy and townhouse comfort, it is rated as Canada's sole hotel in the 1983-84 American issue of *Hideaway Report*, a magazine which seeks out the most enchanting small resorts in the world. The oceanside haven with its own livestock encompasses the lifestyles of the original family emigrants, reflective of a rustic Rothney Cottage, a Chateauguay Farm, a sturdy Drynoch and an elegant Pine Avenue.

Mary Cross Dover, born 1905, is known for the toughness and drive of Ernest, the beauty of her mother Nell, the fierceness of her grandmother Mary Drever and the playfulness of James Macleod. As a newlywed, she found life in Ceylon just grand until late 1938. Then, as frequent dinner guest of the Jewish chief justice to India, Sir Sydney Abrahams, she met boatloads of upper-class European Jews escaping the pending holocaust. It appalled Mary and made an indelible impression upon her.

In June 1939 Mel Dover sent Mary, six-year-old son David, and the Canadian nannie home to Alberta on one of the jammed ships. With the subsequent declaration of war, Mary worked for the Red Cross as a corresponding secretary for the Red Triangle Hostess Council and as Calgary chairman for the national registration of Canadian woman. In 1941 she was made commanding officer of Military District 13 in the Canadian Women's Army Corps. Placing David into Appleby School, Ontario, Mary headed for Ottawa.

Over dinner with Vincent Massey, Canadian high commissioner in London, and Victor Sifton, minister of supply, Mary explained that her recruits had no uniforms and some even had holes in their shoes. As always, she inspired rather than cajoled, and soon the illustrious designer, Creed, was assigned to create the famous swing-skirted uniform for the women's force.

In December 1942 Mary was posted overseas with the first contingent of the CWAC. She met with Winston Churchill's daughter Mary, who was serving in the British ATS. A popular base in London was the home of former prime minister, R.B. Bennett. Mary's brother John, a captain in the 14th Calgary Tank Regiment, often visited her, accompanied by a mob of bicycle-riding soldiers.

In November of 1943 Mary was appointed commanding officer of the 12,000-women CWAC camp at Kitchener, Ontario. At a reunion forty years later, none had forgotten the compelling Lieutenant-Colonel Dover. Loved or resented but always respected by her army, Mary imbued her girls with pride in their uniform and in their nation. In 1944 she was transferred to Ottawa in charge of national recruiting for the CWAC. In 1946 she was awarded the Order of the British Empire in recognition of her service.

In 1947 Mary ran unsuccessfully for the Liberals in the provincial elections. Convinced that women should participate more in government, she won a seat on the all-male Calgary city council. Alderman Dover served from 1948-52 and 1957-60, when council rezoned the city to allow for high-rise buildings. One of the issues she fought but lost was the move to save the old Calgary court house where her grandfather, Justice James F. Macleod, had conducted his hearings.

When Mary moved from the Calgary home she had built at 310-37th Avenue West to her present home of Oksi Hill Garden, Midnapore, fifty kilometres southwest of the city, she had ventured outside the city's boundaries and was disqualified from running as an alderman. Nothing has ever annoyed her more than that. When the boundaries were subsequently extended to include Oksi Hill and her new address became RR #8, Calgary, Mary refused to change it. Today, despite a federal postal system fraught with confusion and delays, mailmen faithfully deliver, on time, her letters to the incorrect address. Following her years as alderman, Mary was awarded an honorary doctorate from the University of Calgary.

Particularly loyal to the memory of James Macleod, Mary supports the Steele Scouts, a group which originated in memory of James's sergeant on the 1870 Red River Expedition. Recognized by the Indians for her untiring interest in their welfare, Mary was also adopted into the Blackfoot nation as a princess. She said, "I relate to the Indians . . . [but] I don't relate to causes. The Indians are not a cause. They are there. I was brought up on them."

On December 15, 1976, Mary was appointed a Member in the Order of Canada, one of the country's highest honours. Outside her foothills home a huge Canadian flag billows and snaps in the wind like a pistol shot, or as Mary once put it, as "an outward and visible sign of Canada's invisible pride in nationhood." Although she is Alberta's spokesman for such occasions as the province's seventy-fifth birthday, or an article in *National Geographic* on Calgary, she will use her influence neither to join nor to support women's movements. She is simply her own person, like Helen Rothney marching Judge Adam Thom to his 1843 court and suing him for back wages.

Today Mary Dover, OBE, OC, CM, lives alone on her Midnapore property south of Calgary overlooking the Rocky Mountains. Her beloved garden is not a formal Pine Avenue "upper garden" or a Grand Métis park primed with nutrients and manicured by gardeners. Even water must be trucked in. The plants at Oksi Hill must be tough, indomitable. Mary continued to walk amongst them when she suffered degenerating hips, as if they gleaned from each other a mutual strength. Despite the harsh weather and challenging conditions, wild roses elbow out juniper, last year's daffodil bulbs push through the near frozen earth. The porcupines have eaten many crabapple trees but some have survived and bloom. The parameters of Mary's garden depend upon the whim of the plants. Once discovering a beautiful tree in the wildness, she cleared away the surrounding thickets to include it. And it is not unusual, if arresting, to see her clad in a shirtwaist silk dress, Drever-white hair swept into a chignon, wielding a chain saw over an unruly hedge. In Mary Cross Dover lives the character of the land.

Margaret Victoria "Marmo" Cross, born 1912, possessed the same statuesque figure and steely backbone as her Drever ancestors, and was described throughout her life as one who loved to race with the bit in her teeth. In 1933, aged twenty-one, she swept through Pine Avenue en route to school in Paris, travelling first class on the CPR lines with letters of introduction around the world. She often visited her guardian and mentor, Prime Minister R.B. Bennett, in Ottawa, Calgary or England.

In 1936 Marmo married Vancouver lawyer Jack Shakespeare and moved for a time to Ottawa. Upon returning to Vancouver she proved a lively force behind civic endeavours such as the Vancouver International Festival. When she, too, developed degenerating hips her courage was an inspiration to her friends. Even then Marmo continued riding only high-strung horses like the big grey named "Legend" who threatened to throw her into roadside ditches.

Marmo loved entertaining in elegant if eccentric ways. As her husband's sixtieth birthday coincided with the four hundredth birthday of William Shakespeare, she and their three children threw an Elizabethan masquerade on the grounds of her Vancouver Shaughnessy home. Wandering minstrels plucked bowed psaltries as guests strolled in towering wigs and plunging bodices. One man dyed his underwear green and went as Robin Hood. Two lumber magnates resorted to a whiskey-tossing feud. Held over twenty years ago, it is still considered one of Vancouver's most memorable bashes.

In 1980 Marmo and Jack Shakespeare were driving north through the Okanagan Valley to Alberta for a Cross-Macleod reunion when a southbound car swerved over the meridian and killed them instantly. Their ashes rest on the wildflower-strewn hill on the a7 Ranche called "Daddy's Knoll." The hill was Ernest and Nell's favourite, for on a clear day one can look in all directions over the a7 Ranche and far beyond the Rocky Mountains to horizons waiting to be discovered.

Born to Ernest and Nell in 1914, Alexander Rothney "Sandy" Cross combines the gentleness of Nell with the renegade spirit of Willie Heber. The former CB&M brewmaster is dedicated to breeding excellence in his Luing, Galloway and Shorthorn herds. From the Depression era on, bachelor Sandy cared for Nell in their 8th Avenue home, quietly assisting his Macleod relatives through their schooling. During the lean years for the painter, Nicholas de Grandmaison, he bought dozens of works so that the artist could subsist. Gifts of land and financing from Sandy to the University of Calgary recently resulted in the building of Rothney Astrophysical Observatory in Priddis, Alberta.

During the fifties, sixties and seventies, the fun-loving Sandy was famous throughout the British Isles for his rollicking trips to the bull sales with Marmo. Brother and sister possessed the same electrifying sense of humour. At the age of sixty, the mellowed brewer married, acquiring an immediate family of his widowed wife Ann Abbot and her five adult children.

The couple built an expansive home with huge picture windows in the Midnapore foothills. There de Grandmaison's paintings bring alive the Blackfoot's expressions of angry pride. When visitors raise the time-worn question of the black Scots: "You Crosses are Indian, aren't you?" Sandy delights in showing them a particularly fierce, handsome portrait of Chief Crowfoot, and says, "That's my uncle." Today, Nicholas de Grandmaison portraits and Charlie Russell cowboys survey the foothills and Rocky Mountains where they were first painted. It is a fitting gallery for a proud race and a western heritage. Sandy and Ann named their land Rothney Farm.

John Munklands (or Monklands) Cross, born in 1916 to Ernest and Nell, has expanded the a7 Ranche by several hundred thousand acres, including leased land. It is over thirty miles in length. Braehead, built by Ernest and Nell Cross, is located at the "Home Ranch" to identify it from the five other ranches the a7 encompasses. The others are the McIntosh, the Flying E., the Blacktail, the Gregory, and the spectacular Bob's Creek, fifty miles from Braehead and reaching into the Rocky Mountains. Geographically the a7 Ranche is one of the largest family-owned ranches in Canada; it is also one of the oldest. Although records have not survived, it is believed that the 1,800 odd calves branded each spring are the progeny of Maggie 13th, the purebred Shorthorn who came west with Ernest and Edmund in 1886 and survived the terrible winter of 1886-87 tied to the side of their sod shack.

The three-storey, seven-bedroom Braehead is spruced up with an indoor swimming pool added on the south side, and it is minus the rambling porch on which Sam Steele and Billie Cochrane sat in 1911, but it is essentially unchanged. In the spacious dining room a towering mahogany cabinet from the Macleods, Isle of Skye, stands against one wall. On a northern hill behind the house the springs to which Willie Heber stormed in 1891 still supply water by gravity. When the water level swells in the May runoff, the overflow pours into the third-floor bathtub and down the drains. One rainy day in 1962, when John and Eleanor were in Calgary preparing for a United Nations Staff Force reception at Braehead, their cat hopped onto the side of the tub, pirouetted over the soap dish and kicked the plug directly into the drain. The rain-swollen springs filled the tub, overflowed and flooded the house. Nature still reigns supreme.

During World War II, John served as a captain in the third wave of troops heading for Dieppe. The contingency was ordered to turn back as it approached the beach. Apart from that time in his life, he has ranched in Alberta. A carbon copy of his father in appearance, and the family historian, John is known internationally for his contributions to the cattle world. His speeches, made over three decades, were almost as short as those of Jim, who carried a stop watch, but they are also memorable for their humour – unless he was speaking on government-proposed beef marketing boards.

Married to Eleanor Leggat of Montreal, John combines the spontaneity of his Macleod heritage with the ranching know-how of the Crosses. The John Crosses and their four grown children still rise before dawn to look after the soil and grasslands as meticulously as they tend their herds. They run the a7 Ranche to turn-of-the-century rhythms, with cattle mainly foraging throughout the winter and field breeding in the spring. These customs rendered the a7 Ranche almost anachronistic during Alberta's last oil boom, when executive ranchers invaded breeding programs and feeder lots with artificial insemination and sophisticated computers. But as faithful stewards to the land, the John Crosses knew that long after the oil ran dry and yet another boom time crashed, the a7 Ranche would remain and flourish. The only threat to their survival is the weather. The 1985 drought has been so drastic that Ernest's turn-of-the-century prediction looms real: "If the grass goes, we go."

Both the fifth and sixth generations of the Cross family are fascinated by the constancy and solidarity of their heritage. They are educated in western private schools and in universities in British Columbia, Alberta, Ontario and Quebec. In the youthful sixth generation, some will run the a7 Ranche and some the family enterprises. Others are heading for careers in business administration, oil exploration, communications, veterinary science. Some have travelled widely, one vagabonded around the world, all are ranch-oriented: "Just living out here you have a lot of time to think." They believe in the responsibility of effecting change through community participation, and the young women are intrigued with the idea of becoming the first woman president of the Stampede, or a premier of Alberta or, for that matter, a prime minister of Canada.

Their visions are not generated from a privileged core but rather from a sense of duty. In seizing their heritage as a challenge, one young Cross cautions, "I don't feel any pressure from my family. It's more a spirit of my ancestry. Whatever I do, I'll do it my way."

Notes

As the narrative of *Braehead* is comprised largely from letters at present inaccessible in private collections, I have acknowledged available sources only. To foonote every unavailable source would be pointlessly tedious even for the most academic reader.

The published sources are recorded in a manner which I hope will be acceptable to historical institutions, authors and scholars, while keeping the text clean as a narrative for the general reader. This method also avoids, for example, documenting every one of the 1,100 letters of Martin Macleod, or the thousands of letters in the CB&M file, Glenbow-Alberta Institute, Alberta.

CHAPTER ONE: 1820-1849

On Lanarkshire, 1595-1800: Mort, *Lanarkshire; Merchant House of Glasgow* pp. 257, 554, 593. On Montreal: Jenkins, *Montreal, Island City of the St. Lawrence; Montreal Herald*, 26 Sept. 1826. On Chateauguay: Sellar, *History of the County of Huntingdon and the seigniories of Chateauguay and Beauharnois*, Cross family on pp. 149, 103, 250, 311, 341, 536; Janet's claim that Lord Selkirk (a Douglas) was an uncle remains unverified. On Lower Canada rebellions: Wade, *The French Canadians*, vol. 1, pp. 155, 188, 202-203. On Adam Thom: Stubbs (who believed that the Durham *Report* was vintage Thom), *Four Recorders of Rupert's Land; Camillus* was found in Special Collections, UBC. On the burning of the Parliament Buildings: *Montreal Gazette* 27 Apr. 1849, 2 May 1849, *Montreal Witness*, 30 Apr. 1849, *Montreal Transcript*, 1 May, 1849, Monet, *The Last Cannon Shot*, pp. 336-39. Biographies on Alexander Cross can be found in: *A Caeclopaedia of Canadian Biography*, or a *Canadian Biographical Dictionary*, Vol. IX, p. 10; *Le Centenniel du barreau de Montréal 1849*, p. 77; *Les Judges de la province de Québec*, p. 137.

CHAPTER TWO: 1821-1849

William Drever's personnel papers: HBCA/MA: C.1/794, B239/g/4-18, 235/d/79-10, B239/a/151 (6 July 1839); Drever's tastes in reading: *The Beaver*, Spring 1983, p. 52. Sound travelling sixty miles in Fort Churchill: Bishop Pinkham memoirs, Glenbow-Alberta Institute. J.J. Hargrave's York Factory report: University of British Columbia Special Collections. Helen Rothney in Insch: Lewis, *A Topographical Dictionary of Scotland*, 1846, vol. 1, pp. 563-64. Thom arrives via New York: Stubbs, *Four Recorders of Rupert's Land*, p. 9, also used extensively for profile of Adam Thom. Observations on the Red River Settlement: Ross, *The Red River Settlement*, pp. 235, 239. Also Hargrave, *Red River*, and Macleod, *Letters of Letitia Hargrave*, p. 146. The letter from Hargrave to her mother on Helen Rothney and Adam Thom, 10 Apr. 1843, is with the Law Society of Manitoba. Drever birthdates: some incorrect on the original records of St. James Church, Winnipeg. William and Helen Drever's early life: Memoirs of Jean Drever Pinkham, Cathedral Holy Church of the Redeemer, Calgary. In 1965, author Catherine Philip interviewed the surviving progeny of Helen Rothney Drever. She combined her material with the memoirs of Jean Drever Pinkham and Bishop Cyprian Pinkham to publish "The Crosses of Alberta," *Chatelaine*, June, July, August, 1965; this work has been most helpful to this chapter. Adam Thom *v.* Helen Rothney: Manitoba Archives, MG2, B4-6, 21 Feb. 1843. The Oregon Treaty: American fur smuggling was escalating to a war with Britain; a battle was averted when Britain forced a furious George Simpson to relinquish the Hudson's Bay Company-owned lands of Oregon, in return for the Americans recognizing the 49th parallel with a southern dip around Vancouver Island. Settlement conditions and the trial of G. Sayer: Ross, *Red River Settlement*, pp. 192-193; pp. 343-351, 364-365, 372-377; also *Winnipeg Free Press*, Feb. 1884.

CHAPTER THREE: 1837-1849

Captain Martin Macleod's letterbooks at the Metropolitan Toronto Public Library contain 1,100 letters to his friends and relatives from 1832-1860. Also used: the unpublished memoirs of Martin's daughter, Maggie Macleod Baldwin, private collection. The *Albion*: Mitchell Library, North Street, Glasgow. On Martin Macleod and Drynoch, Upper Canada: Scadding, *Toronto of Old*, pp. 466-67; Grant, *The Macleods, A History of a Clan*, p. 585; "St. John's Anglican Church, Jefferson." Map of Macleod/Robinson/Baldwin lands: Berchem, *Yonge Street Story*, p. 170.

CHAPTER FOUR: 1850-1869

Alexander Cross and William Lunn papers, private collection. G. Harry Cross memoirs, University of Wyoming, Western History Research Centre. Interviews with octogenarian grandchildren of Alexander and Julia Cross. Advertisement for the Pine Avenue estate: *Centennial Gazette*, 26 Aug. 1867. On Montreal and the politics of the era: Jenkins, *Montreal*; Wade, *The French Canadians*, vol. 1, pp. 276-327; Waite, *Arduous Destiny*.

CHAPTER FIVE: 1850-1869

James's military dispute with Colonel Jackson is found in the State and Military Records, Public Archives of Canada, RG 9, ICI, vol. 152, no. 453; vol. 154, no. 749; vol. 155, no. 856; vol. 155, no. 855; vol. 155, nos.

876, 880, 881, 884; vol. 156, nos. 900, 902, 932, 959; vol. 283, pp. 193-95, pp. 206-207. The letters of Martin Macleod: Metropolitan Toronto Public Library, Canadian History Department; Upper Canada College records; Professor George, "Notes, 1853-1854," Douglas Library, Queen's College, 1853-54; "Queen's College 1851-1852." James's service with the Oak Ridges Cavalry: Sister Annette, *Salute to Canada*, Part III, chapter 6.

CHAPTER SIX: 1850-1868

All undocumented quotes come from the memoirs of Jean Drever Pinkham. Philip, "The Crosses of Alberta," *Chatelaine*, June, July, August, 1965, provided a helpful overview to the chapter. William Drever's personnel files in the Hudson's Bay Company Records, Manitoba Archives: E/6/2/ff50, and his land: ibid., A,E6/2/ff50; General Quarterly Court, 21 Feb. 1867; William's land: Martin, *Hudson's Bay Company Land Tenures* ..., pp. 115, 122; F.W. Morton, *History of the Canadian West*, p. 654. On Sir George Simpson's friendship with Adam Thom, even his two-volume *Journey Round the World* is thought to have been ghost-written by Thom. On the flood: Ross, *Red River Settlement*, pp. 412-16. Thom's departure: Stubbs, *Four Recorders of Rupert's Land*, pp. 40-43. On Sioux to Red River: Jean Drever Pinkham memoirs; Turner, vol. 1, pp. 19-22; Hargrave, *Red River*, pp. 316-320. Christin Drever remembers: *The Albertan*, 5 Dec. 1944. On Portage and Main: Werier, *Winnipeg Tribune*, 29 Oct. 1971; Hargrave, *Red River*, pp. 310-11; Reynolds, "The Man Who Created Portage and Main," pp. 10-18. Drever's plea: "Can the Company ...," ibid., p. 15. On locusts and tornado: Hargrave, *Red River*, pp. 349-40. On the famine: Gunn, *History of Manitoba*, p. 234. On Trinity Church, *Sixty Years and After*, p. 109.

CHAPTER SEVEN: 1869-1870

The most thorough account of the Drevers' involvement in the Red River Rebellion comes from W.L. Morton, *Begg's Red River Journal and Other Papers*, pp. 192, 218, 226, 249, 256, 281, 306, 314-15, 328, 391, 436. On Charles Mair and John Schultz: Hargrave, *Red River*, pp. 450-52, 455; Reynolds, "The Man Who Created Portage and Main," p. 24; Stubbs, *Four Recorders of Rupert's Land*, p. 171. More on the rebellion: Christin Drever interview: *Calgary Herald*, 5 Dec. 1944; taking the fort and descriptions of the jail: Gunn, *Manitoba*, p. 352; the journal of A.W. Graham, Manitoba Archives, MG3-B10; on governor-elect MacDougall in Pembina, Mair's imprisonment and his escape with Willie Drever: Shrive, *Charles Mair, Literary Nationalist*. On the shooting of Thomas Scott: W.L. Morton, *Begg's Red River Journal and Other Papers*; also Graham and Christin Drever's interview. On Red River conditions: *The British Whig*, 16 Mar., 9 and 23 Apr. 1870, Queen's University, Douglas Library, 9/470. Sir John A. Macdonald letters to James Macleod: Public Archives of Canada, MG 26, A, vol. 516, pt. 3, Reel C, 28,13,550; vol. 573, LB 13. Macdonald's "half castes": Wade,

The French Canadians, p. 396. On Willie Drever to Toronto and Ottawa: Gunn, *Manitoba*, pp. 424-25. Wolseley letters: Glenbow-Alberta Institute, A.W867A. On Wolseley's expedition: James Macleod's commission, Public Archives of Canada, RG 9, II, A31; Irvine, University of British Columbia microfilm, no. 365; Gunn, *Manitoba*, pp. 441-53; the Willie Drever and Butler saga: Butler, *Great Lone Land*, pp. 113, 115-36 *passim*; McCourt, *Remember Butler*, pp. 46-48; Mary's message to Ottawa, ibid., p. 49; A.S. Morton, *History of the Canadian West*, p. 391; also interview with Mary Drever Macleod, *Calgary Herald*, 1923. On James Macleod and the "Bummer": Sam Steele speech, Glenbow-Alberta Institute, A. M165A, ff.11; also Steele, *Forty Years in Canada*, pp. 14, 22, 26-27. On liberation day: *Winnipeg Tribune*, Public Archives Canada, RG 18, vol. 3436; *Manitoba News Letter*, 13 Sept. 1870. "Men well led": Steele, *Forty Years in Canada*, p. 31. Wolseley's farewell speech: Steele, ibid., p. 36. On James Macleod's return to Ontario: Turner, *North West Mounted Police 1873-1893*, vol. 1, p. 67. On Butler to Saskatchewan: ibid., p. 69-70.

CHAPTER EIGHT: 1872-1880

The Montreal segment is built from Alexander Cross's papers presently held in a private collection, Aylmer, Quebec. Harry's story and the Colorado section is a condensation of Harry's memoirs written by his daughter, Emma Morton. A copy can be found at the University of Wyoming, Western History Research Centre. On Haileybury: the diary of E. ffolkes, UBC Special Collections.

CHAPTER NINE: 1872-1875

On the Drevers' loss and recompense: Sessional Papers, 35 Vic., 19A, 1872. On the NWMP trek: the reports of James Macleod and of the NWMP veterinary surgeons, published by Coles by respective year, were used extensively; the 1874 diary of Colonel French can be found in the Higgenbotham Collection, Glenbow-Alberta Institute, B1.7, H817. Letters from James Macleod to Mary Drever in the Glenbow-Alberta Institute: 10 July 1874, 28 Sept. 1874, 21 Apr. 1875; Turner, *North West Mounted Police*, vol. 1 (a work written with the help of the NWMP reports), particularly on the Sioux entry to the Red River, J. Schultz in the House of Commons (p. 83), the Cypress Hills Massacre (pp. 22-27), on French and Macleod hiring Willie Drever, pp. 113-14, and the NWMP trek west (pp. 120-98). Correspondence between Sir Alexander Campbell and James Macleod: Ontario Archives, MU471, 8 July 1872, 23 Sept. 1872. On Christin Drever and Judge Johnston: *Calgary Herald*, 5 Dec. 1944. James's summons from Sir John A. Macdonald while on the Isle of Mull: Mackenzie to Richardson, 21 June 1928, A.E. Cross papers, Glenbow-Alberta Institute, M289. The story of James's return to Winnipeg and other events in the life of Mary Drever were supplemented with Philip, "The Crosses of Alberta," *Chatelaine*. The Carscaden memoirs:

Glenbow-Alberta Institute, presently uncatalogued. Colonel French to minister of justice: Public Archives of Canada, 15/5/74193. James to government, "It is quite unnecessary ...": Macleod service file, RG 18, vol. 3436, reg. no. 04; Life in Fort Macleod: Nevitt, *A Winter at Fort Macleod*, p. 58; Turner, *North West Mounted Police*, p. 102. On James's trek to Helena for the payroll: Glenbow-Alberta Institute: James to Mary, 21 Apr. 1875, 12pp; Denny, *The Law Marches West*, p. 67. "Colonel Macleod is the best ..." S.J. Clarke memoirs, Glenbow-Alberta Institute. On the Helena extradition: Turner, *North West Mounted Police*, pp. 228-35; *Helena Weekly Herald*, 29 July 1875; *Hill County Democrat*, 20 Aug. 1926; *Helena Independent*, 18 Nov. 1886, pp. 2-5. French to minister of justice re competency of Brisebois and others: Public Archives of Canada, RG 18, vol. 3, 48a-75. Colonel Selby-Smyth's 1875 report: *Chronicle of the Canadian West*, Historical Society of Alberta, 1975, p. 31.

On Brisebois and Fort Calgary: Dempsey, *Frontier Calgary*, pp. 28-40.

CHAPTER TEN: 1875-1879

I have relied generally on the NWMP reports of James Macleod and Colonel French, reprinted in "Opening Up the West, 1874-1881," Coles Canadiana Collection; also on several hundred letters from James to Mary still in a private collection; and on Turner, *North West Mounted Police*, vol. 1, corresponding years. On Mary's life, conditions in the officers' mess, Bad Boy, the honeymoon, the subsequent trip to Ottawa, and "Auntie": quoted from Philip, "The Crosses of Alberta," *Chatelaine*, June 1965; also interviews in 1981 with Mrs. Norman Macleod, daughter-in-law of James and Mary Macleod. James thanked in House of Commons: Turner, *North West Mounted Police*, p. 253. The Macleod wedding: *Manitoba Free Press*, 3 Aug. 1876. On Stuttaford: James to Mary, Glenbow-Alberta Institute, 29 July 1878. On Treaty No. 7: MacGregor, *Senator Hardisty's Prairies*, 1840-1889, pp. 131-49; Turner, *North West Mounted Police*, pp. 344-57; Speech of James to Blackfoot: Coles NWMP *Reports*, 1877, p. 49-52; Norman Macleod, address to the Historical Society of Alberta: Glenbow-Alberta Institute, 7 Nov. 1958; Mary Macleod speaking on the treaty: Glenbow-Alberta Institute; Price, "Pioneer Interviews," p. 2, A.P94, ff2. Steele on James, "I doubt if anyone ..." *Forty Years in Canada*, p. 115. On James and Walsh: James to Mary, some private, one other: Glenbow-Alberta Institute, 29 July 1878. *New York Times* articles: 5 July 1877, 25 Oct. 1877, p. 2, includes letter of James Macleod to the secretaries of war and of the interior, Washington, 20 Oct. 1877. Reports of the Sitting Bull Indian Commission, Public Archives of Canada, RG 7-G21, vol. 318, f2001, pt.3a. On the starving Indians: James to Mary, Aug. 1879, Glenbow-Alberta Institute. On NWMP costs: French to Irvine, Public Archives of Canada, RG 18, vol. 3437, personnel No. 0-30; Sessional Papers, vol. 13, no. 2, 1880, and vol. 14, no. 1, 1880-81.

Sir John A. Macdonald to James: Public Archives of Canada, 23 June 1879, MG 26A 1(e), vol. 524, pp. 291-94; Macleod to Macdonald: MG 26A, vol. 361, Reel C, 1747, 167099, 11 pp.

CHAPTER ELEVEN: 1876-1885

Harry Cross's memoirs written by Emma Morton, combined with Alexander Cross's papers, form the basis for this chapter. On headmaster John Mills: Briggs, "A career of eminent service in education and agriculture in spite of a serious handicap and many discouraging circumstances: a few facts gleaned from the life and career of James Mills, M.A., LLD," p. 12. On the Ontario Agricultural College: *Annual Report, 1880 and 1881*. On A.E. Cross, gentleman immigrant: Dunae, *Gentlemen Emigrants*, pp. 196-97. ffolkes's diary: University of British Columbia Special Collections; also, "An Emigrant at OAC," *Guelph Alumnus*, vol. iv, 1974. On the Montreal Veterinary College, Dr. Duncan McEachran, and the British American Horse Ranche: Vokaty, "Adventures of Dr. Duncan McNab McEachran in Western Canada," pp. 149-56; also "Canadian Gazette 1881," Jan.-June, vol. 14, no. 45, p. 1564; Turner, *North West Mounted Police*, p. 539. Ernest and Osler: A.E. Cross, speech to the Calgary Historical Society, 23 Oct. 1925. On Wyoming: Huntington-Smith, *War on Powder River*, was invaluable, specifically pp. 15, 22-28; the Cheyenne Club: ibid., p. 12. The tone of Calgary in 1884 is drawn from Dunae, *Gentlemen Emigrants*; *Calgary Herald*, 30 Apr. 1884 (including McEachran's "easy winters"), 12 Nov. 1884. Calgary the "Chicago of the West": *Calgary Herald*, 21 March 1884; L.G. Thomas, "The Rancher and the City," Transactions of the Royal Society of Canada, vol. VI, pp. 206-209. On the Cochrane ranch: A.E. Cross, *Calgary Herald*, 23 Oct. 1925; D.E. Brown, *A History of the Cochrane Area*; Roberts, "The Cochrane Ranch," *Canadian Cattlemen*, vol. 18, no. 3, March 1955; also April 1955, vol. 18, no. 4, p. 18. On Ernest Cross's fascination with the foothills: Calgary Historical Society speech published in the *Calgary Daily Herald*, 22 Dec. 1923. (His original draft remains in a private collection.)

CHAPTER TWELVE: 1880-1888

This chapter was built from the letters of James to Mary Macleod. Unless stated, they (and other letters such as some of Norman Macleod's) remain in private collections. Others from James to Mary in the Glenbow-Alberta Institute on the starving Indians: 29 May 1880, 3 June 1880. Turner, *North West Mounted Police*, continued to provide much information on the West. James's appointment to stipendiary magistrate: Public Archives of Canada, RG 15, vol. 138, ff199. James to Sir John A. Macdonald re Norman: ibid., MG 26A, vol. 210, Reel C1596, 89764. Dewdney to Macdonald re Norman: ibid., MG26A, vol. 211, pp. 89756-770; James to Dewdney re Norman: ibid., MG 26A, vol. 211, pp. 89756-64. The quote on James's character, p. 219, was anonymous, published in the RCMP *Quarterly*, April 1934. On Lord Lorne to the West and life in Fort Macleod: family history, J.P. Turner, pp. 596-97; Coles, "Opening Up the West, 1882", pp. 6-7; on James, Turkey Legs, and the Macleods' party with the Indian princess: quoted from Philip, "The Crosses of Alberta," *Chatelaine*. On Cyprian Pinkham and John McKay: Carrington, *The Anglican Church in Canada*, pp. 162, 185-86, 227, 248, 264. On 1885 Rebellion: James to Mary, Glenbow-Alberta Institute, 17 Nov. 1885; Wade, *French Canadians*, pp. 409-15; Dewdney to Sir John A. Macdonald re Riel's sanity and, "I am glad Macleod was here ...": Pope, *Correspondence of Sir John A. Macdonald*, pp. 365-66. On the Indians' grievances: "Judge Macleod runs this ... country ...": Public Archives of Canada, RG 18, vol. 19, ff249-1888. *The Pentaglot* from Adam Thom, Jean Drever Pinkham memoirs. The reference to "the future bench": L.H. Thomas, *Struggle for Responsible Government in the North-West Territories*, p. 111: "The office of stipendiary magistrate was abolished in 1886 to make way for the supreme court of the NWT 18 Feb. 1887." On first NWT elected assembly: ibid., p. 149.

CHAPTER THIRTEEN: 1886-1887

The Wyoming story comes from the memoirs of Harry Cross and from Huntington-Smith, *War on Powder River*, particularly pp. 31, 38, 44. The Alberta story comes from letters in private collections, and the subsequent roundup from Ernest's speech: Calgary Historical Society, 23 Oct. 1925, and *Calgary Daily Herald*, 22 Dec. 1923. The story of Lincoln School comes from the papers of Alexander Cross and from *Le Sud*, 24 Oct. 1888. The Latin translation of the Crosses tombstone was given by Professor D.J. Guth, University of British Columbia, faculty of law. The Charlie Russell sketch: McCracken, *The Charles M. Russell Book*, p. 217.

CHAPTER FOURTEEN: 1888-1893

Family oral history played a major role from this point on. I have included Harry Cross's story of the Johnson County Massacre because it is an historical incident of renown in the United States. It is supplemented with Huntington-Smith, *War on Powder River*. On Calgary trivia: "Hot hairpins in bottles": MacEwan, *Calgary Cavalcade*, p. 186. On Ernest Cross's move into industry: his extensive letterbooks remain in private collections. However, the A.E. Cross papers, Glenbow-Alberta Institute, M289, were also used to build this and subsequent chapters. Those available in the Glenbow can be found arranged by corresponding year. On early ranching in Alberta and the High River Stockgrowers' Association, I found Kelly, *The Rangemen*, most helpful in substantiating source material in the private collections. The index for Kelly's book, developed by the Glenbow-Alberta Institute, was invaluable. On the Stockgrowers' Association of Alberta: Johnston, *Cowboy Politics*, p. 242. Correspondence between Ernest, Alexander Cross, Hiram Walker and the CPR on his progress in the brewery can be found in the files of A.E. Cross and the Calgary Brewing & Malting Company, Glenbow-Alberta Institute. On the whiskey traders: Gray, *Booze*. On land exemptions: Foran, *Calgary: An Illustrated History*, pp. 32, 33. On the date of the CB&M's first brewing: most historical accounts list it as 1892. However, while the first meeting was held in 1892, the actual distribution of the first green beer occurred on St. Patrick's Day, 1893. See CB&M files, Box 1, ff1-8, Glenbow-Alberta Institute.

CHAPTER FIFTEEN: 1892-1895

This chapter was built from the letters of James to Mary, private collection. Also used: Jean Drever Pinkham memoirs, particularly re the Calgary hospital (pp. 36-37); Philip, "The Crosses of Alberta," *Chatelaine*, and an interview, *Calgary Herald*, 18 Nov. 1933, with Jean Pinkham (includes the mignonette green gown story). On Mary's personality: Price, *Pioneer Interviews*, p. 94. Letters between Mary and Mrs. Inderwick: Glenbow-Alberta Institute, A.138, 9 Apr. 1889, 2 Jan. 1890, 3 Dec. 1891. Also on Inderwick, "A Lady and her Ranch," *The Best from Alberta History*, pp. 65-77. On the fight to keep James Macleod from moving to Calgary: *Macleod Gazette*: 12 June 1892, 11 May 1894. The petition ". . . and 146 others": Glenbow-Alberta Institute, M289. On the funeral of James Macleod: *Winnipeg Free Press*, Sept. 1895. "As a soldier . . .": Steele, *Forty Years in Canada*, pp. 275-76. Governor's general petition: Public Archives of Canada, RG 18, vol. 3436.

CHAPTER SIXTEEN: 1892-1895

Private collections plus the Glenbow-Alberta Institute files of A.E. Cross and the CB&M. The material can be researched in chronological order. On the ffolkes case: A.E. Cross papers, Glenbow-Alberta Institute, A.C. 951-ff88. On Alexander Cross's retirement from the bench: *Montreal Star*, Nov. 1891.On death of Alexander Cross: *Montreal Star*, Sept. 1894.

CHAPTER SEVENTEEN: 1896-1901

Although much of this chapter was built from the letterbooks of A.E. Cross and other material in private collections, it was largely expanded through the source material at the Glenbow-Alberta Institute which mushroomed one-hundred-fold. Information can be found in the CB&M and A.E. Cross files by researching in chronological order. The memoirs of Jean Drever Pinkham and the articles by Philip continued to be of help, as did family oral history. Ernest's article on Hawaii appeared in the *Winnipeg Free Press*, 1897. Ernest to Sir Wilfrid Laurier, a personal note, Public Archives of Canada, Laurier Papers, M626G. On Ernest in politics: his candidacy, *Calgary Herald*, 21 Sept. 1899; the campaign speeches, ibid., 19 Oct. 1899; the results and the subsequent street party, ibid., 14 Nov. 1899. On the debates and speeches, Legislative Assembly, Regina: *Regina Leader*, 13 Apr. 1899.

CHAPTER EIGHTEEN, 1902-1903

Harry Brayne related his own story. The manuscript of historian David Breen, *The Canadian West and the Ranching Frontier, 1875-1922*, was only partially available to me at the time of researching this book, and was used only as a correlating overview. Ernest's House bills: *Regina Leader*, 24 Apr. 1900, 26 Apr. 1900, 10 May 1900, 10 Nov. 1900. On the visit of Lieutenant-Governor Forget: *Calgary Herald*, 24, 30 May 1901; also MacEwan, *Calgary Cavalcade*, pp. 90-91. On the Calgary picnic: *Calgary Herald*, 30 Aug. 1901. On the visit of Duke and Duchess: ibid., 29 Sept. 1901. "Loyalty to crown": ibid., 30 Sept. 1901. Ernest's polo accident and the last great buffalo hunt are stories told by Ernest's sons. No one remembered the exact dates; thus I have taken literary licence for the dates only. On Ottawa treating the West in a "cavalier fashion": *Regina Leader*, 24 Apr. 1902. On Ernest's speech on the division of the provinces: *Regina Leader*, 8 May 1902.

CHAPTER NINETEEN: 1903-1909

This chapter was built with the help of letters and documents from several Cross collections, but the source material in the Glenbow archives, particularly the CB&M and the A.E. Cross files, was significant. The work of Jean Drever Pinkham and of Philip continued to be useful. Harry Brayne stayed with Ernest during the night-long vigil for the diphtheria toxin and the death of his children, also noted in *Calgary Herald*, 26 Sept. 1904. On Bob Edward and "the beer atrocity," *Eye Opener*, 22 Feb. 1907. On Ernest's personal notes to Lougheed re the railroad bonds: for a broader explanation see *Calgary Herald*, 4 June 1908.

CHAPTER TWENTY: 1910-1913

As well as the documentation from the Glenbow-Alberta Institute mentioned in chapter nineteen, the letters written by Nell to Ernest grew into the hundreds during this period. Held in a private collection, they are still filled with the exquisite flowers of the British Columbia coast. On statistics on Alberta's growth and Calgary Petroleum Products: *Frontier Calgary*, Voisey, pp. 238-39. On Nell and the cow: *Calgary Herald*, 1953. On the Pinkhams' trip to the coronation: Jean Drever Pinkham's memoirs, and interviews with her granddaughter, N. Walton, Vancouver. On Mary Macleod: interviews with her grandchildren, and Philip, "The Crosses of Alberta," *Chatelaine*.

CHAPTER TWENTY-ONE: 1914-1919

Generally, private sources plus the files of the CB&M and of A.E. Cross, Glenbow-Alberta Institute. On the oil strike in Turner Valley: *Canadian Annual Review*, pp. 673-76. Aunt Emma Lunn died in July 1916; she had left everything to Selkirk and Lorne Campbell (son of Dean George and Margaret Campbell), both of whom predeceased her. Selkirk's obituary was published in the *Montreal Evening News*, 29 Dec. 1915. On Jean Pinkham and R.B. Bennett forming the Red Cross: Philip, "The Crosses of Alberta," *Chatelaine*. On family members who went to war, including the students from Bishop Pinkham College, Coats, *Frontier Calgary*, p. 148. On prohibition and the druggists: *Canadian Annual Review*, pp. 800-801. On the war ending and the Winnipeg strike: *Globe and Mail*, 20 Feb. 1981. On Uplands, Victoria: a Winnipeg syndicate first invested in Uplands, followed by the Franco Canadian Company of Montreal. Willie Heber Cross's association was with the latter, and for his efforts the Crosses were exempted from paying property taxes as long as they owned Val Rose. Victoria's reaction to the French Crosses comes from interviews with octogenarians and relatives in 1983.

CHAPTER TWENTY-TWO: 1920-1924

A great deal of this chapter was built from interviews with Victorians who remember vividly the 1920s and the Cross families. Boxes of the original papers of Royalite and Imperial Oil, uncatalogued, were found in the main offices of Gulf Canada, Adelaide Street, Toronto. Ernest's letter to Prime Minister Meighen, "(don't give) natural resources to the public": 11 Nov. 1920, Glenbow-Alberta Institute, CB&M file, 1920. Royalite first dividend: *Calgary Herald*, 18 Nov. 1933. Ernest's speech: ibid., 22 Dec. 1923. The clown story about Mary Cross Dover and Jim Cross was published in Gilkes, *Canadian Golden West*, "Call her M'am." On the diamond brooches from the Last Spike: the estate of Lady Northcote (Lord Mount Stephen's daughter) to Captain Bruce Reford, 12 June 1934; *Montreal Gazette*, 22 Oct. 1958; *Saturday Night*, 14 Feb. 1959.

TWENTY-THREE: 1925-1928

On the Victoria scene: interviews with Dolby Gore-Langton Turner, Willie Cross's sister-in-law. On Mary Macleod and the Treaty No. 7 celebrations: Price, Glenbow-Alberta Institute, A.p94, ff2, p. 1. On Mary Macleod as an elderly lady, oral history, and Philip, "The Crosses of Alberta," *Chatelaine*. On the Banff winter carnival: newspapers from Winnipeg and points west during the first two weeks of February 1927. "His Destiny" can be found in the Glenbow-Alberta Institute, with difficulty.

TWENTY-FOUR: 1929-1932

The Glenbow-Alberta Institute files of A.E. Cross and the CB&M continued to be motherlodes supplementing the private collections of letters and documents. On Mary Cross Dover's yellow car in India: *Calgary Herald*, 18 Oct. 1976, p. 7. The film *Tabu* is found in the Hollywood Archives, Los Angeles. On Willie's triumphant arrival at the Saanich Airport, Victoria: *Daily*

Colonist, 24 Feb. 1932. The last days of Ernest Cross were described by his children. The description of the Chateauguay farm comes from my own visit.

EPILOGUE: 1932-1985

Philip, "The Crosses of Alberta," *Chatelaine*, and oral history. Edmund's story came from his children. In Victoria, octogenarians and nonogenarians joined with relatives to spend a candid summer reminiscing about the Willie Heber Crosses and the 1920s. With the exception of Pine Avenue and Rothney Cottage, the homes written about in the book can be seen today across the country. The Bohemian Maid battle between Jim Cross and E.P. Taylor was recorded in *Time*, 21 July 1952. On Mary Cross Dover in India and her subsequent involvements: interviews, 1981; also *National Geographic*: "Calgary: Canada's Not-So-Wild-West," March 1984, photo of Mary Cross Dover, p. 397.

Bibliography

PUBLISHED WORKS

Acheson, T.W. *Canadian Business History, The Social Origins of the Canadian Industrial Elite, 1880-85*. Toronto: McClelland and Stewart, 1972.

Annette, Sister Mary. *Salute to Canada*. Canadian Student Yearbooks, Winnipeg.

Beaverbrook, Lord. *Friends*. London: Heineman, 1959.

Begg, Alexander. *The Creation of Manitoba 1839-1897 or, a history of the Red River troubles*. Toronto: A.H. Hovey, 1871.

_____ . *The Great Canadian North West: its past, history of present conditions and glorious prospects*. Montreal: J. Lovel & Son, 1881

_____ . *Red River Journal and other papers relative to the Red River resistance of 1869-1870*. Edited and introduced by W.L. Morton. Toronto: Champlain Society, 1956.

Bennett, Russell H. *The Compleat Rancher*. Minneapolis: Denison & Co., 1946.

Benson, L.R. "An O.A.C. Student in the 1880's," *Ontario History*, XLII, no. 2, 1950.

Berchem, F.R. *The Yonge Street Story*. Toronto: McGraw-Hill Ryerson, 1977.

Beullac, Pierre, & Surveyer, E. Fabre. *Le Centenaire du Barreau du Montréal*. Montreal: Ducharme, 1949.

Biggar, Emerson Briston. *Canada: A Memorial Volume*. Montreal: Biggar, 1889.

Boam, H. *British Columbia, Its History, People, Commerce, Industries and Resources*. 1912.

Boon, T.C.B. *The Anglican Church from the Bay to the Rockies*. Toronto: Ryerson Press, 1962.

Bosworth, Newton. *Hochelaga depicta – the early history and present state of the city and island of Montreal*. Montreal: W. Grieg, 1839.

Brown, Dee Alexander. *The Fetterman Massacre*. London: Barrie, 1972.

Butler, Sir William Francis. *The Great Lone Land, a tale of travel and adventure in the North-West of America*. London: Gilbert & Rivington, 1872.

Canadian Annual Review of Public Affairs, vols. 1-35: 1901-1938. Toronto: The Canadian Review Company, 1960.

Carrington, P. *The Anglican Church in Canada*. Toronto: Collins, 1963.

Cartwright, Sir Richard. *Reminiscences*. Toronto: William Briggs, 1912.

Chambers, Ernest John. *The Royal Northwest Mounted Police: A Corps History.* Montreal: Mortimer Press, 1906.

Collard, Edward Andrew. *Call Back Yesterdays.* Don Mills, Ontario: Longmans Canada, 1965.

———. *Montreal: The Days That Are No More.* Toronto: Doubleday Canada, 1976.

Cross, A.E. "The Roundup of 1887," *Alberta Historical Review,* vol. 13, 1965. Address first given to the Calgary Historical Society, 1923; original rough copy remains in a private collection.

Creighton, Donald. *Canada's First Century 1867-1967.* Toronto: Macmillan, 1970.

Dempsey, Hugh A., ed. *The Best from Alberta History.* Saskatoon: Western Producer Prairie Books, 1981.

———. *Crowfoot, Chief of the Blackfeet.* Norman: University of Oklahoma Press, 1972.

———. *Men in Scarlet.* Calgary: Historical Society of Alberta and McClelland and Stewart West, 1974.

Dictionary of Canadian Biography, vol. IX, 1861-1870; vol. X, 1871-1880.

Denny, Sir Cecil Edward. Edited by W.B. Cameron. *The Law Marches West.* Toronto: J.M. Dent & Sons (Canada), 1939.

Dent, John Charles. *The Last Forty Years: Canada since the union of 1841.* 2 vols. Edited by G. Virtue. 1881.

Donkin, John G. *Trooper and Redskin in the Far Northwest, 1889.* Toronto: Coles Canadiana Collection, 1973.

Dunae, Patrick A. *Gentlemen Emigrants,* Vancouver: Douglas & McIntyre, 1981.

Duncan, J. ed. *Red Serge Wives.* Centennial Book Committee, 1974.

Elgin-Grey Papers, 1846-1852. Edited with notes by Sir Arthur G. Doughty. 4 vols. Ottawa: Secretary of State, 1937.

Elliott, A.D. (Peter). *Fifty Years.* Edmonton: Alberta Liquor Control Board, 1975.

ffolkes, Edward. *Letters from a Young Emigrant in Manitoba.* London: Kegan Paul, Trench & Co., 1883.

Foothills Echoes. Millarville Historical Society, 1979.

Foran, Max. *Calgary: An Illustrated History.* Toronto: J. Lorimer & Co. and National Museum of Man, 1978.

Fort Macleod, Our Colourful Past 1874-1924. Fort Macleod History Book Committee, 1977.

Forward, C.N., ed. *Residential and Neighbourhood Studies in Victoria.* Western Geographical Series, vol. 15. University of Victoria, 1973.

Friesen, D.W. *From Prairie Grass to Mountain Pass.* History of the Pioneers of Pincher Creek and District, Pincher Creek Historical Society, 1974.

Gilkes, M. *Canadian Golden West,* "Call Her M'am," vol. 13, no.1, circa 1978.

Glasgow, Past and Present. 3 vols. Glasgow: D. Robertson & Co., 1884.

Grant, I.F. *The Macleods, A History of a Clan.* London: Faber & Faber, 1959.

Gray, James H. *Booze.* Toronto: Macmillan of Canada, 1972.

Green, Wilson F. *Red River Revelations.* Winnipeg: Hignell Printing, 1974.

Guelph Alumnus, "An Emigrant at OAC," vol. 4, 1974.

Gunn, Donald. *History of Manitoba.* Ottawa: Maclean, Roger & Co., 1880.

Hamilton, William. *Sheriffdoms of Lanark and Renfrew.* Edited by A. Gardner. Paisley. 1878.

Hardy, William George. *Alberta Golden Jubilee Anthology.* Toronto: McClelland and Stewart, 1955.

Hargrave, Joseph James. *Red River.* Montreal: J. Lovell, 1871.

Healy, William Joseph. *Women of the Red River.* Winnipeg: Bulman Brothers, 1923.

Hebdrie, Lilian Margaret. *Early Days in Montreal, 1870.* Montreal: Mercury Press, 1932.

Higgitt, Commissioner W.L., edited and introduced. *Official Reports of the RNWMP 1874-1885; Law & Order, 1886-1887; Opening up the West 1874-1881; Settlers and Rebels 1882-1885.* Toronto: Coles Canadiana Collection, 1973.

Holy Trinity Church: Sixty Years and After, an Historical Sketch 1868-1945. Winnipeg, 1945.

Horan, John W. *West, Nor'West: A History of Alberta.* Edmonton: Northgate Books, 1945.

Howison, John. *Sketches of Upper Canada.* Edinburgh: Oliver & Boyd, 3rd. ed., 1825.

Huntington-Smith, Helena. *The War on Powder River.* New York: McGraw-Hill, 1966.

Jenkins, Kathleen. *Montreal, Island City of the St. Lawrence.* New York: Doubleday, 1966.

Johnston, Alexander. *Cowboy Politics, The Western Stock Growers' Association and its Predecessors.* 1972.

Kelly, L.V. *The Rangemen.* Toronto: Coles, 1980.

Lanarkshire. Cambridge County Geographies, edited by W. Murison. Cambridge: Cambridge University Press, 1910.

Lewis, S. *A Topographical Dictionary of Scotland, 2 vols., Supplementary Maps of Scotland.* London: S.Lewis & Co., 1846.

Longstretch,Thomas Morris. *The Silent Force.* London: Century, 1927.

Lovell's Montreal Directory 1819-1896. Lovell Litho & Publications Inc., undated.

Lucas, Sir C. *Lord Durham's Report.* 3 vols. Oxford: Oxford University Press, 1912.

MacBeth, Rev. R.G. *The Making of the Canadian West.* Toronto: W. Briggs, 1898.

Martin, Archer. *The Hudson's Bay Company's Land Tenures and the Occupation of Assiniboia by Lord Selkirk's Settlers With a List of Grantees Under the Earl and the Company*. London: Clowes, 1898.

Merchants House of Glasgow. Glasgow: Bell & Bain, 1866.

McCourt, Edward Alexander. *Remember Butler*. Toronto: McClelland and Stewart, 1967.

Macoun, John. *Manitoba and the Great North West*. Guelph, Ontario: World Publishing, 1882.

McCracken, Harold. *The Charles M. Russell Book*. New York: Doubleday, 1957.

MacCulloch, John Arnott. *The Misty Isle of Skye*. Edinburgh: Oliphant, Anderson & Ferrier, 1910.

MacEwan, Grant. *. . . and Mighty Women, Too*. Saskatoon: Western Producer Prairie Books, 1975.

————. *Calgary Cavalcade, from Fort to Fortune*. Edmonton: Institute of Applied Art, 1958.

The McGill News. "George W. Campbell," vol. 6, no.2, March 1925.

MacGregor, James G. *A History of Alberta*. Edmonton: Hurtig, 1972.

Mackenzie, Alexander. *History of the Macleods*. Inverness: A. & W. Mackenzie, 1889.

Macleod, Margaret Arnett, ed. *Letters of Letitia Hargrave*. New York: Greenwood Press, 1969.

MacRae, Archibald Oswald. *History of the Province of Alberta*. 2 vols. Calgary: The Western Canada History Co., 1912.

Mercer, Asa Shinn. *The Banditti of the Plains*. Norman: University of Oklahoma Press, 1954.

Monet, Jaques. *The Last Cannon Shot, A Study of French-Canadian Nationalism, 1837-1850*. Toronto: University of Toronto Press, 1969.

Montreal Chamber of Commerce 1535-1893. "Histoire de Commerce Canadien." Montreal: Editions Elysée, 1975.

Morgan, Henry James. *The Canadian Men and Women of the Time 1842-1913*. Toronto: W. Briggs, 1898.

Morang's Annual Register of Canadian Affairs, 1901. Edited by J. Hopkins. Toronto: George N. Morang, 1902.

Mort, Frederick. *Lanarkshire*. Cambridge: Cambridge University Press, 1910.

Morton, Arthur Silver. *A History of the Canadian West to 1870-1871*. Edited by L.G. Thomas. Toronto: University of Toronto Press, 1973.

National Geographic Magazine, "Calgary: Canada's Not-So-Wild West," vol. 165. no.3, March 1984.

Neatby, Hilda. *Queen's University, 1814-1917*. Vol. 1. Montreal: McGill-Queen's University Press, 1978.

Nevitt, Richard Banington. *A Winter at Fort Macleod*. Edited by Hugh A. Dempsey. 1974.

Nicolson, Alexander. *History of Skye*. Glasgow: A. Maclaren & Sons, 1930.

O'Neill, Moira (Agnes Higginson). "A Lady's Life on a Ranche," *Blackwoods Magazine*, January 1898.

Philip, Catherine. "The Crosses of Alberta," *Chatelaine*, June-August 1965.

Pope, Sir Joseph. *Correspondence of Sir John Macdonald*. Toronto: Oxford University Press, 1921.

Rasporich, A.W., and H.C. Klassen, eds. *Frontier Calgary: Town, City, Region, 1875-1914*. Calgary: University of Calgary and McClelland and Stewart West, 1975.

Reports of the Supreme Court of the North-West Territories. vol. 1, no.1; ed. W. C. Hamilton, QC, 1890.

Reynolds, George F. "The Man who Created the Corner of Portage and Main," Transaction of the Historical and Scientific Society of Manitoba, Series III, no. 26, 1969-70, Winnipeg, 1969.

Roberts, S.L. "The Cochrane Ranch," *Canadian Cattlemen*, vol. 18, no. 3, March 1955; vol. 18, no. 4, April 1955.

Ross, Alexander. *The Red River Settlement, Its Rise, Progress, and Present State*. London: Smith, Elder, 1856.

Roy, P. G. *Les Judges de la province de Québec*, Quebec, 1933.

St. John's Anglican Church, Jefferson, 1848-1973. Richmond Hill, Ontario, 1973.

Sandham, Alfred. *Montreal Past and Present*. Montreal: George Bishop, 1870.

Scadding, Henry. *Toronto of Old*. Toronto: Adam, Stevenson, 1873.

Scottish Burgh Records Society. *Extracts from The Records of the Burgh of Glasgow 1718-1738*, 1899; vol. VI, *1739-1759*, 1911; vol. VII, *1760-80*; vol. X, 1809-22. Edited by Robert Renwick, Glasgow.

Selby-Smyth, Major-General E. "Confidential Report," *A Chronicle of the Canadian West, 1875*. Edited by Stanley W. Horrall. Calgary: Historical Society of Alberta, 1975.

Sellar, Robert. *History of the County of Huntingdon and the Seigniories of Chateauguay and Beauharnois from their First Settlement to the Year 1838*. Huntingdon, Quebec: The Canadian Gleaner, 1888.

Shrive, Norman. *Charles Mair, Literary Nationalist*. Toronto: University of Toronto Press, 1965.

Sixty Years and After: An Historical Sketch of Holy Trinity Parish, Winnipeg. Winnipeg: Dawson Richardson Publications, 1928.

Steele, Sir Samuel Benfield. *Forty Years in Canada, Reminiscences of the Great North-west*. New York: Dodd, Mead, 1915.

Stubbs, Roy St. George. *Four Recorders of Rupert's Land*. Winnipeg: Peguis, 1967.

Tees, Douglas H. *Chronicles of Ogilvy, Renault, 1879-1979*. Montreal: Plow & Watters Printing Canada, 1979.

Thomas, Lewis H. *The Struggle for Responsible Government in the North-West Territories, 1870-1897*. Toronto: University of Toronto Press, 1956.

Thomas, L.G. "The Rancher and the City: Calgary and the Cattlemen,"

Transactions of the Royal Society of Canada, Vol.VI, Series IV, June 1968.

Turner, John Peter. *The North West Mounted Police 1873-1893*. 2 vols. Ottawa: King's Printer, 1950.

Vokaty, Sandra. "The Adventures of Dr. Duncan McNab McEachran in Western Canada," *The Canadian Veterinary Journal*, vol. 20, no. 6, June 1979.

Wade, Mason. *The French Canadians 1760-1967*. Vol. 1, *1760-1911*. Toronto: Macmillan of Canada, 1968.

Waite, P.B. *Arduous Destiny: Canada 1874-1896*. Toronto: McClelland and Stewart, 1971.

Werier, Valerie, "When Portage and Main was Born," *Winnipeg Tribune*, 29 October 1971.

Wood, Kerry. *Queen's Cowboy*. Toronto: Macmillan, 1960.

UNPUBLISHED MANUSCRIPTS AND PAPERS

Annual Reports of the Ontario Agricultural College, 1879-1882.

Baldwin, Margaret (Maggie Macleod). Memoirs 1901. Private collection, Alberta.

Bennett, R.B. Letters to Marmo Cross 0605010 P/A, New Brunswick.

Breen, David. "The Canadian West and the Ranching Frontier, 1875-1922," Ph.D. thesis. University of Alberta, 1972, Vancouver School of Theology Library, microfilm, AW1-R6177. Excerpts seen only.

Briggs, W. "A career of eminent service in education and agriculture in spite of a serious handicap and many discouraging circumstances: a few facts gleaned from the life and career of James Mills, M.A., LLD." Toronto.

Calgary Brewing & Malting Limited. Papers, 127 document boxes, Glenbow-Alberta Institute.

Campbell, Sir Alexander. Papers in Ontario Archives, MU469; Public Archives, MG29.

Carscaden, Joseph. Journal of the NWMP trek, 1874. Glenbow-Alberta Institute. Uncatalogued.

Clarke, S.J. NWMP memoirs. Glenbow-Alberta Institute.

Clulee, Jean. "Architecture of the Chateauguay Valley," Ormstown. Undated.

Cross family. Private collections of letters and documents in Quebec, Alberta, Wyoming, California, British Columbia. The author has compiled a photostat file of much of the material.

Cross, Alfred Ernest. Papers, Glenbow-Alberta Institute, M289, 11 document boxes.

Cross, Helen Rothney ("Nell"). Papers, Glenbow-Alberta Institute.

Cross, Alexander S. 1820-1894. Reford collection, Aylmer, Quebec (private).

George, Professor James. "Notes on Logic taken from the lectures of Professor

George, 1853-1854," Queen's University, Douglas Library.

Graham, A.W. "Notes on the Riel Rebellion, 1869-1870." Hudson's Bay Company Archives, MG 3 B10. Provincial Archives, Manitoba.

Hargrave, James. "Clerk's Report, York Factory, 1828-1829." University of British Columbia Special Collections.

Horseman's Hall of Fame Papers, B1.7, H817, Glenbow-Alberta Institute, Calgary.

Hudson's Bay Company Records, company records of William Drever, 1819-1851. C.1/794; B 239/g/4-18; 235/d/79-10; B239/a/15; E/6/2/ff50; A.E6/2/ff50. Manitoba Provincial Archives.

Inderwick, Mary E. Letters from Mary Drever Macleod, Glenbow-Alberta Institute, Calgary.

Irvine, Acheson G. "Report on the Red River Expedition of 1870 by Assistant Controller Irvine CMG with Preface," University of British Columbia microfilm no. 3655.

Kells, Edna. "Pioneer Interviews" 1935, D 920.K29. Glenbow-Alberta Institute, Calgary.

Lunn, William. Memoirs, Reford collection, Aylmer, Quebec.

Macdonald, Sir John A. Public Archives of Canada: MG 26 A vol. 210, Reel C 1596, p. 88863-65. LB Nov. 24, 1869, Militia Application, pp. 13,550. June 15, 1880 (starving Indians). Sir John to James Macleod on expenses: MG 26 A vol. 524. James Macleod replies to Sir John: MG 26 A vol. 361, Reel C., 1747, 167099, pp. 167099-111. Others: vol. 209, Reel C 1596, pp. 88707-8, 88716. vol. 336, part 2, Reel C 1707, pp. 152990. vol. 516, part 3, Reel C28, pp. 13,550 part 3, Reel C 28. vol. 210, MG 26 A vol. 211. pp. 89756-770.

Macleod, Captain Martin Donald. Letterbooks, Metropolitan Toronto Public Library, Canadian History Department.

Macleod, James F. Court Records of Southern Alberta and Saskatchewan, 1879-1941, notebooks 1889-1894, microfilm, Glenbow-Alberta Institute. State and Military Records, Federal Archives Division, volumes 155, 156, 283 re Chapter 5, James and Colonel Jackson; Personal Papers in Macleod's dispatch box, Calgary (private collection); J.F. Macleod Papers, 1829, 1856-1919, Glenbow-Alberta Institute, Calgary. AM165A; NWMP files, RG 18, Public Archives, Ottawa; approximately five hundred letters from James to Mary, private collections.

Montana Historical Society Archives, Manuscript Collection 53, Box 2, ff17, W.F. Sanders papers.

Morton, E. Memoirs of G. Harry Cross, as recorded by his daughter; condensed from approximately 600 pages (unpaginated). The author was awarded rights to the manuscript; a copy is housed with the University of Wyoming, Laramie.

Pinkham, Bishop Cyprian. Memoirs. Glenbow-Alberta Institute, Calgary.
Pinkham, Jean Drever. Memoirs. Cathedral Holy Church of the Redeemer, Calgary.
Price, Elizabeth B. Mrs. J.F. Pioneer interviews. (Mary) Macleod memoirs circa 1877, Glenbow-Alberta Institute, Calgary. A.P94,f2.
Public Archives of Canada: NWMP business: RG 9: IIA3, 28 April 1870, payment schedule; RG 15: vol. 138 ff199. vol 87, p. 487 (Macleod's payment); RG 18, NWMP file, French to Irvine on police stores, 3437. Personnel file 0-30. vol. 3, 48-75, Brisebois character reference. vol. 3436 48-A, 1875. Indian's grievance hearing in 1888, RG 18, vol. 19 ff. 249, vol. 4, 115-75, vol.7, 345-75; vol. 3436 0-4.
Ranchmen's Club Calgary, 1891-1904. Minute Book.
Reports of the Sitting Bull Indian Commission and other related documents: Public Archives of Canada, RG 7, G21, vol. 318, f2001, pt.3a.
Royalite Papers, Gulf Canada, several boxes, unfiled, of the original papers. Toronto, Ontario.
Sessional Papers. 35 Vic., 19A, 1872, Manitoba; Compensation for Riel Rebellion; Public Accounts, 1879-1881, State of the Militia Report; 1870, National Defence Headquarters, Ottawa.
Thom, Adam. Requests an appeal to the judgement in Rothney *v.* Thom, 16 February 1843. Public Archives of Manitoba, MG 2-B4-6.
Tolley, Grant. Fort Macleod, Private collection of James Macleod letters.
White, Ruth (Macleod). Letters of Norman Macleod, *c.* 1885.

ARCHIVES, LIBRARIES, ASSOCIATIONS
Centre regional des Archives du Québec, Section Archives Judiciaires
City of Lethbrdige Archives, Sir Alexander Galt Museum
Department of National Defence, Ottawa
Douglas Library, Queen's University, Kingston
Glenbow-Alberta Institute, Calgary
Hudson's Bay Archives, Manitoba
Johnson County Museum, Buffalo, Wyoming
Manitoba Provincial Archives
Metropolitan Toronto Public Library, Canadian History Department
McGill University Medical Archives
Montana Historical Society Archives, Helena, Montana
Montreal Bar Association Library
Montreal Civic Archives
Montreal Court House Archives
Provincial Archives of Manitoba
Public Archives of Canada
Public Records Office, Great Britain
State and Military Records, Federal Archives
Teck Mining Company Library, Vancouver, B.C.

University of British Columbia Library: Microfilm, Special Collections and
Law
University of Guelph: Veterinary College, and Archival and Special Col-
lections.
University of Wyoming, Western History Research Centre, Laramie
Western Stock Growers' Association, Alberta
Wyoming State Archives, Museums and Historical Department
Wyoming Stock Growers' Association, Cheyenne

Index